Artful Ownership

Artful Ownership

*Art Law, Valuation, and Commerce in the
United States, Canada, and Mexico*

Aaron Milrad

American Society of Appraisers

Washington, D.C.

2000

ISBN 0-937828-03-3

Printed in the United States of America.

Printed by RR Donnelley & Sons Company, Harrisonburg, VA.

Foreword

This book is the first of a number of new publications sponsored by the American Society of Appraisers (ASA). The society is, as part of its mission, contributing to the growing literature for the professional valuer. The society's intention is to add to the available materials the sorts of books, collected readings, and other publications that can assist appraisers, users of valuation services, and professionals in value-economics, commerce, banking, insurance, law, and government.

While several books are already standard to the study of art law, there has not been, until this book, an overview of legal reasoning from the perspectives of professionals in the valuation of personal properties—especially the fine and decorative arts. Going further, until now there has been no comprehensive overview of case law in the United States and Canada, and there has been no similar overview of Mexican civil codes written for the use of valuers and valuation specialists.

The society is especially pleased that Aaron Milrad has undertaken the task of authoring this book. A lawyer of international reputation, Milrad is also known as a collector and patron of the arts. In 1980, he authored *The Art World: Law, Business & Practice in Canada* with Ella Agnew, and he is known for other publications on the law and the arts. Milrad's membership on boards of trust and advisory groups is exemplary of his innate concern for and appreciation of cultural properties. This new book is not a recitation of legal codes, cases, or interpretations; rather, it is a broadly viewed and lively introduction to interdependent and interconnected areas of study, appreciation, administration, and commerce. The indispensable reference works of Feldman, Lerner and Bresler, Darraby, and Hodes are made more useful to the student of valuation with this new contribution by Milrad.

Although ASA originally saw this project as only an adjunct to ASA's valuation education programs, the society is now persuaded that the book's discussions will also benefit curators and administrators of cultural institutions, government offices, collectors, estates, galleries, academics, accountants, tax advisers, and students of law, social and cultural history, and conservation and preservation. As it does so, it will assist the American Society of Appraisers in fulfilling its responsibilities to the professionals and the public it serves.

AMERICAN SOCIETY OF APPRAISERS
WASHINGTON, DISTRICT OF COLUMBIA
20 JANUARY 2000

Acknowledgments

I met Richard-Raymond Alasko, a respected personal property appraiser with offices in Chicago, Illinois, at the American Society of Appraisers conference in Toronto in 1994. I was a speaker at the conference, and my topic was the ways in which art law concepts differ in Canada and the United States. During an informal discussion with Alasko and Patricia Soucy, a well-known appraiser and lecturer, the idea of creating this book for the ASA was formed. Informal discussions continued over several months to conceptualize the content and to fulfill the opportunity for the ASA to create both an educational tool in the personal-property field and an overview to promote greater cultural harmony and awareness among Canada, the United States, and Mexico.

Throughout the process, the ASA has enthusiastically supported and encouraged my efforts. I am indebted to the society for its support and professionalism.

I am also indebted to a number of ASA members for their support and hard work. Richard-Raymond Alasko was invaluable in his enthusiasm, encouragement, and understanding of the project. Patricia Soucy gave me substantial advice on how to effectively structure the book. I also thank the ASA staff, particularly Ted Baker and Rebecca Maxey, for their assistance in the project.

I owe thanks to a number of others who have contributed significantly to this book. Tim McVittie, of Barber Stewart McVittie & Wallace, insurance brokers, assisted on chapter 7, which covers insurance. Bruce Keilty, of Hunter Keilty Muntz & Beatty Ltd., also offered input and insights on insurance matters.

Juan Pablo Gomez Rivera, an Accredited Senior Appraiser and a member of ASA's Mexico City Chapter (who also happens to be the grandson of the artist Diego Rivera), was a valuable resource on Mexican law and on appraisers, auctions, and the pawn shop business in Mexico. Pablo Torres Hezel, of the law firm of Gutierrez, Diaz de Rivera y Torres, S.C., in Mexico City, provided significant information on various aspects of Mexican law. Roberto Flores Zertuche, a respected lawyer in Mexico City, provided assistance with Mexican law and, in particular, with auctions and tax. I am also grateful to Louis Morton, of Morton Auction House in Mexico City, for his kindness and assistance in providing us with information about the auction process in Mexico.

I am especially grateful to Johanna Hoffmann, of Johanna Hoffmann + Company, for acting as our intermediary and translator in dealing with various members of the Mexican art and law community, as well as for her substantial ongoing involvement in the publicity and promotion of the book. Charis Wahl, my editor, has made certain that "I say what I mean and mean what I say." Any inconsistencies or obscurity in the text are my responsibility, not hers.

Victor Smuckler, of Herzfeld Rubin Attorneys-At-Law, assisted in respect to recent legislation and cases primarily in New York State. Ron Daniels, dean of the University of Toronto Law School, embraced the project with enthusiasm and made it available to interested students at the school. To those students who undertook research—Karen Wintraub, David Surat, and Lainie Appleby—I thank you for your excellent and timely work. Professor Nils Olsen, of the University of Buffalo Law School, was instrumental in arranging for students at that school to assist with researching the U.S. law and cases. To those students—Karmen Kardum and Matthew Clabeaux—I am grateful for your participation and assistance.

Thanks also to Karen E. Carolan, chief of art appraisal services of the U.S. Internal Revenue Service and chair of the Art Advisory Panel, for her assistance.

My law firm, Fraser Milner, has been especially accommodating in permitting me the time and resources to work on this book. I also thank the Fraser Milner law students, past and present, who assisted me in this venture—Jason Annibale, John Russo, Janet O'Brien, Annie Na, Carolyn Decker, Steve Gillespie, Matthew Hibbert, Axel Kindbom, Michael Roland, Alex Tinmouth, Mark Yearwood, Kim Cadario, Scott Burke, Christopher Köddermann, Colin Ground, and especially Cynthia Koller, Greg Hogan, and Nicole St.-Louis, who bore the brunt of the work with unfailing good humor. Thanks also to Chuck Rich for all his help in the creation and revision of the endnotes.

Thanks go to the following people for their constant revisions of the chapters under a tight schedule: Gina Arduini, Connie Cosentino, Barbara Fox, Lucy Gaglia, Laura Garwood, Cecilia Hardeo, Linda Hayes, Jenny Hicks, Wendy Ing, Gladys Leishman, Anita Price, and the staff members of the Document Services Department at Fraser Milner. The library staff of Fraser Milner—Jan Barrett, Linda Boss, Ian Colvin, Trish Richardson, and Natasha Lissovskaia—also assisted with the book; they must be thrilled that this project has finally come to an end. A special thanks to Ian Colvin for his assistance throughout.

Particular publications were of immense help in the preparation of the text: *Art Law,* by Ralph Lerner and Judith Bressler, second edition (Practicing Law Institute, 1998); *Art, Artifact and Architecture Law,* by Jessica L. Darraby (Clark Boardman Callaghan, 1995); *Art Law,* by Frank Feldman, Stephen Weil, and Susan Duke Biederman (Little Brown and Company, 1986, updated 1993); *A Legal Primer on Managing Museum Collections,* by Marie Malaro (Smithsonian Institu tion Press, 1985); the very useful and timely *Artnewsletter* (the international bi-weekly report on the art market); the *Art Newspaper;* the *Entertainment Law Reporter;* and the *International Foundation For Art Research Journal.* On the Canadian side, my earlier book, *The Art World: Law, Business & Practice in Canada* (Merritt Publishing, 1980), coauthored with Ella Agnew, was a useful source for the Canadian part of this work.

The Uniform Standards of Professional Appraisal Practice (USPAP), by The Appraisal Foundation, are reproduced with permission of The Appraisal Foundation. The materials referred to in the text are only a *portion* of the 1999 edition. Complete copies of USPAP (including Advisory Opinions and Statements) are available for purchase from The Appraisal Foundation, 1029 Vermont Avenue, NW, Suite 900, Washington, DC 20005; (202) 347-7722.

Some people are owed my special thanks for assistance above and beyond the call of duty. First and foremost, my assistant at Fraser Milner, Maria Terra, has worked diligently for many months creating the manuscript and its many revisions, prevailing over cantankerous computers, and compiling the diverse materials received from hither and yon. Maria, to you I am deeply indebted.

Steven Muller, a lawyer, friend, and gentleman, assisted me throughout, first with research and later with revisions. Steven, you were there when I needed help. I know how difficult it was for you to be available for this project on an ongoing basis, and I appreciate your skill, patience, fortitude, persistence, and availability.

Finally, to Cheryl Zale, thank you for your encouragement during the many months that this project demanded.

Disclaimer

A diligent attempt has been made to ensure the accuracy of all the information in this publication. Besides my own efforts, I have utilized the services of students and the facilities of the University of Toronto Law School, the University of Buffalo Law School, and my law firm Fraser Milner, as well as research by various interested law students and lawyers and numerous texts, articles, and periodicals both in English and Spanish. Addressing all the issues in detail would have been impossible. Including all relevant legislation and cases would have necessitated an expensive, many-volumed tome that would have required almost daily updating. As it was, the amount of new law and cases that appeared while writing this book was astonishing and has resulted in continuing revision and addition to the text up to the time of editing. There is the possibility that some of the laws and regulations, especially in the taxation area, may have changed in the time lapse between the writing and editing of this book and its ultimate publication.

For that reason, some chapters, such as that on taxation, concentrate on general concepts; where possible, others are written in a more directed fashion, to narrow the issues where appropriate and to try to prevent the book from becoming outdated sooner than it needs to or requiring more frequent updates than would be reasonable. Resources for this book are identified both in the notes and the bibliography and can be consulted by the reader for further information.

If errors are found, I would be grateful if they are brought to the attention of the publisher and author. We will strive to correct them in future editions.

The publication itself is the result of much research from a multitude of sources. Though every effort has been made to be accurate, no warranty as to accuracy can or is given. This publication is intended as a handbook; its purpose is to introduce readers to the problems, concerns, and considerations of each of the topics presented. When dealing with specific issues, the reader should seek professional and legal advice, and no decision or action should be taken by relying on the contents of this book.

Contents

• 8 •

• 9 •

• 10 •

Introduction

This book is a response to the globalization of trade and, in particular, the harmonization of markets in North America. It will consider the laws of Canada, the United States, and Mexico that relate to fine art and art objects and the ways these countries are forging links to market their art and to protect their cultural property. It also will look at sophisticated international legal means of protecting the cultural property of nation states and of retrieving stolen or missing treasures. Peoples and nations throughout the world have increasing understanding and appreciation of their cultural heritage and are demanding the return of exported objects relating to their cultural history. They also are focusing on preventing the further exportation of their cultural property.

This is the first book in the "fine art field" to look at how these matters are being handled in Canada, the United States, and Mexico. It provides an overview of laws and practices, both within those nations and with one another, as well as with the international arts community. Each of the nations has federal and state or provincial governments. Canada and the United States are primarily common-law jurisdictions (i.e., based on English law), although civil law (i.e., Napoleonic law) prevails in the Canadian province of Quebec and is a substantial part of the law of the states of Louisiana and California. Mexican law is civil law. Where appropriate, relevant differences among jurisdictions have been noted.

This book is also about the pleasure, private and shared, of collecting objects of beauty and of appreciating their poetry. It deals extensively with the "commerce" of culture and the technical rules, as well.

Art is precious in numerous ways and can embody different things to different people. But one common thread runs throughout the art world: the law.

The next time you visit a collection of fine art, craft or design, consider how the piece came to be in the institution. If deemed to be a work by a major artist, it must have survived rigorous rounds of authentication. Also, there may have been complex agreements of consignment, purchase, and sale; loan agreements with various lenders; insurance policies and coverages; copyright agreements for reproduction of the work; exhibition agreements; and if the work was donated, tax considerations for the donor and the institution.

What then of the visitor who dares to declare to the owner of a piece, "That's a fake!" The laws of defamation come into play—a possible lawsuit, settlement, public apology, or all three. If it is a fake, on whom does the liability fall? And what of the expert who insists: "That's a reproduction, not an original fine art print!" In addition to all other concerns about such statements, certain jurisdictions have laws governing the sale of multiple prints or copies.

Art issues have a place in almost every legal context: contract and sale of goods laws in respect to purchase and sale and title to the works; criminal law and insurance law, should a piece be damaged or stolen; family law, when works must be appraised and divided between divorcing parties; trusts and estates law, when individuals wish to donate or bequeath works; cultural-property laws every time the work finds a new home or travels outside the country, whether permanently or temporarily, and the repercussions of tax laws on transactions related to an object; and intellectual-property laws, should the work or its image be reproduced. In other words, every transactional step is determined and defined by law—in this context, the laws of Canada, the United States, and Mexico and the international conventions and agreements signed by these countries.

This book also examines ways in which individuals can protect themselves against lawsuits and fraudulent dealings. In the sophisticated art world, the ill-informed buyer, seller, collector, dealer, curator, or valuer is highly vulnerable. The greater the knowledge, the less disruption, aggravation, and expense will be incurred.

The law and the art world are intricately interwoven: art grants benefits, whether aesthetic or pecuniary. Laws preserve and protect our many treasures and promote honesty in their handling.

· 1 ·

Title

As outlined in the introduction, this book is a response to the globalization of trade, especially the art trade, and the harmonization of markets in North America. The beginning point for trade is ownership of the object to be bought, sold, or traded. The concept of ownership will be dealt with under the law of the United States, Canada, and Mexico: how ownership gives rise to various rights, obligations, and responsibilities of an owner in obtaining, keeping, and preventing loss of such ownership.

In law, ownership is often described as having *title*, which refers to "a collection of rights to use and enjoy property, including the right to transmit it to others." It is "the exclusive right of possession, enjoyment, and disposal; involving as an essential attribute the right to control, handle, and dispose."[1] It is a right or interest in things personal, is usually temporary, and is generally applied to property of a personal or movable nature, as opposed to property of a local or immovable character, such as land or houses.[2]

Real estate has a recognized registry system to identify an owner and describe lands and any encumbrances against them. In addition, the buildings on the land can be investigated, inspected, and seen on surveys to exist within the boundaries of the land being purchased, mortgaged, or otherwise administered.

There is no equivalent registry system for personal property, which includes fine and decorative art, jewelry, gemstones, and collectibles. (*Fine art* includes paintings, prints, sculptures, and photography. *Decorative art* includes antique, modern, and contemporary furniture, glass, and ceramics; textiles; and silver and metalware.) Works of art are unique, even in multiples, as each is normally pulled, cast, or created separately and separately numbered. The value of art is based upon the authenticity of the work, as well as the importance of the artist; the image; and the size, material, and condition of the work.

With art properties, the object itself tells the tale. It is the uniqueness of the object that defines the transaction and supports the value. As there are no plans, surveys, or registers, the purchaser buying an original object—a Picasso painting, a Ming vase, a piece of nineteenth century folk art, a diamond—must be satisfied that the object is genuine. A visual inspection alone may not be sufficient to confirm authenticity.

Because of the publicity associated with the high prices at art auctions and booming art sales worldwide, there is a significant amount of art theft and forgery. It has been estimated that the dollar volume of art stolen is second only to that of the international drug trade: many hundreds of millions of dollars worth of art are stolen each year. All classes of art are affected, including contemporary, historical, folk, Asian, First Nations, outsider, and national.

Art faking is another big business. Some say that the young Michelangelo was the first modern art faker, creating phony Greek statues when his own art was still hard to sell. Professional fakers of the twentieth century include David Stein, author of *Three Picassos Before Breakfast*[3] (and faker of the work of many modern artists including Picasso and Chagall); Hans van Meegeren, imprisoned for painting and selling fake Vermeer paintings (many of his "Vermeers" were purchased by the Nazis during the Second World War); and Charles Keeting, who created numerous fake Krieghoffs. Recently, art forgers doctored the archives of the Tate Gallery to designate their forgeries as authentic. Prospective buyers of a forged painting or sculpture will find that the records of the Tate Gallery show the work to be that of the reputed artist (at least until the records are corrected). Fake documentation has often been created in the past, but this appears to be the first case in which false documentation has been insinuated into the archival records of a major museum. (This forged documentation seems to relate to the works of Jean Dubuffet, Ben Nicholson, Alberto Giacometti, and Jacob Epstein, all deceased; and further instances may come to light.) For these reasons, as well as other less dramatic risks, buyers must be vigilant.

Art objects may be sold by professionals such as dealers, auction houses, retailers, etc., or by nonprofessionals in private purchases. What protection is there for a purchaser or other parties to the transaction (auctioneer, seller, valuer)? Are there any guarantees? Are there any warranties? Are there any representations that may be relied upon? Does it make any difference whether the work is sold by a professional or by a nonprofessional? Does an oral contract or statement of origin or authenticity carry the same weight as a written contract or statement? Does the law imply any conditions, terms, warranties, and/or representations? If so, what are they, and whom do they benefit? What rules apply to business transactions apart from criminal laws? This chapter concerns the answers to these and other questions.

CONTRACTS

Canadian, U.S., and Mexican law start with the view that the contract is the first place to look to determine what kind of arrangement exists between a buyer and a seller. In transferring title through sale, it is essential to have a contract, bill of sale, or some other written agreement outlining the deal and the responsibilities of the parties to it. A written contract is the best proof that the vendor is selling, for a stated price and on a stated date, a particular object by a particular creator, and that it has unique features.

The written contract should therefore contain the following information at the very least:

1. the date of the sale;
2. the legal name of the vendor;
3. the legal name of the purchaser;
4. a full and complete description of the item being purchased;
5. the date of creation of the item purchased;
6. the medium (paper, wood, canvas, stone, etc.);
7. the dimensions of the item;
8. the condition of the item;
9. the price and terms of payment (i.e., a deposit of so much and schedule of payments) or notation of payment having been made in full by check;
10. the provenance, or history, of the item—who the prior owners were, and when and where the transfers occurred;
11. the historical cost of the object (i.e., the original price paid or historical development cost);
12. availability of curatorial information;
13. delivery and insurance terms.

Future sellers, purchasers, and valuers will rely heavily on this information; however, if a matter is not dealt with within the contract, various statutes are available to assist the parties.

Commercial Transactions

Canadian Law

In Canada, most commercial transactions are dealt with under the laws of each province. The applicable provincial laws are the Sale of Goods Act[4] (or equivalent), the Personal Property Security Act,[5] and general contract law.

Sale of Goods Act

The Sale of Goods Act of Ontario and similar acts in other common-law provinces generally set out conditions and warranties implied in sales of any goods (these would apply to sales of art objects):

1. the seller has the right to sell the goods—that is, the seller has the title and the authority to sell the goods (Section 13[a]);
2. the buyer will enjoy quiet possession of the goods—that is, the buyer will get valid title to them (Section 13[b]);
3. the goods will be free from any mortgage, lien, or encumbrance in favor of a third party unknown to the buyer before or at the time of the contract of sale (Section 13[c]);
4. where the sale of goods is by description (i.e., defined in a bill of sale), the goods will correspond with that description (Sections 14 and 15);
5. where the goods are different from those described in the bill of sale, the sale will be rescinded and the goods rejected or, if the goods have been accepted and title has passed to the buyer, the buyer may sue for damages but not rescind the transaction (Sections 47 to 50 inclusive).

Statutes dealing with the time within which an action must be brought are important; even when a work differs from that described, action can be brought only within a given time from the date of sale. This "limitation of action" applies not only to misattributions and wrongful descriptions of works sold but also, in some instances, to work purchased in good faith from a vendor who did not have title to the work. (Statutes of limitation are described later in this chapter.)

Sale versus Agreement to Sell

Under the Sale of Goods Act of Ontario, a contract for sale of goods is one made by a seller to transfer ownership of the goods to the buyer for a money consideration called a *price* (Section 2[1]). When the property and goods are transferred from the seller to the buyer, this contract is called a *sale;* however, when the transfer of the property and goods is to take place after the date of the contract or is subject to some unfulfilled condition, the contract is called an *agreement to sell* (Section 2[3]). An agreement to sell becomes a sale on the date of transfer or when the outstanding conditions are fulfilled (Section 2[4]).

Contract Condition and Warranties

When a contract of sale is subject to a condition to be fulfilled by the seller and that condition is not met, the buyer may repudiate the contract and reject the goods, may waive the condition, or may treat the breach of the condition as a breach of warranty rather than as a repudiation of the contract (Section 12[1]). For example, a contract of sale may be subject to the condition that a painting be reframed, a diamond ring be reset, or a sculpture receive a new base. If the seller does not fulfill such a condition, the buyer may accept the sale without the condition or may treat the breach as one of warranty (that is, something against which there may be a claim for damages, rather than one nullifying the contract).

Whether a stipulation in a contract of sale is a condition (the breach of which may give rise to a right to repudiate the contract) or a warranty (the breach of which may give rise to a claim for damages but not to a right to repudiate the contract and reject the goods) depends on the construction of the particular contract. Moreover, a stipulation may actually be a condition, even if it is called a warranty in the contract (Section 12[2]). For example, there may be a "warranty" that a work is an original Picasso, but the work turns out to be either a fake Picasso or a legitimate work by another artist. The courts would treat the warranty as a condition (that is, as a matter that goes to the heart of the contract). As the purchaser would not have purchased this work if it were not a Picasso, he or she is not looking for a reduction in the purchase price; the buyer wants a Picasso. In that circumstance the purchaser has a right to reject the goods and repudiate the contract.

The Ontario Sale of Goods Act also implies a warranty or condition as to quality or fitness in the contract by usage of the trade (Section 15[3]). Therefore, the usage or custom of each trade, as established through historical use or precedent, may be consulted to determine acceptable quality or fitness if not specifically provided in the contract. This implied warranty may be used in the event that the general law does not cover such a situation.

The Personal Property Security Act

The Ontario Personal Property Security Act[6] (OPPSA) provides a system for registration of security interests in personal property in Ontario and is modeled after Article 9 of the U.S. Uniform Commercial Code.[7] In general, the OPPSA applies to any consensual transaction that creates a security interest (s. 2), although certain transactions, such as liens created by statute, are excluded (s. 4).

The OPPSA acts to preserve a creditor's rights and remedies against other persons who claim an interest in the same property. In order to qualify for such protection, a creditor must have a "perfected" security interest. Interests are perfected either by registering the interest (s. 23) or by having possession of the collateral (s. 22). Under the OPPSA, registration is done by filing a financial statement that outlines the debtor and the secured party, a classification of the collateral, and a brief description of the collateral (s. 45).

Part III of the OPPSA sets out the rules governing the priority given to security interests in the same property (called *collateral*). Generally, it gives the first priority to the security interest that is perfected earliest (s. 30).

The OPPSA also

1. outlines how searches may be done to discover whether other parties have registered interests in specific personal properties (s. 43);
2. allows compensation for those who suffer loss or damage as a result of reliance on such a search (s. 44); and
3. dictates the rights and remedies of creditors (Part V), including the right to possess and dispose of collateral on default under a security agreement (ss. 62 and 63).

There are equivalent statutes in other provinces.[8]

U.S. Law

In the United States, as in Canada, the contract of purchase and sale between the respective parties should outline the terms of the transaction. In that regard, the American Uniform Commercial Code[9] (UCC) is the starting point of the law.

The Uniform Commercial Code

The UCC deals with express warranties by the seller (Section 2-313):

1. that any affirmation of fact or promise made by the seller to the buyer that relates to the goods and becomes part of the basis of the bargain creates an express warranty that the goods will conform to the affirmation or promise;
2. that any description of the goods that is part of the basis of the bargain creates an express warranty that the goods will conform to the description.

Subsection 2 goes on to state that the seller need not use terms such as *warrant* or *guarantee* or have a specific intention to make a warranty in order to create an express warranty; however, an affirmation merely of the value of the goods or a statement representing only the seller's opinion or commendation of the goods does not create a warranty.

The difficulty under the UCC is that a claim in the contract that a work is authentic can be interpreted either under Section 2-313(1), as a guarantee of authenticity, or under UCC Section 2-313(2), as only an opinion of authenticity. There is a vast difference between the two in law. In normal circumstances, a purchase of a work is based upon that work having been created by a particular artist; this goes to the heart of the contract. In other words, the sale would not have been made if the work were not by that artist. This is especially true when a professional (a dealer) is selling to a non-professional (an ordinary purchaser or collector).

Often works of questionable authenticity and/or provenance are sold at auctions on a caveat emptor basis, and the presale estimate may be reduced accordingly. Auction houses generally state conditions in their catalogues that limit the representations and responsibility of the auction house. (Auctions and their operations are covered in chapter 5.)

Dealers and dealer associations, on the other hand, take pride in selling authentic goods to a public that can rely upon their professional knowledge. A dealer whose claim of authorship by a particular artist forms the basis of the bargain with the purchaser is rarely giving more than his or her opinion. Yet, in giving that opinion, because he or she *is* a dealer, the dealer is held to have given an express warranty. "As a matter of law, art sellers are deemed to warrant the unwarrantable; they must in essence guarantee 'an opinion' or, under some tests, the 'prevailing opinion' as reconstructed by experts at the time of trial."[10]

The UCC also suggests that a complainant must prove injury resulting from a breach that occurred with the sale. The test appears to be whether the seller's statement was an express warranty or mere puffery, and the code recognizes that some seller's statements are only puffing (Section 2-313[2]). In such cases, the subject matter of the contract must be shown to be different from what was bargained for; for example, if the buyer maintains that he or she was promised an original painting and instead was offered a reproduction of a painting, that must be proved. The purchaser who wishes to terminate the contract has to prove the breach of warranty by the vendor. The UCC gives a "cause of action only against the seller" (Section 2-313).

Statutes of Limitations

Under the UCC, there is a four-year period during which a purchaser may sue for breach of contract (Section 2-725[1]). Generally, an action must be commenced within four years of the occurrence of the cause of action; however, when and how this limitation period begins and ends is a complex legal matter that varies among jurisdictions. For example, it may begin at the time of completion of the contract or on the first date that the purchaser could reasonably know the work was not authentic (for example, by public exhibition of the work or by having it examined by an expert). In the initial agreement, the parties may reduce the limitation period to not less than one year, but they may not extend it.

To date, U.S. courts rarely allow a purchaser to succeed in a breach of warranty action based on authenticity if it arises more than four years after the purchase. They take the position that Section 2-725 is a statutory bar beyond the four years.[11]

Sale by Description

Under U.S. law, when a buyer expressly or by implication makes known to a seller a particular purpose for which goods being purchased are required (so as to show that the buyer relies on the seller's skill or judgment), and where it is within the course of the seller's business to supply such goods, there is an implied condition that the goods will be reasonably fit for that purpose. In the United States, particular cases have indicated that this type of wording applies to the sale of art.[12]

Statutes of Frauds

In addition to statutes of limitations, there are statutes of frauds that require certain types of contracts to be in writing. Under the UCC, the Statute of Frauds (Section 2-201[1]) indicates that:

> except as otherwise provided in this section, a contract for the sale of goods at a price of $500 or more is not enforceable by way of action or defense unless there is some writing sufficient to indicate that a contract has been made between the parties and signed by the party against whom enforcement is sought or by his authorized agent or broker. A writing is not insufficient because it omits or incorrectly states a term agreed upon but the contract is not enforceable under this paragraph beyond the quantity of goods shown in such writing.

Almost any form of writing or initialing has been held to be sufficient. Generally, the courts are more generous to purchasers than to vendors in cases involving the Statute of Frauds. However, it should be borne in mind that:

1. Section 2-201 does *not* apply to the rendering of services for a price, including the commissioning of an artwork;[13]
2. Section 2-201 applies only to contracts for the sale of goods at a price of $500 or more;
3. Section 2-106(1) defines *sale* as "the passing of title from the seller to the buyer for a price";
4. Section 2-105(1) defines *goods* as "all things (including specially manufactured goods) which are movable at the time of identification of the contract for sale."

There are a number of exceptions to the defense of the Statute of Frauds. One in particular, "mutual mistake," is used frequently with apparent success. Mutual mistake arises when both parties to a contract make a mistake about material issues at the time they make the agreement. Mutual mistake allows the contract to be rescinded as if a proper contract were never negotiated by the parties (that is, as if there was never a meeting of minds). This has occurred in a number of recent U.S. cases[14] with regard to contracts for a Balthus drawing, a Matisse drawing, and a Dubuffet that turned out to be fake.

An interesting recent British[15] case of mutual mistake involved two art dealers negotiating for a work of art that was a forgery of a painting by the artist Gabriele Munter. The court held that the purchaser must bear the risk. Both dealers believed the work to be by Munter; however, at the time of the sale, the vendor dealer disclaimed any knowledge of the artist other than that he believed the work to be a Munter. The purchaser relied not on the vendor's opinion but on his own as to the authenticity of the work. It was not a "sale by description" in respect to authorship of the work.

One appeal judge noted that considerable skill and energy has been put into the production of fakes, even during an artist's lifetime. However, this is common knowledge among art dealers and experienced collectors. Therefore, almost any attribution given a work, especially one whose provenance is unknown, may be arguable. "The Court ought to be exceedingly wary in giving a seller's attribution any contractual effect." As well, many dealers habitually deal with one another on the principle of *caveat emptor*, in which transactions the purchaser bears the loss.[16]

This decision, if followed in the United States, would treat dealer opinions of authenticity—at least to other dealers—as personal conclusions only and would therefore be covered in the UCC by Section 2-313(2), under which the seller's opinion or accommodation of goods does not create a warranty and therefore does not go to the heart of the contract so as to allow the contract to be rescinded.

New York State Law

New York State has created specific legislation in respect to the fine arts that removes the uncertainty under the Uniform Commercial Code as to whether a claim of authenticity is a warranty of or only an opinion of authenticity. The New York Arts and Cultural Affairs Law[17] holds the selling art dealer responsible to the innocent nonprofessional buyer for all statements made by the vendor with respect to the authenticity or authorship of a work of art (Sections 13.01–13.07). In short, it turns the seller's opinion into a warranty. Michigan[18] does the same; however, it restricts damages to the return of the purchase money if the vendor's warranty was given in good faith.

New York law also attempts to limit the use of disclaimers to negate or limit the warranty of the vendor. It will hold such a disclaimer to be unreasonable unless it is conspicuous, written, and separate from the warranty and couched in words that clearly and specifically inform the buyer that the seller assumes no risk, liability, or responsibility for the stated material facts concerning the work. Words of general disclaimer

1. do not negate or limit an express warranty and
2. do not protect the vendor if

a. the work of fine art is proved to be a counterfeit, and this was not clearly indicated in the description of the work; or

b. the information provided is proved to be false, mistaken, or erroneous as of the date of sale or exchange (Section 13.01[4] and [5]).

The statute then deals with falsifying certificates of authenticity or similar instruments (Section 13.03) and express warranties on multiples (Section 13.05).

The predecessor to Section 13 of the New York act was used in the case of *Dawson v. Malina*,[19] in which the vendor Malina, a dealer, sold various historical Chinese artworks to Dawson, another dealer. A number of the works were held by experts at the trial to have been improperly described by Malina as to their age and the period in which they were made. The court concluded that in the bills of sale Malina's representations were "without a reasonable basis in fact" for a number of the works. Dawson was therefore entitled to rescind the purchase of those works and to receive a refund of their purchase monies, with interest from the date of purchase.

Tips for Making Auction Purchases and Other Public Purchases

The logical first rule is: know the vendor and know his or her reputation. All the warranties and representations provided by law will not make a dishonest vendor into an honest one.

Second, make certain that you obtain a written document that fully expresses all the representations and warranties.

Third, if there is any doubt, bring in an independent expert to view the work and render an opinion before the purchase.

Finally, offer payment by a series of checks rather than in one lump sum at the time of purchase or delivery.

Quite often, both fakes and stolen works leave a trail that can be uncovered with enough diligence. Rarely is a stolen or fake object offered to the retail trade only once. Usually there is a pattern—both the people and the places involved recur. Checking with the appropriate professional associations, such as the International Foundation for Art Research in New York, would be a good business practice before making any art purchase involving a substantial sum.

AUTHENTICATION AND EXPERT OPINION RISKS

There are significant legal risks for valuers, authenticators, and dealers who make improper or negligent reports, including defamation, fraud or deceit, slander of title, and injurious falsehood. For a discussion of the role and responsibility of valuers, see chapter 4.

An appraiser or valuer is responsible for rendering an estimate of the value of an object at a given time and place, supported by objective facts. "To appraise is to estimate the amount or worth."[20] The valuer will normally require the client to provide evidence of authenticity of the personal property, but he or she does not actually perform authentication. "To authenticate is to establish the genuineness of."[21] However, although there is not an explicit authentication by the valuer, competency is a reasonable expectation.

Defamation

In rendering a certificate of authenticity for a work of art or other art object, there is the risk of the authenticated work turning out to be a fake or not to be a work by the artist. But the reverse also may be true: an opinion may be offered that a work is not authentic, but it may then turn out to be authentic.

These risks lead to the associated risk of defamation for the valuer, art dealer, or expert retained to render an opinion on the authenticity of a work. A statement declaring that a work owned by Mr. X is a fake may result in a negative opinion of Mr. X and thereby affect his reputation. It may also affect the reputation of any expert who previously reached a contradictory conclusion, and it could even affect the artist and his or her market.

An example of a case of defamation is the case of the art dealer Joseph Duveen, who was sued for defamation after claiming that a painting being offered for sale by Andrée Hahn was not an original Leonardo da Vinci even though Duveen had never seen the painting. This resulted in a settlement by Duveen of $60,000.[22]

Canadian Law

In Canada, libel and slander are primarily provincial matters, although defamatory libel is also covered by the federal Criminal Code.[23]

For a statement to be defamatory in Canada, it must harm another's reputation. It can be either libelous or slanderous. *Libel* is defamation in a permanent form, which includes broadcasts preserved in a permanent form. Most provinces also have legislation under which defamation in any kind of broadcasting—preserved or not—is libel. *Slander* is defamation that is spoken or conveyed through gestures.

In an action for defamation, the individual alleging defamation must establish that

1. the statement made was defamatory;
2. the statement referred to him or her specifically; and

3. the statement was conveyed to a third party.

There are several defenses to defamation in Canada.

1. Truth or justification: The author must establish that the statements were true in both fact and substance.
2. Consent: The author must show that the complainant consented to or caused the defamatory statements.
3. Absolute privilege: Defamatory statements made in a judicial, quasi-judicial, or legislative proceeding or report are privileged (that is, not subject to action), based on the rationale that society has a right to be informed of public debate in public forums.
4. Qualified privilege: Defamatory statements made in the discharge of a public or private duty, and published and made available to a person who has some corresponding interest in the information, are protected. However, there must be an absence of malice in order to claim this privilege.
5. Fair comment: Fair and honest expressions made in good faith on matters of public interest are protected. The opinion must be based on known and provable facts. The test involves determining whether the author honestly believed the opinion and whether it is one that could be drawn from known facts. Several provinces and territories have enacted statutory versions of the fair-comment defense. For example, the Ontario Libel and Slander Act[24] (Section 24) states:

> In an action for libel and slander in respect of words consisting partly of allegations of fact and partly of expression of opinion, a defense of fair comment shall not fail by reason only that the truth of every allegation of fact is not proved if the expression of opinion is fair comment having regard to such of the facts alleged or referred to in the words complained of as are proved.

In Quebec, defamation is subject to the province's Civil Code, particularly Article 1053, which states: "Every person capable of discerning right from wrong is responsible for the damage caused by his fault to another; whether by positive act, imprudence, neglect, or want of skill."[25] In Quebec, public interest and the absence of malice can be a complete defense to defamation. Also, in Quebec defamation occurs even if the statements were made only to the defamed party and not to third parties.

U.S. Law

Defamation usually is defined in the United States as a false statement that harms a person's reputation. As in Canadian defamation law, the statement must be directed at and concerning the individual in question.

For a statement to be defamatory, it must be untrue and must cause harm to the reputation of the complainant. Therefore, an untrue statement is not necessarily defamatory (for example, an assertion that the complainant has green eyes when in fact he has blue eyes). However, stating that the complainant sells fakes is defamatory if it is untrue.

Usually, statements of opinion held on reasonable grounds are not actionable. There is always an issue as to whether a statement is fact or opinion. A statement must be "published"—that is, made available to a third party (for example, to an auction house; in a publication, newspaper, or magazine; or on television, radio, the Internet, etc.)—in order to be defamatory.

There are a number of defenses to defamation.

1. Fair comment: This is the right to express opinions (if fairly held) about public officials and members of the art community, etc., in the public eye. It also allows for reasonable satire. Fair comment is the defense most often used by art critics and art writers.
2. Common interest: This is a defense in situations in which the author and the complainant have a common interest and the statement is not made with malice.
3. Privileged statements: Statements made for the protection of the legitimate interests of another party, especially when the information is furnished in response to a request, are not considered defamatory.
4. Public interest: The First Amendment balances private and public interests or public concern. Generally this deals with statements about public figures, who must show that the statement was made with malice—that is, "with knowledge that it was false or made with reckless disregard of whether it was false or not"— for it to be actionable.
5. A private-person complainant must prove fault on the part of the defendant if there is a matter of public concern in the statement. Most American states require that the complainant prove negligence or "gross irresponsibility" on the part of the defendant.
6. The complainant may also have to provide proof of damage, malice, or actual injury in appropriate circumstances.

Fraud or Deceit (Canada and the United States)

The tort of deceit is based on a false representation that results in damage. This tort is sometimes called *fraud* or *fraudulent misrepresentation.* To establish a cause of action for deceit, the complainant must establish

1. that a false statement or representation was made knowingly by the defendant;
2. that the intention to deceive the complainant was present; and

3. that the intention to deceive and materially induce the complainant to act was present, causing him or her damage.

This tort requires a material misstatement of purported fact; therefore, a statement of opinion would not generally be actionable. For it to be actionable, the expert's opinion would have to be made knowing that the statement was false, with a reckless disregard of the statement's truth or falsity, or with conscious ignorance of the truth.

The statement must be intended to induce the complainant to act or refrain from acting on the basis of it. The complainant also must have relied on that statement, and that reliance must have been held to be reasonable. The complainant must also prove damages.

Negligent Misrepresentation (Canada and the United States)

This is similar to fraud but arises only when there is a duty owed by one party to the other, and reliance by the latter is placed on misrepresentation by the former. Whether this relationship exists depends on the facts of the situation. Most often, it arises out of a contract, particularly a contract to render an opinion of value on a work of art or art object. Reasonable care must be taken by the expert, in accordance with the standards set by the professional organization or the custom of the trade. The rule appears to ask: "considering all the circumstances, would a reasonable person have relied on the advice provided by the expert?" Courts also consider the skill and knowledge of the person to whom the advice is given. The plaintiff must prove that damages were caused, both in fact and in law, by the expert's breach of duty of reasonable care.[26]

How far does this duty of reasonable care extend? Does it extend to third parties? Experts have been found liable in cases where they knew their clients were relying on their opinions for the sale of a work to a named third party. Some Canadian provinces and American states have extended the liability of an expert to all foreseeable injuries resulting from the misrepresentation.[27]

Slander of Title (United States) and Disparagement of Goods

A slander of title claim may be brought by an owner of personal property against a valuer or expert based on statements by that expert that cast doubt on the fact or extent of the plaintiff's ownership of a property. The statement must be more than just an opinion, however; the statement of purported fact must be false to the knowledge of the party making the statement. The complainant then must prove damages.

A number of possible defenses to this action exist based on common-law privileges, such as the right to compare products and businesses (which is often used in product and service advertising by comparison tests); the honest belief in the statement; and American state common-law defamation privileges and constitutional privileges under the First Amendment.

There is also an action for disparagement of goods (that is, trade libel). This arises on publication of an intentionally false statement of purported fact regarding a work of art or art object. Again, a reasonable opinion is not actionable.

The complainant must prove both that the statement was false and that it created an injury to his or her monetary interest. The complainant must show at least an intention to cause harm or must prove such recklessness or personal malice as spite, hatred, or ill will. In other words, the complainant must prove more than mere negligence. Defenses to this action are similar to defenses against a charge of slander of title.[28] Defamation or disparagement by an art expert are discussed in more detail in chapter 4.

Injurious Falsehood (Canada)

The Canadian tort of injurious falsehood deals with false and malicious statements about a person's goods or property. (The tort of defamation, by contrast, involves the reputation of a person.) These statements can be spoken or written. This tort goes by various other names: slander of goods or title, trade libel, malicious falsehood, and false and malicious representation. Injurious falsehood emerged toward the end of the sixteenth century when challenges to a person's title to land prejudiced that person's efforts to dispose of the land. The tort's scope was subsequently expanded to include challenges relating to the quality of the land or goods. Today it appears broad enough to encompass any damaging falsehood that interferes with prospective advantage, often economic. It appears to give a remedy not for damages to reputation but for monetary loss.

To establish a cause of action for injurious falsehood, the complainant must establish

1. that the offender made statements disparaging to the complainant's property;
2. that the words were false; and
3. that malice was present.

Moral Rights of Artists

In Canadian, U.S., and Mexican law, artists have *moral rights* in relation to their work. This too is an area of concern for any valuer, as it can affect the value of the property being appraised.

Canadian Law

Under the Canadian Copyright Act,[29] artists have been accorded moral rights in addition to copyright (Sections 14.1, 28.1, and 28.2). The Copyright Act is a federal law applicable to all provinces and territories.

Moral rights include:

1. the right of the artist to prevent his or her work from being altered, defaced, or otherwise modified to the detriment of his or her reputation;
2. the right of the artist to prevent the work from being used in association with a product or service that may be prejudicial to his or her honor or reputation;
3. the right of the artist to be declared the creator or to refuse to be declared the creator of the work.

Remedies for breach of moral rights are all-inclusive and are similar to remedies available for infringement of copyright. These include the right to obtain an injunction, damages (compensation and money), punitive damages, and legal costs.

In some instances, artists have refused to permit their names to be used in association with works they have created because some alteration, modification, or defacement requiring major restoration occurred without their consent.

The artist also has the right to determine when a work of art is completed and worthy of the artist. For instance, an artist may determine that a work is not up to standard and discard the work into a refuse container. If that work is found and the finder wishes to enter it into the marketplace for sale as a work by the artist, the artist has the right to prevent the sale as well as to disclaim the work as being his or her own, thus significantly diminishing the value of the work for commercial purposes.

It should be noted that the artist's rights may extend beyond his or her sale of work; he or she may retain intellectual property rights. For a full discussion of intellectual property rights and copyright issues, see chapter 6, "Copyright."

In Canada, the moral rights of the artist exist for the lifetime of the artist plus fifty years; this is the same term granted for most copyright protection. Recently, the European Union has extended copyright protection to the lifetime of the creator plus seventy years, as has the United States.

Moral rights, like copyright, may descend to heirs and beneficiaries. However, moral rights, unlike copyright, may not be assigned to third parties; they may be utilized or waived only by the artist or the artist's heirs.

U.S. Law

Congress passed the first Copyright Act in 1790. However, up to and even in the Copyright Act of 1976, the moral rights of creators were not recognized. As a result, other areas of the law (such as commercial competition laws, contract laws, as well as libel and slander laws) have extended to cover a libel or slander of the artist or the work of the artist.[30]

In addition, various states have passed legislation to assist artists:

California

The 1979 California Art Preservation Act (California Civil Code S.987)[31] grants rights of paternity and integrity to the artist similar to those under Canadian law, including the prohibition of the mutilation, alteration, or destruction of the artwork and the right of the artist to claim or disclaim authorship.

New York

The 1983 Artists' Authorship Rights Act[32] gives the artist the right to claim or disclaim authorship for just and valid reasons, including unauthorized defacement, mutilation, or other modification of the work without the consent of the artist that would cause damage to the reputation of the artist. (Both the California and New York legislation contain additional rights and concerns.)

Louisiana, Maine, Massachusetts, New Mexico, Pennsylvania, and Rhode Island also have laws dealing with the moral rights of visual artists.

Visual Artists Rights Acts

In December 1990, the United States Congress passed the Visual Artists Rights Act[33] and the Architectural Works Copyright Protection Act.[34] The former grants to the artist moral rights of paternity and integrity; the latter, which covers architectural works created on or after December 1, 1990, deals with the architect's plans or drawings, as well as *architectural work*, being the design of the building as defined by the law.

The creation and passage of moral rights legislation should help prevent the recurrence of past indignities to works of art, such as the repainting by the owners of an Alexander Calder mobile in colors not authorized by the artist or the mutilation of murals or sculptures to accommodate the needs of the owner of a building. Such a case occurred in a Vancouver hotel, where murals created for a dining room were cut into and altered to accommodate food pass-throughs from the kitchen.

Protection of Sellers and Valuers

In view of the foregoing risks, documents memorializing sales and opinions of authorship or value should be composed with consideration of:

1. What is expressed. An appraisal or authentication is an *opinion*, not a statement of fact. The background information must be shown or be readily available to substantiate the opinion. If the opinion is based upon reasonable grounds, the authenticator or valuer would be protected in the event of a dispute.
2. Restricting the use of the opinion to the person requesting the opinion. If it is not so restricted, the opinion may be used by the client for the reliance or comfort of third parties, such as a purchaser from the client. In the event that the opinion is wrong, that purchaser may have a claim against the valuer, dealer, or authenticator even though there was no direct contract between them. It is therefore a benefit to indicate in the appraisal report that the opinion is given for a particular purpose and only for the particular client, and that it may not be used for any other purpose without the prior written permission of the valuer.
3. Indicating that the estimate is based on and restricted to the information made available at the date of the appraisal, and that the estimate is restricted to a particular time (and place, if appropriate).
4. Including the full credentials of the valuer in the appraisal report.
5. Carefully describing the work and, if possible, attaching a photograph of it, so it is clear on what work the opinion is being expressed.
6. Adhering to the specific rules of the Uniform Standards of Professional Appraisal Practice (USPAP) promulgated by The Appraisal Foundation. The American Society of Appraisers, among other professional societies, publishes recommendations on the content appropriate for appraisal reports. In addition, various taxing authorities require an appraisal report to contain certain information.[35]

MEXICO

Commercial Transactions

Mexico has a highly centralized government, and its legal system is founded in the nation's Civil Code.[36] A civil-law system is one based mainly on Roman law, as contrasted with a common-law system (such as that in Canada and the United States), one based mainly on the common law of England.[37] Some of the typical characteristics of a common-law system are legislation by state, provincial, and federal governments and judicial opinions that are commonly regarded as binding or persuasive on a later court dealing with the same or closely related problems.[38]

However, Mexico also has a federal Commercial Code, and problems can arise when it is unclear whether the Civil Code or Commercial Code governs a transaction.[39] The Commercial Code is generally applicable to commercial transactions, but the overlapping of provisions occurs. For example, contract law is dealt with in both codes. If a transaction is commercial in nature, the provisions of the Commercial Code prevail over any contrary provision in the Civil Code. However, the Civil Code can be invoked in situations about which the Commercial Code is silent. If the situation is covered by neither code, Mexican legislators and judges fall back on general legal principles, including common law. There are numerous similarities of concepts given in the Mexican, U.S., and Canadian law in the sale of goods area.

Mexico's Commercial Code defines commercial transactions as all purchases, sales, and rentals entered into for the purpose of commercial profit, involving maintenance, personal property, or merchandise, regardless of their natural state and of whether they have been improved or manufactured (Article 75).

The code defines *merchants* (Article 3) to be persons who, having the legal capacity to engage in acts of commerce, do so as part of their ordinary and customary occupation. Art dealers could be subject to the laws regarding merchants, as "those persons who, either with or without a principal place of business, sporadically perform a mercantile transaction shall be subject to the mercantile laws, even if they are not legally considered merchants" (Article 4). Brokers, bankrupts, and those who have been convicted of crimes against property are barred from engaging in commerce in Mexico (Article 12).

Dealers should note that the Commercial Code states that if an agent contracts in his or her own name, the agent may deal directly with and will be directly liable to the persons with whom he or she deals (Article 284). However, if an agent contracts expressly in the name of the principal, the agent will not incur personal liability, and the agent's rights and obligations will be those under a common mercantile agency pursuant to the provisions of the civil law (Article 285). Moreover, an agent who possesses another person's goods or articles is responsible for their conservation in the condition in which the agent received them. Such responsibility ceases if the destruction or diminution of the merchandise or articles is the result of fortuitous circumstances, *force majeure*, the passage of time, or the inherent nature of the items (Article 295).

The Civil Code also addresses commercial transactions:

1. if the recipient of an asset acted in bad faith and conveyed it to another also acting in bad faith, the owner may retrieve the asset and claim damages from both persons (Article 1885);
2. if a third party receives an asset in good faith, the owner may recover the asset only *if the transfer was gratuitous*—such as a gift (Article 1886);
3. no one may sell that which does not belong to him or her (Article 2269); and
4. the sale of someone else's property is null and void and the seller is liable for damages and losses if he or she acted in bad faith (Article 2270).

The Contract

Both the Commercial and Civil Codes recognize the independence of contract. For a contract to be enforceable, consent of the parties is required, and the contract must relate to some object:

1. The parties must abide by all the conditions of their agreement (Article 372).
2. If the subject matter of a purchase and sales contract is goods, the contract is not perfected until the buyer has inspected and accepted the goods (Article 374).
3. A buyer must pay the price of the goods in accordance with the agreed upon terms and conditions. In the absence of any agreement, payment is in cash. If the buyer delays payment, he or she must pay interest at the legal rate on any outstanding amount (Article 380).
4. If a contract stipulates damages for failure to perform, the injured party may demand performance of the contract or the stipulated damages, but not both (Article 88).
5. If a contract does not specify with sufficient precision the type and quality of the goods to be delivered, the obligor may satisfy his or her obligation by delivering goods of average kind and quality (Article 87).

The Civil Code looks at terms of contract, both express and implied:

1. Parties to a contract may include all terms and conditions they desire, but those requirements essential to the contract, or those necessary by virtue of the nature of the particular contract, are considered to be included even if they are not expressly stated, unless they are specifically waived and such waiver is permitted by law (Article 1839).
2. The seller is obligated to deliver to the buyer the subject of the sale and to guarantee the quality of the asset (Article 2283).
3. The buyer is obligated to comply with all the obligations he or she assumed, particularly that of payment of the price at the time, at the place, and in the manner agreed on (Article 2293).

Warranties

In 1975, the Mexican government enacted the Federal Consumer Protection Act.[40] This act dictates that warranties of any goods and services will be enforced. Previously, warranties were unenforceable.

Burden of Proof

Under the Commercial Code, the person who alleges facts has the burden of proof (Article 1194). Consequently, the complainant must prove his or her actions, and the accused must prove his or her defenses. The person who denies an allegation has the burden of proof if denying the allegation contradicts a legal presumption in favor of his or her adversary (Article 1196).

Limitation Period

Once again, both codes address the issue of limitation of actions. The Civil Code distinguishes between affirmative and negative limitation of action (Article 1136), stating that the acquisition of assets by possession is referred to as an *affirmative limitation* of action; the release from obligations for failure to demand compliance is referred to as a *negative limitation.*

The period of limitation for personal property is three years when the possessor holds the property in good faith, peacefully, and continuously; in the absence of good faith, the limitation period is five years (Article 1153).

In relation to a negative limitation of action, the Civil Code states that unless the claim falls within any exceptions provided by law, the period for barring a claim is ten years from the date when demand for compliance could have been made (Article 1159). Issues may arise as to whether that date is the date of sale or the time of knowledge by the complainant. Certain claims could fall under exceptions elucidated (Article 1161) as being limited to two years:

1. fees, wages, salaries, piece work, or any other remuneration for services rendered. The limitation period begins on the date that services being rendered are terminated;
2. an action by a merchant on a claim to recover the sales price of an item sold to a person not engaged in its resale. If the sale was not on installments, the period of limitation begins from the day the merchandise was delivered.

The Commercial Code also contains relevant provisions involving limitation periods. For example, after one year, an action by retail merchants for sales made on credit is barred (Article 1043).

Statute of Frauds

Certain contracts must be in writing under Mexican law. The Commercial Code (Article 78) states that, generally, contracts must be respected no matter what the terms or conditions: "In mercantile agreements, each party assumes his obligation in the manner and terms he has chosen; the validity of the commercial transaction depends neither on compliance with formalities nor on specific requirements." However, the following are excepted (Article 79):

1. contracts that in accordance with this code or other laws must be in writing or require certain formalities for their effectiveness;
2. contracts entered into in foreign countries where the law requires them to be in writing, in certain form, and executed with certain formalities for their validity, even if not so required by Mexican law.

In either event, contracts that do not meet the respective requirements do not give rise to an obligation or claim pursuable by legal action.

Defamation and Slander

Mexican law recognizes the law of defamation and, possibly to a lesser degree, the law of injurious falsehood. The Civil Code (Article 1161[IV]) holds that claims involving insults, whether spoken or written, are barred after two years. The limitation period begins from the day the insult was heard or known or the day that the injury was caused. Written insults are considered to be libel; spoken insults, slander. Injurious falsehood, which in common law is a separate tort involving slander of title or slander of goods, could be captured by general slander (Article 1161). This is supported by similarly worded statutes of common-law jurisdictions and subsequent case-law interpretation that have held that injurious falsehood can be captured within this general concept of slander.

Moral Rights of Artists

Like Canada, Mexico grants moral rights to creators under its revised Copyright Act. The terms are similar to those in Canadian law, and both are based on the Berne Convention on Copyright.

Negligence and the General Law of Torts

The law of torts in Mexico is much like the law of unjust enrichment in common-law countries. The general law of torts is addressed by one sentence of the Civil Code: "whoever, by acting illicitly or against the good customs and habits, causes damage to another shall be obligated to compensate him, unless he can prove that the damage was caused as a result of the fault or inexcusable negligence of the victim" (Article

1910). The code offers little elaboration apart from a limitation on types of damages that can be claimed (Article 1915). Damages are at the election of the injured party and can take the form either of restoration of the damaged item to its previous condition (which is difficult with regard to art and art objects) or of payment of a liquidated sum for the damages and loss. For general torts, the period of limitation begins from the day the acts were committed. The Civil Code does not recognize damages for pain and suffering.

The Commercial Code elaborates on the concepts of negligence and bad faith, but largely within the context of contract law.

1. In the event of negligence, fault, or bad faith, the responsible party is liable for the loss, damage, or diminution in value of the goods, in addition to any applicable criminal liability (Article 377).
2. Mercantile sales may not be rescinded on the grounds of undue advantage. The injured party, however, has a claim for damages and injuries against the party acting in bad faith or with malice, in the inducement or execution of the contract, in addition to any applicable criminal action (Article 385).
3. Illicit agreements do not create obligations or claims, even when they take place in commercial transactions (Article 77).
4. Those who have been found guilty of "falsity" or other crimes against property are barred from engaging in commerce in Mexico (Article 12).

The Civil Code also addresses improper conduct, in the context of contracts.

1. A contract may be invalid because of a defect in consent, because its purpose or object is illicit, or because consent was not expressed in the manner provided by law (Article 1795). A contract entered into on behalf of another by one not duly authorized to do so is null and void, unless the nonauthorizing party subsequently ratifies it prior to the retraction or acceptance of the offer by the other party. Ratification must conform to the formalities required by law (Article 1802).
2. Consent is invalid if given by mistake, obtained by violence or duress, or exacted by fraud (Article 1812).
3. Deception in contracting is defined as any suggestion or artifice used to induce other parties into error or to keep them in that state; and it is bad faith for one party to deceitfully cover up an error once it has been discovered (Article 1815).
4. Deception or bad faith by one of the parties, or by a third party with the knowledge of one of the parties, on an essential matter of the agreement voids a contract (Article 1816).
5. A party cannot waive a future claim to void a contract on the grounds of fraud or duress (Article 1822).

The Federal Consumer Protection Act also addresses power imbalances between sellers and buyers. The act advocates a relationship between the two parties based on a "principle of truthfulness." The law was enacted after much lobbying from consumer groups concerned about the bad conduct of merchants.

Protection of Valuers

The Civil Code governs some aspects of professional conduct involving art valuers:

1. Valuers cannot purchase the assets from a sale in which they participated (Article 2281).
2. Parties to a contract for professional services can by agreement set the compensation to be paid (Article 2606).
3. Individuals who perform services in professions for which the law requires official accreditation are subject to the penalties specifically imposed for such activities. If individuals do not have accreditation, they are not entitled to any compensation for professional services rendered (Article 2608). Professionals are entitled to their fees regardless of the outcome of the matter of the work assigned to them, unless otherwise agreed (Article 2613).
4. Professionals are responsible to their clients only for negligence, bad faith, or lack of skill, in addition to any penalty incurred in the commission of a crime (Article 2615).

Conflict of Laws

The Commercial Code (Article 13) states that foreigners are free to engage in commerce in accordance with agreements and treaties with the nations of which they are nationals, if provided by the laws pertaining to the rights and obligations of non-nationals. Foreign merchants are governed by the Commercial Code and all the laws of Mexico in their mercantile operations (Article 14). If the foreign merchant is incorporated, it must abide by the applicable provisions of the Commercial Code that deal with foreign corporations.

NOTES

1. *Black's Law Dictionary*, rev. 6th ed., 1106.
2. Ibid., 1382.
3. David Stein, *Trois Picasso avant le petit déjeuner* (Paris: Robert Laffont, 1990).

4. Ontario *Sale of Goods Act*, R.S.O. 1990, c. S-1; British Columbia *Sale of Goods Act*, R.S.B.C. 1996, c. 410; Manitoba *Sale of Goods Act*, R.S.M. 1987, c. S.10.

5. Ontario *Personal Property Security Act*, R.S.O. 1990, c. P.10; Alberta *Personal Property Security Act*, S.A. 1988, c. P4.05; British Columbia *Personal Property Security Act*, R.S.B.C. 1996, c. 359; Manitoba *Personal Property Security Act*, R.S.M. 1987, c. P.35.

6. R.S.O. 1990, c. P.10, as am. S.O. 1991, c. 44, s. 7; 1993, c. 13, s. 2; 1996, c. 5, ss. 1–5.

7. Jacob S. Ziegel and David L. Denomme, *The Ontario Personal Property Security Act: Commentary and Analysis* (Aurora, Ontario, Canada: Canada Law Book, 1994).

8. British Columbia: Personal Property Security Act, R.S.B.C. 1996, c. 359.

Alberta: Personal Property Security Act, S.A. 1988, c. P-4.05.

Saskatchewan: Personal Property Security Act, S.S. 1993, c. P-6.2.

Manitoba: Personal Property Security Act, R.S.M. 1987, c. P35.

New Brunswick: Personal Property Security Act, S.N.B. 1993, c. P-7.1.

Nova Scotia: Personal Property Security Act, S.N.S. 1995-96, c. 13.

(Note: There is no comparable statute for Prince Edward Island or Newfoundland. Personal property security in Quebec is governed by the Civil Code of Quebec.)

9. *Uniform Commercial Code*, as enacted by the various states.

10. Jessica Darraby, *Art, Artifact and Architecture Law* (New York: Clark Boardman Callaghan, 1995), 4–25.

11. *Rosen v. Spanierman*, 711 F. Supp. 749 (S.D.N.Y. 1984), aff'd in part, and vacated in part, remanded 894 F.2d 28 (2d Cir. 1990); *Lawson v. London Art Group*, 708 Fed. Rptr. 2d 226, 228 (6th Cir. 1983); *Balag v. Center Art Gallery—Hawaii, Inc.*, 745 F. Supp. 1556 (D. Hawaii 1990) deals with the sale of fake Dali prints and fake certificates of authenticity by a gallery in Hawaii.

12. See, for example, *McKie v. R.H. Love Galleries, Inc.*, 1990 U.S. Dist. LEXIS 14748 (N.D. Ill. 1990). See also Darraby, *Art, Artifact and Architecture Law*.

13. *National Historic Shrines Foundation Inc. v. Dali*, 4 U.C.C. Rep Serv. 71 (N.Y. Sup. Ct. 1967).

14. See *Arnold Herstand & Co. v. Gallery*, N.Y.L.J. May 5, 1995, at 25 (N.Y. Sup. Ct. App. Div. 1995), rev'd and rem'd 211 A.D., 2d 77, 636 N.Y.S. 2d 74 (1995); *Richard L. Feigen and Co. v. Weil*, Index No. 13935/90 (Sup. Ct. N.Y. County 1992); *Uptown Gallery, Inc. v. Marjorie Weston Doniger*, Index No. 17133/90 (Sup. Ct. N.Y. County 1993).

15. *Harlingdon and Leinster Enterprises Limited v. Christopher Hull Fine Art Ltd.* (1990), 3 W.L.R. 13, (1990) 1 All. E.R. 737 (C.A.).

16. *Leaf v. International Galleries* [1950] 1 all E.R., 693 [1952] KB 86, p. 746.

17. *New York Arts and Cultural Affairs Law* §§13.01, 13.07 (McKinney 1984 and Supp. 1997).

18. *Mich. Comp. Laws Ann.* §442.321–25. (West 1990).

19. *Dawson v. Malina*, 463 F. Supp. 461 (S.D.N.Y. 1978).

20. Ibid., 93.

21. *The Shorter English Oxford Dictionary*, 3d ed., 134.

22. *Hahn v. Duveen*, 133 Misc. 871, 234 N.Y.S. 185 (Sup. Ct. 1929).

23. In the United States, they are state matters, but subject to the federal First Amendment Protection of Speech and to a possible constitutional defense. *Criminal Code*, R.S.C. 1985, c. C-46.

24. *Libel and Slander Act*, R.S.O. 1990, c. L-12.

25. *Quebec Civil Code,* Chap. 64.

26. *Amsterdam v. Daniel Goldreyer Ltd.,* 882 F. Supp 1273 (E.D.N.Y. 1995).

27. *Struna v. Wolf,* 126 Misc. 2d 1031, 484 N.Y.S. 2d 392 (Sup. Ct. 1985).

28. For a full discussion of these concerns see R. C. Lind, Jr., "Legal Risks Associated with Providing Expert Opinions and Authentications" (ALI-ABA Course of Study Problems of Museum Administration, March 20–22, 1991, 191–205). See also Steven Mark Levy, "Liability of the Art Expert for Professional Malpractice," *Wisconsin Law Review* 1991, no. 4 (1991), 596.

29. *Copyright Act*, R.S.C. 1985, c. C-42.

30. *Copyright Revision Act of 1976*, codified as amended at 17 U.S.C.A. §101 (West 1996).

31. *California Art Preservation Act 1979*, California Civil Code, Section 987 (West 1982 and Supp. 1997).

32. New York, *Artists Authorship Rights Act in 1983* (McKinney 1984 and Supp).

33. *Visual Artists Rights Act of 1990*, Pub. L. No. 101-650, tit. VI, 104 Stat. 5089 (1990).

34. *Architectural Works Copyright Protection Act of 1990*, Pub. L. No. 101-650 tit. VII, 104 Stat. 5133 (1991).

35. For a full discussion of the recommended contents of appraisals and the legal concerns for valuers, see chapter 4.

36. Abraham Eckstein and Enrique Zepada Trujillo, *Mexican Civil Code* (St. Paul, Minn.: West Publishing Co., 1996).

37. David M. Walker, ed., *Oxford Companion to Law* (Oxford: Clarendon Press, 1980), 222.

38. Ibid., 253.

39. Eckstein and Zepada Trujillo, *Mexican Civil Code.*

40. *Mexican Federal Law on Consumer Protection Act of Dec. 22, 1992*, c.c. 2248–326.

· 2 ·

Ownership

When dealing with ownership of personal property, the first issue to be resolved is who *is* the owner of the property. Ownership is considered to be the broadest right the law grants. Title links the person to the thing and includes three specific rights:

1. the right to enjoyment of the object;
2. the right to its physical use; and
3. the right to its management.

On gaining ownership of a particular object, the owner may deal with that object to the exclusion of all other parties except those who have equal legal power and control over the property. These "other parties" are described in chapter 3, "Limits on Ownership."

There is no general registry or registration procedure in North America with respect to most personal property. This might result in difficulties should various ownership claims be made. Therefore, prior possession still serves as the principal mode of proving title for personal property.[1]

With respect to original works created by artists, there is a form of property right in addition to title or possession of the object. This is an intellectual right, namely copyright, usually in favor of the creator. This right is not transferred with ownership of the object except with the permission of the artist. Copyright is discussed in detail in chapter 6.

Ownership must be distinguished from possession, for works are often in the possession of persons who are not the owners. For example, a work of art may be lent to a museum for exhibition, held as security for a loan, or come into someone's possession by theft. In such cases the work is in the hands of one party, but title or ownership is held by another party.

OBTAINING TITLE

There are different ways of gaining ownership, and there are different purposes in ownership. Personal property can be acquired by outright purchase, gift, inheritance, a trust, exchange, or possession of abandoned goods (i.e., possessory title). Ownership may be acquired for different purposes—for example, for personal ownership of the property, for resale, for financing, for destruction of the object, for completion of a set or group of works, for completion of a collection, and so forth.

Title Obtained by Purchase

Works may be purchased from a number of sources. These sources may be in different markets and create different levels of market value. A work purchased directly from an artist may be bought at a price below that offered by the retail gallery representing the artist, which may in turn differ from a price paid at auction.

Purchase from the Artist

When purchasing a work directly from the artist who created it, the buyer should receive a proper bill of sale. It should include the following elements:

1. name of the vendor/artist (or the corporation of the artist);
2. confirmation that the vendor is the owner and has the authority to sell the work;
3. description of the purchaser;
4. description of the work being transferred;
5. warranty that the work is free and clear of any liens;
6. the results of any discussion with the artist/creator regarding copyright issues, such as permission to reproduce the work for specific purposes (for example, photographs of the work for insurance purposes, nonprofit use, or reproduction in catalogs, posters, and other venues related to the public exhibition of the work).

Purchase from a Retail Vendor

A purchase from a retail vendor entails the same warranties as a purchase from an artist/vendor with the exception of copyright, which the vendor will not ordinarily own. A retail vendor selling in the ordinary course of business to a bona fide purchaser for value (that is, to a retail buyer for a fair price) can pass title to the purchaser free and clear of any liens, mortgages, or claims against the work that may have been placed on it by the vendor or the vendor's predecessors in title. The one exception, which will be dealt with separately, is stolen goods sold to an innocent purchaser (someone who has no reasonable knowledge of the theft).

Under the U.S. Uniform Commercial Code, in a purchase from an artist or a retail vendor by an innocent purchaser, the innocent purchaser would obtain legal title to the work (Section 9-307), thereby obtaining both ownership and possession of the work. The purchaser becomes the "owner" of the property.

In Canada, most provincial sale of goods acts and personal property security acts provide for a similar result. For instance, the Personal Property Security Act of Ontario provides that:

> A buyer of goods from a seller who sells the goods in the ordinary course of business takes them free from any security interest therein given by the seller, even though it is perfected and the buyer knows of it, unless the buyer also knew that the sale constituted a breach of the security agreement. [Section 28(1)][2]

However, in 1998 only the following Canadian jurisdictions had such acts: British Columbia, Alberta, Saskatchewan, Manitoba, Ontario, New Brunswick, Nova Scotia, and the Yukon.

Consignment

Works of fine and decorative art, collectibles, antiques, and jewelry are often supplied to dealers on a consignment basis. Three types of consignment situations are generally recognized in law:

1. goods delivered to a potential buyer on approval to determine whether the purchaser will purchase the goods (this is called *sale on approval*);
2. goods supplied to a prospective buyer for resale in the course of business; and
3. goods delivered by a principal to an agent (dealer) for sale by the agent in his or her name.

In all of these consignment agreements, title is retained by the supplier of the goods (be it the artist, wholesaler, or collector) until he or she is paid by the vendor. Thus, the dealer acts as an agent to sell the goods. Usually the agent is a retailer who is in the business of selling such goods, while the owner is a private individual, wholesaler, or artist.[3]

Filing or registration of the goods may be required under various personal property statutes. This would be necessary if, for example, the consignment arrangement involved a form of financing, such as an advance against future sales.

In the United States, there are numerous artist/dealer consignment state statutes. These often create a trust relationship between the artist and the dealer resulting in a fiduciary ("trustee") obligation on the dealer.[4] To date, no Canadian jurisdiction has created similar legislation.

In consignment sales made in the ordinary course of business, a bona fide purchaser without notice takes title free and clear of any claim that the owner may have against the vendor, even if the owner is unpaid, or the work sold for less than the amount agreed on between the owner and the agent, or other terms between the original parties were breached in the sale by the vendor/agent.

Purchase or Sale by the Professional Dealer

In the United States, the test of good faith used in the buying or selling of property by professionals is higher than the test applied to the ordinary, bona fide purchaser. In ordinary retail sales (as opposed to public auction sales), U.S. courts, especially those of New York, have determined that the good faith of art merchants and professionals must comprise not only honesty in fact but also reasonable commercial standards of fair dealing in the trade.

For example, *Porter v. Wertz*[5] dealt with a Utrillo painting owned by Samuel Porter. The work was loaned to a purchaser for viewing related to the possible sale of the work. The purchaser turned out to be a scoundrel who, through an accomplice, sold the painting to a major gallery. The gallery, in turn, sold it to an innocent purchaser, who later resold it.

Porter sued the scoundrel and the gallery to recover the painting or its value. The gallery argued that it was an innocent purchaser and should not be held liable.

The court, however, held that the defendant gallery was not an innocent purchaser in the ordinary course of business. It had not made any effort to verify the authority of the vendor to sell the painting, which was inconsistent with "reasonable commercial standards." The gallery was declared to have failed to exercise the sound practice necessary to produce good faith in a buyer in the ordinary course of business.

This decision appears to be relevant to the sale or purchase of property generally, so it applies to dealers of antiques, valuable rugs, jewelry, and unique books as well as to other professionals who must comply with "reasonable commercial standards of fair dealing in the trade."[6]

Title Obtained by Gift

Gifts of works of art, antiques, and other such property are often passed between family members and other loved ones. From time to time, corporations also make gifts of this nature to retiring staff. How does one determine whether an item is a gift or a work on loan?

In a number of cases, retiring employees have taken with them works of art and/or objects of value that were in their offices during their employment. Do such works belong to the occupants and, therefore, do they have the right to take such works? Or are these works part of the office décor and, as such, belong to the corporation? What is required in law to prove that a gift has been made?

In law, the intention of the owner of the work is paramount. Did the owner intend to make a gift, rather than just give up possession of the work? There must be some indication that more than mere possession has been transferred. A signed deed of gift is now often required by public institutions receiving gifts from donors. Often, taxing authorities require such evidence before issuing or accepting a tax receipt indicating that a work has in fact been donated.

Is it necessary that there be a formal transfer of possession? This question arises from time to time when public institutions have been given gifts by donors who then borrow the works. The intention of the donor is paramount, and the best evidence of that intention is a written document of transfer of title. A verbal transfer of title of personal property, although valid in many places, is a poor second: memories fade, parties die, and circumstances change.

Title Obtained by Inheritance

Inheritance is a form of gift. Rather than a lifetime gift, it is a gift from the deceased (the testator) to the beneficiary, either by will or—if there is no will (i.e., on an intestacy)—by the estate laws of the relevant jurisdiction.

One of the concerns with an inheritance (as well as with a lifetime gift) is possible interference by the cultural property laws of the country where the objects are located. For instance, if the beneficiary lives in one country and the testator and the work of art are in another country, an export permit may be required. For example, suppose the testator and the work of art are located in Canada. The work of art is by a deceased artist, is more than fifty years old and has been in the country for more than thirty-five years; however, the beneficiary daughter of the deceased lives in California. Pursuant to the Canadian Cultural Property Export and Import Act,[7] if the work has been determined to be a work of outstanding significance and of national importance, an export permit will be required for the export of that work to the beneficiary. This could result in a significant delay to permit a Canadian institution to attempt to negotiate the purchase of the work from the estate. For a discussion of cultural property laws, see chapter 9.

Title Obtained by Beneficial Trust

A *beneficial owner* is an individual who has the right to use an item but does not hold legal title to it; legal title rests with another individual or in some other legal form, such as a trust. The beneficiary of the trust may receive legal title to the object at some time in the future or may never get it, depending on the terms of the trust. The transfer of property held as a beneficial interest under a trust must be made in writing.

A trust is a property relationship that generally involves three parties: the grantor, the trustee, and the beneficiary. The very nature of a trust is that it is held for a third party. The one who creates a trust is called the grantor, settlor, or trustor. The trustee holds the trust for the benefit of the beneficiary, for whom the trust is being administered. The trustee owns the legal title and holds the property for the beneficiary.

The trust may be one established and operated during the lifetime of the grantor or one established by the will of the grantor that operates only after the death of the grantor. As the beneficiary has an equitable interest in the trust (that is, an interest in the substance of a property but not title to it), there is a fiduciary relationship between the trustee and the beneficiary.

To create a valid trust, an identifiable beneficiary must exist. Beneficiaries need not be specific individuals but may be named from a specified class. Usually the trustee cannot be the sole beneficiary but may be one of the beneficiaries. The trustee has an equitable duty to handle the trust with due care for the benefit of the beneficiary.

There are several other situations in which an individual can be a beneficial owner: chattel mortgages and conditional sales agreements.

Chattel Mortgage

Under a chattel mortgage (a form of security interest), the mortgagee takes a security interest in personal property owned by the mortgagor. The personal property remains in the possession of the mortgagor; however, the mortgagee has the right to seize and sell the property in the event of a default by the mortgagor.

Conditional Sales Agreement

Under a conditional sale, title remains with the vendor until full payment is made by the purchaser, although the purchaser may resell the work in the ordinary course of business. An innocent retail purchaser takes title of the property free and clear of any such security or claim against it, even with registration.

Under a conditional sales agreement, an object is purchased on a time-payment basis. Often these transactions will permit the purchaser to obtain possession of the object purchased but not obtain title until payment is made in full. Prior to payment being made in full, the purchaser is a beneficial owner of the work, but bare legal title may be held by the vendor until full payment has been received, at which time legal title will pass to the purchaser. In the event of default, the vendor has, among other rights, the right to repossess the object.

Title Obtained by Way of Exchange

An exchange is ordinarily the same sort of trade we made as children: I will give you X if you give me Y. I will give you X plus Z if you give me Y.

Commercial art galleries, antique shops, and vendors of property often allow a purchaser to trade in a previously purchased item on a more expensive work, the difference to be paid in cash.

The best evidence of an exchange is the intention to make the exchange, a transfer of property, and documentation of the exchange, preferably a bill of sale showing the total sale, the credit for the trade-in, and the transfer of title to the newly acquired object.

Without written documentation, it is difficult to prove ownership of the newly acquired object and the transfer of the traded object in exchange or partial exchange. Written documentation is especially helpful in respect to any insolvency, bankruptcy, or transfer of business of the vendor. It will ensure that the property is not subject to any creditor of the vendor or any purchaser of the vendor's business.

Possessory Title by Adverse Possession

Possession without right is called *wrongful* or *adverse*.[8] The possession of an object by a person claiming title by adverse possession must be exclusive, open, and continuous. The possession must also be occurring without the permission of the owner. Different states have different statutes of limitations on actions brought by the owner of a work against the possessor. There is no conclusive finding as to whether the expiration of the limitations period extinguishes title or only prevents the real owner of the work from suing for a return of it.

Statutes of limitations for movable or personal property objects are generally provincial laws in Canada and state statutes in the United States. The Mexican Civil and Commercial Codes contain clauses regarding limitations of action.

In the province of Quebec, the Civil Code governs found property.[9] The code provides that in the absence of special legislation, chattels found on the ground, on the public highways, or elsewhere (including on the property of others) without known owner, belong to the owner (unless the owner abandoned them). However, if they are not claimed, they belong to the finder by right of possession. (For a discussion of abandoned property, see chapter 3, "Limits on Ownership.")

Artist or Dealer Abandonment

From time to time, works have been left with a dealer or vendor and the owner can no longer be found. This happens, for example, when artists or customers leave works or valuables with dealers or retailers for resale, the property remains unsold, and the artist or customer can no longer be located.

For goods to be considered abandoned, the owner of the goods must voluntarily relinquish ownership by both intention and action. For instance, someone who has cleared out the garage and sent its contents to a charity for sale would have no claim if one of the works sold to an innocent purchaser turned out to be a valuable treasure.

A number of cases in this area concern artworks removed from buildings by municipal, provincial, or state authorities and warehoused for many years. Did the city, province, or state abandon its rights of ownership? In most cases the courts have determined that there was a voluntary abandonment of possession but not of ownership. Intent is not presumed, and proof of intention and action to abandon the goods must be submitted.[10]

In one U.S. case, *Jiri Mucha v. Charles King*,[11] the son of the Moravian artist Alphonse Mucha sued Charles King for the return of a painting that Alphonse Mucha had painted in or about 1904 and that, as late as 1980, was believed to have been lost. It was a 7-by-7-inch oil painting known as *Quo Vadis,* and it drew its inspiration from the novel of the same name. It depicts, in an art nouveau style, a man and an adoring female slave in a classical pose. The man is a self-portrait.

In 1979, the Newcomb-Macklin Art Gallery in Chicago, to which Alphonse Mucha had consigned the painting in 1920, gave it away to a hot-tub merchant, who sold it to an art dealer. The dealer sold the painting to King in 1981 for $35,000 in cash and merchandise. The painting was in poor condition, and King hired an expert to restore it. King testified that the restored painting might fetch as much as $800,000. The painting was in the restorer's custody pending the outcome of the lawsuit and full payment of the restorer's outstanding fee.

At trial, Mucha won the return of the work, subject to paying King's expenses incurred in having the work restored.

On appeal, King's lawyers argued in part, as follows:

1. that Alphonse Mucha and his heirs were dispossessed of the painting, as the work had been held by Newcomb-Macklin Art Gallery in Chicago for more than five years before the lawsuit was brought. Therefore, Jiri Mucha's right to recover the painting had expired under the five-year Illinois Statute of Limitations applicable to personal property.
2. that Jiri Mucha had abandoned all rights to the painting to the gallery in 1958, when the gallery wrote Mucha advising him that the painting had been with the gallery since 1921 and stored at its expense, and the painting should belong to the gallery to help cover the expenses and charges.

The court determined that there had been a consignment agreement between the artist and the gallery, and that there was no fixed time in the contract for the return of the goods or termination of the agreement. Therefore, the agreement was at the will of the bailee or gallery. (All consignment contracts are *bailment* agreements, if possession of the object is given by the owner to the gallery, dealer, or retailer for resale.[12]) There had been no demand for the return of the goods or any refusal or other act on the part of the gallery, of which the bailor had notice, that was hostile or inconsistent with the bailment arrangement. Only if a denial of the bailment and a conversion of the property had taken place would the Illinois Statute of Limitations start to run.

In this case there was ongoing correspondence between the artist and the gallery, dealing with works to be shipped for exhibition and other matters. This correspondence showed that there was no intention by the artist or his estate to abandon the bailment, nor was there an objection by the gallery. The artist died in 1939, survived by his wife, his son, and his daughter. His wife Marie became the owner of the work and asked the gallery in 1940 to send *Quo Vadis* to New York. Jiri Mucha continued the correspondence thereafter.

The court stated that there did not appear to be any intent by the family to abandon the painting; moreover, that unless the alleged abandonment takes the form of a quit claim deed, there was at least knowledge of the outstanding rights in the work. In fact, the correspondence indicated that the gallery was prepared to return some of Mucha's works upon payment of various storage charges. It was conceded that the statute of limitations did not begin to run until the owner discovered or should have discovered that the gallery had converted the bailed property for its own use. There is some question by the court about whether this concession (that is, that the statute of limitations does not begin to run until the bailor discovers or should have discovered the conversion) should have been made by King. Otherwise, the time frame under the act could start running from the time of the conversion, whether or not discovered by the bailor.

Most states that have dealt with this problem take the view that discovery is necessary for a statute of limitations to begin to run. For example, New Jersey held that artists and their heirs were entitled to invoke the discovery rule when diligently searching or seeking the recovery of a lost or stolen painting.[13]

The full facts of the Mucha case are interesting. In 1979, the gallery owner decided to close down the Newcomb-Macklin Art Gallery and liquidate the contents. A gentleman from Great Lakes Hot Tubs Inc. bought a fan and an ice box from the gallery for $65 and, on his way out, asked whether he could have some of the rolled up paintings he had seen in the basement. The gallery owner gave him the works, including *Quo Vadis*, as a gift.

A year later, the hot-tub merchant sold *Quo Vadis* for $150 to a Chicago art dealer named Tomc who did business under the name "Fly-By-Nite Galleries."

Charles King, a dealer in antiquities who had no place of business but worked out of a shopping bag and had previously done business with Tomc, wanted to buy *Quo Vadis*. A price of $35,000 was agreed on, which King paid in cash, silver candlesticks, and other silver objects over a period of a year, completing the transaction in 1981.

King did not argue that a merchant entrusted with goods is allowed to transfer the entruster's title to a buyer in the ordinary course of business because the owner of Great Lakes Hot Tubs was not an innocent purchaser. He was not a buyer, but the recipient of a gift.

Therefore, he did not obtain Mucha's title to the painting and could not convey title to Fly-By-Nite and thence to King, even if King were a buyer in the ordinary course. (King might have a claim against Tomc for breach of warranty of title, but no such claim was made in the lawsuit, nor was Tomc a party to the action.)

In 1982, a friend of King's wrote to Jiri Mucha seeking information about the content and symbolism of the painting. Jiri Mucha then investigated the transaction and began an action against King in 1983. The letter from King's friend made Jiri Mucha aware of the possible disposition of the painting by the gallery, and he commenced his action within five years both of the receipt of the letter and of the date of the conversion (which was 1982). As a result, Jiri Mucha owned the painting and was entitled to get it back from someone who was not a buyer in the ordinary course of business.

The court also determined that although Mucha's sister was not a party to the action, she retained her 50 percent interest in the painting. Before allowing Mucha to take possession of the painting, the court required that Mucha file an acknowledgment signed by his sister that she was aware of the recovery of the valuable painting, of which she was a 50 percent owner. The court found that there was no abandonment, nor did the statute of limitations prevent the return of the work to the artist's heirs.

Joint Title

Joint title is a common interest in title held by two or more persons. For example, a husband and wife may jointly purchase a work of art, or two museums may join in the purchase of a work of art because the work is too expensive for one institution. (In 1973 the Metropolitan Museum of Art and the Louvre jointly purchased a medieval ivory comb; in 1981 the J. Paul Getty Museum and the Norton Simon Foundation jointly purchased *The Holy Family* by Nicholas Poussin.)

The division of a joint title may pose substantial difficulties, especially on the dissolution of a marriage or partnership.

Community Property Title

Community property is acquired through the effort of both spouses. Both have title to the property, regardless of who paid for it.[14]

Under New York law, marital property encompasses "all property acquired by either or both spouses during the marriage and before the execution of a separation agreement or the commencement of a matrimonial action, regardless of the form in which title is held."[15]

Right of Survivorship

When two individuals (not corporations or trusts) jointly own an object and one of them dies, the surviving owner takes total ownership of the work, free and clear of any beneficiaries of the deceased owner.

Fragmented Title

Parties can own a percentage interest in a property by way of tenancy in common. For example, three people may buy an expensive painting as an investment. Each contributes a part of the purchase price: one of the investors pays half the sale price and becomes half owner, and each of the other two become quarter owners. The legal viability of the standard valuation technique of discounts for fractionalized interests in art has not yet been tested. Discounts for minority ownership and/or lack of control are routine features of business valuation.

Tenancy in common does not give a right of survivorship. Therefore, if one of the owners dies, the other owners do not obtain title to the deceased's portion of the work. The title descends by way of the deceased's will or the operation of law. If there is no will, it descends to the next-of-kin or heirs of the deceased.

There is current discussion and concern by valuers as to the validity of discounting in cases of fragmented title—that is, reducing the value of fractional interests in fine art and art objects if that interest is a minority or noncontrolling interest.

In the United States, gifts are sometimes given to museums on a fractional basis. For example, a collector may own a million-dollar painting that he or she wishes to donate to a museum. For tax reasons, the collector may give the museum only a portion of the work in any given year, say one-tenth of the artwork yearly for ten years. The tax benefit would apply over those ten years, better utilizing the benefit against the donor's income. This form of donation is not permitted under Canadian tax rules.

SPECIAL U.S. LEGISLATION FOR BUYING OR SELLING FINE ART

Print Disclosure Statutes

The art-multiple market has expanded dramatically and contains many variants of limited-edition works. A limited-edition work is a work produced a finite number of times (prints), with the number of times determined in advance by the artist and the prints created by the artist or by the master printer under the guidance of the artist. The edition would be limited both as to the number of public works to be sold and as to the number of artist's and printer's proofs. Each of the public works is numbered with the image number and the edition number and is signed by the artist.

With changes in technology and increased public interest in owning limited-edition works, new variations or "mischiefs" on the concept of the fine art print have entered the marketplace. In some instances, the limited aspect of the print is determined not by quantity but by time. For example, all orders received by a certain date would be filled by the publisher or artist.

Another mischief is the "limited-edition reproduction" by a living artist, who signs and numbers the edition of a work that is not "original" in usual art parlance. Such editions are reproductions (often very good ones) of a pre-existing work done in another medium and recreated by photography (or photolithography as it was sometimes called).

A third situation arises when a limited-edition print is created for a particular geographic area and then reproduced in additional numbers for another geographic area. For instance, a work might be sold in North America as being from an edition of one hundred. However, there might be an additional edition for Europe, or editions on other kinds of paper, or editions numbered in a different way. So the edition is in fact in the thousands, not the one hundred signed on the work purchased by the North American purchaser.

States with large art markets are concerned by this practice and have begun to regulate the market for this type of material. For example, Hawaii became concerned when photomechanical reproductions of existing or forged Salvador Dali works were being produced without the permission of the artist. Arkansas, California, Georgia, Hawaii, Illinois, Maryland, Michigan, Minnesota, New York, Oregon, South Carolina, and Wisconsin have specific legislation regarding this issue, and more than twenty states require some form of disclosure in respect to multiples.[16] Often these statutes apply not only to prints but also to multiple sculptures in an edition. The purpose of such legislation is to compel disclosure, by sellers to buyers, of all relevant information. The legislation varies substantially from state to state; however, the intent is similar—namely, to prevent fraud from being pulled on an innocent buyer who is not a professional.

The New York Arts and Cultural Affairs Statute[17]

This statute applies to art merchants and provides that no merchant shall sell or consign a multiple in, into, or from New York State unless a written description is furnished to the purchaser or consignee prior to the sale or consignment. This document must set out designated descriptive information. If the prospective purchaser requests it, the information must be transmitted to the purchaser prior to payment or to the placement of an order for a multiple. If payment is made by a purchaser prior to delivery of an art multiple, the descriptive information must be supplied at the time of or prior to delivery.

If the purchaser decides to return the multiple based on reasons related to matters contained in the information, the purchaser is entitled to a refund as long as he or she returns the multiple in substantially the condition in which it was received and within thirty days of receiving it. Also, if after payment and delivery it should be found that the information provided is incorrect, the purchaser may be entitled to certain remedies.

With respect to auctions, the information may be furnished in catalogs or other written materials readily available for consultation prior to the sale, provided that the bill of sale, receipt, or invoice describing the transaction makes reference to the catalog and lot number in which the information is supplied.

The New York statute prohibits an art merchant from distributing a catalog, prospectus, flyer, or other written material or advertisement in, into, or from New York State soliciting a direct sale by inviting transmittal of payment for a specific multiple, unless it clearly states, in close physical proximity to the description of the multiple, the descriptive information required by the statute, for the appropriate time period. In lieu of the required information being set out in full at the dealer's premises, the material or advertisement may set forth the information required by the law. For instance, an advertisement might inform the public that "Article 15 of the New York Arts and Cultural Affairs Law" provides for disclosure in writing of certain information concerning multiples of prints and photographs when sold for more than one hundred dollars each, exclusive of frame, prior to the sale. This law requires disclosure of the identity of the artist, the artist's signature, the medium, whether the multiple is a reproduction, when the multiple was produced, use of the *master* (i.e., the mold or plate that produced the multiple), and the number of multiples in the limited edition.

Art merchants regularly engaged in sales and multiples must also post in a conspicuous place in each place of business a sign containing the following information: Article 15 of the New York Arts and Cultural Affairs Law provides for the disclosure in writing of certain information concerning prints and photographs. This information is available to you in accordance with that law.

For a breach of the statute, the art merchant can be held responsible for the funds paid by the purchaser for the work, together with interest from the time of payment, as long as the work is returned in substantially the same condition in which it was received by the purchaser. This remedy does not bar the purchaser from making any claims for damages or for other available remedies.

If the violation by the vendor is willful, the purchaser may recover triple damages, and the court may also award costs. However, if it is found that the purchaser brought the action in bad faith, the court may award appropriate costs to the dealer.

There is no limitation period for bringing an action under the New York statute. However, most of the other statutes provide that the action must be brought within one year after discovery of the breach of the statute and not later than three years after the print was purchased. However, under the UCC (Section 2-725), an action for breach of any contract warranty with respect to sale of goods has a four-year limitation period. When that limitation period starts to run—whether from the date of purchase or from the date of knowledge of the breach of the statute—is an evolving area of litigation. (See chapter 3, "Limits on Ownership," for a discussion of the evolving law on the time requirements for an owner to bring action against an innocent purchaser of a stolen object.)

Under an amendment to the New York Arts and Cultural Affairs Law,[18] sculpture was defined to include three-dimensional fine art objects of media other than glass produced in multiples from a mold, model, cast, form, or other prototype and sold or offered for sale or consigned in, into, or from New York State for an amount in excess of $1,500. The notice to be posted under the act was revised to include information in respect to sculpture being sold for more than $1,500.

Section 15.10, specifically relating to sculpture, was added to the act. It requires that the information provided to a possible purchaser include:

1. the name of the artist;
2. the title of the work;
3. the foundry;
4   the medium;
5. the dimensions;
6. the date produced;
7. the number of the cast; and
8. whether the sculpture was authorized by the artist or, if produced after the artist's death, was authorized in writing by the artist or by the estate, heirs, or other legal representatives of the artist.

Information on works created since January 1, 1991, must also include:

1. whether and how the sculpture and edition are numbered;
2. the size of the edition or proposed edition;
3. the size of any prior edition;
4. whether sculpture casts were produced in excess of the stated size of the edition or proposed edition and, if so, the total number of such excess casts produced, or proposed to be produced, and how they will be numbered; and
5. whether the artist has stated in writing a limitation on the number of additional sculpture casts to be produced in excess of the stated size of the edition or purported edition and, if so, the total number of such excess casts produced or proposed to be produced and how they will be numbered.

For sculptures not made from the master and produced after January 1, 1991, the information also must include:

1. the means by which the copy was made;
2. whether the copy was authorized by the artist, the estate, or the artist's heirs; and
3. whether the copies are of the same material and size as the master.

The legislation also outlines the marks to be used to identify each of the sculptures produced and the records that must be kept in respect to each edition.

The California Resale Royalties Act

This act[19] applies to sales of works of fine art that take place in California after January 1, 1977. The statute covers fine art sold by a seller residing in California as well as sales of fine art taking place in California. Under the act, after the initial sale, on a resale (subject to certain exceptions listed below) during the lifetime of the artist, 5 percent of the sales price is payable to the artist; thereafter it is paid to his or her estate. This right exists for the lifetime of the artist and twenty years thereafter, and the act applies to artists who are American citizens or residents of California for two years. If the artist or the artist's estate cannot be located, the 5 percent is held for the artist by the California Arts Council. The 5 percent of the amount of the sale may be waived only by a written contract providing for an amount in excess of 5 percent. No assignment is permitted to have the effect of creating a waiver, which is prohibited by the act.

The act covers sales of fine art at auction or by a gallery, dealer, broker, museum, or other person acting as the agent for the seller. Any amounts held by any seller or agent for payment to artists pursuant to the act are exempt from seizure by the seller's or agent's creditors.

The act does not apply to work sold for less than $1,000; to initial sales; to a resale for a gross price less than the purchase price paid by the seller; to exchanges of artworks where the fair market value of the work exchanged is less than $1,000; or to various other exceptions.

In determining the value of a work where the California Act may apply, a valuer must decide whether the rights of the artist should be taken into account. Should the painting be valued at 95 percent of fair market value for any owner? Should it be valued at 100 percent of value subject to the 5 percent claim of the artist? The purpose of the appraisal may be significant in this decision.

The valuer must decide also whether other resale rights apply. There are resale rights in favor of artists in a number of countries, including Belgium, France, Italy, Poland, Uruguay, and the Czech Republic, among others. Is the work by an artist who is a resident or citizen of any of these countries? If so, and if the valuer has not taken into account the rights of the artist, does the artist have a right to sue the valuer for negligent appraisal? Does the valuer owe the artist any duty even if the artist is not a party to the contract? Should the valuer know or have known of the legislation and the rights of the artist in the work?

MEXICAN LAW

Although each state in Mexico has its own civil code, Mexico's federal Civil Code[20] applies to the federal district and territories and to all matters over which the federal government has constitutionally asserted its exclusive jurisdiction. All state codes are similar to the federal Civil Code.

Mexicans classify property as movables and immovables, or personal and real property.

Ownership and Title

Canadian and U.S. law recognize the concept that ownership can be divided in time (for example, life estates) and that various interests can be created in property (for example, reversions). Such interests are not acknowledged in Mexican law, nor is there a division of ownership into "equitable" and "legal" title as exists in the common-law jurisdictions of Canada and the United States. For instance, legal title may exist in the trustee, but the equitable ownership of the trust property is in the beneficiary of the trust. In short, Mexico recognizes only the owner of a property, the existing person who holds title to the property. Mexico also does not recognize the right of survivorship in property or joint tenancies. Co-ownership by two or more persons (i.e., tenancy in common) is recognized. A co-owner has the right to force a judicial sale or initiate a physical division of the property.

The owner of property enjoys three rights in Mexico:

1. the right to dispose of the property, whether by sale, gift, bequest, or destruction;
2. the right to the benefits or income produced by the property (such as interest or rent); and
3. the right to use and enjoy the property.

Therefore, property can be bought, sold, gifted, willed, or inherited. Mexican law does not share common-law countries' preoccupation with contracts for consideration. Property other than real property can be transferred without formality, unless it is transferred by a will. Promises to make gifts are not generally enforceable, as there is not a requirement of consideration (that is, any form of payment that is ordinarily required to support the obligation in law of the promisor to proceed with the promise). Property can be acquired by occupation and use if possession is quiet, continuous, and public. This requirement of public possession appears analogous to the Anglo-American requirement of open, notorious, and adverse possession and claim of ownership. For acquisition to be recognized, possession must be for three years in good faith or five years otherwise.

Mexico has imposed mandatory national ownership of all minerals and national art treasures (i.e., pre-Columbian artifacts). Its stringent cultural laws prohibit the export of any national object not exempted by the government. These statutory controls have attracted some international criticism. Legal art scholars criticize art-source countries such as Mexico for failing to define adequately the parameters of these national treasures (i.e., identify, define, and characterize the objects).[21] This problem leads to another: without adequate documentation of national treasures, it becomes a challenge to trace the origin of works that do emerge as the focus of a court battle (in other words, was it merely found in Mexico or is it actually Mexican in origin?).

Under the Mexican Civil Code, possession of property gives rise to the presumption of ownership of that property (Article 798). A person is a possessor of the property if he or she exercises actual control over it (Article 790), although this rule is somewhat modified by the rules concerning bailment. For instance, if the owner of property delivers it to another, pursuant to an arrangement by which he or she grants the other the right to possession of the goods, both parties have possession of the property, one holding title having original possession and the other having derivative possession (Article 791). However, a person who possesses property by virtue of some right other than ownership, as in the case of a bailee, is not presumed to have ownership of the property.

Thus, ownership and possession are distinct; anyone who is an owner also has possessorship as a matter of law, and ownership may be determined independent of possession (Article 803).

Recovery of Possession

A person's possession is protected against those who do not have a better right to the possession (Article 803). Where property is lost, it is to be reinstated to the possessor. If the possession of the property is of dubious legality, the property will be placed on deposit until the right to its possession is determined (Article 803). The possessor of an article acquired in good faith does not lose rights to possession until it is demonstrated that the possessor was aware that his or her possession was wrongful (Article 808). It is to be noted that a person is a possessor in good faith if he or she comes into possession under a good and sufficient title granting the right of possession or if he or she is ignorant of any defects of title that impair the person's legal right to possession (Article 806).

Trusts

Early legislation in Mexico dictated an almost irrevocable agency between donor and trustee. Today, the trustee is viewed as an individual with a duty to manage a trust in accordance with the terms of that trust. In its strict regulation of trusts, Mexico has granted only a few licensed banks the authority to become trustees or fiduciaries. Constructive and resulting trusts (trusts implied by law and not by the creator of the trust) are not recognized in Mexico. The Civil Code, however, in addressing damages for "unjust enrichment," could indirectly invoke these remedial trusts.

Security Interests

Mexican law does recognize some security interests. However, the chattel mortgage, common in the United States and Canada, is not recognized in Mexico, nor is the concept of a floating lien. A *floating lien* or a *floating charge* is a security that is an equitable charge on the assets for the time being of a going concern. It allows the business to be carried on and the property it comprises to be dealt with in the ordinary course of business until the undertaking charged ceases to be a going concern or until the creditor in some way or other intervenes when the charge "crystallizes" (becomes due).[22]

The Civil Code addresses secured transactions, including registration of interests and priority of interests, within a framework much like that of the United States or Canada.

The common security devices for movable property are as follows:

1. The Pledge: This is analogous to the pledge found in U.S. and Canadian law; however, in Mexico, it is necessary to distinguish between the civil pledge and

the commercial pledge, which applies only to movable property. Civil pledges are governed by provisions of the Civil Code, while commercial pledges fall under the Commercial Code. Under the commercial pledge, the creditor, in some cases a third party, must be given actual possession of the property. Under the civil pledge, a constructive or juridical possession is sufficient.[23]

2. The Conditional Sales Contract: There are two types—the sale subject to rescission and the sale with title reserved. They function similarly to the conditional sale under U.S. and Canadian law, with one important exception: under Canadian and U.S. law, such sales can be recorded and thereby become effective against third parties; in Mexico, although some kinds of contracts may be recorded in the public registry, third parties cannot be put on notice of security interests in movables unless the movables can be absolutely identified, typically by serial number. Considerable movables are not protected because of this registration requirement.

3. Transfer of Ownership: Ownership in property is transferred as it is in the United States and Canada. Property can be bought, sold, given away, willed, inherited, or acquired by prescription (adverse possession). A voluntary transfer may be accomplished by contract, written deed, or will, or by physical delivery of movables. As a general rule, no formalities are required for the effective voluntary transfer of property, although some kinds of transactions must be formalized by a notary either recording them in the public registry or otherwise.

Disclosure Statutes

In response to consumer concerns, Mexico enacted the Federal Consumer Protection Act. Under the act, all advertisements or publicity regarding goods and services must be objective, accurate, and truthful. Contracts are subject to the "principle of transparency" and should be clear and precise. The act also requires that merchants provide "truthful and sufficient information" to consumers. The act prohibits misleading advertising, labeling, or markings concerning the origin, uses, properties, or characteristics of personal property.

NOTES

1. Bruce H. Ziff, *Principles of Property Law* (Toronto: Carswell, 1993).
2. See the *Personal Property Security Act*, R.S.O. 1990, c. P.10.
3. Jacob S. Ziegel and David L. Denomme, *Ontario Personal Property Security Act Commentary and Analysis* (Toronto: Canada Law Books, Inc., 1994).

4. For a detailed account of the American statutes, see Franklin Feldman, Stephen E. Weil, and Susan Duke Biederman, *Art Law: Rights and Liabilities of Creators and Collectors* (Boston: Little, Brown and Company, 1986), 361.

5. *Porter v. Wertz*, 68 A.D. 2d 141, 416 N.Y.S. 2d 254 (1979), aff'd 53 N.Y.2d 696, 421 N.E. 2d 500, 439 N.Y.S. 2d 105 (Ct. App. 1981).

6. *New York Arts and Cultural Affairs Law* §13.01 (McKinney 1984 and Supp. 1997).

7. *Canadian Cultural Property Export & Import Act*, R.S.C. 1985, c. C-51 and amendments thereto.

8. *Jowitt's Dictionary of English Law*, 2d ed.

9. *Quebec Civil Code 1991*, chap. 64.

10. *Hoelzer v. City of Stamford*, 933 F.2d 1131 (2d Cir. 1991).

11. *Jiri Mucha v. Charles King*, 702 F.2d 602 (7th Cir. 1986).

12. *Bailment* is "Delivery of personalty for some particular use ..., upon a contract, express or implied, that after the purpose has been fulfilled it shall be redelivered to the person who delivered it, or otherwise dealt with according to his directions or kept until he reclaims it as the case may be. An actual bailment exists where there is either (a) an actual delivery consisting in giving to the bailee or his agent the real possession of the chattel or (b) a 'constructive delivery' consisting of any of these acts which although not truly comprising real possession of the goods transferred, have been held by legal construction equivalent to acts in real delivery." *Black's Law Dictionary*, 6th ed., 192.

13. *O'Keeffe v. Snyder*, 83 N.J. 478 at 497–99, 416 A. 2 862 at 872–73 (1980).

14. Ziff, *Principles of Property Law*.

15. *New York Domestic Relations Law* §236. (McKinney 1984 and Supp. 1997).

16. New York Print Disclosure Act, N.Y. Arts & Cult. Aff. Law §§15.01–15.19 (Mckinney 1984 and Supp. 1997); Cal. Civ Code §1740 (West 1985 and Supp. 1997); Ark. Code Ann. §4-73-301 (Michie 1996); Ga. Code Ann. §10-1-430 (1994); Haw. Rev. Stat. Ann. §481F (New) (Michie 1995); 121½ Ill. Comp. Stat. Ann. §360 (West 1990); Md. Ann. Code §14-501 et seq. (1990); Mich. Comp. Laws Ann. V422.351 et seq. (West 1990); Minn. Stat. Ann. §324.06 et seq. (West 1995); S.C. Code Ann. §39-16-10 et seq. (Law Co-op Supp. 1996).

17. *New York Arts and Cultural Affairs Law*, s.15.

18. Ibid., ss. 11.1, 14.05, 14.06, 14.07, 14.08, 15.01, 15.03, 15.07, 15.09, 15.10, 15.11, 15.13, 15.15.

19. *California Resale Royalties Act*, Cal. Civ. Code §986 (West 1982 Supp. 1997).

20. Abraham Eckstein and Enrique Zepada Trujillo, *Mexican Civil Code* (St. Paul, Minn: West Publishing Co., 1996).

21. See James E. Herget and Jorge Camil, *An Introduction to the Mexican Legal System* (Buffalo: William S. Heinn Co. Inc., 1978), 50.

22. See Sharon A. Williams, *The International and National Protection of Moveable Cultural Property, A Comparative Study* (Dobbs Ferry, N.Y.: Oceana Publications Inc., 1978), 113.

23. *Jowitt's Dictionary of English Law*, 2d ed.

· 3 ·

Limits on Ownership

Ownership of an object entitles the owner to possession of the object. However, from time to time possession is obtained by a party other than the owner and without the permission of the owner. As earlier indicated, such possession is *adverse possession* and may come about through a variety of means. Unfortunately, one of the most common means is by obtaining a stolen object. The object may thus be in the possession of such party but not be accompanied by title or ownership. Issues arise as to the knowledge of the possessor of the stolen goods and any duty that may be required of such possessor at the time that possession is offered to that party. Is there a requirement that the possessor take reasonable care or make reasonable efforts to determine ownership? What if this is not done? Does the original owner who has lost or had the object stolen have a duty to take action to make the world aware of the theft? How long can the possessor of the stolen object lay claim to that object when it is later discovered by the original owner? Are there any intervening laws that try to balance the rights of an innocent possessor or purchaser against the rights of the original owner from whom the object was stolen?

Also, was the work really stolen or was it abandoned? If it was abandoned, what rules apply? How is it proved that there was an intent to abandon and that the work was not simply mislaid? Are there any special rules that apply to abandoned goods? These are some of the issues that will be dealt with in this chapter.

STOLEN OBJECTS

The theft of precious properties has become an epidemic. Stealing art and art objects from individuals and private collections has always been a fact of life; however, art thefts from museums, governments, and even churches are now becoming prevalent. Some of these thefts are facilitated by lack of security, especially for insiders; others have resulted from increased political and economic turmoil, which facilitates theft of cultural property. Even disposing of stolen art has become easier: the increasing value of art objects has contributed to the number of unscrupulous intermediaries willing to risk selling stolen art, forgeries, and reproductions.

Art theft has become so prevalent that Italy recently issued a catalog of stolen art treasures, L'Opera Da Ritrovare (Works to Recover). Organized crime has become interested in art theft because it has become so lucrative ... so lucrative, in fact, that it is probably the third most profitable international criminal industry, after drug smuggling and the illicit arms trade. The thieves have become so organized and skillful that investigators feel increasingly outmaneuvered. Only ten to fifteen percent of stolen art is ever recovered. Few thieves are convicted and their sentences are usually short; few police forces have either art experts or the time to pursue art thieves.[1]

Of late there have been a number of sensational art thefts from public institutions. The National Gallery of Modern Art in Rome was robbed of two van Gogh paintings and one Cézanne painting. The Isabella Stewart Gardner Museum in Boston was robbed of paintings worth as much as $200 million; stolen paintings included works by Vermeer, Rembrandt, Degas, and Monet. *The Scream* by Edvard Munch was stolen from the National Gallery of Norway and later recovered. Eight works by Picasso and Braque, worth more than $60 million, were stolen from a modern art museum in Stockholm, Sweden; most of the stolen artwork has been recovered except for the Braque. The list goes on: twenty paintings by van Gogh from the Rijks museum in Amsterdam; works by Dali and Matisse, worth more than $40 million, from a museum in Rio de Janeiro; three paintings by van Gogh, worth close to $100 million, from the Kroeller-Mueller in the Netherlands; and the largest theft to date from a commercial gallery—works by old masters amounting to $6 million stolen in New York City.

Even churches have not escaped this trend. One thief broke into a Catholic high school south of Buffalo, New York, a few years ago. When he was caught, his automobile trunk was full of religious vessels stolen from Catholic churches throughout the Midwest and upper New York State. The thief had a number of prior arrests, including thefts from at least ten churches in South Dakota; he had continued his art-theft career after he escaped from a South Dakota prison.

Of course, there are also attempts that go awry: in London, a plot to steal art treasures from Britain's National Gallery turned to farce when the three robbers found the wheels of their getaway car clamped because it was illegally parked. None of the thieves had enough cash to pay the fine and get the clamp removed, so they jacked up the car and tried to do it themselves. Police spotted them and searched the car, finding a marked-up plan of the museum indicating a room full of van Gogh paintings worth $240 million.

Often art "insiders" are involved in thefts from both public institutions and private collectors. For instance, a former University of Scranton history professor and expert on Chinese porcelain was given access, because of his credentials, to many public museum storerooms. He "rescued" porcelains from oblivion and donated them to museums where they would be appropriately displayed and appreciated. The Federal Bureau of Investigation found at least a hundred pieces in his apartment.

In another insider case, an employee carried out a series of thefts from the Prado Museum's warehouse in Spain. Stolen items included arms, armor, and fragments of Gothic and Baroque altar pieces.

In Italy, Carmine Benincasa, a university professor and art critic who served as advisor to the Italian minister of culture in the 1980s, was arrested on charges of armed robbery, kidnapping, and conspiracy to commit fraud. Benincasa was charged with defrauding a wealthy fruit merchant by selling him, in April 1993, fake paintings allegedly created by Canaletto, Titian, Rouault, and Toulouse-Lautrec. The paintings were valued at more than $3 million.[2] The magistrate also accused Benincasa of organizing an armed robbery of the purchaser's home. Apparently, after the owner expressed doubts about the works' authenticity to Benincasa, five armed men burst into the purchaser's villa and held the purchaser and his wife at gunpoint for several hours before making off with the paintings. Three of the works were found immediately; the remaining two were still missing at the time of Benincasa's arrest. According to the arresting magistrate, one of the men arrested for taking part in the robbery claimed that Benincasa masterminded the break-in at the purchaser's home in order to erase evidence of the fraud. Benincasa could face up to twenty years in jail if convicted.

Other insiders have included people such as the nurse's aide of James Johnson Sweeney, the first director of the Guggenheim Museum. When he was eighty-five years old, a Joan Miró painting he owned was stolen. Some months later his nurse's aide appeared at a gallery on Madison Avenue with the painting in a shopping bag, offering it for sale. The dealer immediately recognized *Seated Woman*, one of the icons of twentieth-century art. He asked the woman to come back the next day on the pretext that he would have to research the work. A quick call to another art dealer with expertise on Miró identified it as belonging to Sweeney. When the woman returned the next day, she was apprehended and charged by the police; the painting was returned to Sweeney. The year after Sweeney's death, the painting sold at Sotheby's for $900,000.

When the nurse's aide was named in the newspaper as the thief, a New York reader called the police to say that her Remington drawing had disappeared while the nurse's aide had worked for her. Earlier, the International Foundation for Art Research (IFAR) had received an inquiry about the drawing from another collector, who wanted to know if the work had been stolen; at the time it had not been noted as stolen. IFAR called the collector and told him that the work was stolen and from whom. The collector immediately returned the drawing to its owner and was compensated by the thief's embarrassed children.[3]

In addition, we are faced with the ongoing tradition of public museums being ransacked during times of political turmoil. The Kuwait Museum lost many of its finest Middle Eastern and Arabic treasures during the war with Iraq. With the breakup of the Soviet Union, an international black market is swallowing up art treasures from Eastern Europe. Museums in Russia as well as churches and religious sites in the Czech Republic, Slovakia, and other Eastern European countries are being ransacked. Antiquities, religious icons, art objects, and historical art are objects of choice for international gangs and professional thieves. Often these works reappear only years later at auction or for sale by private dealers.

Works stolen in countries suffering political and economic turmoil are often "exported" without proper export documentation. The resulting violation is twofold: first, the theft of the works, and second, their export without proper cultural-property documentation and government clearances. (The examples given in this section will deal only with the issue of stolen property and title to such objects when brought into the marketplace for sale. The cultural property aspect will be dealt with in chapter 9, "Cultural Property Legislation.")

An adjunct to stolen art and art objects is the theft of copyright in such personal property. This includes the reproduction of such works in both two and three dimensions without the knowledge or authority of the copyright holder. The copyright holder may be the original creator of the work or, depending on the time of purchase or transfer of the ownership in the object, it may also be the collector of the work, or the heirs or beneficiaries of the owner, creator, or transferee of such rights. (For a discussion on copyright, see chapter 6, "Copyright.")

Another form of theft is the unauthorized replication or counterfeiting of art and art objects. Such forgeries have appeared with greater frequency in recent years, often due to increased prices in the marketplace for the originals of such works and better means of reproduction now available. Authentication becomes of greater concern than ever before, as does the provenance of the personal property. As will be seen from the various cases discussed in this and other chapters, discussion of the issue of authenticity becomes public most often when works are offered at public auction whose authenticity is questioned either prior to sale or thereafter, giving rise to substantial legal concerns affecting the rights of the owner, the auction house, and the purchaser. (See chapter 5 for examples and a discussion of this concern.)

With art values going up, there is no shortage of intermediaries and dealers prepared to trade in stolen artwork and art objects and even willing to alter them to disguise their identities. Recently, a frieze missing since 1989 was found in a Madison Avenue gallery. Depicting the head of a youth with curly hair, it was a fragment of a 1,900-year-old marble frieze that had been part of a colonnade in an ancient Roman city. Thieves had stolen the fragment from a warehouse in Italy five years earlier. When it was found, the gallery had cut the frieze down in size, removed the excavation identification number, and labeled it as a fragment from a second-century sarcophagus.

While the theft history of a particular artwork or art object may be known to the thief and the receiver of the stolen work, what are the consequences of the sale of the work for value to an innocent purchaser who does not know its past history? Who bears the loss if the work is later identified as stolen? Should it be returned to the original owners free of the claim of the purchaser? Should it remain with the new purchaser who is innocent of wrongdoing? What effect, if any, does theft or disputed title have on value? In either case, one innocent person bears the loss.

The Purchaser

Common Law

In the past, under British, Canadian, and U.S. common law, the buyer bore the risk of void or voidable title: *caveat emptor*, buyer beware, prevailed. However, to deal with today's business realities, mercantile laws were enacted to assist innocent purchasers and to obligate vendors to facilitate proper trade.

In the United States, the Uniform Commercial Code (UCC) offers protection related to warranties of title by the seller—that is, that the title being conveyed is a good title and that the seller has the right to transfer the title free of any security interest, lien, or encumbrance to an innocent purchaser for value (Section 2-312).

In Canada, the various provincial sale of goods acts,[4] factors acts,[5] and personal property security acts[6] provide similar protection to innocent purchasers for value.

In addition to these protections, a responsible purchaser of property should:

1. obtain the provenance of the work and a history as to where the art has been reproduced, has been lent, or has appeared in public.
2. check major purchases with the Art Loss Register and the International Foundation for Art Research (IFAR).
3. purchase from a reputable source and be suspicious of the vendor if the sale is taking place out of the usual fashion in the trade.
4. be aware of a fair price. If the price is well below the norm, there is a duty on the purchaser to be wary.
5. obtain a written bill of sale with the appropriate details as to the creator, title, date, medium, and size of the work.

Such information should be available from the vendor of a work, having been obtained at the time of the original purchase. Also, an original written bill of sale covering the initial purchase by the vendor may be important to the new purchaser.

Title from a Thief

Anyone who obtains objects or goods from a thief can have title and ownership to those objects and goods no greater than the title held by the thief. The thief does not have the right to pass on title of stolen goods; therefore, one who purchases goods from a thief has no greater title to those goods than did the thief and cannot legitimately pass title to a future purchaser. Under the Canadian sale of goods acts, anyone without title to goods does not have a legal right to dispose of the title to the goods. Therefore, such a sale will be void.

In the Canadian case of *Dowe v. J.J. Pawn Shop*,[7] a finder of a lost watch sold it to a pawnshop. The true owners of the watch sued for its return or its value. The pawnshop had relied on the finder having title. However, as the pawnshop owner made no inquiries before he bought the watch, the pawnshop owner was held to have been "willfully blind" and, therefore, not a bona fide purchaser. The watch was returned to the original owner by a decision of the Nova Scotia Supreme Court judge reversing the decision of the adjudicator of the small claims court.

The adjudicator held that "It is well-established common law that a finder, who has possession, is the owner of found goods and has title against all except the true owner. It is also well-established common law that a seller cannot pass a better title than he had himself."[8]

The court then held that,

> However, in as much as possession is prima facie evidence of ownership, and in as much as the defendant in this case is a purchaser for value, the principles of equity prevail. The title of the owner has no priority over the title acquired by the bona fide purchaser, who has done nothing to disentitle himself to the application of equity.[9]

The general division judge ruled that the watch would remain with the defendant.

The original owner of the watch appealed the ruling, arguing that the Sale of Goods Act of Nova Scotia (Section 24) applied:

> For goods that are sold by a person who is not the owner thereof and who does not sell them under the authority or with the consent of the owner, the buyer acquires no better title than the seller had, unless the owner of the goods is by his conduct precluded from denying the seller's authority to sell.

The appellate judge noted that the pawnshop made no inquiries of the vendor as to how the articles in question were acquired. He then went on to indicate that while the pawnshop had good title against nonowners of the watch, the pawnshop could acquire no better title to the goods than the seller had. The seller's interest was subject to the rights of the lawful owners.

The appellate judge then dealt with the duties of the original owner:

> There is no positive act, on behalf of the appellant, which would have led the respondent pawnshop to believe that she was in any way foregoing her right to the watch... the respondent [pawnshop] did not even inquire of the seller as to how he came to acquire the property in question. I cannot accept that this willful blindness can now be used to assist the respondent in acquiring a better title than he might otherwise have.[10]

The watch was thus returned to the original owner.

It is interesting to note that the appellate judge considered the duties of the various parties involved: the original owner had done nothing to disentitle her to the rights to ownership of the watch; on the other hand, the purchaser did not even inquire as to how the vendor came into possession of the watch, which was considered to be "willful blindness."

The facts of every case are carefully considered by the court to determine the conduct of each of the parties making claim to the object and what would be reasonable to expect of each party in the circumstances. This process often appears to result in contradictory decisions in similar cases, but many cases can be reconciled on the basis of what was or was not done by the various parties and what would have been expected of a reasonable person in the circumstances. Often the courts strain to find a legal way to give a just decision based on the facts. This will appear clear in the cases that follow and in the various approaches taken by courts in Canada and the United States to reach a fair result.

Ordinarily, the Canadian sale of goods acts and factors acts enshrine the basic common-law principle that you can't transfer to another person something that you don't have yourself. There are, however, various circumstances under which a nonowner can transfer not just possession but also title. These circumstances generally do not arise in a situation of theft in the usual sense—that is, when a thief has stolen a precious property from an owner. The exceptions generally apply to situations

1. where goods were given by the owner to another party for purposes other than sale and there is an unauthorized sale by that party to a bona fide purchaser;
2. where the seller is in possession of goods or documents of title to the goods and sells them to a person other than the original purchaser; or
3. where the sale is under special common-law or statutory power of sale or an order of the court.[11]

In these situations, nonowners can pass valid title to a purchaser, as the vendor has a voidable title rather than a void title.

A *voidable act* is one that was originally valid but may later be voided; it is valid until the "fatal vice" in the transaction has been judicially ascertained and declared. A *void act* is one that was invalid from the beginning and, therefore, is ineffectual and has no legal force or binding effect. In law, a void title is unable to support the purpose for which it was intended (a transfer of title). The thief at all times has a void title and cannot pass a good title to a purchaser. Nothing can cure a void act, whereas a voidable one has an imperfection or defect that can be cured by an act or confirmation by the appropriate party. (For example, inaction on the part of a legal owner may stop that owner from claiming back property.)

Several provinces in Canada have laws providing that if property is stolen (but not obtained by fraud or other wrongful means), it will revert to the original owner or his or her representatives on conviction of the thief. For example, this concept is seen in the British Columbia Sale of Goods Act (Section 58).[12]

The Canadian Criminal Code (Section 739)[13] states that if any property stolen by a convicted thief was sold to an innocent purchaser, the courts may, on the application of the innocent purchaser and after restitution of the property has been made to the rightful owner, order the convicted thief to pay to the purchaser an amount not exceeding that paid by the purchaser for the property.

Disclaimers

Vendors may try to protect themselves by make disclaimers regarding a work. For example, auction houses include disclaimers in their conditions of sale. Disclaimers may exclude various implied warranties—for instance, as to the condition of the goods—as the goods were available to be examined by prospective purchasers. *Merchantability*—i.e., that the goods are of the general kind described and are reasonably fit for the purpose for which they have been sold—may be disclaimed; so too, may title or a reduction of rights by a purchaser in the event that title in the work is not clear. For instance, the remedy may be restricted to a return of the purchase price, not to any increased value of the work or the right to receive the work. Auction houses usually have a time limit within which a complaint may be made by a purchaser, especially as to the authenticity or provenance of a work purchased. The courts apply strict interpretation on these restrictions, and if they are uncertain or unclear, the courts are loath to enforce them against an innocent purchaser who has a right to expect what has been bargained for.

The True Owner

If an art object has been stolen, is there any duty incumbent on the true owner after the theft has come to light? The courts are still dealing with this extremely difficult question. For instance, if a work has been stolen, ought the true owner to make inquiries about the theft? Is the owner responsible for informing the outside world of the theft? If the theft is kept secret by the owner (that is, if the owner does not wish to go public with the information), thus preventing the marketplace from knowing that the work is stolen, is he or she violating this responsibility? If so, when the work appears in the market in the future, is it tainted? Consider a situation in which the owner has not given notice of a theft and the work is ultimately sold through a number of hands to a bona fide purchaser. Even if the title is void, is there a statute of limitations prohibition on the original owner from questioning the possession and ownership of the work by the new innocent purchaser? Does the time limit for bringing a court action apply to works that have been stolen with the intent of preventing them from being returned to the original owner?

If an owner has a duty to make the marketplace aware of a theft, does this duty arise when the theft occurs or when the owner becomes aware of the theft? For example, the work may be stolen from a museum, library, or university that does not become aware of the theft for some years. Such situations have occurred with insider thefts from universities and museums: students or curators sell works in a clandestine fashion to dealers or collectors who either do not know that the work is stolen or become parties to the theft and sell the works to innocent buyers.

Courts in both Canada and the United States have held that the original owner has a duty to report the work as stolen and to make efforts to obtain its retrieval, at least from the time the owner becomes aware that the work has been stolen.

The question then arises—what are sufficient efforts? In a prominent U.S. case, *Menzel v. List*,[14] a number of these areas were canvassed by the court. Erna Menzel and her husband purchased a painting by Marc Chagall at an auction in Brussels in 1932. The Germans invaded Belgium in 1940, and the Menzels fled, leaving behind their possessions, including the Chagall painting. They returned six years later to find that German authorities had removed the painting and left a receipt for it.

In 1955, the work reappeared, having been purchased by Klaus Perls and his wife, who owned an art gallery in New York. They purchased the work from a Parisian art gallery. The Perls were innocent purchasers who made no inquiries and knew nothing about the history of the work. They relied on the reputation of the Paris gallery as to the painting's authenticity and title.

In October 1955, Perls sold the painting to Albert List. In 1962, Menzel noticed a reproduction of the Chagall in an art book, with a note to the effect that the work was part of the Albert List collection. Menzel contacted List and asked him to return the painting. When he refused, Menzel instituted action against him. List, in turn, added the Perls to the action, alleging that if he was liable for returning the work, then the Perls breached the implied warranty of title in selling the painting to him.

The jury brought a verdict in favor of Menzel, and List was directed to return the painting or pay Menzel its current value, which was found to be $22,500. List returned the painting. In addition, the jury found for List, the innocent purchaser, against the Perls in the amount of $22,500, the current value of the painting, plus costs.

The Perls appealed, and the amount payable to List was reduced to $4,000, being the original purchase price, together with interest from the date of purchase. List then appealed the reduced judgment, as the painting was worth $22,500 at the time of the judgment.

The court held that Menzel's action was not barred by the statute of limitations of either Belgium or New York, as her cause of action arose not upon the theft of the painting but from the date of her discovery of the whereabouts of the work and the refusal of the then "owner" to return it.

Upon the further appeal by List, the court held that List was entitled to the fair market value of the work ($22,500), not just the original purchase price plus interest. The court reasoned that List lost the painting and, therefore, lost its current market value, which would have been its worth if proper title had been given to him in the original purchase.

In the end, Menzel got back her painting, and List was awarded the fair market value of the work. The Perls were left having to seek redress from the Parisian art dealer.

With the internationalization of art purchases and sales and the expanding market for stolen art and antiques, works stolen in one country may well be sold in another to purchasers unaware of the theft. Also, the laws of the different countries and jurisdictions differ in respect to stolen works and the consequences of such thefts. Therefore, purchasers must take great care to ascertain the provenance of a work, its title, the country of origin of its original owner, and the cultural property laws that may affect the legitimate sale and export of such works.

Checking title to a work is not an easy task. At the very least, inquiries should be made of the International Foundation for Art Research (IFAR) and other monitoring organizations and police forces before the transaction is completed. A warranty of title, even in writing, by the vendor is only as valid as the vendor is reputable; therefore, it is essential to deal with legitimate dealers.

The New York courts have applied the principle established in the Menzel case that damages will take into account any appreciation in value of the work. This was held in *Koerner v. Davis.*[15] Henry Koerner, an artist, brought an action to recover the value of one of his paintings, which had been stolen in 1964. It had re-emerged at auction in 1983 and was sold to one of the defendants.

In 1964, Koerner apparently brought his painting to New York for framing. He accidentally left the painting in a taxi; the taxi driver kept the painting. Koerner had insured the work for $1,000, and he received that amount from the insurer. In

1983, the work was consigned to the William Doyle Galleries Inc. by Robert Hessler and sold at auction to David J. Davis for $1,200.

At the time of the sale, the auction house knew neither the provenance of the work nor the identity of the artist. After Davis purchased the work, he attempted to ascertain its provenance by writing to various specialists in the field. He was able to determine that Koerner was the artist, and one of his inquiry letters to an expert was forwarded to Koerner for his information. Sometime thereafter, Koerner called Davis and explained the history of the painting and its theft, and demanded its return. Davis refused and placed it with the Gertrude Stein Gallery for sale. Koerner demanded that both Davis and the gallery return the painting to him. The gallery returned the painting to Davis, who did not return it to Koerner. Koerner then commenced an action against Davis and the Gertrude Stein Gallery to recover the work or its fair market value. In the face of the action, Davis delivered the work to Tom Ledell, a Los Angeles antique dealer, for resale. Ledell died, and the painting disappeared once again.

At trial, the court determined that Koerner never voluntarily relinquished title to the painting: it was stolen from him when it was left in the taxi, especially as he had asked the taxi driver to wait for him to return to the taxi. The driver instead sped away with the painting in the car.

It was clear, too, that when Davis purchased the painting, he had no knowledge of who the artist was, of the provenance of the work, or that it was stolen. Nonetheless, Davis had no rights in the painting as against Koerner. The court held that "where property is taken by direct larceny, rather than by trickery or false pretenses, no title to such property is conveyed. To put it another way, a possessor of property originally taken by direct larceny possesses a title that is void and not merely voidable."[16] Thus, in the Koerner case, as the work was taken by direct larceny, title never passed from Koerner; therefore, no one in the chain of possession thereafter ever had legal title to it. When Koerner demanded the return of the painting from Davis and he refused, this was a wrongful conversion of the painting, for which Davis was responsible. The Gertrude Stein Gallery was also held liable for conversion when it disposed of Koerner's painting by returning it to Davis. By having full knowledge of the competing claims to the painting but not returning it to its true owner, and by rendering control over the property to another, the gallery converted the painting.

The defendants then argued that Koerner had been paid $1,000 under the insurance policy on the painting; therefore, his rights to the painting were now held by the insurer who had paid him. The court held that if the plaintiff had in fact received the full value of the work from the insurer, the defendants would be correct. However, the insured value of $1,000 was found to be about one-third of the true value of the work at that time. The court also held that when an owner receives insurance proceeds that do not cover the full value of the lost or stolen property, that person still has rights and interests in the property, and they have not passed to the insurance company.

An expert testified that the work would now command a market price of $30,000 because the reputation of the artist had grown during the intervening years. The court accepted the $30,000 value at the time that Koerner sent the demand letters to Davis and the Gertrude Stein Gallery. Judgment was therefore rendered in favor of Koerner in the amount of $30,000.

As we have seen above, in void title cases there has never been a meeting of the minds so as to form an actual agreed-upon contract, nor has there been a mistake of fact or a fraud. In those situations, the contract between the parties is void. However, in cases of voidable title, the innocent purchaser's rights would ordinarily prevail, subject to the law of the jurisdiction of the transaction.

The results may differ between civil-law and common-law jurisdictions, and different rules may apply. For example, in Canada, Quebec cases must be interpreted based on the Quebec Civil Code and ecclesiastical or canon law. In the United States, rules in California and Louisiana may differ from those in states such as New York, which has specialized legislation in respect to precious properties.

A responsible owner should photograph the work and put transparencies or prints in safekeeping so that, if the work is stolen, its likeness can be reproduced by the authorities and professional associations. A notice of theft without photographs is significantly limited in value. Photographs are also essential to an owner for making an insurance claim, and often for the purchase of an insurance contract.

The Statutes of Limitations

Statutes of limitations exist in various states and provinces. They have a fixed term of two, three, or (as in most Canadian jurisdictions) six years within which a claim can be brought forward for actions involving a civil wrong. The issue to consider is: when does this term begin for the original owner?

In Canada, the statute of limitations and its operation have not been as extensively litigated as they have in the United States. The northeastern United States, especially New York, has been the center of trade in art properties since at least the 1950s. A number of situations have required court clarifications. New York and New Jersey courts have taken various approaches to deal with and try to balance the rights of an innocent owner against the rights of an innocent purchaser of a stolen object that may have passed through a number of hands before reaching the innocent purchaser.

In Canada, the period limited by statute for bringing an action usually begins on the date of accrual of the cause of action, that is, when all the elements of civil wrong existed so that a prima facie case can be proved.[17] Whether the cause of action has accrued is independent of whether a complainant knows it has accrued or whether the complainant can give evidence as to the cause of action at that time.

However, recent British cases—that of *Anns and Others v. London Borough of Merton*,[18] in particular—cast uncertainty on this principle. In this case it was held that a cause did not accrue until a person capable of suing discovered, or ought to have discovered, the damage.[19]

A Supreme Court of Canada case, *Central Trust Co. v. Rafuse et al.*,[20] was decided on this basis. It involved a claim of negligence against a firm of Nova Scotia solicitors acting on a mortgage loan to a company. The court determined that, generally, a cause of action arises when the material facts on which it is based have been discovered or ought to have been discovered by the plaintiff, by the exercise of reasonable diligence.

The Supreme Court of Canada reaffirmed that discoverability rule in 1997 in *Peixeiro v. Haberman*.[21] Justice John C. Major wrote for a unanimous court:

> In balancing the defendant's legitimate interest in respecting limitations periods and the interest of the plaintiffs, the fundamental unfairness of requiring a plaintiff to bring a cause of action before he could reasonably have discovered that he had a cause of action is a compelling consideration.

It would therefore appear that this is now the test in tort matters in the common-law provinces in Canada (all provinces except Quebec). The reasoning in this "discovery rule" is similar to that of many jurisdictions in the United States.

Ordinarily, the six-year limitation period in Canada applies to art thefts, but the limitation period may be postponed, suspended, or extended. For instance, the limitation period affecting the Crown or a public authority may be different from that affecting ordinary individuals. As well, the commencement of a limitation period may be postponed in cases of complainants who are underage or have a disability and in cases where the accused are either trustees or guilty of fraud.[22]

If a statute of limitations does apply, the owner is barred from claiming the return of the work. The intent of a statute of limitations is to have a fixed time frame within which a claim can be made, after which the owner is precluded from reclaiming the work. The innocent purchaser, even if he or she has purchased the work from a thief, is entitled to keep the work free of the claim of the original, rightful owner.

In *Erisoty v. Rizik*,[23] in the state of New York, the court outlined the various tests for the applicability of the statute of limitations. (A full discussion of that case appears later in this chapter.)

Courts have used three basic approaches in determining whether an original owner should be able to maintain an action for the return of stolen goods against a bona fide purchaser beyond the codified limitation period:

1. the demand and refusal rule;[24]

2. the Laches approach,[25] which is based on delay attended by or inducing a change of condition or relation (i.e., a lack of diligence on the part of the complainant to the injury, prejudice, or disadvantage of the accused); and
3. the discovery rule.[26]

The Demand and the Refusal Requirement

The statute of limitations period on the claim to recover stolen property from a good faith purchaser does not begin to run until the possessor refuses to return the object upon demand.

In the case of *Menzel v. List*,[27] discussed above, List, the innocent purchaser, pleaded that the applicable three-year statute of limitations prevented the owner from retaking possession of the work. The painting was stolen in 1941; in 1955, List obtained possession of the work as an innocent purchaser. The court held that the cause of action against a person who unlawfully comes by a chattel arises on the defendant's refusal to convey the chattel upon demand. (Here the action was brought within three years of List's refusal to return the painting to Menzel.)

In *DeWeerth v. Baldinger*,[28] a Monet landscape owned by Gerda DeWeerth disappeared from storage in Germany after American soldiers occupied the family home in 1945. In 1981, DeWeerth learned the painting had been exhibited in 1970 at a gallery in New York City and had been included in the exhibition catalog. The lender of the work was not identified in the catalog.

After several rounds of litigation, the gallery was ordered to disclose the identity of the lender. (The gallery was reluctant because it had sold the work to the lender originally.) DeWeerth then sought the return of the painting from the lender, Edith Baldinger, who denied that DeWeerth had a right to the painting. Baldinger claimed to have received a good title from the gallery when she bought the painting in 1957. The gallery, brought into the action as a third party, pleaded that it had acquired the painting in 1956 from a Swiss art dealer. Baldinger and the gallery asserted that the statute of limitations had now run, barring the action. Also, the equitable doctrine of Laches was asserted (that is, DeWeerth had allowed the work to become "free floating" in the marketplace by not seeking the work through advertising; she had therefore given up rights to it).

The court held that New York state law applied to the action. Under New York law, actions that accrue within the state are governed by the state statute of limitations. New York legislation required that the action be brought within three years of the time that the action accrued. The date of accrual is the date upon which the identity of the party from whom recovery is sought becomes known.

Where the owner proceeds against one who innocently purchases the property in good faith from a thief, the limitation period begins only when the owner demands return of the property and the purchaser refuses,[29] even if it is many years after the theft occurred. Until demand and refusal, the purchaser in good faith is not considered a wrongdoer.

In the DeWeerth case, it was undisputed that DeWeerth initiated the suit within three years of the date that Baldinger refused DeWeerth's demand for the return of the Monet.

Where demand and refusal are necessary to start a limitation period, the demand may not be unreasonably delayed. While this proscription against unreasonable delay has been referred to as "Laches," the New York courts have explained that the doctrine refers solely to an excused lapse of time. The DeWeerth case indicated that the owner is obligated to make a demand for the return of the work without unreasonable delay and to use due diligence to locate the stolen work. The court indicated that an obligation to attempt to locate the stolen property is consistent with New York's treatment of a good faith purchaser. The purpose of the rule, whereby demand and refusal are substantive elements of a conversion action against a good faith purchaser, is to protect the innocent party by giving the purchaser notice before he or she is held liable.

This rule may disadvantage the good faith purchaser; however, if demand is indefinitely postponed, the good faith purchaser will remain exposed to a suit long after an action against innocent parties or even against a thief will be time-barred. This rule is especially appropriate with respect to stolen art. Much art is kept in private collections, unadvertised and unavailable to the public. An owner seeking to recover such property will almost never learn of its whereabouts by chance; yet, the location of stolen art may frequently be discovered through investigation.

In the DeWeerth case, the court also stated that other jurisdictions have adopted limitations rules that encourage property owners to search for the missing goods. In virtually every state except New York, an action for conversion accrues when a good faith purchaser acquires stolen property; demand and refusal are unnecessary. In these states the owners must find the current possessor within the statutory period before the action is barred. Obviously, this creates an incentive to find one's stolen property.[30]

In this case, the court held that the efforts by DeWeerth were minimal. She did not take advantage of the programs available for listing the work as stolen with the various authorities, governments, and agencies. The court felt that to require a good faith purchaser who has owned the painting for thirty years to defend would be unjust and that New York law avoids this injustice by requiring a property owner to use reasonable diligence to locate his or her property. In this case, DeWeerth failed to meet that burden and, therefore, the judgment of the district court was reversed by the New York Court of Appeals.[31]

Thus, though the statute of limitations in various jurisdictions does not transfer title, the successful use of the statute of limitations prevents title being asserted by the prior owner, and that ultimately means that the present owner can pass good title to the work in future transactions.

The Laches Approach

In *Solomon R. Guggenheim Foundation v. Lubell*[32] the lower court found that the efforts made by the Guggenheim Museum to recover a Chagall gouache were not sufficient. The work was proclaimed to be worth about $200,000 and had been created by Marc Chagall in 1912 as a study for an oil painting. The museum alleged that the work had been stolen in the 1960s by person or persons unknown. The museum learned that the work was in the possession of the defendant, Rachel Lubell, in August 1985. On January 9, 1986, the museum demanded that Lubell return the gouache, but she refused.

Lubell responded that she and her late husband had purchased the work in May 1967, from a reputable Manhattan gallery, for $17,000. At no time did she or her husband know of any defects on the gallery's title. She then raised the three-year statute of limitations, the defense of Laches, the defense of adverse possession, and her status as a good faith purchaser for value.

She then moved for summary judgment, as the statute of limitations had expired since the theft with no effort being taken by the Guggenheim to obtain the painting's return. The court granted the motion and dismissed the action. The Guggenheim had never reported the theft to the police or to industry organizations; the museum had offered no proof that the work had been stolen; and no insurance claim had been made, because the theft could not be proven.

The museum appealed, and the lower court's decision was overturned. The court held that the use of the statute of limitations was incorrect. Instead, it would have substituted a Laches standard. "It then went on to dilute the due diligence standard of DeWeerth as automatically applicable. It instructed the lower court to examine the actions taken by the original owner [the museum] as whether reasonable or not, and whether in accord with industry practice at the time."[33]

The defense of Laches is based on an unwarranted delay that would give rise to an assumption that the complainant has waived his or her rights. Typically, a complainant, knowing of his or her rights, does nothing to pursue them and unreasonably delays exercising them. This inaction, it is argued, usually works to the detriment of an innocent party. In this instance, Lubell would need to show that she was prejudiced by the museum's delay in demanding the return of the work.

This case also concluded that the federal court of appeals in the DeWeerth case should not have imposed a duty of reasonable or due diligence on the original owners for the purposes of the statute of limitations. There was, however, a recognition that a true owner who has discovered the location of a stolen or lost property cannot unreasonably delay making demand for the return of the property.

Although the due-diligence requirement on original owners has been all but abolished in New York State, it does continue in other jurisdictions. The jury is still out with respect to future requirements of the original owners and new innocent purchasers in these cases.

For example, the case of *Erisoty v. Rizik*[34] involved a work by Giaquinto Corrado purchased by Stephen Erisoty at an auction on April 16, 1989. The work turned out to have been stolen in July 1960 from the Washington, D.C., home of Jacqueline and Phillip Rizik. It was one of three works by Giaquinto and two works by other artists stolen at that time. (The other works were not an issue in this case.)

A day after the theft, the Riziks reported the theft to the District of Columbia Metropolitan Police Department. (Photographs of the stolen works were not then available.) The FBI was informed of the theft the same day and commenced an investigation. Soon after the burglary, the Rizik family provided photographs of the stolen works and other related documents to the police. The paintings were covered by the homeowner's insurance policy issued by Maryland Casualty Company, and shortly after the burglary, the Riziks filed a proof of loss with the company. Maryland Casualty paid the Riziks $15,000 to compensate for the loss of the three Giaquintos.

Local law enforcement authorities dissuaded Phillip Rizik from hiring a private investigator and assured him that the district police, the FBI, and Interpol would do everything necessary to try to recover the works. From time to time there was contact among the Rizik family, the police, and FBI as to possible tips, updates, and continuing investigation, until approximately 1979. There was no contact thereafter until August 1993, when the FBI informed Jacqueline Rizik that the painting at issue had been located. Until September 1992, the Riziks had not published any announcements or notices of the theft of the paintings in any newspapers, magazines, art journals, or other periodicals.

From 1961 to 1991, Jacqueline or Phillip Rizik periodically visited museums to look for the stolen paintings but did not provide any museums with photographs or other documents identifying the stolen paintings. Nor did they provide any auction house with photographs of the stolen paintings from 1960 to 1993 or contact any auction house regarding the paintings from 1971 to 1993. The Riziks were neither art collectors nor participants in the fine art community, and they had no real knowledge of periodicals in that field.

In March 1988, a woman hired a cleaning and removal service to remove unwanted furniture from her home in Philadelphia. The woman removed what she wanted, leaving the remainder to be disposed of. The house was to be left in a "broom clean" condition. While removing the unwanted furniture, the owner of the cleaning service came across a trash bag behind a dresser, which contained the stolen painting. At the time of discovery, the painting was in five pieces. The owner of the cleaning service removed the pieces from the house and thereafter entered into an agreement with Ellen Gerber, an antique store owner, to try to identify the painter and the painting and to estimate its value in exchange for a ten percent finder's fee.

Gerber contacted the Philadelphia Museum of Art and was referred to its curator of European paintings prior to 1900. At her meeting with the curator, Gerber was advised that the painting was in extremely fragile condition and that if it continued to be moved it would be destroyed or suffer major damage. She was asked to leave the artwork at the Philadelphia Museum of Art to be examined by the museum's conservators and to have its condition stabilized by mounting it on a piece of Styrofoam. She agreed.

To obtain information about the painting, the curator contacted various world experts, but none was able to provide any information regarding provenance. They knew only that it was probably a work by Giaquinto.

The cleaning-service owner then arranged for the work to be sold at auction in Philadelphia. No evidence as to the cleaning-service owner's title to the painting was ever given to the museum or the auction house.

Prior to the sale, the auction house prepared a brochure describing the works in the auction. The catalog, which included a reproduction of the painting, was distributed to auction attendees and anyone requesting a catalog prior to the auction. The auction house also placed advertisements in several periodicals and newspapers announcing that there was a painting by Giaquinto in the auction. The work was on public display at the auction house for two days prior to the sale.

Stephen Erisoty learned that the painting would be sold at auction when he received in the mail a brochure from the auction house. He previewed the painting at the auction premises prior to the sale and was told by the auctioneer that the work had been at the Philadelphia Museum of Art; the museum had attributed the work to Giaquinto. Erisoty was not told the name of the consignor of the work. The auction house catalog contained a condition (number 5) as follows: "The auctioneer … assumes no risk, liability, or responsibility for the authenticity of the authorship of any property identified in this catalog. All merchandise is sold as is, where is, with no warranties or guarantees, whether specified or not. Not responsible for typographical errors."

On April 16, 1989, the work was purchased at auction for $25,000 by the wife of Gregory Erisoty on behalf of a group of investors. The total price paid, including the commission, was $29,050.

Stephen Erisoty, a member of the purchaser group, was a restorer and expended substantial time and effort over a four-year period restoring the work.

At this point, the Riziks were still unaware of what had happened to their painting. In 1992, Jacqueline Rizik learned of the International Foundation for Art Research (IFAR) and its art theft services. That year she reported to IFAR the theft of the three paintings by Giaquinto, and she authorized IFAR to publish a report that the

Riziks were offering a reward for information leading to the recovery of the work. There was an announcement of the theft of the three works, including photographs, dimensions, and titles, in the September 1992 issue of *IFAR Report*. Parties at the Philadelphia Museum of Art saw the announcement in the IFAR publication and advised IFAR that they believed it had been sold at auction in 1989. IFAR passed this information on to the FBI in July 1993. The FBI contacted the auction house, which told the FBI that the painting had, in fact, been sold to the Erisoty group.

In September 1993, the FBI went to the Stephen Erisoty home and demanded the return of the painting. When the FBI told Erisoty that he had no choice, Erisoty handed over the painting, even though he claimed that he had lawfully purchased it.

The FBI notified the Rizik family that the painting had been recovered and would be returned to Jacqueline Rizik after she reached an agreement with the Maryland Casualty Company regarding a release. The insurance company agreed to release the painting to the Riziks in exchange for $5,000, one-third of the amount paid in 1960 by the insurer for the loss of the three works. The FBI returned the work to the Rizik residence in Washington, D.C.

Erisoty demanded, in an exchange of letters and ultimately an action, that the work be returned to the Erisoty group. In 1962, although the work was insured for $5,000, the fair market value, based on an appraisal, was approximately $9,000 to $10,000. In 1993 the work had an appraised fair market value of $200,000.

The parties focused their efforts largely on whether the Riziks' efforts to locate the painting were sufficiently reasonable and diligent to overcome the statute of limitations time frame. The Erisoty group alleged that the Riziks did not proceed diligently, even though it conceded that the Riziks had a right to the painting and would have title to it but for their failure to act diligently.

Counsel for the Erisoty group also made two other arguments. The first dealt with the contention that the Riziks gave up title to the work to the Maryland Casualty Company, when they were paid $5,000 in 1960. The Erisoty lawyer cited a New York State opinion that when a claim is paid under a theft policy the "insurance company takes an assignment of ownership of its assured."[35]

In response to this, the court indicated that there was not sufficient evidence to prove that title had passed to the insurance company, and that title was returned to the Riziks only on their $5,000 reimbursement of the insurance company in 1993. The court also held that even if there was evidence of such an assignment, the way insurance companies conduct business evidences a recognition of the insured's ongoing interest and desire for the return of its property. The actions of the insurance company, in cooperating with the insured and accepting the payment of $5,000 for the return of title without question, assumes a recognition of the insured's interest in the work by the insurance company. In any event, the Riziks retained a very real interest in the painting and in its value pending its recovery.

The second argument made by the Erisoty group was that a bone fide purchaser of a painting that has been entrusted to an art dealer should be able to acquire good title against the true owner. However, the court held that this statement is merely an articulation of the principle of entrustment, which provides that entrusting possession of goods to a merchant who deals in that kind of goods gives the merchant the power to transfer all the rights of the entrustor to a buyer in the ordinary course of business. Here the original theft of the painting resulted in a void title, and the principle stands that a bona fide purchaser of a chattel from a thief gets nothing. Title could not vest in the cleaning-service owner through his taking of the painting, and the plaintiffs' subsequent purchase of the painting put them in no better position than the cleaning-service owner.

The court then looked at "the center piece of the litigation"—whether the Riziks' efforts to locate the painting were sufficient to preserve their right to claim title. First, the court had to review the Erisoty group's contention that the Riziks should be barred from asserting their rights to the painting due to the statute of limitations. The court then had to determine the applicable statute and when it began to run. Given the facts of the case, the statute would permit the Riziks either two years or three years, depending on the applicable law, following the Erisoty group's acquisition of the painting in April 1989. The Riziks did not act within either time frame and would be time barred unless other principles were invoked.

The court held that the statute of limitations may be *tolled* (that is, the bar of the action by statute of limitations removed) if strict enforcement would work an injustice on victims of crime (for example, should an original owner be unable to locate stolen art work for many years despite reasonable search efforts).

The court then set out the three different approaches to determine whether an original owner should be able to maintain a replevin action (an action brought to recover possession of goods unlawfully taken) against a bona fide purchaser beyond the codified limitation period: the demand and refusal rule; the Laches approach, which we have already discussed; and the discovery rule, which follows.

The Discovery Rule

Under the discovery rule an original owner's cause of action does not accrue "until the injured party discovers, or by exercise of reasonable diligence and intelligence should have discovered, facts which form the basis of a cause of action." (The court cited the O'Keeffe case,[36] which is discussed below.) In the stolen-art context such facts include the identity of the possessor of the paintings, and the O'Keeffe case held that where a court finds that an owner has diligently searched for a stolen painting but "cannot find it or discover the identity of the possessor, the statute of limitations will not begin to run."[37]

The court found that "the discovery rule shifts the emphasis from the conduct of the possessor to the conduct of the owner. The focus of the inquiry will no longer be whether the possessor has met the test of adverse possession but whether the owner has acted with due diligence in pursuing his or her property."[38] The burden of proving due diligence rests on the original owner.

The court therefore held that the Riziks' efforts must be "measured by the standard of 'reasonable due diligence' and not by a standard of discoverability."[39]

In addition, the court noted this was not a case of replevin (an original owner suing an innocent purchaser for the return of a work) but a case in which the innocent purchaser was suing the original owner for the return of a work. The court, however, proceeded along the lines of a replevin action, and the discovery rule still rested with the original owner. Looking at prior cases, the court affirmed that the discovery rule is highly fact-sensitive and flexible.

After consideration of the law and the unique facts of the case, the court found that the search efforts of the original owners were reasonable and diligent in the circumstances and that they satisfied the discovery rule. In addition, the balance of equities was in favor of the original owners: the innocent purchasers had purchased the painting without inquiring as to the painting's prior ownership or the identity of the consignor; nor did they make any inquiry to art or law enforcement agencies after learning that the painting was originally in five pieces and that suspicious circumstances surrounded the work. In short, the Erisoty group took a gamble in the purchase of the work at the auction house. The original owners, on the other hand, suffered an intrusive crime, subsequently contacted the FBI, remained in contact with the agency for many years, and finally set in motion the process of recovering the painting through their diligence in contacting IFAR, when they became aware of its existence.

The judgment went on to indicate that the discovery rule is fact-sensitive, so as to adjust the level of scrutiny to that appropriate to the identity of the parties. What are reasonable efforts for an individual relatively unfamiliar with the art world may not be reasonable for a savvy collector, gallery, or museum.

This comment will have significant impact on future cases, as there is obviously a higher duty on an art-related professional than on a nonprofessional, especially one who was not the original purchaser but merely a spouse or successor in title.

Though the court concluded that the Riziks were entitled to maintain possession and ownership of the work, it also gave rights to the plaintiffs to claim against the defendants any increase in the value of the work through the restoration efforts of Stephen Erisoty. (However, later on summary judgment, the court denied Erisoty any compensation for the restoration holding there was no unjust enrichment of the Riziks and, in any event, the restoration was at the risk of Erisoty.[40]) At the time of writing, Erisoty's lawsuit against the auction house and consignor to recover the purchase price paid on behalf of the investment group was still pending.[41]

(As a matter of interest, various statutes of limitations that could have been applied in the case included those of the District of Columbia or Maryland, each of which had a three-year limitation period, and that of Pennsylvania, which had a two-year limitation period. Under Pennsylvania law, the Pennsylvania limitation period applied; however, inasmuch as the Riziks did not locate the painting until more than three years after the Erisoty group gained possession, the distinction between the two- or three-year limitation period was insignificant.)

The equitable balance in this case was quite distinct from cases such as DeWeerth, in which a sophisticated art collector, who had lost a valuable oil painting by Claude Monet in 1945, failed to seek assistance from the law enforcement agencies; failed to contact any of several post-war agencies created for the specific purpose of locating art lost during the war; and conducted no search during a twenty-four-year period, while for thirty years the painting hung in the New York apartment of a good faith purchaser and on two occasions was displayed in public exhibitions.

The court in the Erisoty case cited *O'Keeffe v. Snyder*,[42] which has become central to the application of the discovery rule. In that case, the artist Georgia O'Keeffe brought an action to recover three of her paintings that had disappeared from a New York City gallery in 1946. O'Keeffe had never reported the theft to police, because she did not feel they would be helpful in recovering stolen art. Nor was there any notice published of the theft, but there were discussions by O'Keeffe with various art world acquaintances. In 1972, O'Keeffe allowed her secretary to report the theft of the three works to the American Dealers Association, which had established an inventory of stolen art as a resource for collectors, dealers, and authorities.

In September 1975, O'Keeffe learned that the paintings were up for sale on consignment in a New York gallery. She was then able to obtain information that the paintings were claimed by Barry Snyder, the owner of the Princeton Gallery of Fine Art. She demanded the return of the paintings in February 1976; Snyder refused. O'Keeffe commenced an action for the return of the paintings (replevin) immediately thereafter.

Snyder defended the action, arguing that the six-year statute of limitations of the state of New Jersey prevented O'Keeffe from bringing the action. The trial judge, however, concluded that Snyder had failed to satisfy the concept of "open and notorious" required to obtain adverse possession of goods, because between the theft in 1946 and 1973 the paintings were never displayed in public. However, the court granted Snyder judgment because it held that O'Keeffe's action was barred by the statute of limitations; more than six years had run from the date of the theft to the time of bringing of the action.

An intermediate appellate court reversed this decision. It held that the statute of limitations did not run until all the elements of adverse possession were established. As the paintings were never openly exhibited until 1973, the six-year statute of limitations did not begin to run until 1973. Since the action was commenced in 1976, it was commenced within the appropriate time frame.

The New Jersey Supreme Court subsequently reversed and remanded the case to determine whether the paintings had actually been stolen.

The court determined that O'Keeffe should be given the benefit of the discovery rule. The doctrine of adverse possession was created primarily for real property and was not easily applied to personal property; unlike real property, jewelry and works of art do not have a fixed location, are portable, and can be concealed easily. It is difficult for the true owner to receive notice of possession of these goods. Accordingly, the Supreme Court dispensed with the tests for adverse possession, stating that these tests were not a fair and reasonable means of resolving this kind of dispute.

The court held that the discovery rule should be applied instead. The discovery rule provides that a cause of action does not accrue until the injured party discovers, or by the exercise of due diligence should have discovered, the facts constituting the basis of the action. The court explained that the rule would avoid the harshness that might result from a mechanical application of any statute of limitations. The New Jersey Supreme Court proposed that the trial court consider whether O'Keeffe exercised due diligence in recovering her paintings, whether there was an effective means of alerting the art world to the theft, and whether registering with an art-theft archive would give a prudent purchaser notice of the theft.

The New Jersey court was more inclined to favor the innocent purchaser and to look to the free transfer of personal property in the marketplace. It refrained from imposing on an art dealer the duty to investigate title before making a purchase; this was substantially different from the New York courts and the approach taken in *Porter v. Wertz*,[43] in which a duty of care was placed on the art dealer to investigate title. The O'Keeffe court placed a burden on the owner, the victim of the theft, to exercise due diligence in seeking to recover the stolen property. The dissenting judgment correctly argued that the major shortcoming of the discovery rule is its failure to consider whether the purchaser exercises due care and reasonable prudence.

In a recent article, law professor Franklin Feldman observed that a New York statute that has direct applicability to any claim brought by non–New York residents has been overlooked. He states that Section 2.02 of the New York Civil Practice Law and Rules (CPLR) known as the "borrowing statute" provides that:

> An action based upon a cause of action accruing without the state cannot be commenced after the expiration of the time limited by the laws of either the state or the place without the state where the cause of action accrued, except that where the cause of action accrued in favor of a resident of the state the time limited by the laws of the state shall apply.[44]

Feldman goes on to state:

> Thus, where the cause of action arose outside of New York and the plaintiff is a nonresident of New York, the applicable statute of limitation is limited to the time period prescribed by that of the plaintiff's residence. As is obvious, in many situations, this would significantly restrict the claim of a non-New York Holocaust victim to recover his stolen art if the suit were instituted in New York as would be required if the defendant were located here.[45]

The courts are continually faced with trying to resolve, in a Solomon-like manner, the duties and responsibilities of innocent purchasers with those of original innocent owners of art properties. The facts of each case must determine the thinking of the court. The courts attempt to reach the right result through different means and different tests, taking into account the conduct of the parties, the state or provincial statutes, and the common law. Good business ethics is the best way for vendors to minimize the problem, and good "personal housekeeping" by owners of art objects—having proper inventories, storage, controls, and insurance—will reduce the need for courts to act as arbiters.

California

California has legislation governing the accrual of a cause of action in the case of a stolen artwork or artifact. It provides that an action must be brought within three years of "the discovery of the whereabouts" of the work "by the aggrieved party." This discovery may occur only after many years and still give rights to the original owner even if purchased by a good faith purchaser years earlier.[46]

When the California Statute of Limitations was amended in 1983 to include a discovery accrual rule, however, the law did not deal with thefts that may have occurred prior to the 1983 amendment.

In *Naftzger v. American Numismatic Society*,[47] the court of appeals held that actual discovery by the original owner of the identity of the possessor of the property (in this case, a coin collection) was implicit in the pre-1983 version of the statute of limitations, and that the diligence of the original owner was not a component of the pre-1983 discovery rule.

In *Society of California Pioneers v. Baker*,[48] the court determined that the statute of limitations runs anew each time a new purchaser for value obtains possession of the stolen item (in this case an antique cane head), as long as each of these innocent purchasers holds the stolen object for less than the three-year statute of limitations requirement. Thus, if one innocent purchaser held the work for two years and nine months, and then sold it to another innocent purchaser, who held it for two years and seven months, the sale would recommence the time period under the statute of limitations.

The court also decided that fair and reasonable duties of the original owner and theft victim would be what would be fair and reasonable in the community of the original owner.

These decisions are consistent with most recent U.S. case law on the subject of statute of limitations, which holds that the owner is not affected by the statute of limitations until he or she learns that the object has been stolen and is in the possession of a particular person, or until the owner has demanded the return of the object and the new owner, usually a bona fide purchaser, refuses to return it.[49]

A number of states besides California have now passed legislation containing discovery rules dealing with stolen art, including Indiana, New Jersey, Ohio, Oklahoma, and Pennsylvania.

New York State Statutory Proposal

There is a proposal in New York State that would relate back to January 1, 1998, to add two new sections (206[E] and 214 [D]) to the Civil Practice Law and Rules.[50] These sections would provide that both actions for the recovery of damages associated with the detaining of stolen cultural objects and the three-year limitation period within which such actions must be commenced shall be determined solely in accordance with Title N of the Arts and Cultural Affairs Law (Section 38.01 ff).[51]

There is serious concern that even many years after an object enters legitimate commerce, those who purchased it in good faith may not be protected from a claim by the original owner. The proposed statute attempts to balance the rights of the theft victim and the rights of good faith purchasers. The legislation includes the setting up of an art registry. A theft victim who reports the theft to the art registry within three years of the theft (or, in the case of objects stolen before the setting up of the registry, three years after the date when the registry system goes into effect) could not be adversely affected by the legislation.

If the theft victim filed a theft report with a computerized cultural-objects registry within three years of the theft, no cause of action against the person in good faith possession would accrue until the date when the claimant discovered the object's whereabouts. The claimant would then have three years to commence a court action.

If the claimant filed no theft report within three years of the theft, the cause of action accrues on the third anniversary of the theft; three years thereafter (that is, six years after the theft), the claim would be time-barred.

If a purchaser consults the registry before or after acquiring a cultural object and receives a favorable search report (written confirmation that no theft report has been filed), the claimant's cause of action accrues on the earliest of three dates—the date of the search report, the date of discovery of that theft, or the third anniversary of the theft—and generally would be time-barred three years thereafter.

If a theft report is filed within three years of the theft and someone has request-ed or subsequently requests a search report, the registry would notify law enforce-ment agencies and the claimant. Similar notification would be made if a theft re-port were filed between three and six years after the theft but not more than three years after the registry's issuance of a favorable search report.

There would be certain transition rules, and theft reports filed before the effec-tive date would be grandfathered, giving those theft victims automatic protection under the new law.

The advantages of the proposed statute are:

1. The theft victim who registers the theft in a timely manner protects his or her rights until the discovery of an object's whereabouts. This protection is compara-ble to the current rights of theft victims under New York's "demand and refusal" rule.

2. It could no longer be argued that a theft victim who files a theft report delayed unreasonably before locating the object or bringing suit.

3. Notification requirements imposed on the registry will facilitate the return of cultural objects to the rightful owner.

4. A purchaser would be able to determine, before acquiring a cultural object, whether it is listed with the registry as missing or stolen.

5. A purchaser would know, generally within six years of acquiring a cultural ob-ject, that his or her title to the object no longer could be challenged.

6. Clarity would be brought to an area of the law in which there is great ambiguity and uncertainty both for theft victims and purchasers.

There would also be separate protection for claims made for the return of paint-ings, sculpture, and other cultural objects stolen in connection with the Holocaust. These would be protected until three years after a survivor or family member dis-covers an object's whereabouts, providing a theft report is on file with a cultural objects registry before the effective date of the proposed statute or is filed within three years after the effective date.

The cultural objects registry would consist of a computerized database of more than fifty thousand cultural objects that have been reported missing or stolen.

Under New York's Uniform Commercial Code, a good faith buyer of stolen property has four years from the date of the sale to bring an action against a seller for breach of the seller's implied warranty of title. Generally speaking, the proposed statute would preserve such claims until the first anniversary of the date when the buyer relinquishes a stolen cultural object or pays damages to a claimant whose claim is not time-barred.

The statute's proponents believe that if the statute is enacted, it will serve as a model for other jurisdictions. Computer technology may create opportunities to solve some of these legal problems by enabling the creation of a registry system similar to those already in existence for personal property security registrations and for automobile licensing. It will be interesting to see, if and when this legislation is approved, if it will be a catalyst for similar legislation in other states, Canada, and perhaps ultimately worldwide, to deal with the international market in stolen art.

Nazi Confiscated Art

The possession and ownership of significant numbers of artworks has been affected by the Second World War. Hitler intended to create his own museum, and he and senior members of his staff wanted to enhance their own art collections by confiscating master works from private collections in conquered countries; this motivated a significant number art thefts. The works that were stolen were often hidden for years or placed in collections that were not open to the public, which makes it more difficult to identify the original owners. Only recently have such works begun to reenter the art market, giving rise to conflicting claims of ownership.[52]

The repatriation and return of art confiscated by the Nazi regime or sold to the Nazis under duress has been a continuing and difficult area of legal concern. The art affected has, in some cases, passed through many hands, which increases the number of innocent purchasers who would bear loss if the works were returned to their original owners. Works that have been purchased by museums or given to them as gifts may previously have been owned by families exterminated in the Holocaust. What law is applicable to transactions involving art that originated in one country and passed through the hands of purchasers in various other countries, ending in a third or fourth country? The choice of law will determine the applicability of a particular statute of limitations.

In 1998, forty-four nations and thirteen nongovernmental organizations met formally at the Washington Conference on Holocaust-Era Assets (November 30–December 3, 1998) and the National Archive Symposium on Records and Research Relating to Holocaust-Era Assets (December 4, 1998) to discuss the problems posed by unsettled questions of assets, including art and art objects.

The following principles with respect to Nazi-confiscated art[53] emerged as a consensus of the participants.

1. Art that was confiscated by the Nazis and not subsequently restituted should be identified.
2. Relevant records and archives should be open and accessible to researchers, in accordance with the guidelines of the International Conference on Archives.
3. Resources and personnel should be made available to facilitate the identification of all art confiscated by the Nazis and not subsequently restituted.

4. In establishing that a work of art was confiscated by the Nazis and not subsequently restituted, an agreement should be made to excuse unavoidable gaps or ambiguities in the provenance in light of the passage of time and the circumstances of the Holocaust era.
5. When art is found to have been confiscated by the Nazis and not subsequently restituted, every effort should be made to publicize the known facts in order to locate its pre-war owners or their heirs.
6. Efforts should be made to establish a central registry of such information.
7. Prewar owners and their heirs should be encouraged to come forward and make known their claims to art that was confiscated by the Nazis and not subsequently restituted.
8. If the prewar owners of such art—or their heirs—can be identified, steps should be taken expeditiously to achieve a just and fair solution, recognizing that this may vary according to the facts and circumstances surrounding a specific case.
9. If the prewar owners (or heirs) of art that is found to have been confiscated by the Nazis cannot be identified, steps should be taken expeditiously to achieve a just and fair solution.
10. Commissions or other bodies established to identify art that was confiscated by the Nazis and to assist in addressing ownership issues should have a balanced membership.
11. Nations are encouraged to develop national processes to implement these principles, particularly as they relate to alternative dispute resolution mechanisms for resolving ownership issues.

The conference did not make a point of focusing on the differences between civil- and common-law systems regarding good title to chattels. When the issue was brought up, it was usually to say that no statutes of limitations should apply to art looted by the Nazis and their collaborators.

Russia made news by stating it was open to claims from individuals through their governments, but it defended its controversial law nationalizing all the art the Soviets found on German soil at the end of the war.

New Restitution Guidelines for Holocaust-Era Art in Museums

In June of 1998 the Association of Art Museum Directors (AAMD) adopted guidelines for American museums to deal with works of art confiscated during World War II and not yet returned to their legitimate owner. The guidelines are not binding but carry the force of the AAMD's 175 member museums in the United States, Canada, and Mexico.

Guidelines[54]

The Association of Art Museum Directors (AAMD) has developed the following guidelines to assist museums in resolving claims, reconciling the interest of individuals or their heirs who were dispossessed of works of art with the fiduciary and legal obligations and responsibilities of art museums and their trustees to the public for whom they hold works of art in trust.

A. Research Regarding Existing Collections

1. As part of the standard research on each work of art in their collections, members of the AAMD, if they have not already done so, should begin immediately to review the provenance of works in their collections to attempt to ascertain whether any were unlawfully confiscated during the Nazi/World War II era and never restituted.
2. Member museums should search their own records thoroughly and, in addition, should take all reasonable steps to contact established archives, databases, art dealers, auction houses, donors, art historians, and other scholars and researchers who may be able to provide Nazi/World War II era provenance information.
3. AAMD recognizes that research regarding Nazi/World War II era provenance may take years to complete, may be inconclusive, and may require additional funding. The AAMD Art Issues Committee will address the matter of such research and how to facilitate it.

B. Future Gifts, Bequests, and Purchases

1. As part of the standard research on each work of art,
   a. member museums should ask donors of works of art (or executors in the case of bequests) to provide as much provenance information as possible with regard to the Nazi/World War II era; and
   b. member museums should ask sellers of works of art to provide as much provenance information as possible with regard to the Nazi/World War II era.
2. Where the Nazi/World War II era provenance is incomplete for a gift, bequest, or purchase, the museum should search available records and consult appropriate databases of unlawfully confiscated art.
   a. In the absence of evidence of unlawful confiscation, the work is presumed not to have been confiscated, and the acquisition may proceed.
   b. If there is evidence of unlawful confiscation but there is no evidence of restitution, the museum should not proceed to acquire the object and should take appropriate further action.
3. Consistent with current museum practice, member museums should publish, display, or otherwise make accessible all recent gifts, bequests, and purchases, thereby making them available for further research, examination, and study.

4. When purchasing works of art, museums should seek representations and warranties from the seller that the seller has valid title and that the work of art is free from any claims.

C. Access to Museum Records

1. Member museums should facilitate access to the Nazi/World War II era provenance information of all works of art in their collections.
2. Although a linked database of all museum holdings throughout the United States does not exist at this time, individual museums are establishing Web sites with information about collections. Others are making their holdings accessible through printed publications or archives. To assist research, AAMD is exploring the linkage of existing sites that contain collection information.

D. Discovery of Unlawfully Confiscated Works of Art

1. If a member museum determines that a work of art in its collection was illegally confiscated during the Nazi/World War II era and not restituted, the museum should make such information public.
2. In the event that a legitimate claimant comes forward, the museum should offer to resolve the matter in an equitable, appropriate, and mutually agreeable manner.
3. In the event that no legitimate claimant comes forward, the museum should acknowledge the history of the work of art on labels and publications referring to such a work.

E. Response to Claims Against the Museum

1. If a member museum receives a claim against a work of art in its collection related to an illegal confiscation during the Nazi/World War II era, it should seek to review such a claim promptly and thoroughly. The museum should request evidence of ownership from the claimant in order to assist in determining the provenance of the work of art.
2. If after working with the claimant to determine the provenance, a member museum should determine that a work of art in its collection was illegally confiscated during the Nazi/World War II era and not restituted, the museum should offer to resolve the matter in an equitable, appropriate, and mutually agreeable manner.
3. AAMD recommends that member museums consider using mediation wherever reasonably practical to help resolve claims regarding art illegally confiscated during the Nazi/World War II era and not restituted.

F. Incoming Loans

1. In preparing for exhibitions, member museums should endeavor to review provenance information regarding incoming loans.
2. Member museums should not borrow works of art known to have been illegally confiscated during the Nazi/World War II era and not restituted unless the matter has been otherwise resolved (for example, guideline D3 above).

U.S. Law

The federal statutes of the United States (U.S. Code) contain various provisions relating to theft, stolen property, and cultural property, the most important of which are outlined below.

The National Stolen Property Act

The National Stolen Property Act,[55] first enacted in 1934, was created as part of title 18 (Crimes and Criminal Procedure), chapter 113 (Stolen Property), of the U.S. Code provisions regarding, among other things, transportation of stolen property and the sale or receipt of stolen property.

Transportation of stolen goods: Whoever transports in interstate or foreign commerce any goods of the value of $5,000 or more, knowing the goods to have been stolen, converted, or taken by fraud, shall be fined and/or imprisoned for not more than ten years (Section 2314).[56]

Sale or receipt of stolen goods: Whoever receives, possesses, conceals, stores, or sells any goods of the value of $5,000 or more, or pledges or accepts as security for a loan any goods of the value of $500 or more that have crossed a state or United States boundary after being stolen, knowing the goods to have been stolen, shall be fined and/or imprisoned for not more than ten years (Section 2315).

National Stolen Property Act has been held to apply to dealings in pre-Columbian artifacts. These were classified as stolen because the Mexican government enacted a law declaring national ownership of its patrimony. However, the courts have also held that, as a declaration of national ownership is necessary before illegal exportation of an article can be considered theft, and as Mexico did not make a clear and unequivocal declaration as to its ownership of all pre-Columbian artifacts until 1972, the law would not apply to pre-1972 dealings in such artifacts.[57] In Canada, there is also the Cultural Property Export and Import Act, which deals with illegal import and export of cultural artifacts. This is discussed in chapter 9, "Cultural Property Legislation."

Theft of major artwork: A person who (a) steals or obtains by fraud any object of cultural heritage from the care, custody, or control of a museum or (b) knowing that an object of cultural heritage has been stolen or obtained by fraud (whether or not the person knows that the object was taken from a museum), receives, conceals, exhibits, or disposes of the object shall be fined and/or imprisoned for not more than ten years (Section 668). "Museum" refers to a museum situated in the United States, and "object of cultural heritage" is defined as an object that is more than one hundred years old and worth more than $5,000, or an object worth at least $100,000. The limitation period for the prosecution of an offense under Section 668 is twenty years (Section 3294). This statute and cases under it are discussed more fully in chapter 9, "Cultural Property Legislation."

United States Customs rules prohibit the importation into the United States of pre-Columbian monumental or architectural sculpture or murals exported from the *country of origin* (that is, the country in which such sculpture or mural was discovered). *Pre-Columbian monumental or architectural sculpture or mural* means any stone carving or wall art that is the product of a pre-Columbian Indian culture of Latin America subject to export control by the country of origin.[58]

Mexican Law

The Federal Civil Code of Mexico[59] deals with title of stolen objects and related law in Section 6. Under the code, possession of property could give rise to the presumption of ownership (Article 798). A person is a possessor of property if he or she exercises actual control over the object (Article 790). Generally, ownership and possession are distinct; for example, an object may be possessed by a bailee but owned by another.

Possession is protected against those without a better right of possession (Article 803). Lost property is to be reinstated to the possessor. However, possession acquired in good faith is recognized until it is demonstrated that the possessor is aware that his possession is wrongful (Article 808). A person is a possessor in good faith if he or she comes into possession under a good and sufficient title granting the right of possession or if he or she is ignorant of defects in title that impair the legal right to possession (Article 806).

The possessor of lost or stolen property can recover possession from a purchaser in good faith who acquired the property at an auction or from a merchant only if he or she reimburses what the purchaser paid for it. The possessor may then claim from the seller the amount paid to recover the property (Article 799).

An owner who is in bad faith possession but did not obtain possession through the commission of a criminal act is obliged to return all or part of the benefits he or she obtained. The owner may also be compelled to compensate for the loss or deterioration (other than natural wear and tear) of the property, depending on the length of possession (Articles 812 and 813).

A person who obtains possession through the commission of a criminal act must restore all the benefits produced by the property and must also compensate for the loss or deterioration of the property (Article 814).

Personal property acquired by prescription (adverse possession) is covered in Articles 1135–1180 of the code. If the adverse possession is under a claim of ownership, peaceful, continuous, and public, the prescription period is three years if the possessor holds the property in good faith and five years in the absence of good faith or if possession was acquired by force.

If possession is obtained through a criminal act, the possession is considered to be held in bad faith, and the prescription period begins to run from the end of the penalty imposed. Prescription is interrupted if the possessor is deprived of possession for more than one year or if the possessor expressly or implicitly acknowledges the right of the person against whom the statute is running.

Limitation

Neither the Mexican Civil Code nor the Mexican Commercial Code contains specific provisions governing limitation periods for the recovery of stolen property. The general limitation period under both codes is ten years, except for tort actions, for which the limitation period is two years. It would thus appear that a limitation period for abandoned goods might be ten years, whereas for stolen goods it might be two years if it were considered a tort. Under Mexican law, torts includes intentional torts, negligence, deprivation of goods, and interference with business interests. Therefore, a claim for recovery of stolen goods might sometimes constitute an action in tort—for example, where the complainant alleges an illegal sale and purchase were knowingly carried out. Although civil liability for the commission of the tort is barred after two years, this does not affect criminal actions arising from the conduct of the parties.

The Mexican Civil Code (Article 1135) defines the limitation of action concept: "Limitations of actions is the means whereby one can acquire property or be released from an obligation by the passage of a specified period of time and under conditions established by law." The acquisition of assets by possession is referred to as *affirmative limitations* of actions; the release from obligations for failure to demand compliance is referred to as *negative limitations* (Article 1136). Only those assets and obligations in the stream of commerce can be subject to the limitation of actions, except those specifically exempted by law (Article 1137).

The running of statute of limitations shall be interrupted

1. if the possessor is deprived of possession of the property or of the enjoyment of a right for more than one year or

2. by the commencement of any action or proceeding whereof the possessor or obligor is notified (Article 1168).

Actions derived from commercial transactions are barred in accordance with the limitation provisions of the Commercial Code; the limitation period in mercantile matters begins on the day when an action could legally have been exercised through judicial proceedings (Article 1040). Where the code does not establish a shorter period for barring a claim in an ordinary commercial matter, the period of limitations is ten years (Article 1047).

Once it is determined that a purchaser cannot retain the purchase goods (for example, when eviction occurs), the general rule is that the seller must reimburse the purchaser the full cost of the goods sold to him (Articles 2119–2143).

Finally, the Commercial Code provides for recovery against bad faith sellers in commercial transactions (Articles 377 and 385).

No one may sell that which does not belong to him or her (Article 2269); a sale of someone else's property is null and void. The seller is liable for damages and losses if he or she acted in bad faith, subject to applicable title provisions relating to the Public Registry and bona fide purchaser (Article 2270).

The Civil Code outlines the rights of the various parties when the transferor acted in either good or bad faith and the responsibilities of the transferor in either case (Articles 2125–2127).

THE LAW RELATING TO ABANDONED GOODS

Common Law—Classification of Found Property

In common law, found property is classified into four categories:

1. abandoned property;
2. lost property;
3. mislaid property; and
4. treasure trove.

These categories comprise different entitlements to ownership.[60]

Abandoned Property—U.S. Law

Property is abandoned when its owner gives it up absolutely, voluntarily relinquishing possession with the intention of terminating ownership and without vesting it in any other person.[61] An act of abandonment includes both the intention to abandon and the external manifestation of abandonment in fulfillment of that intention.[62]

It has been repeatedly held by the courts that intention is the most important factor in determining whether abandonment has occurred, as there can be no abandonment without the intention to abandon. Abandonment is therefore tantamount to throwing away property. The finder of an abandoned object has a right to title to the object against all others, including the former owner.[63] Such a finder would acquire title by *occupancy*, namely by taking possession of "property without an owner" with the intention of appropriating the property for her or his own use.

Special rules of abandonment apply in some cases. For example, the U.S. government may not abandon its title to certain of its property without an act of Congress, although it may abandon the use of such property.[64] Also, *wrecks* (defined narrowly as property cast on shore after a shipwreck and broadly as shipwrecked goods in general) may be treated somewhat differently from other abandoned property. In British common law, a wreck belonged to the Crown unless it was reclaimed by the true owner within a year and a day from the date the goods were seized by the finder. Although that is also accepted in the United States, it has been held in some cases that no length of time will divest the owner of property found afloat in the sea.[65] Modern courts tend to take the view that, once abandoned, a wreck has no owner.

Lost Property

Property is legally "lost" when the owner has parted with its possession involuntarily, whether through negligence, carelessness, or inadvertence, and does not know its location. Thus, an object that was voluntarily laid down is not lost, even if the owner has forgotten where it is. (Such an object is classified as "mislaid" property and is discussed below.)

In common law, the finder of lost property acquires title to the property if he or she appropriates it with the intention of taking possession. Merely finding the property does not result in acquisition of title. The title so acquired is good against all but the true owner of the property. However, as is discussed below, this common-law rule has been superseded in many jurisdictions by statutes setting out detailed procedures for dealing with lost goods.

Mislaid Property

When the owner of property voluntarily and intentionally puts property somewhere and subsequently forgets where it is, the property is mislaid. Thus, for example, an art object found carefully concealed is more likely mislaid than lost. In common law, the finder of mislaid property acquires no ownership of the property; it belongs to the owner of the premises on which the property is found, against all but the true owner.[66]

Treasure Trove

Treasure trove may be seen as a type of mislaid or lost property. It is usually defined as any found gold, silver, coin, or currency concealed by the owner. In order for property to be classified as treasure trove, its owner must be unknown or likely to be dead, as the treasure has been hidden for a long time.[67] Usually, if the owner can be identified, the property is not treasure trove. The finder of treasure trove takes title to it against all but the true owner. Some jurisdictions have declined to recognize the concept of treasure trove.[68]

Shipwrecks

There has been substantial interest in sunken ships and the artifacts found within and about sunken ships in recent years. The discovery of the *Titanic* has led to discussions as to the appropriateness of removing artifacts from sunken ships. As well, it has attracted the interest of treasure hunters who seek the lost bullion and treasures of abandoned ships.

In the United States, both the federal government and individual states have passed legislation as "trustees of the public interest" to ensure protection of the historical and archaeological significance of shipwrecks.[69]

Historically, the British and Canadian courts have found that title to abandoned property found on or under the sea is vested in the Crown. The U.S. rule, however, was that title to such recovered ships and artifacts belonged to the finder unless there was legislation providing that it belonged to the state or federal government. In either situation, the property must have been abandoned; that is, the owner must have expressly and publicly abandoned the property or items recovered from ships sunk long ago, and no owner appears to claim them.[70]

The U.S. federal government passed the Antiquities Act of 1906[71] and the Archaeological Resources Protection Act[72] of 1979 to assert title to ancient vessels sunk near the coast. The Antiquities Act was an attempt by the United States Congress to deter the plunder of historic American sites. It established a screening process to limit and control access to sites on federal land and required that antiquities be housed in museums or universities.[73] However, in *Treasure of Salvors Inc. v. Unidentified Wrecked and Abandoned Vessel,* the court of appeals ruled that the Antiquities Act applied only to lands owned or controlled by the federal government. Ships outside the territorial waters of the United States are free of any claim by the United States and are "up for grabs."[74] For a wreck to fall within the concept of the act, there are three tests that must be met:

1. the wreck must be abandoned;
2. it must be located on the submerged lands of the state in issue; and

3. it must be embedded in the sea floor or determined eligible for listing in the National Register of Historic Places (National Register).

The act then provides that the federal government of the United States may assert title to such wrecks. If title is so asserted, the government may then transfer title to the wreck to the appropriate state for administration, management, and regulation.

Congress then enacted the Abandoned Shipwreck Act of 1987 to protect underwater archaeological treasures in state waters.[75]

The test for abandonment is the common-law rule of renunciation of title or abandonment inferred by lapse of time and, in the case of wrecks, the failure to pursue salvage efforts by the owner.[76]

Archaeological Resources Protection Act[77]

The Archaeological Resources Protection Act gave more precise identification than the earlier Antiquities Act to items of cultural significance and their protection. It established a structure to oversee excavation of these items. The *archaeological resources* were defined as objects more than one hundred years old that constitute "material remains of past human life or activities which are of archaeological significance" and can be removed from federal lands only pursuant to a government permit. If the object is found on tribal land, removal also requires the consent of the tribe, and the object remains the property of the landowner; it must be held in a museum or university and cannot be sold in the private market except to qualifying institutions.[78]

Place of Finding

In applying the law regarding found property, the place where the object was found may be of significance. This is because property located in a privately owned place is considered to be in the constructive possession and protection of the owner of the place; thus, such property cannot be lost. As property that is not lost cannot be found, the law regarding found goods has no application where a chattel is found in a private place.

In general, when property is found in a place that is not private and is classified as lost property, the finder is not affected by the ownership of the place where it is found.[79] However, if the object has been buried or embedded in the soil, the owner of the land takes title against the finder but not against the true owner. Treasure trove is an exception to this rule: the owner of the soil in which treasure trove is found does not acquire title to the treasure by virtue of being the owner of the soil.[80]

Duties and Liabilities of Finder to Owner

In general, the finder of property must restore the property to its owner if such owner is known. If the owner is unknown, the finder must follow any procedure required by statute for discovering the owner and give any claimant a fair opportunity to inspect the property. It has also been held that the finder of *lost* property, by taking possession, assumes the duties of a bailee without compensation.[81] Such a finder may therefore be liable for any damages caused to the property as a result of not properly carrying out the duties of a bailee, for example, protecting the object.

Statutory Control of Lost (or Found) Goods

Lost property is under statutory control in many jurisdictions. For example, Iowa Code chapter 556F prescribes the following: Any person who finds lost goods or money whose value is at least five dollars must inform the owner, if known. The finder is entitled to ten percent of the value of the goods or money restored to the owner. When the owner is unknown, the finder must, within five days of finding the property, take the property to the county auditor, who enters the description and value of the property, along with the finder's affidavit, into the lost-property book. The finder must then advertise the finding of the property, posting notices at the locations and with the frequency stipulated by the statute. If no person claims the property within twelve months of such posting, the right to property vests irrevocably in the finder. If there is a claimant and the claimant and the finder cannot agree upon true ownership, the matter is to be resolved before a district judge. The statute also stipulates the penalty for failure to comply with the statutory procedure. (Iowa has statutes dealing with property presumed to have been abandoned, also, as in the case of unclaimed funds in a bank account.)

Laws regarding lost goods differ from jurisdiction to jurisdiction. For example, under Michigan's Lost Goods Act, if the true owner is not found within the prescribed time, the value of the goods is divided evenly between the finder and the township in which the goods were found.[82]

Statutes and Common Law

There are two views as to the scope of the application of statutes such as the Iowa Code discussed above. One view is that such statutes apply only to found property classified under common law as lost property;[83] the other view is that statutes concerning lost property apply to *all* found property, regardless of its common-law category.[84]

In the former view, lost-goods statutes do not apply to mislaid or abandoned property or to treasure trove (if the jurisdiction recognizes treasure trove); the ordinary rules of common law apply to these categories of found goods. In the latter, broader view, lost-goods statutes have superseded common law, and no preliminary classification of found property is necessary before applying them. The court in the *Willsmore* case stated that such an expansive interpretation of the Lost Goods Act was desirable because, unlike common law, the act provides certainty of title by vesting clear title after a set period of time; encourages honesty in finders by providing penalties for not complying with the act; provides protection to the finder; and generally provides "a reasonable method of uniting goods with their true owner, and a plan which benefits the people of the state through their local governments."[85]

CANADIAN LAW

The Common-Law Provinces

It is a settled law in the common-law provinces of Canada (all except Quebec) that a finder of goods acquires a good title against all but the true owner.[86] However, there are some preliminary concepts to consider before applying this rule.

The finder of a chattel acquires no title unless it is abandoned or lost. *Abandonment* is defined as occurring when "there is 'giving up, a total desertion, and absolute relinquishment' of private goods by the former owner," and it "may arise when the owner with the specific intent of desertion and relinquishment casts away or leaves behind his property."[87] It follows that a finder of abandoned property acquires title against all the world, including the previous owner.

With regard to found property that is not abandoned, British and Canadian cases do not appear to distinguish between mislaid or forgotten property on the one hand and lost property on the other; they generally apply the same law of found property to both categories. (The two categories are distinguished in the United States, where finding of lost property is governed by statutes.)

A finder acquires no title by the mere fact of finding. Only by physically taking possession and having the intention to take possession does a finder acquire title. Furthermore, a finder who takes possession acquires only limited rights if he or she does so with dishonest intention or while trespassing.

Once a finder takes possession of a lost chattel, the finder legally becomes, and assumes the obligation of, a bailee for the true owner.[88] These obligations include taking reasonable steps to locate the true owner, exercising due care for the safety of the chattel, and returning the chattel to the true owner on demand. The finder will be liable for any damage caused by not performing these obligations. The general rule that a finder who takes custody of found property acquires good title against all but the true owner is subject to two exceptions: if the property was found embedded in land or if it was found by an employee in the course of his or her job.

Place of Finding

A finder does not acquire title if the property was found embedded in or attached to land, unless the finder is the owner of the land. Where a person owns land or a house with a manifest intention to exercise control over it and the things on or in it, anything found on the land or in the house is presumed to belong to the owner. Thus, property found in a place that is privately occupied in general belongs to the owner of the property.[89] However, a finder of property lying unattached on the surface of privately owned land may acquire title to the property if its location was not under sufficient control by the owner.[90] Where property is found in a public place, title belongs to the finder, against all but the true owner.

Employee's Finding

Property found by an employee in the course of employment belongs to the employer.[91] There is obvious difficulty determining when an employee is in the course of employment. Where property was found in a private place by an employee of the owner of the place, this rule is often used to support the rule that such property belongs to the owner.

Treasure Trove

Under British common law, which Canada has inherited, treasure trove is defined as money, coin, gold, silver, plate, or bullion hidden and embedded in the earth or other private place with its true owner unknown.[92] Treasure trove belongs to the Crown unless the person who hid the treasure is discovered, in which case the treasure belongs to that person.

Note that treasure trove excludes treasure not embedded in the earth or not hidden. Therefore, treasure scattered in the sea or not embedded in the earth belongs to the finder, not to the Crown.[93] Wrecks found unembedded in the sea—property that has been cast ashore, including flotsam, jetsam, lagan, and derelict found in or on the shores of the sea or any tidal water or inland waters of Canada—generally belong to the finder. The Canada Shipping Act (Part VI) sets out the procedure that the finder of a wreck must follow.[94]

The Province of Nova Scotia has a statute dealing with treasure trove: the Treasure Trove Act.[95] Under this act, which does not define *treasure trove* but refers in various sections to "any precious stones or metals in a state other than their natural state or any treasure or treasure trove," the governor in council may issue a license granting a person the right to search for treasure in the parts of Nova Scotia specified in the license. The act further stipulates that when a person, whether licensed or not, discovers treasure, he or she shall forthwith make a report to the minister of mines and energy in the manner set out in the act. Under the act, a license-holder who discovers treasure may be allowed to keep the treasure on payment of a royalty at the rate prescribed by the license. (The act does not address the issue of whether an unlicensed person who discovers and recovers treasure can also retain it on payment.)

The British law of treasure trove was generally considered impossible to enforce, because under that law, the Crown has the right to buried antiquities only if it can prove that the treasure was hidden with the intention of recovery and if the descendants of the person who buried it cannot be found. This means that coroners' juries often had to decide what the dead were thinking when they buried their goods. If the Crown won, it offered the finder a reward; if it lost, it could have no further claim. For this reason, the British law is taken to favor the finder.

Found treasure is now governed in Great Britain by the Treasure Trove Act, which came into force in 1997. The act abolishes the common-law definition of treasure trove, redefining it as any object at least three hundred years old that contains more than ten percent precious metal. Under the act, the Crown automatically receives hidden treasure, and the finder is compensated. It is now an offense not to declare a find within two weeks of its discovery, punishable by a maximum penalty of three months' imprisonment and a £5,000 fine. The act, which enjoyed strong support in Parliament, is expected to affect thousands of professional and amateur archaeologists, who fear that the new law will be much less favorable to them than the common law.

Quebec Civil Code[96]

The Civil Code of Quebec treats found property as follows:

1. A movable property that is lost or forgotten in the hands of a third person or in a public place continues to belong to its owner (Article 969).
2. The finder of a thing shall attempt to find its owner; if the owner is found, the finder shall return the item to him or her (Article 940).
3. The holder, including the state or a municipality, of a found thing, may sell it if it is not claimed within sixty days (Article 942).
4. The owner of a lost or forgotten thing may "revendicate" it (that is, receive its return), as long as his or her right of ownership has not been prescribed, by paying the cost of its administration and, where applicable, the value of any work done. The holder of the thing may retain it until payment has been made (Article 946).

These provisions have been interpreted to mean that ownership of found property remains with the owner, who can claim it any time, provided that his or her right to do so has not been prescribed and that the finder does not acquire ownership, unless by prescription (by adverse possession). The period for acquisition of ownership is generally ten years (Article 2917), but the law of prescription is complex and allows for many causes for interruption. In addition, an owner's right to claim the property is subject to the finder's right to compensation, although the code does not set out the precise manner or amount of compensation. The property belongs neither to the government nor to the owner of the property on which it was found.

A movable property without an owner, including abandoned property, belongs to the person who appropriates it for himself or herself by occupation. If an abandoned movable property is not appropriated by anybody, it belongs to the municipality or to the state. Treasure is a special type of property without an owner (Article 938): treasure belongs to the finder if the finder finds it on his or her own land. If it is found on the land of another, one half belongs to the owner of the land and one half to the finder, unless the finder was acting for the owner.

It should be noted, however, that found things are in most cases governed by special legislation, which supersedes the code.

THE LAW OF MEXICO

The Mexican Federal Civil Code provides that possession of property gives rise to the presumption of ownership of the property (Article 798). The rule is somewhat modified by rules such as those having to do with bailees (that is, if the owner of the property delivers it to another pursuant to an arrangement, both parties have possession of the property, the owner holding title and having original possession and the bailee having derivative possession). The person who possesses property by virtue of some right distinct from ownership is presumed not to have ownership. This means that ownership and possession are distinct; ownership may be determined independent of possession (Article 803).

A person who has right of possession is protected against those who do not have a better right (Article 803). Where property is lost, it is to be reinstated to the possessor. If possession of property is of dubious legality, the property will be placed on deposit until the right to its possession is determined (Article 803). However, possession acquired in good faith is recognized until it is demonstrated that the possessor is aware that the possession is wrongful (Article 808). A person is a possessor in good faith if he or she comes into possession under a good and sufficient title granting him or her the right of possession or if the person is ignorant of defects in title that impair his or her legal right of possession (Article 806).

The possessor of lost or stolen property cannot recover possession from a purchaser in good faith who acquires the property at an auction or from a merchant unless the possessor reimburses the purchaser what he or she paid for it. The possessor may then claim from the seller the amount paid to recover the property (Article 799).

A person who is in bad faith possession as owner, but did not obtain possession through the commission of a criminal act, is obliged to return all or a portion of the benefits obtained. He or she may also be compelled to compensate for the loss or deterioration (other than natural wear and tear) of the property, depending on the length of possession (Articles 812 and 813).

A person who obtains possession through the commission of a criminal act must restore all the benefits produced by the property and compensate for the loss or deterioration of the property (Article 814).

Adverse Possession

Ownership of personal property can be acquired by adverse possession (Articles 1135–1180) if the adverse possession is under a claim of ownership that is peaceful, continuous, and public and if it continues for the required length of time: three years if the possessor holds the property in good faith, five years in the absence of good faith or where possession was acquired by force. If possession is obtained through a criminal act, possession is considered to be held in bad faith, and the time for prescription runs from the end of the penalty imposed. Prescription is interrupted if the possessor is deprived of possession for more than one year or if the possessor acknowledges expressly or by implication the right of the person against whom the statute is running.

Possession of property is lost by abandonment (Article 828). Personal property that has been lost or abandoned and whose owner is unknown is "unclaimed" property (Article 774). Anyone who finds unclaimed property must deliver it within three days to the appropriate authority (Article 775), which will have it appraised and will post notices, setting the date of auction in case no claimant appears (Articles 776 and 777). If there is a claimant, a judge will decide whether the claimant is the rightful owner (Article 779). If no claimant appears and no one is adjudged to be the owner, then the property will be sold: one quarter of the proceeds will be given to the finder, the remainder to public charity (Article 781).

Treasure Trove

Treasure trove is defined in the Mexican Civil Code as a "hidden deposit of money, jewels, or other precious objects whose legitimate owners are unknown" (Article 875). The finder of treasure trove is entitled to it if it is found on the finder's property (Article 877). However, if it is found on lands belonging to someone other than the finder, the finder is entitled to one half, and the owner of the land to the other half (Article 877). Treasure trove discovered on someone else's land as a result of work carried out without permission of the owner of the land belongs wholly to the owner of the land (Article 881).

If the objects found are of intrinsic value to science or the arts, they will become the property of the state, and their fair money value will be distributed to the appropriate parties (Article 878).

Expropriation of Cultural Property

The Mexican government has the power to expropriate private property that is considered noteworthy and constitutes a symbol and expression of national culture (Article 833). The present owner of such property may not sell or alter it in any way without authorization from the president of the republic granted through the secretary of public education and fine arts (Article 834). A violation of this law is punishable as a crime (Article 835).

The federal government's power to expropriate cultural property extends to treasure trove: if the objects found are of intrinsic value to science or the arts, they will become the property of the state, and their fair money value will be distributed to the appropriate parties (Article 878).

NOTES

1. "New Weapons against Art Theft," *The Star-Ledger,* Newark, N.J., 8 August 1993, sec. 1, p. 40.

2. "Canadian Court Tackles Illegal Art Imports," *Art Newsletter* 20, no. 1, (September 6, 1994), 7–8.

3. Connie Lowenthal, "The Nurse's Aide Did It," *Wall Street Journal,* July 26, 1991.

4. See *Ontario Sale of Goods Act*, R.S.O. 1990, c. S.1.

5. See *Ontario Factors Act*, R.S.O. 1990, c. F.1.

6. See *Ontario Personal Property Security Act*, R.S.O. 1990, c. P.10.

7. *Dowe v. J.J. Pawn Shop* [1994] 129 N.S.R. (2nd) 363 (N.S.S.C.).

8. Ibid., p. 364.

9. Ibid.

10. Ibid., p. 365

11. See Gerald Henry Louis Fridman, *Sale of Goods in Canada*, 4th ed. (Toronto: Carswell, 1985), 121–22.

12. *British Columbia Sale of Goods Act*, R.S.B.C. 1996, c. 410.

13. *Criminal Code*, R.S.C. 1985, c. C-46, s. 739.

14. *Menzel v. List*, 49 Misc. 2d 300, 267 N.Y.S. 2d 804 (Sup. Ct. 1966), modified as to damages, 28 A.D. 2d 516, 279 N.Y.S. 2d 608 (1967), rev'd as to modifications, 24 N.Y. 2d 91, 246 N.E. 2d 742, 298 N.Y.S. 2d 979 (1969).

15. *Koerner v. Davis,* No. 85 Civ. 0752 (S.D.N.Y. May 21, 1987).

16. Ibid.

17. Jeremy S. Williams, *Limitation of Actions in Canada*, 2d ed. (Toronto: Butterworth, 1980).

18. *Anns and Others v. London Borough of Merton,* (1977) 2 All E. R. 492 (H.L.). (This case was later overruled by *Murphy v. Brentwood District Council,* [1990] 2 All E. R. 908 [H.L.], but not on the statute of limitations issue.)

19. Williams, *Limitation of Actions,* 9.

20. *Central Trust Co. v. Rafuse et al.,* (1988) 1 S.C.R. 1206, a rehearing of, (1986) 2 S.C.R. 147, 31 D.L.R. (4th) 481.

21. *Peixeira v. Haberman,* (1995), 25 O.R. (3d) 1 (C.A.).

22. Williams, *Limitation of Actions,* 13.

23. *Erisoty v. Rizik,* no. 93-6215, 1995 U.S. Dist. LEXIS 2096 (E.D.Pa. Feb. 23, 1995), aff'd, no. 95-1807, 1996 U.S. App. LEXIS 14999 (3d Cir. May 7, 1996).

24. *DeWeerth v. Baldinger,* 836 F.2d 103 (2d Cir. 1987), rev'd 658 F. Supp. 688 (S.D.N.Y. 1987), cert. denied, 486 U.S. 1056, 108 S. Ct. 2823, 100 L. Ed. 924 (1988), remanded, 804 F. Supp. 539 (S.D.N.Y. 1992), rev'd, 38 F.3d 1266 (2d Cir.), cert. denied, 115 S. Ct. 512, 130 L. Ed. 2d 419 (1994).

25. See *Republic of Turkey v. Metropolitan Museum of Art,* 762 F. Supp. 44 (S.D.N.Y. 1990). See also *Solomon R. Guggenheim Foundation v. Lubell,* 77 N.Y. 2d 311, 569 N.E. 2d 426, 567 N.Y.S. 2d 623 (1991), aff'g 153 A.D. 2d 143, 550 N.Y.S. 2d 618 (1990) (modifying an order from the Supreme Court, N.Y. County, entered Feb. 14, 1989, which denied a motion by plaintiff for discovery and inspection and granted a cross-motion by defendant for summary judgment), and *Erisoty.*

26. *O'Keeffe v. Snyder,* 83 N.J. 478, 416A. 2d 862 (1980).

27. *Menzel.*

28. *DeWeerth.*

29. *Menzel.*

30. See *O'Keeffe.*

31. For discussion of the case see Franklin Feldman, Stephen E. Weil, and Susan Duke Biederman, *Art Law: Rights and Liabilities of Creators and Collectors,* 1993 supplement (Boston: Little, Brown and Company, 1993), Sections 11.2.4 and 11.2.4(a).

32. *Guggenheim Foundation* (modifying an order from the Supreme Court, N.Y. County, entered Feb. 14, 1989, that denied a motion by plaintiff for discovery and inspection and granted a cross-motion by defendant for summary judgment).

33. Feldman, Weil, and Duke, *Art Law,* 414.

34. *Erisoty.*

35. See *Spillane v. Liberty Mutual Insurance,* 317 N.Y.S. 2nd 203, 206 (N.Y. Civ. Ct. 1970), affirmed 327 N.Y.S. 2d 701 (N.Y. App. term 1971), 7.

36. *O'Keeffe,* 8.

37. Ibid.

38. Ibid.

39. Ibid, 9.

40. See *Erisoty.*

41. Laurie Attias, "French Museum Paintings Pursued by War Victim's Heirs," *Art Newsletter* XXII, no. 17 (April 22, 1997): 6–8.

42. *O'Keeffe.*

43. *Porter v. Wertz,* 68 A.D. 2d 141, 416 N.Y.S. 2d 254 (1979), aff'd, 53 N.Y. 2d 696, 421 N.E. 2d 500, 439 N.Y.S. 2d 105 (Ct. App. 1981).

44. Franklin Feldman, "New York's Statute of Limitations with Respect to Stolen Art and Holocaust Claims," *IFAR Journal* 1, no. 2 (Summer 1998), 16. See also *Insurance Company of North America v. ABB Power Generation, Inc.*, 91 N.Y. 2nd 180 (1997).

45. Ibid.

46. *California Civil Process Code*, Section 338 (C) (West 1982 & Supp. 1997).

47. *Nafzger v. American Numismatic Society*, 42 Cal. App. 4th 421, 49 Cal. Rptr. 2d 784 (Ct. App. 1996).

48. *Society of California Pioneers v. Baker*, 43 Cal. App. 4th 774, 50 Cal. Rptr. 2d 865 (1996).

49. For discussion of these cases see the *IFAR reports* 17, no. 5 (May 1996), particularly Carla J. Shapreau, "Rule in Cases to Recover Stolen Art," 2–3, and John Merryman, "Reversals in Two California Cases Prompt Debate on Time Limits," 4–5.

50. New York Civil Practice Law and Rules (McKinney 1984 and Supp. 1997).

51. *New York Arts and Cultural Affairs Law* §13.01 (McKinney 1984 and Supp. 1997).

52. See Lynn H. Nicholas, *The Rape of Europa* (New York: Vintage Books, 1995) for a carefully researched account of "The Fate of Europe's Treasures in the Third Reich and the Second World War."

53. U.S. Department of State Washington Conference on Holocaust-Era Assets held at the U.S. Holocaust Memorial Museum, and notes provided by Constance Lowenthal, director, Commission for Art Recovery, American Jewish Congress, New York, 1995. See also "Principles with Respect to Nazi Confiscated Art," *IFAR Journal* 2, no. 1 (Winter 1998/99): 8.

54. *IFAR Journal* 1, no. 3 (Autumn 1998), 20.

55. *The National Stolen Property Act*, 18 U.S.C. §2314 (1982).

56. See *United States v. Hollinshead*, 495 F.2d 1154 (9th Cir. 1974), the first cultural property case prosecuted under this provision. See also *United States v. McClain*, 545 F.2d 988 (5th Cir. 1977), 593 F.2d 658 (5th Cir. 1979).

57. Ibid.

58. *The Pre-Columbian Art Act, 1972,* codified at 19 U.S.C. §2091–95 (1988).

59. Abraham Eckstein and Enrique Zepada Trujillo, *Mexican Civil Code* (St. Paul, Minn.: West Publishing Co., 1996).

60. See *Benjamin v. Lindner Aviation, Inc.*, 534 N.W. 2d 400 (Iowa 1995), 406, for a succinct explanation of the common-law classification of found goods.

61. *Dober v. Ukase Inc. Co.,* 10 P. 2d 356 (Oregon S.C. 1932).

62. *Roebuck v. Mecosta County Rd. Commission*, 229 N.W. 2d 343 (1975).

63. *Ritz v. Selma United Methodist Church*, 467 N.W. 2d 266 (Iowa S.C. 1991).

64. *U.S. v. Warmsprings Irr. Dist.*, 38 F. Supp. 239 (Oregon Dist. Ct. 1940).

65. *Wilkie v. Two Hundred and Five Boxes of Sugar*, 29 F. Cas. No. 1247, Bee 82 No. 17 662 (South Carolina Dist. Ct. 1796).

66. *Ritz*, 269.

67. *Jackson v. Steinberg*, 205 P. 2d 562 (Oregon S.C. 1949).

68. *Willsmore v. Oceola*, 308 N.W. 2d 796 (Mich. App. 1981), 800.

69. For a detailed list of the states and the legislation, see Marilyn Phelan, "A Synopsis of the Laws Protecting Our Cultural Heritage," *New England Law Review* 28 (1993), 63.

70. See *Maritime Underwater Surveys Inc. v. The Unidentified, Wrecked & Abandoned Sailing Vessel*, 531 N.E. 2d (Mass. 1988). See also *Treasure of Salvors Inc. v. Unidentified Wrecked and Abandoned Vessel*, 569 F. 2d 330 (5th Cir. 1978).

71. *Antiquities Act of 1906*, Ch. 3060, §2, 34 Stat. 225 (1906), codified as amended at 16 U.S.C. §§431–33m (1988).

72. *Archaeological Resources Protection Act of 1979*, Pub. L. No. 96-95, §2, 93 Stat. 721 (1979), codified at 16 U.S.C. §§470aa-70mm (1988).

73. Quoted from Susan B. Bruning, "Native American Art and Antiquities: A Legal Primer for Collectors," *IFAR Journal* 17 (1998): 3.

74. *Treasure of Salvors Inc.*

75. 43 U.S.C., Section 2101–06.

76. *Deep Sea Research*, 102 F.3d, 33 FF. See also "Treasurer Salvors Win a Victory in the Ninth Circuit," *IFAR Journal* 1, no. 1 (Spring 1998), 19. Reproduced from C. Shapreau, *Art Antiquity and Law* II, issue I (March 1997). See also *Zych v. Unidentified Wrecked and Abandoned Vessel*, 755, F. Supp. 213, 216 (N.D. ill 1990), amended 1991, WL 2536 (1991). See also *Zych v. Unidentified Wrecked and Abandoned Vessel*, believed to be the Capital SB "Seabird," 811, F. Supp. 1300, 1314 (N.D. ill 1992) affirmed, 19F.3d, 1136 (7th Cir.).

77. Archaeological Resources Protection Act of 1979, *16 U.S.C.* S. 470aa-47011.

78. Bruning, "Native American Art and Antiquities."

79. *In Re Savarino*, 1 F. Supp. 331 (D. Ct. N.Y. 1932).

80. *Groover v. Tippins*, 170 S.E. 634 (Ga. App.). The owner of the soil in which treasure trove is found does not acquire title to the treasure by virtue of being the owner of the soil.

81. *Dolitsky v. Dollar Savings Bank*, 118 N.Y.S. 2d 65 (1952).

82. *Willsmore.*

83. See *Benjamin v. Lindner Aviation, Inc.*, 534 N.W. 2d 400 (Iowa 1995). See also *Bishop v. Ellsworth,* 234 N.E. 2d 49 (Ill. App. 3rd Dist. 1968).

84. *Willsmore.*

85. Ibid., 804.

86. *Bird v. The Town of Fort Frances,* (1949) O.R. 292 (H.C.). This rule is said to originate in the British case of *Armory v. Delamirie*, 1 Stra. 505 (1722).

87. W. B. Raishenbush and R. A. Brown, *The Law of Personal Property*, 3d ed. (Chicago: Callaghan & Co., 1975), 8–9. This definition was adopted in the recent case of *Ontario v. Mar-Dive Corp.*, O.J. No. 4471 (QL) (Gen. Div. 1996).

88. *Trachuk v. Olinek*, 4 W.W.R. 137 (Alta. Q.B. 1996).

89. *Grafstein v. Holme*, O.R. 354 (Ont. H.C. 1957); affirmed O.R. 296 (Ont. C.A. 1958).

90. *Kowal v. Ellis*, 2 W.W.R. 761 (Man. C.A. 1977).

91. *White v. Alton-Lewis et al.*, 4 O.R. (2d) 741 (Co. Ct. 1974).

92. *Halsbury's Laws of England*, 4th ed., vol. 8 (Cumm. Supp.), §1513.

93. *Mar-Dive Corp.*

94. *Canada Shipping Act*, R.S.C. 1985, c. S-9.

95. *Treasure Trove Act,* R.S.N.S. 1989, c. 477.

96. *Quebec Civil Code* 1991, chap. 64.

· 4 ·

Role and Responsibility
of Valuers

The professional valuer is often an essential element in commercial transactions involving art and art objects. Reliable valuation data are integral to purchases, sales, donations, gifts, insurance, and the administration of personal property. Tax and estate planning are often dependent on professional estimates of property values.

Art and antique dealers estimate various values: the retail value of the work to be sold; trade-in values on works forming part of the payment for a new work purchased; time payment values, if the work is being purchased over time; and discount values given for cash payment in full. Insurance values have to be estimated according to the wording of the relevant policy: "replacement value," "replacement value new," or "depreciated value."

A result of an auction sale establishes a price. In some auction catalogs, presale estimates are stated for each work being auctioned and are called *estimates.* The seller and the auction house also establish private *reserve prices* below which a particular work will not be sold. *Final results,* the sum of the purchase price plus the commission to the auction house and buyer premium, are used by auction houses to predict responses for similar properties in subsequent sales.

Valuations of personal property are needed to estimate capital-gains tax on sales; tax benefits for donations or for estate and death-duties purposes, such as bequests; and insurance coverage of the estate assets.

What we in North America call *appraisers,* much of the rest of the world calls *valuers,* and the appraisal process is called *valuation.* However, in this text there is a difference between *valuation* and *appraisal. Valuation* is:

1. the calculation of a certain property's worth for tax purposes;
2. the cost given to something;
3. the assessed value of an item.

Appraisal is defined as "the process of estimating property value by seeking an expert analysis rather than by selling."[1] An *appraisal report* is the written (or verbal) report explaining the process and result of that analysis. In other words, appraisal is the estimation of the value of a property at a given time and place for a specific purpose, supported in a report by objective facts.

THE VALUER

In the United States, Canada, and Mexico, there are numerous valuers of personal property and a number of professional appraisal organizations.

A large number of self-appointed valuers do not belong to any professional association. These parties are unregulated, untested, and not subject to any association's organizational or educational requirements, standards, or codes of conduct. Some of these valuers are also art dealers, who may be members of dealer associations with various standards and requirements for buying and selling; however, most are not.

WHAT MAKES A VALUER "PROFESSIONAL"?

The usual ingredients to establish a profession are:

1. Education—in a body of knowledge.
2. Recognized methods.
3. Specialized vocabulary.

In 1986–87, various nationally recognized U.S. and Canadian professional valuer associations created The Appraisal Foundation and developed the Uniform Standards of Professional Appraisal Practice (USPAP),[2] which became the standards for The Appraisal Foundation. The Appraisal Foundation, a not-for-profit educational organization, was founded in 1987 to foster professionalism in appraising through the promotion of appraisal standards and the assessing of valuer qualifications. The foundation accomplishes this through two independent boards, the Appraiser Qualifications Board (AQB) and the Appraisal Standards Board (ASB), both of which are appointed and funded by the foundation's Board of Trustees. The AQB establishes minimum education, experience, and examination criteria for valuers. The ASB promulgates the generally accepted standards of the appraisal profession, interpreting and publishing such practices and issuing advisory opinions on appraisal practices and other professional matters as they emerge.

In 1989, the U.S. Congress enacted the Financial Institutions Reform, Recovery and Enforcement Act (FIRREA),[3] which requires that appraisals prepared by state-certified and licensed real property valuers be performed in conformance with USPAP. Personal-property valuers are not required to be licensed.

The Uniform Standards of Professional Appraisal Practice and various publications that deal with it are available from The Appraisal Foundation. Standards 7 and 8 were specifically established for, and directed to, personal-property valuation. Those standards—and the rules governing ethics, competency, departure, jurisdictional exceptions, and supplemental standards—set the minimal performance guidelines for the valuation of personal property.

In 1994, the Appraisal Institute of Canada adopted a new Uniform Standards of Appraisal Practice[4] setting out the ethical and professional requirements its members must meet.

International appraisal standards are being composed by the International Valuation Standards Committee (IVSC); these standards will combine the professional interests of the European Union, the Pacific Rim Nations, and developing countries with those of Canada, the United States, and Mexico. Founded in 1981, the IVSC comprises national valuation societies and institutions representing their respective states. The principal IVSC objective is to formulate and publish, in the public interest, valuation standards and procedural guidance for the valuation of assets for use in financial statements and to promote their worldwide acceptance and observance. The second objective is to harmonize standards among the world's states and to make disclosures of differences in standards statements and/or applications of standards as they occur.

THE VALUER-CLIENT RELATIONSHIP

In establishing the valuer-client relationship, it is imperative that various preliminary matters be clarified to the satisfaction of both parties.

1. The client must choose a valuer in whom he or she has confidence as to qualifications, knowledge, and integrity. The valuer and the client must also be comfortable in dealing with each other, and the valuer must believe in the integrity of the client and of the proposed scope of work.
2. Background facts should be provided to the valuer in a clear manner, because an appraisal report based on partial or false facts or assumptions will ultimately invalidate the appraisal and harm the credibility of the valuer. These background facts include not only those associated with the assignment but also

those underlying the object itself, such as its history, condition, provenance, authenticity, and ownership. The facts must include the client's right to deal with the object to be appraised and his or her authority to hire a valuer.

THE APPRAISAL CONTRACT

The relationship between the client and the professional valuer is as important as—and similar to—the relationship between a client and a lawyer, an accountant, or anyone else dealing with confidential information. The parties should acknowledge that their relationship will be a professional one, subject to due diligence required of the valuer and requirements of confidentiality, free of conflict of interest, and noncompetitive. They should establish the fee for services and time of payment, as well as any added fee for, or restriction of use of, the appraisal report by third parties.

Because the contract is important, it should be in writing. It may require the involvement of a lawyer, especially if the client is not the owner but an agent for the owner. A contract in writing establishes the guidelines for the appraisal and can also set out the independence of the parties to the transaction, especially if the appraisal report is to be relied on by a third party.[5]

The following matters should be included in any such contract:

1. an indication of the qualifications and independence of the valuer. This may take the form of a schedule, including a resume of the valuer's credentials, history, and independence.
2. the authority of the client to authorize the appraisal.
3. the parameters of the work to be done by the valuer, the purpose and scope of the assignment, the intended use and user of the appraisal report, and the expectations of client and valuer, including the fact that the valuer is proceeding on the assumption that the work or object is authentic. The valuer may restrict the use of the appraisal report to specified parties to avoid misuse by unintended parties. (The reasoning in the case *Foxley v. Sotheby's Inc.*[6] illustrates that the inclusion of a disclaimer and the wording of it *is* significant to both the client and the valuer. See note 6 for a discussion of the case.)
4. the fee to be paid to the valuer and the time and place of such payment.
5. the location of the object and a listing of all background materials, photographs, and information on the object that will be available to the valuer.
6. the valuer's disbursements (for travel, telephone, faxes, etc.) to be paid by the client, and what proof will be required for reimbursement.
7. whether the valuer will be available as an expert witness if required and, if so, on what terms. What are the valuer's credentials, experience, and history as an expert witness?

8. the time frame for the appraisal.
9. the format of the appraisal.
10. an indication of what laws will apply to the contract and how disputes, if any, will be settled.

The American Society of Appraisers College of Fellows opinion on contractual conditions[7] also suggests the following inclusions in the contract:

11. that any use by the client of the appraisal report is contingent on payment of all fees in accordance with the agreed terms.
12. that fees are in no way contingent upon the value(s) estimated by the valuer. (This is also required by both American and Canadian tax authorities.) For performing the services rendered at the fee charged, the valuer expressly limits his or her liability to five times the amount of the fee paid or $25,000, whichever is less.
13. that the valuer expressly disclaims liability as an insurer or guarantor. A client seeking greater protection from loss or damage than is provided for in the contract should obtain appropriate insurance.
14. that the valuer is to be afforded ready access to the property to be appraised.
15. that fees quoted in appraisal engagement letters are due and payable irrespective of whether the valuer's conclusions coincide with the client's expectations.
16. that unless specifically brought to his or her attention, the valuer will assume there are no hidden or unexpected conditions of the property that adversely affect the value.
17. that if, in the future, the valuer is required or compelled to produce documentation to support testimony in regard to work performed for the client, the client shall reimburse the valuer for all costs, including legal fees, preparation and travel time, court deposition or court time, and expenses incurred.
18. that the client shall indemnify the valuer and his or her employees, agents, and subcontractors against all claims made by any third party and against any judgment for loss, damage, or expenses related to the performance services by the valuer.
19. that in the event of a dispute, mediation and—if necessary—binding arbitration should be undertaken to settle any dispute.

THE UNIFORM STANDARDS OF PROFESSIONAL APPRAISAL PRACTICE

USPAP sets out the ethical and professional expectations of the Appraisal Standards Board for the conduct of valuers. The standards contain binding requirements as well as specific requirements to which the Departure Rule may apply under certain conditions (discussed later). However, no departure is permitted from the Preamble, Ethics Rule, Competency Rule, or Definition Section.[8]

Preamble

The USPAP preamble includes the following: "It is essential that professional appraisers develop and communicate their analysis, opinions, and conclusions to intended users of their services in a manner that is meaningful and not misleading. The importance of the role of the appraiser places ethical obligations on those who serve in this capacity." It goes on to provide the requirements of "integrity, impartiality, objectivity, independent judgment, and ethical conduct."

Ethics Rule

The Ethics Rule in USPAP is divided into four sections: conduct, management, confidentiality, and recordkeeping. The ethics provisions comprise the following:

1. **Conduct**—deals with ethical conduct, which includes impartiality, objectivity, and independence and prohibits accommodation of personal interests.
2. **Management**—deals with compensation of the valuer. It is unethical to accept compensation that is contingent on the reporting of a predetermined value or a direction in value that favors the cause of the client, the amount of the value estimate, the attainment of a stipulated result, or the occurrence of a subsequent event.

   The payment of undisclosed fees, commissions, or things of value in connection with the procurement of appraisal, review, or consulting assignments is unethical.

   Advertising for or soliciting appraisal assignments in a manner that is false, misleading, or exaggerated is unethical.

   The restriction on contingent compensation in the first paragraph of this section does not apply to consulting assignments where the valuer is not acting in a disinterested manner and would not reasonably be perceived as performing a service that requires impartiality. This permitted contingent compensation must be properly disclosed in the report.

3. **Confidentiality**—deals with the protection of the confidential nature of the valuer-client relationship.
4. **Recordkeeping**—deals with a written work file for each assignment, including a recording of oral testimony given, reports provided, and all other data necessary to support the valuer's opinions and conclusions and to show compliance with the rule and other applicable standards. Work files must be retained for five years after preparation and two years after final disposition of any judicial proceeding where testimony was given, whichever period expires last.

Competency Rule

USPAP also includes a Competency Rule "that places an immediate responsibility on the appraiser prior to acceptance of an assignment as well as during the performance of an assignment."[9] Prior to accepting an assignment or agreeing to perform one, a valuer must properly identify the problem to be addressed and ensure that he or she has the knowledge and experience necessary to complete the assignment competently. Alternatively, the valuer may

1. disclose his or her lack of knowledge to the client before accepting the assignment;
2. take all steps necessary to complete the assignment competently; and
3. describe the lack of knowledge and/or experience and the steps taken to complete the assignment competently in the report.[10]

Departure Rule

This rule permits departure or exceptions from sections of USPAP that are classified as special requirements rather than binding requirements.[11]

CODES OF CONDUCT

USPAP has established a uniform standard for valuers, including a Code of Conduct. In addition, most professional appraisal societies have established codes of conduct for their members.

The 1999 edition of USPAP introduces a fifth prefatory rule concerning supplemental standards. The rule states that in addition to USPAP, other standards may apply to an assignment, such as standards set by clients, employers, government, and/or professional appraisal organizations. The rule makes a valuer and his or her client responsible for deciding whether any supplemental standards apply and, if they do, for following them.

DUE DILIGENCE

Due diligence is defined as "such measure of prudence as is properly to be expected from and ordinarily exercised by a reasonable and prudent person under the particular circumstances; not measured by any absolute standard, but depending on the relative facts of the special case."[12] There are two stages of due diligence:

1. investigation or information collection—understanding the property to be valued, assessing factors involved in appraisal, and considering market and economic conditions;
2. verification—examining and analyzing financial information, clarifying risks and opportunities, and drawing conclusions.

A duty of care arises out of the contract of appraisal. It entitles a client to rely on an expert's representations and sets out the extent of the expert's responsibility, his or her understanding of the scope of the opinion, and his or her professional qualifications.

The duty of care is one of a specialist or expert, and the duty is to act with care, consistent with that special knowledge or skill. The standard of care is the standard that would be required of that particular profession, similar to the standard that applies to other professionals such as lawyers, doctors, architects, engineers, and so forth within the context of their professions.[13]

In the analysis of sales history of the subject property, a valuer must exercise due diligence, but such due diligence need not necessarily include a search of the public record; it depends on the nature and scope of the assignment. If certain information is unavailable, comments on the efforts undertaken by the valuer to obtain the information are required to be cited.

WHAT DOES A VALUER DO?

USPAP defines *appraisal* as the act or process of developing an opinion of value.[14] USPAP Standard 7, "Personal Property Appraisal, Development," states that "In developing a personal property appraisal, an appraiser must be aware of, understand, and correctly employ those recognized methods and techniques that are necessary to produce a credible appraisal."[15] USPAP Standards Rule 7-1, from which departure is not permitted, states:

In developing a personal property appraisal, an appraiser must:

(a) be aware of, understand and correctly employ those recognized methods and techniques that are necessary to produce a credible appraisal;

(b) not commit a substantial error of omission or commission that significantly affects an appraisal;

(c) not render appraisal services in a careless or negligent manner, such as making a series of errrors that, although individually might not significantly affect the results of an appraisal, in the aggregate affect the credibility of those results.[16]

In developing a personal property appraisal, a valuer must consider the purpose and intended use of the appraisal report and follow specific appraisal requirements set out in USPAP Standards Rule 7-2. These requirements include:

1. adequately identify the property to be valued. This means employing a method of identification that must adequately describe the property as it is understood in its market.
2. define the purpose and intended use and users of the appraisal report, including all general and specific limiting conditions.
3. identify the effective date of the appraisal.
4. select and define the type of value consistent with the purpose of the appraisal. For example, if the value to be estimated is market value, the valuer must clearly indicate whether the estimate is the most probable price
    a. in terms of cash;
    b. in terms of financial arrangements equivalent to cash; or
    c. in such other terms as may be precisely defined.
    For example, if an estimate of value is based on submarket financing or on financing with unusual conditions or incentives, the terms of such financing must be clearly set forth, their contributions (positive or negative) to value must be described and estimated, and the market data supporting the valuation estimate must be described and explained.
5. collect, verify, analyze, and reconcile such data as are available, adequately identified, and described to indicate a value conclusion.
6. value the property by an appropriate appraisal method or technique.
7. use pertinent information in items 1 through 6 above in the development of a personal property appraisal.

USPAP Standards Rule 7-3 recognizes that personal property has several measurable marketplaces. The valuer must identify, define, and analyze the appropriate market consistent with the purpose and intended use of the appraisal report. In other words, the valuer must recognize that there are distinct levels of trade, each with its own market value. A property may have one value at the wholesale level of trade and another value at commercial galleries and dealerships or at auctions under varying conditions. For example, properties sold at auction can be liquidated in an orderly or a forced manner, and their values may represent any of a number of market levels.[17] Therefore, the valuer must consider the property within the appropriate market context.

Some examples of cases in which the relevancy of market data is explored are *Anselmo v. Commissioner,*[18] *Hunter v. Commissioner,*[19] and *Lio v. Commissioner.*[20] All three cases deal with relevant markets for the various works that were donated by the parties involved and the appropriate amount of tax deductions available to the donors. These cases tested reliance on and sufficiency or insufficiency of the data from varying market sites considered in an appraisal.

A specific value may be considered for a particular work in respect to its history or popularity. For instance, the court in *Purdue v. Commissioner* indicated that an appraisal could rely on the "romantic appeal and glamour" that certain objects had because of the publicity surrounding their creation or discovery, even if their value when measured by a quality standard would be considerably less.[21]

THE APPRAISAL REPORT

The results of the development of an appraisal are presented in a report provided in writing or verbally. In either instance, the rules and standards of USPAP apply. The report describes the manner in which the valuation was reached. Therefore, the report must contain sufficient information for a reader to understand it properly. USPAP—particularly Standard 8—deals with these requirements in detail.

The Getty Information Institute has also proposed a useful object identification format to describe art objects. This format is described in chapter 7, "Insurance."

Standard 8 of USPAP specifies requisite elements for a professional appraisal report, including:

1. description of the personal property being appraised;
2. identification of the ownership interest of the property being appraised;
3. a statement of the purpose and intended use and users of the appraisal report;
4. a definition of the value being considered, consistent with the purpose of the appraisal;
5. the effective date of the appraisal and the date of the report;
6. a description of the extent of the process of collecting, confirming, and reporting data;
7. all assumptions and limiting conditions that affect the analyses, opinions, conclusions, and valuations;
8. the information considered, the appraisal procedures followed, and the reasoning that supports the analysis, opinions, conclusions, and valuations;

9. where appropriate, comparable sales data, auction results, offers from reputable firms, or other such information. If not included in the narrative of the report, they must be referenced in the report and maintained with the field notes;
10. where appropriate, an explanation and support of the analysis of the highest and best use;
11. where appropriate, an explanation and support of the analysis of the appropriate market;
12. an explanation and support of the exclusion of any of the usual valuation approaches;
13. any additional information that may be appropriate to show compliance with, or clearly identify and explain permitted departures from, the requirements of Standard 7;
14. a signed certification in accordance with Standards Rule 8-3.

The personal-property professional valuer who has complied with USPAP certifies the report with a series of statements that underline the objectivity and independence of the valuer and the appraisal process.

Therefore, in following the appropriate professional methodology, the appraisal generally should include the requirements of Standard 8 of USPAP and generally the following:

1. the name of the client;
2. a description of the property, including the subject matter; medium; edition number; artist; creation date; size; interest transferred; cost, date, and manner of acquisition; history of the work (provenance); photographs and reproductions of the work in publications; exhibition history of the property and the artist; and standing of the artist;
3. representations and warranties by the owner and the valuer;
4. the qualifications of the valuer; and
5. the statement of value.

THE LEGAL LIABILITY OF THE PROFESSIONAL VALUER

Like any other professional who has special knowledge, skill, and training, the valuer has a duty to act with reasonable care and in a manner consistent with that special knowledge, skill, and training to avoid liability in tort law.

A tort is an act of commission or of omission that may arise through negligent misstatement or misrepresentation. Liability for negligence may extend beyond the client-valuer relationship, depending on the valuer's terms and form of employment and on the knowledge of the parties. For example, the valuer may have been engaged by a lawyer for a client, an estate, or for sale purposes to provide an appraisal report to a potential purchaser or seller. All these parties have a right to rely on the appraisal report provided, even though they may not be the client and may not have paid the valuer for the appraisal.

Therefore, it is imperative that the valuer outline in the appraisal report the name of the client and the purposes for which the appraisal report has been prepared, as well as any limiting factors on the appraisal report and its use.

An example of a negligent appraisal claim is the case of *Struna v. Wolf.*[22] The issue presented to the court was whether the Metropolitan Museum of Art was liable when its curator allegedly made a negligent appraisal of a work. An individual, who unbeknownst to the curator of the museum was not the actual owner of the artwork but rather the consignee who initially purchased the work, relied on the curator's alleged negligent statements as to the work's authenticity and value. The plaintiff sued to recover the balance claimed to be owed on a contract to purchase a sculpture, *La Femme Assise* by Elie Nadelman.

There were various facts in dispute, including whether or not the curator rendered such an appraisal of the work and whether in any event there was any contract and contractual liability. The court determined there was no contractual relationship between the museum and the party suing under the alleged contract. However, the court went on to determine whether or not there was a cause of action for negligent appraisal in this case.

The court determined that "a claim for negligent appraisal is in essence a claim for negligence representation." With respect to liability for negligent statements, the law is "although it is a broad general rule that an action will not lie for negligent misrepresentations, there may be liability for damages resulting from the negligent utterance of words under certain circumstances. Thus, in some cases a negligent statement may be the basis for a recovery of damages. Liability in such cases arises only where there is a duty, if one speaks at all, to give the correct information. This involves many considerations. There must be knowledge, or its equivalent, that the information is desired for a serious purpose; that the person to whom it is given intends to rely on and act on it; and that, if the information is false or erroneous, using it could cause injury to a person or property. Finally, the relationship of the parties, arising out of contract or otherwise, must be such that in morals and good conscience, the one has the right to rely on the other for information and the person giving the information owes a duty to give it with care."[23]

Generally, therefore, negligent words are not actionable unless they are uttered directly, with knowledge or notice that they will be acted on, to one to whom the speaker is bound by some relation of duty (arising out of public calling, contract, or otherwise) to act with care if he or she acts at all—or unless the speaker has a duty to give the correct information if he or she speaks at all.[24]

Judge David B. Saxe found that

> under the facts presented here, the requisite elements necessary for tort feasibility for a negligent appraisal are lacking and the defendant therefore cannot be found liable as a matter of law.... The plaintiff fails to show how the museum could have known that the plaintiff planned to act in reliance upon any statements of appraisal made by the curator.[25]

In order to state a claim for negligent misrepresentation (or negligent appraisal), it is essential that a complainant demonstrate that the speaker made the negligent statement "with knowledge or notice that it will be acted upon."[26]

Moreover, these cases routinely require the existence of a special relationship between the parties creating a duty of care owed to the complainant, thus entitling the complainant to rely on the defendant's representations. Whether or not a special relationship exists depends on many considerations; but, as demonstrated in the previously discussed cases, a special relationship arises out of a contract where the offender in question is specifically employed for the purpose of rendering an appraisal to the complainant, knowing that he or she intends to rely on it.

In *Struna v. Wolf*, on the other hand, by the plaintiff's own admission, it appeared that the plaintiff was acting at arm's length (that is, independently and not as a participant in the transaction) in attempting to achieve a sale of the sculpture to the museum. This relationship between the parties thus appears to be the very antithesis of the special relationship, which would support holding the defendant to a higher duty of care than is otherwise required. Therefore, the court determined, the museum could not be held liable to the plaintiff based on any claim that its curator rendered a negligent appraisal.

The negligence of a valuer falls in Canada and the United States under provincial or state law, unless it is criminal in nature, in which case it may also involve a breach of a federal statute. Art experts are increasingly being sued for malpractice by clients who believe they have been misled, especially when appraisal values have been successfully attacked in the courts or by government agencies. Such claims include negligence, breach of fiduciary duty, and conflict of interest.

Though defenses are available—assumption of risk, contributory negligence, and even the expiration of a limitation period under the statute of limitations—a valuer is usually wise to avoid litigation with a client or former client. Regardless of the outcome, litigation is always costly to the valuer, both in reputation and in fees paid.

Negligence

The most common action against a valuer, as against any professional advisor, is for negligence. The law of negligence requires that the complainant prove that there was a duty to exercise reasonable skill and knowledge on the part of the valuer; that there was a breach of that duty; and that the breach gave rise to the resulting injury, be it financial and/or to the reputation of the client or the party relying on the appraisal, causing actual loss or damage to that party.

The legal concerns for a valuer were outlined in the U.S. decision of *Estate of Querbach v. A&B Appraisal Service.*[27] The defendant, A&B Appraisal Service, was retained to appraise the tangible property of the deceased. The impetus for the appraisal was federal estate tax and New Jersey inheritance tax. The valuer was to estimate values for individual items, which a residual beneficiary might then choose as a portion of his or her inheritance from the estate.

The valuer made a room-by-room and item-by-item appraisal of the tangible personal property at the home of the deceased, excluding only some antique clocks. One of the items listed in the living room was "three small, unframed oil paintings, $50 each—$150." An acquaintance of the plaintiff, when being shown through the residence of the deceased, expressed an interest in purchasing one of the three small unframed oil paintings. After receiving the appraisal report from A&B, the plaintiff sold the painting for $50.

When the buyer took the painting to be framed, the proprietor asked whether the painting was insured and recommended that it be appraised. A valuer estimated the value of the painting to be $14,800. When the plaintiff was advised of the appraisal value, he brought an action against the original valuer, A&B Appraisal Service, for damages. The plaintiff alleged that A&B was negligent in failing to exercise due care and failing to follow procedures and standards of professional valuers, thereby causing the plaintiff damage equal to the real value of the work.

Among other defenses, the defendant alleged that this was not a work appraised by him; however, evidence proved that, in fact, it had been appraised by the defendant.

The plaintiff alleged that the painting was by J. F. Cropsey, "a renowned American artist of the Hudson River School."[28] A&B took the position that such authenticity was not proved. The court, however, found the painting to be authentic after hearing expert evidence, including the fact that the picture was signed "J. F. Cropsey, 1882." Moreover, on the back of the painting was a remnant of a paper label, typical of the artist, stating "St. Lawrence J. F. Cropsey, 57 West...." The artist was known to have had a studio at an address that corresponded with the partial address on the label fragment.

The court then stated it could find no precedent that set out professional standards and procedures for identifying and evaluating fine art. However, the defendant represented himself to be a member of a professional valuer association that had a code of ethics and professional conduct encompassing certain standards to be upheld by its members. As well, the defendant had been advised that the appraisal would be used for Internal Revenue Services purposes. The court stated that the criteria for appraisals of fine art for federal tax purposes are clear.[29]

The court stated that "the public has a right to expect that persons holding themselves out to be appraisers of 'fine art' are competent to recognize or utilize accepted professional procedures to identify and evaluate 'fine art'."[30]

In this instance, the defendant was held to have failed in his professional responsibility: he neither recognized J. F. Cropsey as a noted American painter nor determined whether the artist's name had any significance in the art world. He also failed to see that the painting was a fine example of the Hudson River School. He obviously made no close examination of either the painting or its reverse.

As a result, the court found that the defendant was negligent and "breached his duty to the plaintiff to make a professional appraisal of the painting." Judgment was entered against the defendant for the amount of $14,700 (being the net amount of the plaintiff's lost profit), together with prejudgment simple interest at 12 percent per annum.

The valuer's obligation to give competent service is as follows:[31]

> It is not proper for an appraiser to accept an engagement to make an appraisal of property of a type he is not qualified to appraise or in a field outside his society membership classification, unless (a) he fully acquaints the client with the limitations of his qualifications, or (b) he associates himself with another appraiser or appraisers who possess the required qualifications.

In the recent Canadian case of *Buchanan v. Copeland et al.,*[32] the Ontario Divisional Court dealt with a situation in which both the buyer and seller agreed that the purchase price of a property would be estimated by a valuer "with no room for appeal or independent review of any kind."[33] The valuer delivered his appraisal report, estimating the value of the property at $45,700. Instead of accepting the valuer's valuation, the buyer continued the litigation and later obtained admissions from the valuer that he had made mistakes in his evaluation and that he had changed his mind as to market value, which he now estimated at $20,000.

The court held that the admissions did not affect the price to be paid. The court determined that the submission on behalf of the respondent (buyer) that it was an implied term of the agreement that the parties would be bound only by an appraisal whose underlying quality was "unimpeachable" was unreasonable.

Any such term would have completely negated the purpose of the agreement, which was to settle the dispute between the parties and avoid further costly litigation. In situations of any complexity, of which this was one, it is doubtful whether any appraisal can be unimpeachable. The result might have been different if [the appraiser] on his own initiative had sought to correct errors shortly after delivering his valuation, but here, the mistakes were brought out in cross-examination in a review which the parties had agreed should not take place.[34]

The court then reversed the lower court judgment, which had substituted the revised lower valuation of $20,000 and replaced it with the valuer's original higher appraised value of $45,700.

The interesting question that remains is whether the buyer is precluded from suing the valuer on the erroneous appraisal because of the terms of the original contract between the buyer and the seller.

Restrictions on the Use of the Appraisal Report

To limit possible lawsuits by third parties who are not parties to the contract with the valuer, a valuer should specify in the appraisal document the extent to which it may be used and by whom it may be used. For example, it might be stated that the appraisal report may be used only for a specific purpose and only by the contracting client or by the client of the party retaining the valuer, in the case of a law firm retaining the valuer on behalf of a client. There are standard statements in USPAP that treat intended use and intended users.

The law both in Canada and the United States has been developing to permit awards against professionals whose works might be used by "foreseeable" parties such as bankers, potential buyers, lenders, and so forth. Thus, an unrestricted appraisal report is vulnerable to future actions by third parties who are or could be intended beneficiaries, even if they are unknown to the valuer.

The California Court of Appeals expressly extended the rules of professional liability to valuers in the case of *Soderberg v. McKinney*.[35] Although the case involved a certified real-estate valuer, neither the language nor the intent of the opinion indicates any limitations that would exclude personal-property valuers. The court held that third parties, even if unknown to the valuer at the time of appraisal, could successfully assert negligent misrepresentation claims if they belonged to a particular group or class for whom the information was of benefit.

Defamation or Disparagement

Any art expert, including a valuer, who publicly questions the authenticity or value of a work runs the risk of being sued for defamation or disparagement. Defamation is an invasion of an individual's personal reputation; disparagement is an invasion of his interest in property.

An example of defamation is the case cited in chapter 1 of the art dealer Joseph Duveen, who, in 1929, was sued for defamation[36] after claiming that a painting owned by Andrée Hahn was not an original Leonardo da Vinci. Hahn was offering the painting for sale. In fact, Duveen had never seen the work. At trial, the jury could not agree on a result, and before the retrial, the matter was settled out of court by Lord Duveen for $60,000—a great deal of money in 1929.

Suppose a valuer undervalues a work that the client believes to be a masterpiece. If the valuer is wrong, the painting's reputation has been diminished, and the owner can sue for disparagement of title or quality.

Seven elements are required for the client to be successful in such a case. It must be shown that

1. a legally protected interest was affected by the falsehood,
2. the falsehood was of injurious character,
3. the matter was untrue,
4. the matter was published,
5. there was reasonably foreseeable reliance on the falsehood by a third party,
6. the recipient understood it as disparaging of the plaintiff's property, and
7. special damages resulted from pecuniary loss.

The defenses of the valuer may include:

1. the valuer was acting in good faith,
2. the statement was true,
3. the accuracy of the valuation has been verified by statements by other credible valuers, or
4. the client consented to having the appraisal made. (By giving such consent, it can be argued, the owner is seeking the valuer's opinion on the work regardless of whether it is favorable.)

Valuers should consider the following safeguards:

1. The valuer should include in the appraisal report a statement disclaiming liability and giving no warranty of accuracy.

2. When taking on the responsibility for the appraisal, the valuer may wish to include in the appraisal agreement both a release, from the client, and an indemnification in respect to the appraisal opinion given, as long as it is given in good faith. The valuer will have to assess whether this will cause difficulty with the client and/or result in loss of business.

3. The valuer should have some form of malpractice-liability insurance. Various insurance companies offer professional liability coverage with reasonable limits for valuers. The wording of the policy should be reviewed carefully to make certain that the coverage is sufficiently broad to protect the valuer with regard to his or her responsibility to both the client and third parties.

THE VALUER AS EXPERT WITNESS

In case of litigation, valuers may be required to appear as expert witnesses. The valuer must provide credentials to support his or her claim of expertise. The expert witness must bring forward all relevant facts with honesty and integrity; therefore, thorough preparation for testimony is essential. Ultimately, the expert for one side or the other will be the more credible witness, and his or her testimony will be accepted by the court. Any weakness in one's appraisal should be admitted, and the assumptions giving rise to the appraisal should be clearly enunciated.

The valuer is *not* an advocate; that is the role of the lawyer. Nor is the valuer the judge. Ultimately, based on all the evidence presented by the parties, the judge rules on the credibility of the various opinions and the one or more opinions that the judge is prepared to accept as being more credible.

What Is an Expert Witness?

An *expert witness* is one who is qualified to give expert evidence. This expert evidence may consist of opinion evidence and has been defined by the Supreme Court of Canada as "any inference from observed fact."[37]

It has been stated that "opinion evidence given by experts differs from that given by lay witnesses in this respect: the expert opinion is not something that the court could reach without the additional knowledge, training, or experience which the expert possesses."[38]

"In the case of an expert opinion, the court must say: the opinion in question is not one which I could reach. It requires knowledge, training, and experience which I do not have. So I will hear that opinion."[39]

Qualifying the Expert

The Supreme Court of Canada has also ruled that counsel presenting an expert witness must qualify the expert in all the areas in which the expert is to give opinion evidence. "If this is done, no question as to the admissibility of the opinion will arise." If the witness is so qualified—"in an area" and not just as a "valuer" or whatsoever—then there will be less likelihood of an objection being taken to the "expertness" of the witness.[40] Robert White, Q.C., in *The Art of Using Expert Evidence*,[41] has provided a checklist on the approach for presenting a witness to give expert evidence at a trial.

1. Advise the court that a witness is to be presented to give opinion evidence or observations on a particular subject or in a specific area.
2. Examine the witness as to his or her qualifications and the methods by which he or she has obtained them.
3. Direct the witness's attention to the specific areas in question and establish such evidence from his or her examination that will enable a court to conclude two things:
   a. that the subject of the expert evidence is outside the skill or knowledge of the trier of fact,
   b. that the witness has the expertise necessary to give evidence of the observation or to give the opinion.
4. Invite the court to accept the witness's expert evidence in the areas specified.

Ultimately, it is up to the court to determine whether or not a witness is an expert qualified to render an expert opinion. It is important that the valuer provide the lawyer with sufficient biographical material to enable the lawyer to present the court with sufficient professional qualifications to so qualify the expert. This includes information on the educational background of the valuer; the experience of the valuer in the field; various lectures given, articles and books written, teaching experience, membership in various professional organizations associated with his field of expertise, and experience in any related field such as museums, art galleries, auction houses, government arts agencies, private dealing, and sales; and the past use of professional opinion and expert testimony given by the valuer for other credible individuals and organizations in prior court cases, arbitration, or other hearings.

THE VALUER AS CONSULTANT, DEALER, OR BROKER

Occasionally, valuers are retained to recommend a particular course of conduct for a client rather than to provide a valuation. The client—who could be anything from an estate to a corporate collector to a trustee in bankruptcy—may wish direction on how or where or when to buy or sell an object or collection. And the assignment may ultimately lead to a request for a valuation once the course of conduct is determined or the object or collection found. Can the valuer also receive a fee as the dealer or agent on the sale or purchase of the personal property? Is there an inherent conflict of interest in acting as a dealer to buy an object and then acting as a valuer of that object for the client?

These are some of the current issues and concerns being considered and debated within the appraisal profession in an attempt to reach a consensus as to the required competence and ethical standards for valuers when acting as consultants, dealers, or brokers.

Issues arise as to the ethical and professional responsibilities of the valuer in such a retainer. What, if any, standards and ethics are applicable to consulting engagements? What form of payment is acceptable; for example, can the valuer as consultant be paid on a percentage or contingent fee basis? Does the valuer as consultant become the advocate for the client? If so, does this then cause the valuer/consultant to lose objectivity in providing a later valuation of the object or collection for the client? Should the valuer refuse to provide such valuation and request that it be provided by an independent valuer? If not, does the valuer/consultant have different standards to follow in the role as valuer than those applicable to acting as consultant? How credible will the testimony of a valuer/consultant be in a court or arbitration hearing involving the object or collection purchased or sold?[42]

There are some guidelines that can be spelled out. Based on USPAP, it is clear that a consultant cannot also provide an "independent" appraisal. In a property-tax case, a valuer/consultant cannot provide an appraisal that he or she prepared and expect it to be taken as an independent appraisal. And a valuer cannot accept a contingent fee for an appraisal even if it is part of a consulting assignment.

MEXICAN LAW

The Mexican Commercial Code[43] makes specific reference to appraisals in the context of legal proceedings. Chapter 20, "The Weight of Evidence," deals with the weight to be accorded appraisals in legal actions. Appraisals are conclusive proof

(Article 1300). Where there are other expert opinions, including written ones, the validity of such opinions is determined by the judge (Article 1301). In the case of foreclosure, assets (including art) are sold after an appraisal by two certified *corredores publicos* (public brokers) or two similar experts. The corredores publicos are expert witnesses, certified by the Secretariat of Commerce and Industrial Development (SECOFI), with licenses reviewed every three years.

The Federal Law of Public Brokering (Article 6) establishes the functions of a public broker. They are facilitators; commercial mediators; valuers of goods, services, rights, and obligations; and expediters. They give traders legal counsel on trade-related activities. They can, on request of the parties, act as arbiters of controversies derived from trade acts, contracts, or agreements. They also can act as public warrantors to certify the validity of contracts and commercial agreements (excluding real estate). Each party is entitled to an expert. In case of disagreement, the judge will designate a third such expert. In order for an expert to testify, he or she must have a professional degree in the particular field in which the expert will give an opinion, if such a degree is required for the exercise of the particular profession (Article 1252).

In instances of commercial arbitration, the arbitration tribunal may, unless otherwise agreed by the parties, appoint one or more experts to inform it on specific matters. The tribunal also may request that the parties involved provide the expert with all relevant information (Article 1442). The expert might also be asked to participate in the hearing to allow the parties to question the expert's evidence.

Independent valuers can be licensed as specialists in particular areas based on education, experience, and an examination administered by the licensing commission, La Comisión Nacional Bancaria y de Valores (CNByV). Licenses are renewable every two years.

Tax

In Mexico, there is no income tax, but there is capital gains tax on the sale of personal property by individuals. Appraisals are therefore necessary. There is also capital gains tax payable on gains by a corporation. The tax is adjusted for inflation by a special formula.

There is no tax on donations to charitable institutions or on estates or inheritance. Therefore, no appraisals are necessary. (Taxation is discussed in chapter 8.)

Pawnshops in Mexico

Special not-for-profit pawnshops have existed in Mexico for more than three hundred years. For-profit or private pawnshops are a more recent type of business venture. They are widely used for transactions involving all sorts of art and other objects and are subject to extensive regulations. The pawnshops have valuers who estimate prices of art and other objects for the purposes of their business, which is similar to Canadian and American pawnshops. However, the profits of these not-for-profit pawnshops are used for charitable-type purposes, such as relief of poverty, assistance for the aged, and help for hospitals. The main not-for-profit pawnshop in Mexico City is the Nacional Monte de Piedad (National Mount of Piety), which receives movable goods to guarantee repayment of a monetary loan that the pawnshop makes to the client.

In a pawnshop, the goods are delivered to the guaranty creditor, who then acquires the following rights:

1. the right to redeem the debt by means of the sale of the pawned goods;
2. the right to demand that restitution be made to it of the pawned goods if they come to be held by anyone else, including the debtor;
3. the right to be indemnified for any expenses that it may incur to preserve the goods; and
4. the right to demand from the debtor some other goods, or the repayment of the debt, if the pawned goods are lost or damaged due to causes not imputable to the creditor according to Article 2873 of the Codigo Civil (Civil Code).[44]

Conversely, the creditor is also responsible for certain obligations, which it acquires with the guarantee:

1. the duty to keep the pawned goods as if they were its own, answering for any damages and deterioration to which they are subject while under its care, if these are due to its fault or negligence, and
2. the duty of restoring the goods to the debtor once the loan has been repaid wholly, including interest if such had been stipulated and any expenses incurred on behalf of the debtor in preserving the goods (according to Article 2876 of the Codigo Civil).

Upon pawning the goods, the debtor receives a payment slip to document the transaction. It includes general data about the debtor and the pawned goods, the amount lent by the creditor, the period of time granted for the repayment of the debt, the interest rate (if any), and so forth. Without this payment slip, it is impossible to recover the pawned goods. At the end of a certain period of time, the creditor is empowered to sell the pawned goods, without judicial intervention, and to repay the debt with the proceeds of the sale.

In Mexico, the valuer is in the fullest sense a professional member of the cultural community, faced with numerous questions and issues of title, use enjoyment, and value.

NOTES

1. American Society of Appraisers, *Glossary of Appraisal Terms* (Unpublished first draft: 1998), 10.

2. Appraisal Standards Board of The Appraisal Foundation, *Uniform Standards of Professional Appraisal Practice* (Washington, D.C.: The Appraisal Foundation, 1999), foreword.

3. The Financial Institutions Reform, Recovery and Enforcement Act (FIRREA)—Public Law: 101-73.

4. Appraisal Standards Board of The Appraisal Foundation, *Uniform Standards of Professional Appraisal Practice* (Washington, D.C.: The Appraisal Foundation, 1996).

5. A valuable checklist for an appraiser-client contract is outlined in Jessica L. Darraby, *Art, Artifact and Architecture Law* (New York: Clark Boardman Callaghan, 1995).

6. *Foxley v. Sotheby's Inc.*, 893 F. Supp. 1224 (S.D.N.Y. 1995). In *Foxley v. Sotheby's Inc.*, Sotheby's provided two appraisals to Foxley on a painting purportedly by Mary Cassatt, the authenticity of which later became an issue. The Sotheby's appraisal agreements set forth this disclaimer: "our appraisal … is not to be deemed a representation or warranty with respect to the authenticity of authorship … genuineness … or attribution." (Sotheby's Inc. appraisal agreements at page 1.) The appraisal agreement also included an exculpatory clause, which released Sotheby's from liability stemming from appraisals. It stated: "in consideration of our furnishing the appraisal, you hereby release Sotheby's … from any liability or damages whatsoever rising out of or related to the appraisal … unless … due to Sotheby's gross negligence or bad faith." The court indicated that generally exculpatory clauses that are explicit in a contract foreclose damage claims alleging reliance on the subject matter disclaimed. However, the court ruled that sufficient facts existed to support Foxley's claim that Sotheby's was negligent in performing the two appraisals and these claims would be permitted to proceed to trial.

On reargument brought by Sotheby's, it was argued that the court had erred in finding that "Sotheby's had a duty to authenticate the painting notwithstanding the explicit provisions in the appraisal agreements stating that Sotheby's was not performing an authentication and as a result of the disclaimer it is immune from suit."

The court, however, stated that:

> The Court does not, in its earlier opinion or in this one, require appraisals to include authentication of the article appraised. However, in the absence of an explicit disclaimer that the customer agreed that the appraisal fully assumes authenticity and other indicia of genuineness, liability may attach from an appraisal performed with gross negligence or bad faith. The assumption of authenticity for appraisal purposes can be rebutted by supportable allegations of gross negligence or bad faith including fraudulent appraisal. This is particularly true where the valuer was aware of significant doubt as to the authenticity of the work in question.

Defendant's alleged knowledge of the painting's inauthenticity at the time of the appraisals, if proven at trial, necessarily gives rise to liability. Rendering an appraisal of the painting at $650,000 in the face of knowledge of inauthenticity would clearly constitute—not merely gross negligence but also mala fides. [p. 1237]

Finally, Sotheby's arguments, taken at face value, would insulate all appraisals from any claims of gross negligence or fraud based on inauthenticity. Sotheby's argues that appraisals accompanied by disclaimers can never be negligently performed if the claim is based on the fact that the artwork in question is inauthentic. Defendant's concern that this holding will burden valuers with a duty to authenticate is unfounded. Appraisals of inauthentic artwork do not give rise to liability where they explicitly disclaim authentication and where a plaintiff cannot demonstrate that the valuer had, or should have had, knowledge of inauthenticity. [p. 1237]

7. ASA College of Fellows, *Opinions,* vol. 1, 1975–1996 (Herndon, Va.: American Society of Appraisers, 1997), 35.

8. Appraisal Standards Board, *Uniform Standards* (1996), 2–5.

9. Appraisal Standards Board, *Uniform Standards* (1999), preamble, 1.

10. Ibid., 5.

11. Ibid., 6.

12. Elizabeth Shultis, "Due Diligence in the Appraisal of Personal Property," American Society of Appraisers International Appraisal Conference Proceedings, Toronto, June 16–19, 1996, Tab 1, p. 2.

13. See *Estate of Querbach v. A&B Appraisal Service,* below, for a discussion of negligence.

14. Appraisal Standards Board, *Uniform Standards* (1999), footnote, 10.

15. Ibid., 43.

16. Ibid.

17. In the case of *Estate of Querbach v. A&B Appraisal Service,* the valuer failed to recognize a J. F. Cropsey painting as being by the painter nor did the valuer estimate whether the artist's name had any significance in the art world. He also failed to note that the painting was a fine example of the Hudson River School of Art. As a result, the court found the defendant negligent in that he "breached his duty to the plaintiff to make a professional appraisal of the painting." [American Society of Appraisers, "Value and Market Level Definitions," *The Appraisal of Personal Property: Principles, Theories, and Practice Methods for the Professional Appraiser,* eds. Patricia C. Soucy and Janella N. Smyth (Herndon, Va.: American Society of Appraisers, 1994). See also Judith Bresler, "Expert Art Opinions and Liabilities," *IFAR Journal* II, no. 3 (Summer 1999), 12.

18. *Anselmo v. Commissioner,* 80 T.C. 872, affirmed 757 f.2d 1208 (11th Cir. 1985). Reproduced in American Society of Appraisers, *Appraisal of Personal Property,* 188.

19. *Hunter v. Commissioner,* 51 TCM (CCH) 1533 (1986-308). Reproduced in American Society of Appraisers, *Appraisal of Personal Property,* 188–89.

20. *Lio v. Commissioner,* 85 T.C. 56 (1985). Reproduced in American Society of Appraisers, *Appraisal of Personal Property,* 89.

21. *Purdue v. Commissioner,* 62 T.C.M. (CCH) 845 (1991). However, the courts have decided that the Murphy case itself is "not appropriate for publication and may not be cited to or by the courts of this circuit" (United States Court of Appeals for the 9th Circuit except as provided by the 9th Circuit Rule 36-3). Cited with approval in *Murphy v. Commissioner,* 1993 U.S. App. LEXIS 26485, 73 A.F.T.R. 2d (RIA) 418.

22. *Struna v. Wolf,* 126 MISC. 2d 1031, 481 N.Y.S. 2d 392 (Sup. Ct. 1985), unpaginated.

23. Ibid.

24. 24 N.Y. Jur., Fraud and Deceit, sec. 153; *International Products Co. v. Erie Railroad Co.,* 244 N.Y. 331 (1927), cert. denied 275 U.S. 527 (1927).

25. *Struna v. Wolf.*

26. *White v. Guarante,* 43 N.Y. 2d. at 363; *Courteen Seed Co. v. Hong Kong & Shanghai Banking Corp.,* 245 N.Y. 377 (1927).

27. *Estate of Querbach v. A&B Appraisal Service,* No. L089362-85 (N.J. Sup. Ct. Bergen County 1987). Also reproduced in full in Franklin Feldman, Steven E. Weil, and Susan Duke Biederman, *Art Law: Rights and Liabilities of Creators and Collectors,* 1993 Supplement (Boston: Little, Brown and Company, 1993), 468.

28. Franklin Feldman et al., *Art Law 1993 Supplement* (Boston: Little, Brown and Company, 1993), 470.

29. Rev. Proc. 66-49 1966-2CB1257.

30. Feldman, *Art Law,* 471.

31. American Society of Appraisers, *Principles of Appraisal Practice and Code of Ethics* (Herndon, Va.: ASA, 1994), 5.

32. *Buchanan v. Copeland et al.* [1997] 155 D.L.R. (4th) 765 (Ont. Ct. Gen. Div.).

33. Ibid., 765.

34. Ibid., 767.

35. *Soderberg v. McKinney,* 52 Cal. Rptr. 2d 635 (Cal. Ct. A.).

36. *Hahn v. Duveen,* 133 Misc. 871, 234 N.Y.S. 185 (Sup. Ct. 1929).

37. *Regina v. Abbey* [1982] 2 S.C.R. 24.

38. Robert B. White, *The Art of Using Expert Evidence* (Toronto: Canada Law Book Inc., 1997), 16. See also *William Daubert v. Merrell Dow Pharmaceuticals Inc.,* 509 U.S. 579, 113 S. Ct. 2786, 1993 U.S. Lexis 4408, containing a discussion of expert evidence.

39. White, *The Art of Using Expert Evidence,* 16.

40. Ibid., 39–40.

41. For a discussion of the expert appraiser, the American judicial system, and relevant state and federal rules of evidence, see Santo J. Sottilare, "The Appraisal Expert and the Judicial System," in *The Appraisal of Personal Property* (Herndon, Va.: American Society of Appraisers, 1994), 34–48.

42. For a discussion of the risk of the testimony of the appraiser being held to be invalid because of the contingent fee of the appraiser, see *City and County of Denver Colorado and Board of Equalization of the City and County of Denver v. Board of Assessment Appeals of the State of Colorado and Constellation Properties et al.,* 96 SC 785 (S. C. of Colorado, November 10, 1997). For a discussion of these issues see Frederick L. Iusi, "Consulting Issues—Personal Property Discipline," *1998 American Society of Appraisers International Appraisal Conference Handbook,* Opening Educational Seminar (Herndon, Va.: American Society of Appraisers, 1998).

43. Abraham Eckstein and Enrique Zepada Trujillo, *The Mexican Commercial Code* (St. Paul, Minn.: West Publishing Co., 1996).

44. Ibid.

· 5 ·

Auction and Other Marketplaces

There is much romance surrounding auctions and auction participation. We have all heard about wonderful bargains obtained at auctions, knowledgeable purchasers buying unknown works that turn out to be masterpieces. Such is the mythology. Auctions are also thought of as the place to obtain bargains by purchasing in competition with the professionals: one can obtain an object at the price a dealer would pay and save the dealer commission of one-third to one-half the price of the work on the retail market.

Auctions, it is said, exist because of the "three Ds"—death, disaster, and divorce—and the associated need to liquidate collections. Under these rather harsh circumstances, few masterpieces slip by unnoticed at auction. Rarely does one know whether the property has been placed into the auction under compulsion or by the free will of the consignor, which may result in a lower or higher reserve on the work and affect its ultimate sale price. One may be bidding against nonprofessionals, who do not necessarily know value; even when bidding against a dealer, it is difficult to know whether the dealer is bidding on his or her own behalf or as an agent for a collector who will pay a bidding fee. If a dealer is bidding on behalf of a collector, one is competing not for a wholesale price but against the collector for a retail price or even more. Even if the dealer is bidding for his or her own gallery, one does not know why. For example, the dealer may have presold the property to a client and may be prepared to pay handsomely, knowing that he or she is assured of a profit. Perhaps the work is from a period that is required for the gallery's stock and for which the dealer is prepared to pay a premium. Works are often purchased for a reason quite apart from quality or price.

It is, therefore, not unusual to see works sold at auction substantially below or above retail prices. Dealers often lament that a successful bidder could have bought a similar work at their galleries for less than was paid at auction, although dealer prices are generally above auction results.

When a work is sold at auction at a bargain price, it may be for a good reason. For example, the work may have been repaired or restored and not be the pristine work a purchaser assumed he or she was getting, or the dealer's inventory might be full.

In the past, the atmosphere of an auction was that of a gaming room. Trying to identify the "players" and to recognize their bidding technique was a favorite pastime. Knowing who was bidding on a particular work could influence other bidders: why was this knowledgeable dealer bidding on this minor work? What did the bidder know that the auction house did not? Was it the great long shot to be purchased for a pittance only to be revealed as a long-lost masterpiece worth thousands of times its purchase price? However, the bidders one can see at an auction may be only part of the action; with the advent of telephone and electronic bidding, it is not necessary for a bidder to be in the auction room.

Consequently, auction results by themselves are often an inadequate basis for estimating a market value of any particular work of art or object. Often they are no more than one indicator of a price achieved at a particular time and place of a particular object of personal property. The properties at auction are often subject to disclaimers outlined in the catalogs, which in themselves contradict the assumption of an open market. Rarely does the catalog provide information as to the condition of the object, whether it has ever been damaged, and if so, whether it has been restored. The auction house does not usually offer an opportunity for extended payments (as is usually done at commercial galleries). And—most important in estimating fair market value—auction results do not reveal whether the buyer is the ultimate consumer or an agent or dealer buying "at wholesale" with an intent to resell at a higher price.

Today professional publications, electronic publications, Web sites, and Internet auction services document sales and results and track the results of various "schools" and individual artists at auction. Auctions are now rather like a stock-market trading floor: quotations are given and results predicted on the basis of analyses of past auction sales. Specialized services can be subscribed to and reports received on a regular or as needed basis. Internet services not only document the objects that have been sold and the prices received worldwide but also provide a prospective purchaser with details of any works by a particular artist coming to auction, including reproductions of the work as well as the auction history. Books and Internet services list the artists who have been the hottest sellers at auction; what schools to avoid because they are overpriced; what artists and types of art and decorative art might be underpriced and should be purchased now for future gain.[1] In short, auction sales are reported and analyzed like the commodities exchange they have become.

Auction houses deal in billions of dollars of art, antiques, decorative art, and gems. However, the auction market is not regulated to the same extent that the stock and commodities markets are, and the auction market is not considered a perfect market.

Recently, auction houses entering into joint purchasing agreements with private dealers to purchase art collections have blurred the auction market. After Sotheby's and the Acquavella Gallery in New York jointly purchased the inventory of the Pierre Matisse Gallery after the death of the dealer, Pierre Matisse, a number of the works purchased were sold privately by the Acquavella Gallery. Others were auctioned by Sotheby's. This led to concerns of conflict of interest and, ultimately, to further regulation of auctions, at least in New York, by requiring disclosure of the interest of an auction house in any work being sold by it.

Further confusion has been caused recently by auction houses purchasing private dealers. For instance, Sotheby's has purchased both the famous André Emmerich Gallery in New York (thereafter closed by Sotheby's) and a fifty percent interest in the Contemporary Art Gallery of Jeffrey Dietch (Dietch Projects) in New York. Christie's also has purchased private dealers, including Spinks in London.

TYPES OF AUCTIONS

The form of the auction has varied from time to time, and different styles of auction have developed in different countries.

The *Dutch auction* is a now uncommon form that involves a descending price system. The auctioneer determines what he or she believes is a high starting figure and asks for bids on the price established. If no bid is received, the auctioneer will lower the bid at intervals until a bid is received. Among the subspecies of the Dutch auction is one in which the highest bidder's offer is accepted only if the bidder remains the highest bidder in the descending phase of the auction.

The *ascending-bid auction system* is used by major auction houses worldwide for the sale of art objects. Normally, works are offered for sale with an unpublished reserve price and a published high and low estimate, indicating that the work is expected to sell in the range between "X" and "Y." Usually the reserve is below or at the lower estimate. For example, on a work estimated to be worth from $100,000 to $125,000, the reserve would usually be less than $100,000.

Depending on the expected sales price of a work, increments in bidding are set by the auction house, at anywhere from $10 to $100,000 or more.

Another variety of ascending-bid auction has both an ascent and a time limit. For instance, in *candle auctions,* which are held primarily in Britain, the last bidder before the candle goes out is the successful bidder. Other time auctions use an hourglass or clock. Such auctions are often used in rural England for the sale of lands or of the right to farm or tenant lands.[2]

ABOUT AUCTIONS

Catalog

There are terms and conditions that are peculiar to auction sales; these are set out in the catalog. The description of each work must be carefully read and cross-referenced to the glossary of terms in the catalog. For instance, there are vast differences among works described as follows:

(1) Winslow Homer;
(2) W. Homer, or attributed to Winslow Homer;
(3) school of W. Homer;
(4) manner of Winslow Homer, or circle of Winslow Homer;
(5) in the style of Winslow Homer;
(6) studio of W. Homer;
(7) Homer; and
(8) after Winslow Homer.

Of all these descriptions, only the first would describe a work of art actually by, and warranted to be by, Winslow Homer. Moreover, even "Winslow Homer" may carry a restricted warranty rather than a warranty or guarantee as to the actual artist. For instance, following the name of the artist, one catalog indicated that

> the work is ascribed to the named artist, either by an outside expert or by our own staff, and such ascription is accepted as reliable by the gallery. This is our highest category of authenticity in the present catalog, and is assigned only upon exercise of our best judgment; no unqualified statement as to authorship is made or intended.[3]

Instead of buying a painting, one may be buying a lawsuit.

There is also a difference between the phrases "signed" and "bears signature." "Signed" usually means that in the "qualified opinion" of the auction house, the signature of the artist is genuine; in the case of "bears signature," the auction house is less sure.

Similarly, "dated" means that it is the "qualified opinion" of the auction house that the work was executed at the time of the date; "bears date" indicates that it may have been dated but not necessarily executed at that time.

Each catalog at each auction sets out the conditions of that particular auction. These conditions of sale generally also contain information regarding the warranties (which are usually restricted or limited in nature and are less than what would normally be provided under general sale of goods laws), the representations and obligations of the auction house, and the purchaser's right to return the personal property in the event that it is not as represented in the catalog. (Often auction houses try to restrict this right to a five-year term from the time of purchase, and only to the original purchaser of record at the auction.) Courts have held that the warranties that would ordinarily be present in a sale of goods may be altered between the parties by contract. Thus, the auction contract with the consignor of personal property will in most cases contain restrictive language as to the responsibility and continued liability of the auction house, including restricting its role as fiduciary or trustee for and on behalf of the consignor. Often these restrictions in the contract also relate to the right of the auction house to cancel the sale in the event that the authenticity of the work is questioned by a purchaser on reasonable grounds or that the consignor's title to the personal property may be suspect or put into question after the property has been received or sold by the auction house. (See the discussion of consignment contracts later in this chapter.) The conditions also set out the obligations of a purchaser in purchasing personal property at the auction, as well as the rights of the auction house in the event of nonpayment by the purchaser.

Reserve Bids

The reserve bid is normally placed on a work by a consignor in consultation with the auction house, and it establishes a minimum amount for which the work may be sold. The existence of a reserve bid is generally indicated in the catalog by an asterisk next to the description of the work. Alternatively, there may be a general statement in the catalog indicating that each sale is "subject to any reserve bid placed...by the vendor."

When a bid is received from the floor that is below the reserve, the auctioneer will normally bid on behalf of the reserve bidder up to the next multiple, and then await a further bid from the floor. This is generally done until just before the reserve price is reached; the action then remains with the floor, subject to bids by the auctioneer on behalf of telephone bidders and persons who have placed advance or absentee bids. Traditionally, if the reserve price was not reached, that fact was not announced at the auction; however, government pressure, especially regulations created by the Department of Consumer Affairs of New York City, now requires that such notice be given to the floor.[4]

An auction catalog will also often contain a provision stating that any lot may be withdrawn from sale without prior notice. As the catalog is often prepared and distributed well in advance of the sale, a lot may have been privately sold or withdrawn by the time of the auction or there may have been a title or condition problem or some other issue that resulted in the work being removed from the auction.

Presale Estimates

As a convenience to customers, auction house catalogs usually contain presale estimates of the price range anticipated for each work. Prospective purchasers can see the auctioneer's anticipated spread. This will sometimes give a clue as to the reserve bid, as the reserve is generally less than the presale estimate.

Catalog Services

The catalogs of each auction house may be purchased on a yearly basis; they will be automatically sent in advance of sales. The ultimate sale results are available immediately after the sale, followed by a mailing to the catalog subscriber disclosing the successful bid on each work sold and omitting works not sold (which are called works "brought in" or "B.I.'d."). These price lists also indicate which works were unsold because they did not reach the reserve price; often this is done by omitting the lot number of the unsold work from the price list. Postsale results also note salesroom announcements that relate to offered properties.

Electronic Auctions

Today's auction salesroom has expanded to the Internet, and sales now take place on the World Wide Web. Old concerns must now be dealt with in a new way worldwide including verification of ownership, existence, and condition of the object being offered for sale, as well as security of the purchaser and the purchaser's credit card or credit facilities. These matters are now being addressed in e-commerce generally and will soon facilitate better use of the Internet for auctions on a worldwide basis.

Auction House Commissions

Until recently, the vendor paid the auctioneer's commission; as a result, the auctioneer's obligation was to the vendor. First in Britain, and more recently in the

United States, then Canada (but not Mexico), the major auction houses have instituted a commission for both vendor and purchaser. Auction houses may use different approaches to calculate their fees. The commission now paid by a purchaser is generally fifteen percent of the sales price, less as the amount paid for the property rises. The vendor commission is usually ten percent, and it too may vary downward depending on the price of the work. For example, Sotheby's charges fifteen percent of a successful bid price up to $50,000 and ten percent on any sale above $50,000.

Art dealers have questioned the legality of auction houses accepting payment from both buyer and vendor as, by law, the auction house is supposed to be the agent for the seller. The concern is that the practice might give rise to divided loyalties and to conflict with trust or agency laws. However, their efforts to attack this practice have not been successful.

Collectors bidding at such auctions must bear in mind that not only will a buyer's premium be added to the price of the work purchased but any applicable sales taxes will be calculated on the price of the work plus the commission. (In Canada, this includes both provincial sales taxes, where applicable, and the federal goods and services tax. In the United States and Mexico, state sales taxes will be added where applicable; for example, Mexico City sales tax is eight percent.)

Resale Rights of the Artist

Vendors and auction houses must consider possible resale rights of creators. Sometimes known as the *droit de suite*,[5] these rights were an attempt by the French government in 1920 to permit an artist to receive a portion of the resale price of his or her work. Originally, it was a percentage of the sale price each time the work was sold at a public auction. The rights continued for the same term as the copyright, namely the life of the artist plus fifty years. This has now been raised to seventy years in the European Community.

Resale rights exist in different forms in a number of European countries. They do not exist in Mexico or Canada and, in the United States, they exist only in the state of California. There has been much discussion as to the expansion of the *droit de suite* to other states and even federally in the United States. Although similar discussion has taken place in Canada, no such right was introduced in the recent amendments to the Canadian Copyright Act.[6]

The California Resale Royalties Act

The California Resale Royalties Act provides that the right to resale is an inalienable right of the artist for his or her lifetime plus twenty years. After death it inures to the heirs, legatees, and personal representatives of the artist. It applies to paintings, sculpture, drawings, and works of art in glass.

The royalty has been set at five percent of the gross amount of the sale price, which must be withheld and paid to the artist or the estate of the artist. No royalty is payable if the gross sale price is less than $1,000 or less than that paid by the seller.[7]

The law applies to artists who are American citizens or residents of California for more than two years. For the statute to be applicable, the seller must either be a resident of the State of California at the time of the sale or the sale itself must take place in California. Thus, auction houses (and galleries) in California are required to make the appropriate inquiries and payments.

Under the California statute, *droit de suite* does not apply to the first sale of a work when legal title is sold by the artist to the first purchaser. The act is designed to apply only to resales.

The Preview

Wise bidders generally will not bid on an item unless they have attended the preview and carefully examined the work. Often a work may differ from the catalog reproduction: the color may be different, scratches may not have been revealed by the photograph, or the work may have been repaired or restored.

Especially worrisome at auctions is the purchase of framed fine art prints and works on paper—watercolors, gouaches, and drawings. How carefully have the works been framed? Is the mat nonacidic, or is it one of the colorful pulp-paper mats that over the years bleed both color and acid, permanently staining or damaging the work? Prints also may be permanently damaged by being *dry mounted*— cemented to a cardboard backing and then framed. Like a postage stamp, the back of a print is as important to a collector as is the front. The margins on a work should be considered: have they been cut down, perhaps to fit a particular frame or wall area? This may be hidden by a mat. At a recent auction of Inuit prints, for example, one of the bidders insisted on having the frames removed. When the auctioneer complied, it was found that the margins on many of the works had been cut to fit standard-size frames and that some of the prints had been dry mounted.

Another problem that arises with framed prints and works on paper is the closeness of the work to the glass covering it. If the work is pressed against the glass, parts of the image may become affixed to the inside of the glass rather than to the paper.

In a recent case, a Matisse crayon drawing had been improperly framed. When the frame was removed, much of the crayon remained on the glass rather than on the paper. Fortunately, a qualified restorer was able to transfer the crayon back to the work without permanent damage. Similarly, in Toronto, an important Degas pastel was found to have been framed under Plexiglas rather than glass. (Generally, Plexiglas is to be avoided with a pastel, as an electric charge can build up within the Plexiglas if it is cleaned or dusted from time to time. This charge can pull the pastels off the paper.) In this instance, an informed framer spotted the problem before damage occurred, and it was corrected; however, often damage does occur and cannot be corrected.

Therefore, a wise buyer will ask the auction house to have the frame and cover removed before bidding so that the work can be inspected. A refusal to do so by the auction house could be a warning against bidding on that particular work.

THE LAW OF SALE AT AUCTION

Canadian Law

To a great extent, Canadian auction sales are governed by British common law. (Many jurisdictions in the United States are governed by similar law.) Recently, the Province of Alberta enacted the Fair Trading Act, which went into effect September 1, 1999.[8]

This act replaces The Public Auction Act of 1981. The new act deals in part with public auctions; the licensing of auctioneers; the conduct of public auctions, including bidding rules; the proof of ownership of goods being offered for sale; the payment of funds to consignors within twenty-one days; and provisions that all proceeds of sale from auctions must be placed in a trust fund. Civil and criminal penalties are provided for breach of the act.[9]

In addition, most common-law provinces have a sale of goods act, which regulates sales by auction. For instance, the Ontario Sale of Goods Act[10] indicates the following:

1. Where the goods are put up for sale in lots, each lot is considered a separate sale.
2. The sale is complete when the auctioneer announces it is complete by the fall of the hammer or in any other customary manner. Until such announcement, any bidder may retract his or her bid. (This is rarely known by bidders, who believe, erroneously, that once they have bid they are automatically bound by their bid.)
3. Where a sale is not declared to be subject to a reserve bid, it is not lawful for the seller to bid himself or herself, for the seller to employ a person to bid for him or her, or for the auctioneer knowingly to take any bid from the seller or any person acting for the seller. Any sale contravening this rule may be treated as

fraudulent by the buyer and would entitle the buyer to the return of his or her purchase price.

4. A sale may be declared to be subject to a "reserved or upset price" by or on behalf of the seller. This implies that reserve-bid information would have to be noted in the catalog or announced by the auctioneer prior to the work being auctioned.

5. Only when a right to bid is expressly reserved can the seller, or anyone on the seller's behalf, bid.

The rules of the common law apply, as long as they are not inconsistent with the act. Therefore, rules relating to the law of principal and agent (that is, the auction-eer acts as agent for the owner and has the right to sell), fraud, misrepresentation, duress or coercion, mistake, or other invalidating cause apply to contracts for the sale of goods.

Under the Ontario Sale of Goods Act and similar acts in other provinces, there are various implied conditions and warranties:

1. that the seller has the right to sell the goods;
2. that the buyer will have and enjoy quiet possession (that is, ownership will not be attacked);
3. that the goods will be free of any mortgage or encumbrance in favor of a third party that is not known to the buyer before or at the time the contract of purchase is made; and
4. when the sale of goods is by description (for example, as described in the auction house catalog), the goods will correspond with that description.

The act generally gives the purchaser the right, should the goods be different from those advertised, to rescind the sale and reject the goods or, if the goods have been accepted and title has passed to the buyer, to sue for damages but not rescind the transaction. Where the work differs from its description, if sufficient time has passed from the date of sale (six years in Ontario), any action is at an end. This applies not only in regard to misattributions and wrongful descriptions of works sold at auction but also, in some instances, to a work purchased in good faith from a vendor who does not have title to the work.

U.S. Law

The Uniform Commercial Code (UCC),[11] especially Sections 2-312 and 2-328, applies to and supplements any contractual laws of auctions. Laws applicable to auctions also have been passed by the city of New York and the state of Illinois. Illinois' revised statutes,[12] like the Ontario law, deal with warranties applicable to the sale, title, merchantability, and fitness.

Warranties

A warranty is generally defined in law as "a promise that a proposition of fact is true."[13] It is also

> a statement or representation made by the seller of goods, contemporaneously with and as a part of the contract of sale, though collateral to the express object of it, having reference to the character, quality, or title of the goods, by which he promises or undertakes that certain facts are or shall be as he then represents them.[14]

It is also defined as "a promise or agreement by a seller that an article sold has certain qualities or that the seller has good title thereto"[15] and as "a statement of fact representing the quality or character of goods sold, made by the seller to induce the sale and relied on by the buyer."[16]

There are specific warranties expressed at the time of the sale; implied warranties, which are implied by the nature or type of sale or implied by law; collateral warranties; continuing warranties; promissory warranties; and various other warranties created in law, some or all of which may be applicable to the sale of personal property.[17]

Any relevant warranties expressly made by the auctioneer, if given negligently or falsely and proved to be untrue, would give rise to a claim for rescission and the return of the funds to the purchaser. Where there is any doubt as to the proper party to be sued, the auctioneer, the auction house, and the vendor (if he or she is known) should all be joined as party defendants.

Warranty of Title

In the 1984 case of *Abrams v. Sotheby Park Bernet, Inc.,*[18] Sotheby's sold a number of major Hebrew books and manuscripts known to have been in the possession of a Hebrew seminary in Germany and smuggled out of Germany before the Second World War. There was concern as to how these works came to be in the hands of the seminary and whether they had been improperly or illegally transferred as a consequence of the Second World War. Who held legal ownership and title to the works? Could title be given to purchasers from the auction house? Sotheby's at first refused to identify the consignor.

The attorney general of the State of New York sought to void the sale under both the New York state law relating to consumer fraud and the Military Restitution Laws[19] arising from the Second World War. These laws hold that there is a presumption that a transfer of property without proper payment or consideration during specific years in parts of Germany is void, having occurred because of duress.

Ultimately, Sotheby's was able to obtain the return of approximately thirty of the fifty-nine manuscripts and books sold at the auction. It agreed that it would donate them to institutions for the study of Jewish cultural and religious history. However, if any buyer could demonstrate that the item purchased by that buyer at the Sotheby's auction was also available in an institution for public use, it would not have to be returned, the sale would not be canceled, and the funds received by Sotheby's would be given to various institutions to purchase historical Jewish materials.

Also, the consignor, Professor Alexander Guttmann, a teacher at Hebrew Union College, was to receive $900,000, approximately half the amount raised at the Sotheby's auction. These funds were raised from a separate sale at the Jewish Theological Seminary of two of the documents. This settlement caused great concern to Hebrew Union College, which questioned Guttmann's ownership and therefore his right to receive the funds. He was subsequently dismissed from the college.

Issues as to title arise constantly, and auction houses have responded by revising their conditions in respect to responsibility for warranting title from time to time. These restrictions are examined carefully by courts and must be reasonable in the circumstances.[20]

In *Kelly v. Brooks*,[21] a purchaser claimed that the painting that he had purchased at auction was of questionable authenticity. However, the purchaser had signed the bill of sale containing a written disclaimer indicating the property was sold "as is and that neither the auction house nor the consignor made any guarantees, warranties, or representations, expressed or implied with respect to the property purchased, especially in respect to no representation as to the work being genuine or as to its attribution...."[22]

The court determined that the disclaimer was "clear and unequivocal" and that as the agreement had been signed by the plaintiff, there could not be a defense that the disclaimer was not brought to the attention of the plaintiff.

It is interesting to note that the classic definition of *caveat emptor* comes from the British case *Wallis v. Russell*,[23] reported in 1902. The judge in that case stated that the doctrine applies "to the purchase of specific things, i.e. to a horse or a picture, upon which the buyer can and usually does exercise his own judgment."[24] In addition to pointing out the care that must be taken by someone choosing a specific object, the judge, by choosing horses and pictures to illustrate his point, is suggesting that the risk for the purchaser of either is comparable.

With the vast amounts of money being spent at auctions, it seems odd that—compared to a stock exchange—the auction market is almost completely unregulated. As stated earlier, there appears to be an opportunity and need for governments to regulate auction procedures and auctioneers more closely to ensure that they operate in a legitimate and proper manner. There are numerous auction houses throughout the country, many of them "storefront" operations, with great potential for abuse.

THE CONSIGNOR AND THE AUCTION HOUSE

Advertisements for Auctions

The auctioneer is a fiduciary (that is, in a trust position) for the seller and is obliged to notify the public of the time, place, and manner of sale. The advertisement, however, is no more than an invitation to attend and bid. It has no contractual value. If a sale does not take place, a prospective purchaser has no remedy for things such as loss of time, travel expenses, etc., in Canada and Britain, and in most, if not all, of the United States.

The fiduciary relationship between the consignor and the auction house also determines that auction proceeds are to be treated as "trust funds." The New York Supreme Court in *Edwards v. Sorsmen's Sales Co.*[25] so determined based on the consignment contract of the auction house, which stated that the "net proceeds of the auction received were to be remitted within forty-five days." The court determined that the requirement to remit was more than a mere obligation to pay a debt; indeed, it was money entrusted to the agent for a particular purpose, namely, to remit to the vendor. In law, it was thereby held by the auction house as a trust in favor of the vendor until he or she was paid.

Consignment Contracts

The vendor supplies goods to the auction house on consignment. The auction house is therefore a bailee of the consigned goods. It must use reasonable care to safeguard the works delivered to it and would be responsible to the consignor if the works were lost or damaged as a result of the negligence of the house, its agents, or its employees. It is subject to the usual rules of bailment law.

Recently in Canada, Xerox Canada Finance Inc. brought an action against Wilson's Industrial Auctioneers Ltd.[26] Xerox had consigned equipment to the auctioneer, which was sold at auction. When the sale took place, the auctioneer was in serious financial difficulties and later went out of business without paying the money over to Xerox. The auctioneer had never segregated the proceeds of the consigned goods from its own money. The auctioneer used the proceeds from the consignment sale to carry on its own business.

The auctioneer's assets were seized and later liquidated.

The issue before the court was whether Ernest Sloan Wilson, the principal and directing mind of Wilson Industrial Auctioneers Ltd., was personally liable for having allowed the proceeds of the consignment sale to be lost with his company's money. Wilson argued that he never acted in a personal capacity with respect to the consignment goods.

The Ontario Court found that Wilson was personally liable. The court confirmed that an auctioneer is an agent of the consignor. The money paid by the buyer belongs to the consignor, and the auctioneer is a fiduciary in respect of the money. Where the risk of losing the consignor's money is evident, the auctioneer must take steps to keep the money safe from seizure by the auctioneer's creditors. The money in this case was lost because Wilson allowed the funds to be used as if they were company money when he knew of the risk of the funds being seized by company creditors. Wilson knew for some time that his company could not meet its obligations.

Wilson failed in his personal duty to keep the funds safe from loss. He had a duty to direct that the consignor's money be kept separate from the company funds. Wilson could not use the corporate structure to avoid fulfilling the duties connected with his business.

Modification of Fiduciary Duty of Auction House

An auctioneer's fiduciary obligation may be modified by the provisions of the consignment contract of the auction house. Recent American cases have determined that the fiduciary obligations of the auction house may be varied and restricted by the consignment contract between the parties. In the recent case of *Greenwood v. Koven,*[27] the consignor, Jane Koven, agreed to sell through Christie's auction house a pastel allegedly created by Georges Braque, the well-known twentieth-century French painter and co-inventor, with Picasso, of cubism. Koven had purchased the work many years earlier from a New York gallery. In December 1989, she entered into a Christie's standard consignment contract with some provisions removed. It was Christie's opinion that the work was an original Braque and offered it for sale at auction in May 1990. It was sold to a well-known art collector at the New York auction for $600,000.

Christie's then remitted the sale proceeds to Koven. In and around the time of the sale, there was some question raised about the authenticity of the work. Christie's then took it upon itself to obtain authentication of the work. It retained and received a report from an independent French expert on Braque who was the son of the man who had been granted Braque's moral rights (i.e., *droit moral*), which the court held gave him the right to authenticate works as being by Braque or not. In his opinion, the work was not by Braque.

Christie's then unilaterally rescinded the sale and refunded the purchase price to the purchaser. When Koven refused to return the proceeds to Christie's, the auction house brought the matter to the attention of its insurers, who sued Koven in the New York Federal District Court for the return of the sale proceeds. Koven claimed that Christie's was her agent and had a fiduciary duty to her and, as a result, it should not have investigated the authenticity of the pastel nor rescinded the sale and returned the funds to the purchaser.

The court determined that Christie's did not breach the duty of undivided loyalty when it undertook to investigate the purchaser's concern about the authenticity of the work. According to the court, the law recognizes that Christie's fiduciary responsibilities may be modified by agreement, and, in this instance, the modified consignment agreement allowed Christie's to investigate the authenticity of the consigned artwork even after the sale. The agreement also provided that Christie's had the right in its discretion to seek the views of any expert in respect to the work. It also had the right to rescind the sale if it determined that "the offering for sale of any property has subjected or may subject Christie's and/or seller to liability … including under the warranty of authenticity" as stated in the consignment agreement.

The court determined that Christie's duty of undivided loyalty to Koven was thus modified by the consignment agreement. Christie's investigation of the authenticity of the work, based on the complaint of the purchaser, was appropriate under the terms of the agreement. Christie's also had the right to rescind the sale when it determined in its sole discretion and judgment that it might incur liability as a result of the sale—namely, an action by the purchaser for the return of the funds. The contract terms gave Christie's alone the right to make a determination of its potential liability, and because that determination was made with an honest belief, Christie's was protected. The court went on to determine that if the consignment vendor wished to have greater protection than that given by the auction house, she should have sought such protection in the consignment agreement initially.[28]

The Consignment Contract

Each auction house has its own consignment contract. This contract is the starting place for determining the obligations and warranties undertaken by each party. Consignment contracts usually will

1. specify that the auction house will act as agent at a public auction and will have discretion as to how and when the work is auctioned;
2. establish the commission;
3. set out the settlement time (when payment is to be made);
4. establish a reserve on each work by a formula outlined in the contract, unless otherwise agreed upon;
5. include vendor's representations, warranties, and indemnities as follows:
   a. a representation of ownership by the vendor;
   b. a representation by the vendor that the work is free and clear of encumbrances and that there are no restrictions on the vendor's right to make the sale; and
   c. an indemnity by the vendor that the auction house is held harmless for all claims, damages, and awards relating to any breach of representation by the

vendor and that these representations and warranties survive the completion of the transaction.

6. determine which party is to bear various expenses, including catalog illustration, shipping, customs, insurance, and service charges;
7. establish responsibility for loss or damage;
8. establish limited liability for the auction house, indicating the amount for which the auction house will be liable in case of loss or damage;
9. note the right of the vendor to withdraw the work up to a certain date only;
10. establish the right of rescission by the auction house, in the event the property is inaccurately described or is a counterfeit or forgery, and the right of the auction house to investigate authenticity;
11. if the work does not sell at auction, give the auction house exclusive right for sixty days following the auction to try to sell the work privately for an agreed-upon price (this is called a *private treaty sale*);
12. specify that the auction house will return unsold property to the unsuccessful vendor;
13. cover estimates and catalog descriptions;
14. outline the use of the name of the vendor, unless otherwise agreed, and the status of the vendor (principal or agent);
15. include legal terms and conditions dealing with amendments to the contract, notices, waiver, and the law applicable to the contract;
16. note copyright status (ordinarily, when a work is sold at auction, the object only is sold, not the copyright in the object); and
17. establish a price guarantee and advances of funds to vendors.

Right of Return

What right does a purchaser of personal property have to return a work purchased at auction if its authenticity is questioned?

A recent case dealing with this concern occurred in 1994 when Sotheby's was sued by William C. Foxley, an art collector and owner of the Foxley Cattle Company.[29] In 1987, he purchased a work called *Lydia Reclining on a Divan* through Sotheby's for more than $600,000 (U.S.). The painting was sold as a work by Mary Cassatt.[30] In 1989, Sotheby's reappraised the painting for Foxley at $650,000. In 1993, it reappraised the Cassatt once again at $650,000.

In 1993, Foxley sent the painting and other works to Sotheby's for sale by auction. Only two days before the auction, in December 1993, Sotheby's advised Foxley to withdraw the work to "clear up questions of attribution." (Indeed, in 1994, the Cassatt Foundation had ruled against including the painting in its yearly revised catalog raisonné.) Needless to say, Foxley was upset with the Sotheby request, stating that he had been assured by a member of Sotheby's at the time of his purchase that the purchase price would be refunded if a problem arose with the authenticity of the work. He also was supposed to have earlier received a copy of a report by Adelyn Breeskin, considered at that time an authority on the works of Mary Cassatt, which dealt with the authenticity and the importance of the Cassatt work purchased by Foxley. However, Foxley did not receive that report until 1993, and only after he had notified Sotheby's that it had failed to provide the report earlier. Then, for the first time, he read in the report that the Breeskin opinion on the Cassatt painting was based only on having seen a transparency of the work and not on seeing the actual work itself. Foxley alleged that had he known that fact before the auction, he would never have bid on the painting.

Foxley asked for the return of the purchase price. Sotheby's refused, and Foxley sued approximately seven years after the purchase at auction alleging a number of legal theories, including breach of warranty of authenticity of the painting. Sotheby's argued that the warranty of authenticity set out in its auction catalog was for a five-year period only and that the time had expired in December 1992. The court agreed and also held that this was a sale of goods at auction and therefore governed by the Uniform Commercial Code (N.Y. UCC, SS 2-328, 2-102, 2-105 and Section 2-725; McKinney 1990). It also held that the applicable statute of limitations expired as of December 1991, four years after the auction. Therefore, Foxley was prevented from asserting his claims of breach of warranty in the catalog.

The court accepted Sotheby's argument that the purpose of its appraisal reports was value only; the reports were not authentications and therefore did not attempt to prove authorship of the artwork. This was clear from Sotheby's disclaimer language in its appraisal contracts, which stated that "the appraisal was not deemed to be a representation or warranty with respect to the authenticity of authorship...genuineness or attribution."[31]

The court also looked at the exculpatory language in the appraisal agreement, which provided that "in consideration of our furnishing the appraisal, you hereby release Sotheby's...from any liability or damage whatsoever rising out of or related to the appraisal...unless...due to Sotheby's gross negligence or bad faith."[32]

However, the court did find that sufficient facts existed to support two claims, namely, that the 1989 and 1993 appraisals of the painting were negligently performed, in that Sotheby's twice reappraised the Cassatt painting at $650,000 when in fact it might have been worthless.[33]

Sotheby's sought reargument of the two causes of action, which alleged gross negligence and/or bad faith with respect to the two appraisals received from Sotheby's. Sotheby's argued that the court erred in finding that "Sotheby's had a duty to authenticate the painting notwithstanding the explicit provisions in the appraisal agreements stating that Sotheby's was not performing an authentication." Sotheby's contended that it was immune from any action as a result of the disclaimer contained within each appraisal agreement.

The court stated:

> The Court does not in its earlier opinion or in this one, require appraisals to include authentication of the article appraised. However, in the absence of an explicit disclaimer that the customer agreed that the appraisal fully assumes authenticity and other indicia of genuineness, liability may attach from an appraisal performed with gross negligence or bad faith. The assumption of authenticity for appraisal purposes can be rebutted by supportable allegations of gross negligence or bad faith including fraudulent appraisal. This is particularly true where the appraiser, itself, was aware of significant doubt as to the authenticity of the work in question.[34]

The court went on to state that the "defendant's alleged knowledge of the painting's inauthenticity at the time of the appraisals, if proven at trial, necessarily gives rise to liability. Rendering an appraisal of the painting at $650,000 in the face of knowledge of inauthenticity would clearly constitute not merely gross negligence but also *mala fides*."[35]

The court also provided the following hypothetical example:

> If an appraiser knew that an alleged family heirloom diamond ring was made of cubic zirconium, then a $100,000 appraisal is simply fraudulent. One cannot presume authenticity in the face of facts to the contrary. This is a very different concept than requiring an appraiser to authenticate an object during an appraisal.[36]

Lawyers for Sotheby's had also argued that Foxley, as a knowledgeable collector, should have sought an independent opinion on authenticity. The court, however, held that "Sotheby's arguments taken at face value would insulate all appraisals from any claims of gross negligence or fraud based on authenticity."[37]

PRICE GUARANTEES

Recently, in order to attract business, auction houses have at times made available to vendors guarantees as to the ultimate price of the sale of the works at auction. The usual arrangement is that a guarantee will be given for a certain amount; any amount received above the guarantee will be shared between the auction house and the vendor.

LOANS TO PURCHASERS AND VENDORS

Auction houses sometimes make loan advances against the anticipated proceeds of a sale to assist financially strapped vendors in need of funds in advance of the auction, which may not take place for some months. This occurs in divorce settlements, bankruptcy, or demands by creditors, such as the federal government pressing for payment of overdue income tax. Interest is generally charged by the auction house on such advanced funds.

Loans are also made by auction houses to buyers to assist in the purchase of works at auction. This occurs when the potential buyer will receive funds, either from the auction of works of the buyer or from other sources after the time of purchase. The auction house will accept this future income as collateral for both the loan and the interest to be charged on it.

Sotheby's lent money to at least one buyer with the loan secured by the painting purchased until such loan was repaid. The successful buyer was Alan Bond, the Australian financier, who purchased the Vincent van Gogh painting, *Irises*, in November 1987 for a then record price of $53.9 million (U.S.). Sotheby's, it was reported, lent approximately fifty percent of the purchase price to Bond. Bond was unable to complete his purchase due to financial difficulties, and Sotheby's later resold the work to the Getty Museum.

PUFFING

It is noted in the Ontario Sale of Goods Act[38] that unless there is a notification by the vendor that the vendor and his or her agents will be bidding on the work, such bids may not be accepted. Even if there is such notice, the owner is not entitled to engage in "trap bidding" to artificially inflate the price. When an unauthorized bid from the owner is accepted, the Sale of Goods Act permits the buyer to rescind.

The same is true under the United States Uniform Commercial Code,[39] which provides that an auctioneer may not knowingly receive a bid on the seller's behalf. Normally, the seller may not procure such a bid without prior notice to the buyer that the seller has retained the right to do so. U.S. case law also has indicated that fictitious bids are fraudulent and illegal.[40]

A device used for price enhancement is

the employment of a puffer or bybidder who makes fictitious bids in order to raise prices. A puffer has been defined as a person who, without having any intention to purchase, is employed by the seller at an auction to raise the price by fictitious bids...while he himself has secured from risk by a secret understanding with the seller that he shall not be bound by his bids. One who bids at a public sale not because of any desire to purchase but merely to run up the price is not considered a puffer, however, if his bid is recognized as the highest and he can be compelled to accept and pay for the property. It has been broadly held by judicial pronouncement that puffing is forbidden by law and that contracts resulting from such tactics are void, or voidable as contrary to public policy.[41]

MOCK AUCTIONS

A mock auction is one in which the seller alone or in collusion with a buyer or buyers pretends to consummate a sale, but no real sale takes place. Such an "auction" could be used to artificially inflate the value of a particular work, or the work of a particular artist or school, by establishing falsely inflated market prices.

Anything constituting a mock auction is illegal by statute in both New York and California. In Canada, such an auction may be illegal under the Criminal Code. The Criminal Code may also apply if a purchaser deprecates the quality of goods in order to obtain them at a better price. This is usually called *chill* or *damp* bidding. Such bidding may give rise to an action for defamation, such as slander of goods or title.

RINGS

Another illegal tactic is for a group of bidders to agree not to bid against each other for certain works. Once these works are acquired as cheaply as possible at the auction, a second auction (known as a *private* or *knock out* auction) is held among the dealers involved. Any profits or losses resulting from this knock out auction are divided among the participants. In England, this was known as *rings*. The British Act of 1927 made such bidding illegal.[42] In Canada, this may be prohibited by provisions in the Criminal Code dealing with conspiracy. Policing such conduct, however, is almost impossible. The reserve bid was developed to neutralize ring control over prices.

In the United States, chill bidding, including rings, is also illegal under the common law.

One recent case tried in New York dealt with the early-American furniture dealers Bernard and S. Dean Levy Inc. and Thomas Schwenke Inc., a Connecticut antique dealer.[43] It appears that the two galleries had "refrained from bidding against each other" in a 1986 sale at Christie's auction house. The item that they were interested in was a Chippendale mahogany late-eighteenth-century chest. It appears that an agent in the employ of Levy's bought the piece at the Christie's sale for $30,800 (U.S.). Afterward, in a car parked outside the auction house, it was privately auctioned again, to the Levy firm, for the increased price of $38,000 (U.S.). The two dealers pleaded guilty to the charge of federal conspiracy to restrain trade.

The court indicated that *pooling* (rigging an auction in a dealer's favor, often to the detriment of the seller) is a type of ring. In a pool, dealers band together and agree not to bid against one another. As only one dealer bids for an item, its price is depressed. Later, pool members hold a private auction amongst themselves. The amount paid above the auction price is divided among the dealers in the pool, as in the Levy and Schwenke case.

In related cases:[44]

William Barrett Numismatics Ltd., which was a Montreal-based corporation, pleaded guilty in April 1995 to a charge of collusive bidding at a major auction of rare bank notes from the archives of the American Bank Note Company. The auction was held at Christie's New York in November 1990. Barrett paid a $125,000 criminal fine.

That same year, Mel Steinberg Inc., a San Anselmo, California, rare bank note dealer, also pleaded guilty to the same charge at the same auction and paid a $50,000 criminal fine.

The ongoing grand jury investigation into collusive bidding at auctions of numismatic items, conducted by the New York field office, netted another guilty plea for the same Christie's auction in March 1996 from Inmobiliaria Samisu S.A., a Dominican Republic–based corporation owned by Isaac Rudman, a leading numismatics collector. Rudman paid a $55,000 criminal fine. All coconspirators "agreed to refrain from bidding against one another," according to Justice Department documents.[45]

In 1997, the attorney general of the state of New York again became concerned about the possibility of price fixing and restraint of trade by a dealer ring operating at auction houses in New York. He subpoenaed the records of major New York commercial dealers in respect to their bidding and partnering at major auction houses to determine whether some agreement or conspiracy existed among them. The auction houses and the dealers have denied any such involvement or arrangement. Any equivalent to a ring would be contrary to the Sherman Antitrust Act.

OTHER LAWS RELEVANT TO AUCTION PRACTICES

Canadian Law

In various common-law provinces, acts such as the Ontario Business Practices Act[46] deal with unfair trade practices. The Ontario act deals with false, misleading, or deceptive consumer representations, especially as they relate to a particular standard, quality, grade, or style of goods. It also deals with misleading statements of opinion on which a consumer relies, to his or her detriment. The act indicates that no person shall engage in any unfair practice, including the actions noted above, and states that a contract induced by such conduct may be rescinded. The act also indicates that one cannot contract out of the terms of the statute. There do not appear to have been any cases to date under the statute concerning auctions or auction sales.

The Criminal Code of Canada[47] also affects auction sales in Canada. The federal Criminal Code applies to deliberate, false, or misleading statements or conduct as a form of false pretenses or fraud. Exaggerated commendation or deprecation of quality is not a false pretense under the act unless it is so extreme that it amounts to a fraudulent misrepresentation of fact. This has to be determined on the facts of each situation. The Criminal Code also contains provisions that make it illegal to enter into an agreement, whether oral or written, for the purchase or sale of goods without a bona fide intention of buying or selling them, when this is done to profit from rising or falling prices.

U.S. Law

In the United States, various criminal actions may be brought under federal and state laws, as a combination and restraint of trade, if there is sufficient proof of such a ring; other civil laws deal with fraud and unfair competition.

New York City, one of the major auction centers of the world, has established regulations for auctions and auctioneers.[48] These regulations deal with

1. the need to have a written contract between a consignor and an auction house;
2. full disclosure in respect to fees and other charges;
3. a warranty of title by the consignor;
4. an indemnity by the consignor of the auction house against any defects of title, and acknowledgment that the intended beneficiary of that warranty is the ultimate purchaser;

5. disclosure of any interest by the auction house in the item being sold;
6. requirements that the auction catalog include, among other information, whether the consignor is entitled to any rebate commission, whether the consignor may bid on the property offered for sale, whether there is a reserve on the work being auctioned, and whether a loan has been made to the consignor or prospective buyer; and
7. rules of conduct of the auction, including when the auctioneer may bid on a work (usually not once the reserve price has been reached), warranty of title, disclosure of the existence of any reserve price on any work being offered, and an admission of "nonsale" (when a work does not reach its reserve and is brought in unsold and returned to the consignor).

On December 17, 1997, Diana D. Brooks, valuer and chief executive of Sotheby's, revealed the company's new policy for auction and consignments based on recommendations received from a panel assisgned to review the Sotheby's operation due to allegations of misconduct in its European operations.

Under the new policy, Sotheby's would

1. refuse to handle art in all categories without valid export documents;
2. require consignors to sign a warranty that the goods being consigned have not been illegally exported;
3. refuse to do business with prospective vendors who have not agreed to sign statements that the items offered have come to them by legitimate means only;
4. require dealers with large consignments to sign warranties confirming that the works have been legally exported from their countries of origin;
5. create a six-person compliance department to review the history of all objects sent for auction that may have crossed borders and, therefore, be subject to potential import/export and cultural-property restrictions.

The review committee also recommended various changes to existing auction practices:

1. announcing from the rostrum the fact that a lot has gone unsold, and
2. banning auctioneers from making fictitious bids by pointing at people or places in the salesroom.

THE LAW OF AUCTIONS IN MEXICO

Specific rules have been created for commercial auction sales in the Federal District of Mexico.[49]

1. The holding of commercial auction sales in establishments that have been authorized to that effect is authorized by these rules.
2. Commercial negotiators who wish to hold an auction must previously have applied for a license from the Federal District Department. The request must contain the following data:
   a. the name of the applicant, who must be a Mexican citizen or a corporation organized according to Mexican law with a Mexican chairperson;
   b. the location of the establishment;
   c. the type of articles that will be sold;
   d. the manner and time of the sales, with the understanding that these are to be held at least every three months.
3. Once the application is submitted, the department will indicate the amount of guarantee that the applicant must provide according to the importance of the negotiation.
4. Auctions may involve goods from the negotiator or from third parties that entrust the goods to the negotiator for their sale.
5. All negotiators who effect the sale of objects or merchandise that are the property of third parties must, prior to the announcement of the sale, confirm the ownership that the interested parties claim with respect to them, under their most strict responsibility.
6. All sales effected by means of an auction must be paid for at that time, and with hard currency, save such instances when the owner of the item up for bids has given his authorization previously and when the negotiator that carries out the auction agrees to effect the sale under his or her responsibility. This includes the payment of the goods to the owner in the event of default.
7. The negotiator who receives from a third party objects or merchandise to be sold by means of an auction has a duty to care for the goods and keep them safe. All damage and deterioration that the goods suffer are the responsibility of the negotiator, except for acts of God.
8. Before agreeing to sell objects or merchandise that is the property of third parties, the negotiator must inspect the goods for quality and for the possibility of sale. If the sale cannot be effected after the goods are accepted, the negotiator does not have the right to claim any amount whatsoever from their owner as a fee or storing expenses of any other kind, unless agreed prior to the acceptance.

9. The commercial negotiators who receive goods from third parties must have a contract with the owner covering the amount of the fee plus the sale expenses; if these were not agreed upon, the negotiators will not be able to charge above ten percent of the product of the sale.

   When charged, the fee and the expenses cannot exceed fifteen percent of the total cash price obtained from the auction sale of the goods.

   The percentages previously mentioned include publicity expenses, preparation of the sale, commissions, fees, and so forth. No other amounts may be collected aside from those, for any reason.

10. All sales to be effected by means of an auction must be announced by the selling negotiator at least thirty days prior to its holding. In the respective announcements, the goods up for bids, their quality, and their current state must be detailed. If the object is an art object, its origin and merits must also be stated.

11. To be legally sold at auction, all objects must be publicly exhibited for at least six days prior to the date of the auction.

12. The infraction of any of the requirements expressed in articles 9 and 10 of these rules makes the negotiator responsible for all damages and deterioration caused to the buyers as well as to any third-party seller.

13. The value of the sold items will be the security for the selling negotiator for the contracted amount of the fee and expenses, as well as for the taxes that he or she may have to pay because of the transaction. The negotiator may apply the amounts obtained from the sale of the goods directly to the payment of the contracted amount at the time the sale is effected.

14. The taxes on each sale must be deducted from the price by the negotiator and must be held by him or her to be paid to the proper fiscal authorities (currently an eight percent income tax on the sales price and a value-added tax or VAT of fifteen percent on the commission).

15. The buyers of auctioned objects do not have any rights against the negotiator if all the requisites set in these rules are fulfilled, unless it is proven that the purchased object does not meet the conditions and quality that were announced at the time of the auction.

16. During the holding of an auction, all the items up for bid must be visible to the interested parties. As the auctioneer announces each item, he or she must also repeat its qualities, condition, and, if applicable, origin.

17. The representative of the negotiator who presides over the auctions (the auctioneer) cannot adjudicate the property of any item (that is, terminate the bidding) as long as there are bidders that improve on the price of the sale; previous to the adjudication, he or she must repeat three times the amount to be paid for the item so that the licensing authorities may be convinced as to the legitimacy of the sale.

18. When so desired by a third party who entrusts objects or merchandise to be sold at an auction, a minimum price may be established (the reserve price). If the negotiator acts contrary to such a disposition, he or she must immediately round out or pay the difference to the owner.
19. No auction may be held without being properly verified by the appropriate official appointed by the Federal District Department, who must witness the auction.
20. A certifying document will be made for every auction in which the number and necessary data for every item are stated, together with their original appraised value, the price paid for them, and any other pertinent facts. This document will be signed by the representative of the selling negotiator and by the official or officials designated by the Federal District Department to verify the sales. To this document must be added the notices or catalogs through which the sale was announced.
21. The infringement of any of the precepts herein contained will be penalized by the head of the Federal District Department, with a fine ranging from one hundred to five thousand pesos in addition to any civil or penal responsibilities that may have been incurred, or with the revocation of the license, according to the seriousness of the offense.

The law above is complemented by a transitional article stating that the head of the Federal District Department is empowered to provide the necessary measures for implementing and defining the rules enumerated.

BUYING AND SELLING THROUGH A COMMERCIAL DEALER

Creators as well as private and corporate collectors often use a dealer rather than an auction house for the sale of art and art objects. Prices will be retail and not the usually lower auction price. The work will not usually be put into a catalog or shown at a public preview as it would for an auction sale. Most works and objects for resale by the dealer are taken on a consignment basis; the dealer is an agent working for and on behalf of the vendor. Rarely does a dealer purchase a work for inventory from a private seller.

For artists, there are special benefits and concerns that come with selling through a dealer rather than privately. Dealers often have a special knowledge of particular collectors who may wish to purchase a particular kind of work or a collection being offered; they may also know which collections require works of the kind being offered to round out the collection.

Well-known collectors may use private dealers and agents to consummate sales when in some financial difficulty, preferring not to have this information become public.

The most important concerns for the owner are the history and financial capability of the dealer. Membership in a professional association is a possible guide, as is the dealer's reputation among professionals in the field.

Consignment Agreements

The dealer will ordinarily require that the vendor provide sufficient information and warranties to reassure the dealer that the vendor has title to the work or object and that the object is genuine.

The dealer will wish to establish with the owner the *end price* (the final price to the buyer) and any discounts that the dealer may make available to a prospective purchaser. The terms of purchase also will be established; for example, whether the vendor is prepared to accept payment on a time basis, at whose risk should those payments not be made, and at what point in the time-payment period will the object be given to the purchaser and title transferred.

The vendor will wish to ascertain that the object is fully insured by the dealer while in the hands of the dealer or out on approval to prospective purchasers.

A written contract outlining the various rights and responsibilities of the parties should include the following:

1. the warranty of authority to sell, especially if it is an estate sale;
2. a warranty that the title is free and clear of all encumbrances;
3. a warranty as to the authenticity of the work;
4. a determination of an acceptable end price, any discounts, and who absorbs them;
5. a determination as to whether time payments are agreeable to the vendor and on what basis;
6. the time term of the consignment to the dealer, as well as any rights of renewal, and by whom;
7. the warranty of the dealer as to sufficient all-risks insurance to cover the work while in the hands of the dealer or out on exhibition or approval;
8. payment of the funds as they are received and how they are to be split;
9. confidentiality regarding the transaction and name of the vendor;
10. the rate of commission or fee to be charged by the dealer and when and how it is to be payable;
11. the right of the dealer to accept a work on trade; and, if so, how and when payment will be made to the vendor (Can the dealer hold off payment to the vendor until the work is sold, or is such a transaction at the risk of the dealer?);
12. payment for advertising, reframing, or any necessary restoration of the work;

13. if agreeable, the right of the gallery to purchase the work on its own behalf and, if so, at what price or discount;
14. any guarantee by the dealer in respect to the sale and price to be received;
15. any advance to the vendor prior to the sale of the work; and
16. whether the consignment contract has turned into a financing arrangement and, therefore, requires appropriate registration or filing to be effective against a third party (such as a defaulting purchaser in a time-payment arrangement, who has possession of the goods).

Purchasing from a Dealer: The Bill of Sale

When purchasing fine or decorative art through a commercial art dealer, it is important that the buyer obtain a proper and complete bill of sale. It should contain as much detail as possible about both the work and the artist. It should, at the very least, indicate the full name of the artist or studio or manufactory; the title of the work; the medium; the date of the work; the ownership history of the work, if possible; and any exhibitions in which the work has appeared. It should be signed by the dealer.

The more representations contained in the bill of sale, the more protection there is for the purchaser. This is especially true in respect to the authenticity of a work and its past ownership.

Price

The price and payment terms—as well as any discount given the purchaser—should be specifically shown on the bill of sale. Discounts may be given for cash, for prompt payment, or to an art consultant or important collector and good client.

Condition

The physical condition of the work must be examined carefully. Condition is essential to any determination of value, and it is up to the purchaser to be satisfied as to the condition of the object being purchased. (Rarely will there be any representation made as to condition by a vendor/dealer.)

With today's technology, it is possible to discover restorations that cannot be seen by the naked eye. Thus, an expert should be retained to determine the condition of an object before purchase. In some instances, works by the historical Canadian painter Cornelius Krieghoff have been so restored that there is little left of the original hand of the artist; yet they sell for tens of thousands of dollars.

Recently a buyer purchased a work by a well-known historical Canadian painter only to find that the central figures—two young children playing in and around a pond—had been added by another hand and were not by the original artist. This information was revealed only when the work was taken to a restorer to restore another aspect of the work.

Restoration and condition concerns are not restricted to historical objects. When Canadian Inuit prints first came to market in the 1960s, they were inexpensive. As a result, many were framed inexpensively and, often, improperly. It is only as the artists become famous and many of the prints are worth substantial sums of money that they are being examined as to condition. Sadly, a number have been dry mounted, cut down to fit a frame, or put into mats and backings that are not acid free. One of the most valuable Inuit prints to date was framed up against the front glass; much of the image has now transferred to the glass from the paper.

Similarly, if masking or transparent tape is affixed to the back of the work, it will ultimately affect condition—at least of the back of the work and perhaps the front because of acid leaching—and reduce value.

Condition and control of condition are essential to all works and objects. It is sometimes difficult to estimate value based on sales of similar works or even prints from the same edition because of variations in condition.

The Dealer

For purchasers as well as vendors, the credibility of the commercial art dealer is essential. Is the dealer a member in good standing of an appropriate professional association that has a code of ethics that members must adhere to? Such associations are the American Dealers Association in the United States, the Professional Art Dealers Association in Canada, and the Canadian Antique Dealers Association. There are also various associations for dealers specializing in postage stamps, coins, and other collectibles.

PURCHASING DIRECTLY FROM THE ARTIST

The professional artist will usually have his or her works handled by a commercial art dealer. This enables the artist to have his or her works shown to the largest possible audience in a favorable manner. It also frees the artist of the difficulties and embarrassment connected with attempting to sell his or her own works, leaving the artist free to do what the artist does best, namely, creating art. There are special rules in respect to consignment arrangements between artists and dealers. In many jurisdictions, the dealer becomes a trustee for and on behalf of the artist, especially in respect to the receipt of funds for the sale of work created by the artist.[50]

Suffice it to say that creators, especially well-known creators of art objects, may have ongoing contractual relationships with commercial galleries. Often these contracts require that the artist produce a certain number of works for the gallery within a certain period of time. The gallery generally has exclusive jurisdiction for the sale of the works in a given geographic area and for a set time period.

Sometimes, however, contracts permit artists to sell work directly, as well as through the gallery, although galleries often try to prevent such sales so as to maintain control of both market and price. A gallery's commission may be from one-third to one-half of the ultimate sale price. Private, direct sales by the artist may be for prices below those offered through the gallery, thereby affecting the credibility of retail prices of the artist's work.

In the event an artist is permitted by contract or arrangement with the gallery to sell directly, there are a number of concerns that a purchaser should bear in mind.

1. There may be an ownership concern. For instance, if the work is being created for a gallery exhibition, the dealer may have contractual or other rights to that work. If so, is this a concern to a purchaser who is not a party to the contract? A bona fide purchaser for value would not ordinarily be concerned about such a restriction; however, is the purchaser a bona fide purchaser for value if the purchase price is well below market or retail price as established by the gallery?

2. In the purchase of the work, a proper bill of sale should be obtained from the artist. It should set out the transfer of the property and full particulars of the work or object being purchased. This document not only is evidence of ownership but also is vital to establishing the authenticity of the work.

   The creator should warrant that this is an original work created by the artist and outline the details of the work. For instance, if it is a multiple, the bill of sale should set out the number of the work being purchased, the edition size, the total numbers in both the artist's proofs and any variant editions. This is required by law in New York but not in many other jurisdictions, including Canada.

3. The purchase of an artwork transfers title to the object; however, without proper documentation, copyright is not transferred to the purchaser but remains with the creator. The same is true of moral rights.

   If the purchaser is purchasing the work with the intent of reproducing it, he or she should be aware that if the work is still under copyright, an owner is not permitted to reproduce it without permission of the artist. Ordinarily, a work of art is under the artist's copyright for the life of the artist plus fifty years (seventy years in the United States and seventy-five years in Mexico). Exceptions as to ownership of copyright include copyright in portraits, lithographs, and works for hire, but these are not usually relevant in the purchase of an existing work of art from the artist's inventory.

For example, if an owner wishes to reproduce a work for commercial or advertising purposes, the permission of the artist or, if the artist is deceased, of the estate of the artist would be required. Failing such permission, the artist or estate may bring an action for breach of copyright for unauthorized reproduction of the work. Remedies permitted by law include damages and even an injunction preventing the reproduction of the work.

Copyright would also be breached if an owner reproduced a substantial part of the work in any medium without permission of the artist or his estate.

Often a purchaser, especially a corporate or government purchaser, will negotiate a right to reproduce the work in the future, usually for an additional fee payable to the artist. The fee could be a one-time payment or a fee paid for each use of the work, depending on the use made of the artwork. For instance, if it is reproduced in color on a magazine or book cover, the reproduction fee would be higher than for a black-and-white reproduction in the interior of a book or corporate annual report.

Moreover, a work is usually reproduced from a slide or transparency, on which the photographer usually holds copyright. As a result, if a photograph, slide, or transparency of a work is given by the artist to the purchaser, copyright permission must still be obtained from the copyright owner of that photograph in order to reproduce it. Often the artist is also the photographer of the work, and a warranty and permission should form part of the original purchase agreement of the work.

4. The establishment of a purchase price for a work may require some negotiation, especially if a gallery is not involved in the sale. If the purchaser is buying the work with immediate payment, this is of benefit to the artist. Ordinarily, a purchase through a gallery would permit the purchaser to pay for the work over a period of time, without interest, and would result in delayed partial payments to the artist.

If the artist does not have a dealer and sells directly to the public, the price charged may become the market price of the work.

Market price is always difficult to establish, for vendors, purchasers, and valuers. It may have different meanings for different people at different times. For instance, a market price established by the artist for a work is a unilateral determination as to what the market will bear. A "market value" to a valuer would encompass the view of the artist and sales by the artist, but it would also take into consideration all the other relevant markets in which the work has appeared and the market price of other works by the artist.

The Public Commission

Often government agencies and departments have a budget for public art. For example, there was often a budgetary amount, usually one percent of building costs, for art contracts for public buildings being built by Canadian provincial and federal governments. Works would be commissioned for a particular site often through an art consultant and art committee. Similarly, in Albany, New York, some years back, then Governor Nelson Rockefeller established an art program that brought art by some of the finest living American artists to public government spaces.

A "public" work can be preexisting; but most often, it is work commissioned for a specific site in or near a building. (Sculpture to be placed in or about the grounds of the building is sometimes called "plop art.") In Toronto, when the new City Hall was built, the architect wished to have a Henry Moore sculpture for the front plaza. Ultimately, Moore created *Three Way Piece*, known as the "Archer," to stand in the plaza outside City Hall. The sculpture was vilified by various politicians and became a civic election issue: the sculpture was supported by the mayor at that time, who ultimately lost the election, in part because of his support for the sculpture.

In recent years, transportation systems, particularly subways, have commissioned works of art for specific stations. Most notable among them are a recent project in Buffalo, New York, and various art projects in the subway lines of Toronto. Artworks are also commissioned for pavilions at world fairs and Olympics. Both the Calgary Olympics in Canada and the Atlanta and Los Angeles Olympics in the United States had substantial cultural and art components. Recently, Toronto has commissioned significant artworks such as a unique terrazzo floor and a unique 100-foot metal tree pole with birds, bird holes, and light from within for its new Convention Centre as an integral part of the construction.

In selecting art for public projects, numerous questions should be answered in the contract.

1. Who are the contracting parties, and who will be responsible? For example, is the artist incorporated? If so, the artist's corporation should warrant it will hire the artist to do the work, but who gives the warranties?
2. What are the obligations of the artist?
3. When must the work be completed?
4. If the work is to be constructed as part of a building, who is responsible for the site being of correct size and orientation and for the issuance of building and

other necessary permits? Can the site be available to the artist within the time framed by the contract? If not, what are the consequences? What if the space is not correct? Is the artist entitled to a cancellation fee?

5. Who has copyright on the work?
6. Who will maintain the work?
7. Is the artist using any subtrades, for instance, a fabricator, engineer, or foundry? How can the commissioner ensure compliance and receive protection from default?
8. If the work is later damaged, does the artist have the first right to be retained for any repair work?
9. Who is responsible for transportation, insurance, crating, and shipping? Are there any union concerns?
10. Is there a right to reject the work by the patron, and if so, what happens to the work?
11. Is ownership reserved by the artist until payment is made in full?
12. Is there a warranty given by the artist? If so, what for?
13. Does the artist have the right to create additional versions of the work for sale to others?
14. Does the artist have the right to create reproductions?
15. Does the patron have the right to create reproductions? If so, on what basis and in what media (photographs, posters, three-dimensional reproductions, etc.)?
16. How is the price to be established? What relationship does it bear to the artist's market price?

The price of a public commission is often determined by the budget available rather than the market price of a work by the artist. Work created for a public commission is generally of a size and for a purpose quite different from the usual work created by an artist. Valuing such works of art is extremely difficult, both for contract purposes and, ultimately, for a valuer. There are usually few similar examples of works by the artist for comparison, and questions arise as to the valuation process.

Recently, the value of donations of various public works by private patrons has been questioned by Revenue Canada. The valuation criteria of such works were at issue: If the work is unique and not similar to prior works by the artist, what valuation criteria are to be used by the valuer?[51]

17. When are payments to be made to the artist?
18. Is the art project subject to construction liens for nonpayment to the artist or his or her subtrades?
19. Who is responsible for insuring the work?
20. Can the work be removed from the site and/or put in storage?

21. What happens to the work if the building is destroyed?
22. What happens to the work if the building is sold?
23. What if the owner or employees want the work moved? Does the artist have the right to keep it in situ?

The facts of each situation must be carefully considered, and the contract must be tailored to it. The rights and obligations of the parties must be balanced both in a fair contract and, ultimately, in the quality of artwork contracted for by the parties.

The case of *Serra v. The United States General Services Administration* is an example of such a problem.[52]

A commission was awarded to Richard Serra by the United States Government for a sculpture to be located in the Federal Plaza in lower Manhattan. The sculpture was entitled Tilted Arc. The price paid was $175,000. Under the terms of the contract, the government was to own all preliminary drawings, sketches, and models, as well as the work. The work was a 120-foot long piece of "rusty steel," twelve feet tall, positioned so that it blocked access to people wishing to cut diagonally across the plaza.

The government received many complaints, both in respect to the look of the work and to its interference with pedestrian traffic. The government wished to remove the sculpture, and Serra brought an action to prevent its removal on the grounds that it was site-specific (i.e., that the removal of the work would in effect destroy it). This would violate both the contract and the artist's constitutional rights.

The case touched on a number of jurisdictional problems as well as governmental rights and obligations. Ultimately, the court held that the decision to relocate the sculpture was a "valid content-neutral determination" that had nothing to do with the artist's right under the First Amendment to freedom of speech. The court found that the government had not attempted to ban Serra's sculpture and that the contract had given full ownership of the models, sketches, and physical object to the government.

The court of appeals affirmed the decision and concluded that the artistic expression belonged to the government rather than to Serra. Even if Serra retained some First Amendment interest in the continued display of the structure, its removal by the government was a permissible restriction. The government had a right and interest to keep the plaza free from obstruction, and the relocation of the sculpture did not preclude Serra from communicating his ideas.

Various state laws deal with moral rights, including the right of artists to have works kept at specific sites. For instance, the California Art Preservation Act[53] deals with works of art such as murals and site-specific sculptures incorporated in or about buildings. Removal is permitted if the work can be removed without sustaining damage. The building owner has an obligation to use its best efforts to notify the artist of the intention to remove such a work. If the work cannot be removed from the building or site without substantial physical damage or destruction—unless the moral rights provisions in the work are expressly reserved to the artist by a written instrument signed by the building owner—the work can be removed.

The Federal Visual Artists Rights Act of 1990[54] provides greater protection for the art and the artist. For example, a building owner may remove a work only if the artist had consented to its installation prior to June 1, 1991, or if both artist and building owner had signed a written agreement after that date acknowledging that removal of the work may damage it and accepting such eventuality.

Various other states, including Connecticut, Louisiana, Maine, Massachusetts, Nevada, New Jersey, New Mexico, and Pennsylvania, have moral-rights legislation that may affect site-specific works. Each statute must be looked at carefully to determine what rights are available to the artist and to the owner of the site in which the artwork is being placed.

As a result, contract provisions are crucial if rights other than those provided by statute are to be provided to either the artist or the owner of the site. Any such terms will affect the future use of the work and the flexibility of the owner to deal with the site.

In Canada, there have been no cases reported that give the artist a right to have works specifically sited. In fact, works created for public authorities and governments, including major outdoor sculptures, have been removed without the authority or even the knowledge of the artist. Recently, a major sculpture by Robert Murray was removed from its site at the Vancouver airport without the consent of the artist, and John Nugent had a work removed from a government-agency building in Winnipeg without his consent and permission.

The question to be answered is: What is fair in the circumstances, and how much control can an artist have in public contracts? Ideally, the issue should be dealt with in the "call to tenders," so an artist would know at the outset what conditions were attached to the commission and could use that information when deciding if he or she wishes to tender for it.

The Private Commission

From time to time, a private collector or corporation may wish to enter into a contract with an artist for the creation of a particular work, be it art, craft, jewelry, or artifact, for a particular purpose, for example, a photograph of a retiring president or official or a painted portrait of a retiring judge. A glass sculptor may be asked to create an edition of a glasswork to be given as an annual award for a particular purpose; a sculptor may be asked by a developer to create a site-specific sculpture for a new building.

Throughout history, artists existed through the patronage of the church or a particular noble family. Even today, it is not uncommon for artists to have a particular private or corporate patron, especially during the their formative years: often the patron pays a stipend to the artist on a periodic or annual basis in return for all or part of the artist's output. In such a situation, the artist has little bargaining power. However, later when the artist becomes better known and is sought out for commissions, the artist's bargaining position improves.

Today, in contracting with an artist, it is essential to know whether the artist is represented by a commercial gallery. If so, the contract between the dealer and the artist may stipulate that the dealer has control of commission contracts. If so, the gallery, not the artist, will negotiate the contract and fee; therefore, the existence of such an agreement between artist and dealer must be determined at the outset.

Whether the work is being directed through a dealer or with the artist, the commission contract must clearly set out the parties to the contract and the rights of those parties. The following concerns must be considered in such a contract.

1. Who has artistic control of the work? Who has the right to approve the work? If the patron is to approve the work, what are the criteria for approval? For instance, if the work is a portrait, the sitter may have input on the type and quality of the image he or she wishes to see. However, the sitter may not be the commissioner but only the subject matter of the commission. Does this person have any rights within the contract? If the sitter is not a party to the contract, he or she may well have no rights to interfere in the commission.

2. How is the satisfaction of the commissioning party to be determined? If the contract indicates the work is "to be done to the satisfaction of the patron," British and Canadian law—and in all probability the law of most American states—would hold that the opinion of the commissioning party is paramount, even when it is unreasonable. Therefore, contracts should indicate that the approval of the patron must be on a "reasonable basis" rather than on the basis of his or her "satisfaction." The problem is, of course, that satisfaction can be determined only after the work has been created. It would therefore make sense for the artist to obtain as much of the fee as possible up front, as patrons can be difficult.

   Take, for example, the famous case of the portrait of Winston Churchill by Graham Sutherland. The completed portrait was not to the satisfaction of the Churchill family and was destroyed. Former President of the United States Lyndon Johnson also was not satisfied with his official portrait and refused to accept it.

On the other hand, consider the Ontario patron who commissioned an artist to paint his portrait. The artist had photographs taken of the client, but after painting the facial aspects of the portrait, the artist lost the photographs. Nevertheless, he completed the portrait, and it was, aesthetically, a fine example of his work. When the portrait was delivered to the patron, however, he was shocked to discover that instead of portraying his head of white hair, the artist had painted him bald. Needless to say, the portrait was rejected, and the artist did not receive the balance of the fee owing.

A number of questions arise: Does the artist have the right to sell this rejected work to another? Would it be an embarrassment to the patron? Might there be a possible action by the patron for defamation or invasion of privacy? Could the patron prevent the work from being exhibited in public? If so, would this right extend to the estate of the patron? Such questions will, no doubt, have to be dealt with by the courts in the not-too-distant future.

3. What is the time of delivery? This should be specified, perhaps with a penalty clause inserted for late delivery, especially if the work is to be created for the opening of a new building.

4. If the work is to be site-specific, who is responsible for ensuring that the site will be exactly as promised if it is yet to be constructed? Recently, a site-specific work was created for inclusion in a particular area of a building being constructed in Ottawa. When the steel and electronic sculpture was brought to be installed, it was found that the space was smaller than originally planned, and the work was too large for the finished site. The work was fabricated as an integral unit and could not be altered.

What would be the consequences of this situation? For instance, would the commissioning party be responsible for a new work to be created to fit the space? Would the artist have any obligation to prepare such a work? Was the commissioning party responsible for final payment, even though the work as created could not be installed? Did the commissioning party have the right to place the work in another site? If possible, all these issues should be addressed in the negotiation leading up to the contract.

5. Can the artist attend and install the work on the site? Would this create a union concern? Often builders have agreements with unions that only union labor can be used on the site. Does the artist have to join a construction union?

6. Can the work be moved or resold by the patron, even if it is site-specific? There are unique moral-rights laws in various jurisdictions that may give artists rights that must be considered for contract purposes.

7. How is payment to be made, and at what stages of the commission? Often, a deposit of at least one-third is paid on signing the contract. If there is a maquette

created by the artist, a further payment is often due at that time; final payment is made on acceptance of the final work by the commissioner.

8. Who owns the maquette and preliminary drawings? If the commissioner owns them, is the artist owed an additional fee for these works?

9. Who is responsible for various expenses such as insurance, cost of travel, crating, installation, etc.?

10. What if the contract is awarded and preliminary work is done, but the final drawings or maquette are not acceptable to the client? Should the commissioner be able to cancel? If so, should a cancellation fee be paid to the artist?

11. Who will own copyright on the final work and on any maquette or drawings? If the patron wishes to use the image of the work for publicity and promotion, copyright and moral rights will have to be negotiated. A separate fee may be payable to the artist and a separate licensing agreement may be negotiated.

12. Should there be an obligation on the commissioner to maintain the work, especially if it is a public mural or sculpture and/or one with moving parts? Should the artist have first right to repair the work? If so, at what fee?

13. Is there a warranty by the artist on the work, especially if it is kinetic?

14. What if either the artist or the patron dies during the period of the contract? Is the agreement terminated? What if the artist dies when the work is half built? Can a substitute be brought in to complete the work? If so, who is the creator of the work, and who holds copyright? Should insurance on the life of the artist be considered by the patron?

15. Can the artist have access to the work to photograph for his own publicity and promotion purposes? If so, this right should be provided for in the agreement.

16. Might the patron wish to reproduce the work for commercial purposes—posters, postcards, reproductions, calendars, etc.? If so, the artist may insist that a fee be paid for this right and an acknowledgment of the artist as creator appear on or adjacent to each image.

17. Are there any safety or other special concerns for the patron? For example, the builders of Skydome, the multipurpose sports facility in Toronto, commissioned a "light sculpture." When it was installed, however, the blinking lights caused difficulties for the batters. The sculpture was disconnected during games and often not reconnected thereafter. This unforeseen situation had to be negotiated among the artist, builders, and patron donor of the work.

18. Many of the concerns regarding public commissions outlined earlier in this chapter are equally applicable to private commissions and should be considered for contract purposes.

NOTES

1. An example of such service is Richard Polsky, *Art Market Guide: Contemporary American Art* (New York: D.A.P. Distributed Art Publishers, 1995).

2. For a discussion of the history and types of auctions, see Brian W. Harvey and Franklin Meisel, *Auctions—Law and Practice* (London: Butterworth and Company, 1985), in particular chapter 1. See also Ralph Cassidy Jr., *Auctions and Auctioneering* (Los Angeles: University of California Press, 1967), especially chapter 2.

3. For a terminology example, see Christie's Auction Catalogues General Glossary, e.g., Christie's *South Kensington Twentieth Century Art,* June 18, 1999, p. 3.

4. *New York City Administrative Code*, title 20, chapter 2, subsection 13, rule 20 (McKinney 1984 and Supp. 1997).

5. See Franklin Feldman, Stephen E. Weil, and Susan Duke Biederman, *Art Law: Rights and Liabilities of Creators and Collectors,* chap. 6 (Boston: Little, Brown and Co., 1986) for articles and a discussion of the European and American experience.

6. *Copyright Act*, R.S.C. 1985, c. C-42. *Droit de suite* is discussed in more detail in chapter 6, "Copyright."

7. *California Civil Code*, Section 986 (1988).

8. *Fair Trading Act*, 2nd Sess., 24th Leg., Alberta (1998).

9. Ibid., pt. 12, sec. 121 ff.

10. *Sale of Goods Act,* R.S.O. 1990, c. S.1.

11. *Uniform Commercial Code*, as enacted by various states.

12. *Illinois Compiled Statutes*, chap. 1.2½, paragraphs 1100–04.

13. *Black's Law Dictionary,* 6th ed. (1990), 1586.

14. *Black's Law Dictionary,* rev. 4th ed. (1968), 1757.

15. Ibid., 1758.

16. *Black's Law Dictionary,* 6th ed., 1586.

17. *Ibid.*, 1588–89.

18. *Abrams v. Sotheby Parke Bernet, Inc.*, N.Y.L.J. at 6, col. 2 (Sup. Ct. N.Y. County 1984).

19. Article 5 of *Military Restitution Laws,* no. 59, and Article 4 of the *Berlin Restitution Law.*

20. *Weiscz v. Parke-Bernet Galleries, Inc.*, 67 Misc. 2d 1077, 325 N.Y.S. 2d 576 (N.Y. City Civ. Ct. 1971), rev'd, 77 Misc. 2d 80, 351 N.Y.S. 2d 911 (App. Term 1974).

21. *Kelly v. Brooks*, 92 Civ. 729, 1993 U.S. Dist. LEXIS 3385 (S.D.N.Y. March 19, 1993).

22. Ibid.

23. *Wallis v. Russell,* 2 Ir. R. 585, 36 I.L.T.R. 67 (Ireland C.A. 1902).

24. *Wallis v. Russell,* 2 Ir. R. 586, 36 I.L.T.R. 67 (Ireland C.A. 1902).

25. *Edwards v. Sorsmen's Sales Co.*, 560 N.Y.S. 2d 165 (Sup. Ct. 1989).

26. *Xerox Canada Finance Inc. v. Wilson's Industrial Auctioneers Ltd.*, 34 B.L.R. (2d) 135 (Ont. Gen. Div. 1997).

27. *Greenwood v. Koven*, 880 F. Supp 186 (S.D.Y.N.Y. 1995).

28. For a discussion of French moral rights and a critique of the judgment in this case, see Franklin Feldman, "The French Law of Experts: A Corrected View," *IFAR Journal* (Spring 1998), 6.

29. *William Foxley v. Sotheby Inc.*, 893 F. Supp. 1224, 1226 and 1236 (S.D.N.Y. 1995) US Dist. Lexis 5332.

30. Unlike the Koven case, Foxley had not been reimbursed by the auction house.

31. *Foxley*, 1235.

32. Ibid., 1236.

33. Ibid.

34. *William Foxley v. Sotheby Inc.*, 893 F. Supp. 1224, 1226 and 1236 (S.D.N.Y. 1995) US Dist. Lexis 8211.

35. Ibid.

36. Ibid., 1237

37. Ibid.

38. *Sale of Goods Act.*

39. *Uniform Commercial Code*, Section 2-328(4).

40. See *Nevada Nat'l Leasing Co. v. Hereford*, 36 Cal. 3d 146, 680 P.2d 1077 (1984); *Berg v. Hogan*, 322 N.W. 2d 448 (N.D. 1982); *Feaster Trucking Serv., Inc. v. Parks-Davis Auctioneers, Inc.*, 211 Kan. 78, 505 P.2d 612 (1973).

41. Ralph Cassady, Jr., *Auctions and Auctioneering* (Berkeley: University of California Press, 1967), 212.

42. The Auctions Bidding Agreements Act, 1927 and 1969. For a full discussion of auction rings and the full text of the Auctions Bidding Agreements Act, 1927, 1969, see Brian W. Harvey, *Auction Law and Practice* (London: Franklin Meisel, Butterworth and Company, 1985), 144.

43. The facts of the case were reported in the *Wall Street Journal,* August 20, 1991.

44. Judd Tully, "What Is Antitrust Anyway?" *Art and Auction* (October 1997), 135.

45. Ibid.

46. *Business Practices Act*, R.S.O. 1990, c. B. 18.

47. *Criminal Code*, R.S.C. 1985, c. C-46.

48. *New York City Administrative Code. Auctioneer Rules*, title 20, chap. 2, subchap. 13.

49. The rules are as follows: When referring to "objects," the law may be construed to mean one-of-a-kind items, such as art objects.

50. The artist/dealer relationship is, however, largely outside the purview of this book.

51. See chapter 8, "Taxation," for appraisal requirements by tax authorities for donation purposes.

52. *Serra v. United States Gen. Servs. Admin.*, 667 F. Supp. 1042 (S.D.N.Y. 1987), aff'd, 847 F. 2d 1045 (2d Cir. 1988). See also *Serra v. United States Gen. Servs. Admin.*, 664 F. Supp. 798 (S.D.N.Y. 1987).

53. *California Art Preservation Act*, California Civil Code, sec. 987 (West 1982 and Supp. 1997).

54. *Federal Visual Artists Rights Act of 1990*, 17. U.S.C.A. S. 101 ff. (West 1996 and Supp. 1997).

· 6 ·

Copyright

Copyright is an intellectual-property right. (Intellectual property also includes patents, trademarks, industrial designs, and design patents.) A right created by the intellect is distinguished from a personal property or a real-property right. Real-property rights relate to ownership of the object or property. Personal-property rights are the rights to reproduce that personal property—copyright is distinct from ownership of the material object in which the copyright is embedded. Transfer of the object itself does not ordinarily transfer any right of copyright in that object.

Copyright gives creators protection and control of their creations and of the various rights that flow from such creations: control of reproduction rights, exhibition rights, and the right to royalties. Moral rights may also flow from copyright; they comprise the right to be known as the author of the work and the right to prevent the work from being altered or mutilated (and, in Canada, used in association with a product or service) to the prejudice of the honor or reputation of the artist.

What is copyright? Who owns copyright, and for how long? How does one get copyright? Can one lose copyright? What rights flow from it? Can these rights be valued? If so, on what basis? These are some of the significant questions that will be dealt with in this chapter.

WHAT IS COPYRIGHT?

Essentially, copyright is a monopoly, usually in favor of the creator; it applies to works that are original, dramatic, musical, literary, or artistic. The artist's original idea must be fixed in a tangible form or medium of expression, for example, writing, drawing, painting, sculpture, or musical score. Copyright protects that expression of the idea, not the idea itself. Thus, it is the content of paintings, drawings, sculptures, photographs, motion pictures, maps, CD-ROMs, digital video disks, videos, toys, fabric design, and original decorative objects that is protected.

Canada, the United States, and Mexico all are members of the Berne Convention for the Protection of Literary and Artistic Works,[1] the international convention on copyright. Each has a copyright act (or a copyright revision act) implementing the provisions of the Berne Convention. Under these copyright acts, copyright protection is available to a creator domiciled within the country and also to a citizen or subject of, or a person ordinarily resident in, a treaty country. In the case of a published work, if the country of first publication was a treaty country at the time of publication, it too is protected.

In accordance with the Berne Convention, in Canada and Mexico the sale of an object occurs without the transfer of copyright unless specifically provided by the artist.

Prior to the 1976 revision of the U.S. Copyright Act (which went into effect January 1, 1978),[2] the transfer of an object without a mention of copyright interest in the conveyance led to a presumption in law that the purchaser obtained any existing copyright in the object as well as the right to possess the object itself. Under the revision, this presumption was reversed.

RIGHTS OF THE COPYRIGHT HOLDER

Generally the copyright holder has the sole right to produce or reproduce the work, or any substantial part thereof, in any material form. The copyright owner also has the right to adapt, to distribute, to perform, and to display the work. For instance, an artist who owns copyright in his or her work can control its reproduction in photographs, books, videos, TV, film, CD-ROM, and any other means of reproduction, as well as its reproduction on clothing, jewelry, or other merchandise.

Generally speaking, in both Canada and the United States, the first owner of copyright is the creator. However, there are exceptions to this rule:

1. When the work has been created by a full-time employee in an employee/employer situation, the employer would own copyright. It is sometimes difficult to determine whether there is an employment relationship or the creator is a freelance or independent contractor. In the latter case, the contractor would ordinarily own the copyright. It is sometimes also difficult to determine whether an employee made an original work within the scope of the employee's employment. If so, the copyright belongs to the employer. If not, it belongs to the employee, especially if made after hours.

2. In the United States, commissioned works for uses prescribed by statute and expressly agreed to in writing by the parties are considered to be works made for hire. In such a case, the commissioner owns copyright in the work. There are nine categories of such commissioned works, including contributions to collective works, parts of motion pictures or other audio-video works, atlases, etc. It should be noted, however, that under U.S. law, a commissioned portrait is not a work made for hire.

3. In Canada, the exceptions to the creator being the first owner of copyright include the above employee-employer relationship and the following:

   a. If the work has been created for Her Majesty the Queen by a province or the federal government or any agency of either, the Crown owns the copyright. This is an important exception, as it affects independent artists who do work for federal or provincial governments, national museums, and Crown agencies. (Copyright on the work of employee artists is already owned by these entities.)

   b. The commissioner owns the copyright on certain commissioned works, including graphics and fine art graphics, portraits, and photographs, unless there is an agreement to the contrary.[3]

It is possible for the owner of copyright to sell or rent the copyright. The sale, which is called *assignment,* must be in writing and must name the parties, disclose the original work in which the copyright is being sold or rented, and include the price to be paid.

Copyright is rented by way of license. A license may be for different purposes, time periods, and geographic areas. For instance, an artist may license the reproduction of a painting for poster use in North America, for a book cover in Europe, and for a calendar in Japan. All these rights may be licensed for different time periods under different financial arrangements. Any such exclusive license must be in writing. Thus the Copyright Act permits fragmentation of the copyright.

TERM OF THE COPYRIGHT

Under the 1976 U.S. Copyright Act, the term of copyright was for the life of the creator plus fifty years. In 1998, the duration of copyrights in the United States was lengthened by an additional twenty years by the Sonny Bono Copyright Term Extension Act signed by President Bill Clinton on October 27, 1998, and named in memory of the late Congressman Sonny Bono, who was part of the performing duo "Sonny and Cher." This extended term of seventy years after death was earlier instituted in the European Union countries and applies to non-European works only as long as they are protected by copyright in their own countries of origin. Thus, if the

United States had not passed this twenty-year extension, American works would enter the public domain in Europe upon the expiration of the fifty-year term after death. Now they will be protected in Europe as well as the United States for an additional twenty years.

When a work is "prepared by two or more authors with the intention that their contributions be merged into inseparable or interdependent parts of a unitary whole,"[4] the resulting *joint copyright* exists for the life of the last surviving author plus seventy years. This extension is available for works created since 1978 by natural identified authors. The Sonny Bono Act adds twenty years to the duration of works created prior to 1978 by extending the renewal term of those works to sixty-seven years from the old forty-seven years, thus making the total duration of the copyright term ninety-five years rather than the old seventy-five years. Similarly, copyright for works created before 1978 but not published or registered until 1978 or later will now last through the year 2047 and must be published by the end of 2002 or the copyright will expire at the end of that year. For works unpublished from and after 1978, the duration of copyright is now 120 years from creation rather than the old 100 years from creation. Alternative terms apply for works for hire and works of unknown authors (95 years from first publication or 120 years from creation, whichever is longer).[5]

In Canada, if the copyright is owned by Her Majesty the Queen, its term is fifty years (Section 12). Also, if a corporation other than one owned or controlled by the artist/creator owns the copyright in photographs, the term of copyright in those photographs is fifty years (Section 10).

Until recently, Canada provided a fifty-year term of copyright from the post-humous publication of any work. In 1997, this was changed to a term of fifty years from the end of the calendar year in which the creator died, regardless of when or if the work was published after the death of the author. Canada has not yet extended this term to seventy years.

Mexico, by a law of December 5, 1996, as amended, increased copyright protection from the life of the creator plus fifty years thereafter to the life of the creator plus seventy-five years thereafter. For works published posthumously, the term is for seventy-five years after publication.[6]

GETTING COPYRIGHT

Copyright is given automatically to the creator in all Berne Convention countries on the expression of an original work of art (music, literary work, or drama, as defined in the acts). This copyright exists from the moment of creation. Neither registration nor the use of the copyright symbol (©) or the word *copyright* is needed to secure copyright.

However, in the United States, this applies only to works publicly distributed with the authority of the copyright holder after the adoption of the Berne Convention Implementation Act.[7] This act became effective March 1, 1989. Works distributed in public prior to that date required a copyright notice.[8]

Nonetheless, often it is recommended that a creator place a notice of copyright on the work in a place that is conspicuous but that does not alter the image of the work. The usual notice would comprise the word *copyright* and/or the copyright symbol (©), the year of the work's first publication, and the name of the owner of the copyright. Placing the copyright information on the object will prevent any infringer from claiming to be innocent of infringement and thus reduce or avoid damages.

ARCHITECTURAL WORK

Under the Mexican and Canadian Copyright Acts, architectural works are protected. In the United States, a separate act called the Architectural Works Copyright Protection Act provides copyright protection for the life of the creator plus fifty years (extended now to seventy years) on all architectural works created on or after December 1, 1990. Architectural work is defined as a design of a building as embodied in any tangible medium of expression, including a building, architectural plans, or drawings. Architectural work includes the overall form as well as the arrangement and composition of spaces and elements in the design but does not include individual standard features.[9]

There is a specific exemption in the Copyright Acts of Canada and the United States to permit the distribution or display of paintings, photographs, or other works of art, including engravings that are not architectural drawings or plans of public buildings and architectural works.[10]

Neither the author nor the copyright owner of an architectural work may prevent the owner of the building from altering or destroying it.[11]

The Canadian act permits the making or publishing of paintings, drawings, engravings, photographs, or cinematography of a work of sculpture or artistic craftsmanship if permanently situated in a public place or building. (The issue then is to determine what is a "public" place.)

The term of the copyright under the U.S. act is for the life of the creator plus seventy years if the creator of the protected, constructed architectural work died in 1990 or thereafter.

PUBLIC DOMAIN

It is not an infringement for someone to copy a work that is in the public domain. Copyright falls into the public domain after the term of the copyright is complete. In countries that belong only to the Universal Copyright Convention[12] (a convention that requires specific formalities to be followed for copyright protection), if the formalities of the convention are not followed (that is, copyright is not registered or the copyright notice, year of publication, and name of the copyright owner are not placed on the work or in a conspicuous place), the copyright may fall immediately into the public domain.[13] Also, facts are public domain by their very nature, and not copyrightable. However, the expression of facts, if original within the meaning of the Copyright Act, is copyrightable.

Photography of Public Domain Art

A landmark case under the prior act dealing with the formalities required to protect a work of art—in this instance, the famous Pablo Picasso Public Sculpture installed on the Plaza of the Civic Centre in the City of Chicago—is the case of *"The Letter Edged in Black Press" Inc. v. Public Building Commission.*[14]

Picasso created a maquette (model) of the proposed Chicago sculpture. There was no copyright notice on the work. An aluminum model of the design with some slight revisions was prepared as a guide for the construction of the sculpture and was approved by Picasso from a photograph of that model. Though offered $100,000 for the work, Picasso refused the sum, as he wished to donate the work to the city of Chicago, which he did by way of a deed of gift that included the maquette and the right to create the monumental sculpture for the Civic Centre. He also gave the Public Building Commission the right to reproduce the work. As part of the campaign to raise funds for the work, the maquette was placed on public exhibition at the Chicago Art Institute. No copyright notice was affixed to the maquette. The following notice was, however, posted in the Art Institute: "The rights of reproduction are the property of the Public Building Commission of Chicago. © 1966. All Rights Reserved."[15]

Press photographers attended the showing at the invitation of the commission and the Art Institute, which later published pictures of the maquette and the aluminum model in Chicago newspapers and magazines with national and international circulations. In addition, the commission supplied photographs of the maquette and the uncopyrighted architect's aluminum model to members of the public who requested them for publication.

The second showing took place when the U.S. Steel Corporation, with the knowledge of the commission, completed a 12½-foot wooden model of the sculpture and invited the press to photograph it. There was no copyright notice on this model, and the pictures were published for both publicity and for articles in various magazines, all without any copyright notice.

Later the maquette was displayed at the Tate Gallery in London and in a catalog published by it with a picture of the maquette. Neither on the maquette nor on the photograph in the catalog did any copyright notice appear.

On August 15, 1967, the actual completed monumental sculpture was dedicated in ceremonies on the Civic Centre Plaza. The sculpture itself bore the following copyright "©1967 PUBLIC BUILDING COMMISSION OF CHICAGO ALL RIGHTS RESERVED."

In conjunction with the dedication, a commemorative souvenir booklet of "The Chicago Picasso" dedication ceremonies was prepared by the commission. This booklet contained drawings from photographs of the maquette and the aluminum model and was distributed to ninety-six honored guests. Neither the booklet nor the photographs shown therein bore any copyright notice. Also, on the day of dedication, the U.S. Steel Public Relations Office sent out a press release and a photograph of the monumental sculpture. The photograph bore no copyright notice.

Subsequent to the dedication, the Art Institute published its annual report containing an uncopyrighted picture of the maquette. It also continued selling a photograph of the maquette on a postcard, many copies of which were sold. Thereafter, however, the commission asked the Art Institute to stop selling the postcard, and the Art Institute complied with this request.

The commission later stated its policy that no individuals should be restricted from full personal enjoyment of the sculpture, including the right to take photographs and make paintings, etchings, and models of the same for personal, noncommercial purposes. The commission also had a policy of granting licenses to copy the sculpture for commercial purposes for a nominal fee and a royalty on copies sold.

Finally, on January 12, 1968, the Public Building Commission filed its application with the registrar of copyright requesting copyright on the monumental sculpture entitled "The Chicago Picasso." In due course, the certificate of copyright registration was issued to the Public Building Commission.

The plaintiff, the Letter Edged in Black Press Inc., sought a declaratory judgment invalidating the copyright of the defendant, The Public Building Commission. The plaintiff was a publisher who desired to market a copy of the sculpture, maintaining that the defendant's copyright was invalid because the sculpture was in the public domain. The defendant, the Public Building Commission, asserted that "The Chicago Picasso" had never been in the public domain. It submitted that the attaching of the notice to the monumental sculpture and a later registration of the copyright were sufficient to obtain a statutory copyright.

The plaintiff, however, took the position that any attempt to establish a statutory copyright must fail if "The Chicago Picasso" was in the public domain prior to the copyright notice being placed on the monumental sculpture and that such a conclusion is inescapable given the statutory admonition of 17 U.S.C. § 8 that "no copyright shall subsist in the original text of any work which is in the public domain."

In order to determine how a work comes to be in the public domain, the court found it necessary to explore the basis of copyright protection. It concluded that the common-law copyright arises on the creation of any work of art and protects against unauthorized copying and publishing. The common-law copyright is terminated, however, by publication of the work by the proprietor of the copyright. On termination of the common-law copyright, the work falls into the public domain if statutory protection is not obtained by the giving of the requisite notice. In the United States, a common-law copyright is terminated upon the first publication.

An exception to this rule is that a limited publication does not divest the holder of his or her common-law protection, and generally a limited communication is one where the contents of the copyrighted material is communicated to a definite select group and for a limited purpose without the right of reproduction, distribution, or sale.

In applying the general principles of copyright law to the facts of the case, the court was persuaded that the copyright to the work known as "The Chicago Picasso" was invalid. It determined that general publication occurred without the requisite notice, and therefore, the common-law protection was lost on publication and the work was thrust into the public domain.

The court found that when the maquette was published without the statutory notice, Picasso's work was forever lost to the public domain. When the monumental sculpture was finally completed, it could not be copyrighted, for it was a mere copy (albeit on a grand scale) of the maquette, a work already in the public domain. At the time of the display of the maquette, there was no restriction on copying, no guards preventing copying, and both citizens and the press were freely allowed to photograph the maquette and publish those photographs in major newspapers and magazines.

Other defenses raised were also set aside by the court, including one of "fair use" as well as a defense that the publication of pictures of the models constituted an infringement. The court made short shrift of this defense on the basis that instead of objecting to uncopyrighted publication, the commission itself disregarded its own instructions, did not object to the uncopyrighted publications, and in some cases actively engaged in the distribution of the uncopyrighted pictures promoting "The Chicago Picasso."

A New York federal judge recently dismissed a case brought by the Bridgeman Art Library, Ltd., which claimed to have exclusive rights in photographic transparencies of a substantial number of well-known works of art located in museums around the world.[16] Bridgeman transformed those transparencies into digital images in which Bridgeman also claimed exclusive rights.

Bridgeman contended that the defendant, Corel Corporation, was marketing compact discs in the United States and abroad that contained digital images of a significant number of the same works of art that Bridgeman claimed must have been copied from its transparencies. Bridgeman alleged that Corel was thus infringing on Bridgeman's copyrights in the United States, the United Kingdom, and Canada. Bridgeman also claimed that this conduct was a violation of the Lanham Act and also was actionable at common law.

Bridgeman was in the business of acquiring rights to market reproductions of public domain works of art owned by museums and other collections. It obtained these rights either from the owners of the underlying works of art or freelance photographers it hired. It maintained a library of these reproductions in the form of large-format colored transparencies and digital files.

Bridgeman also attached a color correction strip to each transparency to ensure that the image was a genuine reflection of the original work as it existed in the circumstances in which it was photographed. The photographer attested that the photographs were authored by him or her and that the photographer had a copyright in the photographs. The photographer then assigned the copyright to Bridgeman, which then distributed the images as transparencies and digital images on CD-ROM, which were then licensed to various clients. (Low resolution CD-ROM images generally were provided to clients of Bridgeman without charge.)

Corel is a Canadian corporation engaged chiefly in the creation and marketing of computer software products including a set of seven CD-ROMs known as "Corel Professional Photos CD-ROM Masters I-VII." The product contains seven hundred digital reproductions of well-known paintings by European masters. Corel maintained that it obtained the images for its masters from another supplier and was told that the slides were created from lithograph images owned by the supplier's president.

The court determined that the law to be applied is the law of the state with the most significant relationship to the property and the parties. The Berne Convention defined the country of origin of a particular work as the country in which the work first was published. At issue here were nearly 124 photographs produced either by the museums owning the original works of art or by freelance photographers employed by Bridgeman, which is based in the United Kingdom, where the photographs were first published. Therefore, the court concluded that the United Kingdom had the most significant relationship to the issue of copyrightability and its law would apply to the issue of copyrightability. The second element, namely the infringement, if it occurred would have been in the United States and would therefore be dealt with under United States law.

The court determined the issue of copyrightability under the British Copyright Designs and Patents Act of 1988. Using British precedent, the court stated that although it takes great skill and judgment and labor to produce a good copy of a painting, no one would reasonably contend that the copy painting or enlargement was an original artist work in which the copier is entitled to claim copyright. Skill, labor, or judgment merely in the process of copying cannot confer originality.

Result under United Kingdom Law

As a result, Bridgeman's images are not copyrightable under the United Kingdom act since they were substantially exact reproductions of public domain works, albeit in a different medium.

In respect to the argument that the color bars gave originality to the work, the court determined that there was no copying of the color bar by Corel, only of the image itself.

Also, there was no direct evidence that Corel copied the Bridgeman images.

Result under U.S. Law

The court also opined that under U.S. law the results would be the same in respect to the U.S. originality test, which requires "a distinguishable variation" between the work sought to be copyrighted and the underlying work.

Following the decision, the court was "bombarded with additional submissions." Among other grounds raised for a reargument and reconsideration was one based on an unsolicited letter from Professor William Patry, author of a copyright law treatise that argued that the court erred in applying the law of the United Kingdom to the issue of copyrightability. The plaintiff then moved for an order permitting the filing of an amicus brief by one of its associates to address the United Kingdom law issue. The court granted leave for the submission of the amicus brief and invited the parties to respond to Patry's letter.

After argument, District Judge Lewis A. Kaplan determined that U.S. law governs originality and copyrightability since the "convention makes clear that the holder of, for example, British copyright who sues for an infringement in a United States court is entitled to the same remedies as holders of the United States copyrights and, as this court previously held to the determination of infringement under the same rule of law."[17] Although there is a broad scope for copyright in photographs because "a very modest expression of personality will constitute sufficient originality,"[18] Kaplan stated, "as the Nimmers have written, there 'appear to be at least two situations in which a photograph should be denied copyright for a lack of originality'; one of which is directly relevant here: where a photograph of a photograph or other printed matter is made that amounts to nothing more than slavish copying."[19]

The judge continued, "There is little doubt that many photographs, probably the overwhelming majority, reflect at least the modest amount of originality required for copyright protection. Elements of originality…may include posing the subjects, lighting, angle, selection of film and camera, evoking the desired expression, and almost any other variant involved." But "slavish copying," although doubtless requiring technical skill and effort, does not qualify. As the U.S. Supreme Court indicated in *Feist*, "sweat of the brow" alone is not the "creative spark" that is the sine qua non of originality.[20]

Kaplan further stated,

In this case, the plaintiff by its own admission has labored to create 'slavish copies' of public domain works of art. While it may be assumed that this required both skill and effort, there was no spark of originality—indeed, the point of the exercise was to reproduce the underlying works with absolute fidelity. Copyright is not available in these circumstances.[21]

More on United Kingdom Law

The judge also determined that "While the court's conclusion as to the law governing copyrightability renders the point moot, the court is persuaded that the plaintiff's copyright claim would fail even if the governing law were that of the United Kingdom."[22]

The decision and dismissal of this claim may give stock photo agencies, art museums, and museum photography archives, which license archival materials for fees, serious future concerns as well as challenges to such user fees by third-party users.[23]

How Far Will This Case Be Extended?

Questions arise as to the extension of this decision to other copyright areas. For instance, will there be a loss of copyright for photographs of artworks not in the public domain? The same reasoning would also appear to apply to the copyright of the photographers in photographs of these works. What about photographs of public sculptures, buildings, monuments, and towers, if such photographs are exact replications of such public works and therefore determined not to be original? Will museum and photo licensing contracts have to change from contracts that charge license fees to contracts that charge for access? How binding will these agreements be on third parties? Will there now be an open season for reproduction of such material on the Internet by anyone who wishes to do so from any source whatsoever?

In respect to the creator/photographer, will it be possible to turn the photographs taken into something that is original? How original is "original"? Will a bad photograph be more original than a good photograph of the artwork or public work? These are just some of the questions that arise as a result of this decision.

INFRINGEMENT

There is an infringement of the rights of the owner of the copyright if, without permission of the owner, one does something only the owner is permitted to do, for example, produce or reproduce the work or any substantial part thereof in any material form. It is not an infringement if something less than a substantial part of the work is taken.

Other relevant exceptions to the rights of the copyright owner include:

1. "fair dealing" for private-study research, criticism, review, or newspaper summary in Canada and "fair use" in the United States for similar and broader purposes;
2. a creator who no longer owns copyright can make use of the sketch, model, cast, or plan if he or she does not repeat or imitate the main design of the original work.

Fair Use

Under the United States Copyright Act, guidelines have been set out to determine fair use:

1. the purpose and character of the use (including whether the use is of a commercial nature or is for not-for-profit educational purposes);
2. the nature of the copyrighted work;
3. the amount and substantiality of the portion used in relation to the work as a whole; and
4. the effect of the use on the potential market for the original work.

Remedies for Infringement

Both civil and criminal penalties are provided for breach of copyright. All remedies available in normal civil cases are available for breach of copyright, including interim injunctions, injunctions, and damages. The innocent infringer, however, is not subject to a claim for damages but only to an injunction to prevent the infringement from continuing.

Recent cases in the United States involving the sculptor Jeff Koons outline some of the copyright issues and difficulties for artists.[24] Koons was held liable for copyright infringement three times, each in connection with sculptures created by him for a 1988 exhibition entitled "Banality Show" that took place at the Sonnabend Gallery in New York.

Jeff Koons is part of the "pop art" movement, raising everyday objects of popular culture to high art through recontextualization, thereby showing the banality of present-day society in North America.

The first case involved a Koons sculpture of polychromed wood called *String of Puppies*. It was a sculptural version of a photograph by Art Rogers of Jim and Mary Scanlon and their eight puppies. The photograph had been published in a local newspaper and then exhibited in a museum and reproduced as a note card.

The photographer, Rogers, sued Jeff Koons and the gallery for breach of copyright in his photograph. Koons admitted at trial that the source of his sculpture, *String of Puppies*, was the note card reproduced from Rogers' photograph. He also admitted that he had directed his workers to carve the sculpture to copy the photograph. Four such sculptures were made by Koons; three had been sold for a total of $367,000 and the fourth was still owned by Koons.

The district court found that the sculptures infringed the Rogers photograph and entered a permanent injunction barring Koons and the gallery from selling any works or derivative works based on the photograph. It also required that Koons deliver up all infringing articles to Rogers, including the fourth sculpture.

Koons had alleged that the photograph by Rogers was not original and, therefore, could not be protected under copyright. The trial judge, however, observed that the elements of originality in a photograph may include "posing the subjects, lighting, angle, selection of film and camera, evoking the desired expression, and almost any other variant involved." Rogers had posed the group for the photograph and had taken and printed the picture. His work was sufficient to meet the concept of originality under the Copyright Act; he therefore had a valid copyright in the photograph. There was direct evidence of copying by Koons' own admission, and the court held that his sculpture was substantially similar to the copyrighted work.

The judge held that there was no copyright protection of an idea, in this case the idea of a couple seated on the bench with eight puppies. However, there was protection for Rogers' expression of the idea "as caught in the placement, in the particular light, and in the expression of the subjects…that gives the photograph its charming and unique character."[25] The court held that Koons had used the identical expression of the idea created by Rogers.

The court rejected Koons' defense of fair use, i.e., that his sculpture was a satire or parody of society at large, which would entitle the user to a more extensive use of the copied work than is ordinarily allowed. The judge determined that the sculpture was not a parody of the photograph, as the photograph was not the object of the alleged parody. Rather, the original content of the photograph was taken, not an imitation or parody of Rogers' style.

The court determined that Koons' copying of the photograph was done in bad faith and primarily for profit. Therefore, in addition to Koons giving up the infringed materials, Rogers would have the right to damages. In view of Koons' willful behavior in copying the work, Rogers might also seek statutory damages in lieu of, and greater than, an award of actual damages and apportioned profits.

Koons was successfully sued in two other cases. The first was brought by United Features Syndicates for breach of copyright in the "Garfield" comic strip character, "Odie."[26] In Koons' sculpture *Wild Boy and Puppy*, the puppy was virtually identical to Odie. Koons admitted copying the Garfield comic. Again, the court rejected his defense of fair use, applying the same analysis as in *Rogers v. Koons*.

The third case was brought by Barbara Campbell, a photographer who alleged that her photograph *Boys with Pig* was infringed by Koons' sculpture *Ushering in Banality*, which was based on the photographic composition by Campbell.[27] The court rejected the fair-use defense, and found that the case was substantially identical to *Rogers v. Koons*.

It is interesting to note that in the *Rogers* case, the judge commented that

> the copying was so deliberate as to suggest that the defendants [Koons and the gallery] resolved so long as they were significant players in the art business, and the copies they produced bettered the price of the copied works by one thousand to one, their piracy of a less well-known artist's work would escape being sullied by an accusation of plagiarism.[28]

This, the court held, is not to be permitted. Thus, copyright exists in an original work of a creator irrespective of whether the creator is well-known. Copyright has the same protection for unknowns as for works created by art "superstars."[29]

Sometimes the threat of a copyright action is sufficient to stop an infringement. For instance, Canada's national newspaper, *The Globe and Mail*, reported on October 4, 1995:

> WINNIPEG—Local bakers call it goofy. But most of them say they'll abide by an order from Walt Disney Co. not to use images such as Mickey Mouse on birthday cakes. Disney has threatened to take legal action against any bakery that uses its characters without permission. Bakers were told of the order last week by phone and through the newsletter of the Retail Bakers Association of America, said Ignazio Scaletta, manager of Goodies Bake Shop in Winnipeg. "We're not going to make the cakes any more. I don't want to face a legal tort, pardon the pun." Disney spokesman Chuck Champlin said the

company is attempting to protect its copyright. "It's not like we're sending out storm troopers." He said only bakeries that have bought cake pans sanctioned by Disney can legally use its images.[30]

REGISTRATION OF COPYRIGHTS

Neither registration nor a copyright notice is now required to protect copyright in the United States for original works publicly distributed, by authority of the copyright holder, on or after March 1, 1989 (when the U.S. Berne Convention Implementation Act of 1988 took effect).

U.S. Law

Recording and registration are prerequisites to infringement suits except for actions for infringement of copyright in Berne Convention works whose country of origin is not the United States. (This would exempt Canada and Mexico from registration requirements.) The copyright owner must register the work and record any transfer as a condition of bringing or continuing an infringement suit.

RESALE RIGHTS: DROIT DE SUITE

The *droit de suite* (resale rights) is intended to allow an artist to participate in any appreciation in the value of his or her works on resale. The concept was established in France, where the right applies for the lifetime of the artist plus fifty years.

Germany followed the French model by giving the artist a designated percentage of the resale price. In Italy, the artist receives a percentage of the difference between the seller's purchase price and the resale price when the work is sold at a gain. This system is confusing and difficult to enforce.

The European Union has been negotiating with member states to have a unified system of *droit de suite* that would require a resale royalty right throughout the union available to artists during their lifetime plus seventy years thereafter. (As previously noted, in the European Union countries as well as the United States, copyright now runs for the life of the artist plus seventy years.) Various art dealers in Paris and London have denounced this proposal. They fear this new concept would drive the contemporary art market out of Europe because it would be expensive for Britain and France. (The proposed rates represent an increase over France's existing 3 percent *droit de suite*.) Moreover, they argue that these resale rights ultimately benefit the famous and wealthy artists whose works make up a majority of the works resold and very little would get into the hands of less well-known artists.

Alhough resale rights have been debated from time to time in Canada, no such rights have been added either to the Copyright Act or to any specific federal or provincial statutes. In Mexico, no resale rights are provided under the Copyright Act or in other statutes.

In the United States, there are no resale rights provided under the Copyright Act or under any federal statutes. Various states, including New York, have from time to time introduced resale royalty bills; but only California has passed a re-sale-right statute.[31] Various artists from time to time create contracts with a purchaser giving the artist resale rights in the event of the resale of the work by the purchaser. However, these contracts are generally binding or enforceable only on the parties to the contract.

California Resale Royalties Act[32]

The California Resale Royalties Act provides that when a work of fine art is sold and the seller resides in California or the sale takes place in California, the seller or the seller's agent shall pay to the artist or to the artist's agent five percent of the sale price (Section 986[a]). Note that the five percent is on the amount of the sale, not on the amount of the increased value of the work. The artist may waive this right only by a contract in writing that provides for an amount in excess of five percent, but the artist may not waive any rights below five percent. The artist may assign the right to collect the royalty to another entity or individual. Upon the death of the artist, the rights and duties inure to the heirs of the artist for twenty years from the date of death (Subsection 7).

When a work of fine art is sold at auction or by a gallery, dealer, broker, museum, or other person acting as agent for the seller, the agent must withhold the five percent, locate the artist, and pay it to the artist (Section 986[a][1]). If the seller or agent is unable to locate and pay the artist within ninety days, an amount equal to five percent of the amount of the sale is transferred to the Arts Council (Subsection 2).

If the five percent is not paid as above noted, the artist may bring an action for damages within three years after the date of sale or within one year after the date of discovery of the sale, whichever is longer (Subsection 3). The prevailing party in the action shall be entitled to reasonable lawyer's fees to be determined by the court.

The Arts Council has a duty to attempt to locate any artist for whom it has received money. If the artist cannot be located or does not file a written claim for the money within seven years of the date of the sale, the right of the artist termi-nates, and the money is transferred to the council for use in acquiring fine art pursuant to the Art and Public Buildings Program (Subsection 5).

Any money held by a seller or agent as a resale payment for an artist is exempt from enforcement of a money judgment by the creditors of the seller or agent (Subsection 6). Thus the funds are fully available to the artist and are not subject to the creditors of the vendor.

The five percent holdback does not apply

1. to the initial sale of a work, if legal title to the work was vested in the artist;
2. to a resale of a work for a gross sale price of less than $1,000;
3. to a transfer of a work exchanged for one or more other works or for a combina-tion of cash, other property, and one or more works, if the fair-market value of the property exchanged is less than $1,000;
4. to a resale after the death of the artist, other than as above provided;
5. to the resale of a work for a gross sale price less than the purchase price paid by the seller;
6. to the resale of a work by dealer to a purchaser within ten years of the initial sale of the work by the artist to an art dealer, providing all intervening resales are between art dealers; or
7. to a sale of a work of stained glass if the work has been permanently attached to real property and is sold as part of that property (Subsection [b] 1-7).

An *artist* is defined as a person who creates a work of fine art and who, at the time of the resale, is a citizen of the United States or has been a resident of Califor-nia for a minimum of two years (Subsection C[1]). *Fine art* is defined as an original painting, sculpture, drawing, or work of art in glass (Subsection C[2]).

NAFTA AND INTELLECTUAL PROPERTY

The North American Free Trade Agreement (NAFTA)[33] (Chapter XVII) requires members to guarantee that their nation's laws will include the defense of intellectual property and procedures as well as remedies to prevent present and future breaches of copyright and intellectual-property rights.

The defenses required by NAFTA include civil and criminal penalties and enforcement of intellectual-property rights at the border of the country. It also requires internal enforcement of copyright owned by foreigners, to prevent black-market and bootlegged products violating the copyright of the creator.

NAFTA put pressure on Mexico to establish and enforce intellectual-property rights for foreign nationals, especially those of NAFTA members. As a result of joining NAFTA, Mexico passed the Industrial Property Law[34] (*ley de propiedad industrial*) in 1991 and the Federal Copyright Law[35] (*ley federal del Derecho de autor*) in December 1996. Two institutes were created: the Institute of Industrial Property, an agency within the Ministry of Commerce and Industrial Promotion, and the National Copyright Institute, a government agency reporting to the Ministry of Education. Mexico now pays greater attention to the protection and enforcement of copyright as required under NAFTA.

Under NAFTA, each party shall enforce the intellectual-property rights of the nationals of another party, at least to the extent of giving effect to the substantive provisions of the Berne Convention (Article 17.01). If a party to NAFTA has not acceded to the specified text of any such provisions on or before the date of entry into force of the NAFTA agreement, it shall make every effort to accede.

"Each party shall accord to nationals of any party treatment no less favorable than that it accords to its own nationals with regard to the protection and enforcement of all intellectual-property rights [Article 1703(1)]. No party may, as a condition of according such national treatment, require rightholders to comply with any formalities or conditions in order to acquire rights in respect of copyright and related rights [Article 1703(2)]—for example, filing or registration is not required to obtain copyright."

However, the party may vary from this in relation to its judicial and administrative procedures for protection or enforcement of intellectual-property rights. This includes any procedure that requires a national of another party to designate for service of process an address in the party's home territory or to appoint an agent in the party's home territory, as long as such variance is consistent with the relevant convention, is necessary to secure compliance with measures not inconsistent with this chapter of the act, and is not applicable to a matter that would constitute a disguised restriction on trade (Article 1703[3]).

Each party is specifically required to protect works covered by Article 2 of the Berne Convention,

> including any other works that embody original expression within the meaning of that convention (Article 1705[1]). Each party also shall pursuant to article 1705(2) provide to authors and their successors in interest those rights enumerated in the Berne Convention in respect to works covered by paragraph 1, including the right to authorize or prohibit
>
> a. the importation into a party's territory copies of the work made without the rightholder's authorization;
> b. the first public distribution of the original and each copy of the work by sale, rental, or otherwise; and
> c. the communication of the work to the public.

This article also deals with computer programs.

Each party shall provide (Article 1705[3]) that, for copyright and related rights,

a. any person acquiring or holding economic rights may freely and separately transfer such rights by contract for purposes of their exploitation and enjoyment by the transferee; and
b. any person acquiring or holding such economic rights by virtue of a contract, including contracts of employment underlying the creation of the works and sound recordings, shall be able to exercise those rights in his or her own name and enjoy fully the benefits derived from those rights.

If the time frame for protection for a work other than a photographic work or work of applied art is other than the natural life of a person, then the term shall be no less than fifty years from the end of the calendar year in which the first authorized publication of the work took place or, failing such authorized publication taking place within fifty years from the making of the work, fifty years from the end of the calendar year of its making (Article 1705[4]).

Canada, the United States, and Mexico have all acceded to the NAFTA requirements as they relate to copyright, including the enforcement of these rights. (Effective action must be taken against any act of infringement of intellectual-property rights [Article 1714]; such procedures are to be fair and equitable, and both civil and criminal penalties are to be provided.)

Each party will also adopt procedures to enable a rightholder who has valid grounds for suspecting the possible importation of pirated copyright goods to lodge an application in writing for the suspension by the Customs Administration of the release of any such goods into free circulation, and appropriate rights are given to the authorities for this purpose (Article 1718). Mexico was required to comply with Article 1718 within three years of the date of signing the NAFTA Agreement.

MORAL RIGHTS

Under the Berne Convention, moral rights of authors, as well as copyright, are to be protected. In Canada and in Mexico, moral rights are contained in the Copyright Act. In the United States, they are set out in the Visual Artists Rights Act.[36] That act grants the moral rights of paternity and integrity to the creator of a work of visual art. It amends the Copyright Act of 1976 to embody the moral rights provided by the Berne Convention in the context of works of visual art.

U.S. Law

The Visual Artists Rights Act was enacted in 1990 and took effect in 1991. It uses the Copyright Act as the structure from which these rights arise. It covers works of visual art, including paintings, drawings, prints, sculpture, and still photography produced for exhibition purposes. The works must exist in single copies or in a limited edition of not more than two hundred copies, consecutively numbered and signed by the artist.

Specifically excluded are posters; maps; globes; charts; technical drawings; diagrams; models; applied art; motion pictures and other audiovisual works; books; magazines; newspapers; periodicals; databases; electronic information services and publications; advertising, merchandising, promotional and packaging material; works for hire; and any work not subject to copyright protection.

Unlike the moral rights given by the Berne Convention and the copyright laws of Canada and Mexico for all creators, including creators of original literary and artistic works, the moral rights provisions of the Visual Artists Rights Act are limited to authors of works of visual art.

Moral rights in works created after 1991 exist for the lifetime of the creator only. The rights conferred by the act may not be transferred but may be waived by the author in a written instrument signed by the author identifying the work and uses to which the waiver applies (S.106A[e][i]). Works created before June 1, 1991, are dealt with differently unless as of June 1, 1991, the author was the owner of the work. (S. 106A[d][2]).

The most relevant aspects of the act for the purposes of this chapter are

1. the definition of *work of visual art* (Section 101);
2. the rights of attribution and integrity (Section 106A);
3. removal of works of visual art from buildings (Section 113);
4. preemption of state legislation (Section 301);
5. infringement actions (Section 501[a]); and
6. fair use (Section 107).

The act states that moral rights are exercisable by the author of the work of art, whether or not the author is the copyright owner (Section 603). Only the author of the work of visual arts has the moral rights conferred by the act. These rights are not available for a work for hire. The authors of a joint work of visual arts are co-owners of these rights.

The act grants to the creator the rights of attribution (that is, paternity) and integrity. Both rights, however, are subject to the fair use provisions of the Copyright Act.

Right of Attribution

This right includes

1. the right to be identified as the creator;
2. the right to prevent the use of the creator's name as author of a work not created by him or her; and
3. the right to prevent the use of the creator's name as author of a work by the creator if it has been distorted, mutilated, or modified so as to be prejudicial to the creator's honor or reputation.

Right of Integrity

This right includes

1. the right of the author to prevent any distortion, mutilation, or modification of a work of art that is prejudicial to his or her honor or reputation;
2. the right of the author to prevent any intentional or gross or negligent destruction of a work of recognized stature (this right is narrower than that provided in the Berne Convention).

The right of integrity is subject to the following exceptions:

1. a work of visual art incorporated in a building in such a way that removing the work of art from the building would cause the work's destruction, distortion, or mutilation, if the author consented to such work's installation either
   a. before June 1, 1991, or
   b. in a written instrument signed on or after June 1, 1991, by the author and the owner of the building, specifying that the installation may subject the work to destruction, distortion, or mutilation by its removal;
2. a work of visual art that can be removed from the building without causing harm, provided that the building owner either
   a. makes an unsuccessful good-faith attempt to notify the author of the work's intended removal or
   b. notifies the author, who fails to remove the work or to pay for its removal;
3. any modification of a work that is a result of the passage of time or the inherent nature of the materials;
4. any modification as a result of the conservation of the work or of the public presentation of the work, including lighting and placement, unless the modification was caused by gross negligence; and
5. various reproductions, depictions, portrayals, or other uses of the work described as an exception to the definition of "work of visual art" in the act.

A recent case, *John Carter, John Swing and John Veronis v. Helmsley-Spear Inc.*,[37] was brought under the Visual Artists Rights Act by three artists working together under the name of "Three Js" or "J x 3" to create sculptures and other works of visual art.

In 1991, they agreed to design, create, and install a sculptural work in the lobby of a building under the management of Sig Management Company in Queens, New York. The artists were granted the right to design, color, and style the work to be installed. By the contract, the management company had the right to determine the location of the parts of the artwork. The contract provided that the artists would receive credit as creators of the sculpture and artworks and would own the copyright in the works.

As the installation was being created, the artists were paid a weekly stipend by Sig and then by its successor partnership, Helmsley-Spear, Inc. While the work was under construction, the management company allegedly announced its intention to remove or materially alter the artwork. An action was then brought by the artists "to prevent any intentional distortion, mutilation, or other modification of the work that will be prejudicial to…[the creators'] honor or reputation, and any intentional distortion, mutilation, or modification of that work that is a violation of that right."[38]

After reviewing the provisions of the act, the judge noted that the artwork at issue consisted of a "number of sculptural elements including artwork attached to the ceiling and the floor; interactive art; a vast mosaic covering the majority of the floor and portions of the walls, several sculptural elements, and the interior of three elevators that opened into the lobby."[39] With the exception of certain items, such as a building directory and the entrance steps, the lobby installation was held to be a single work of art whose elements were interrelated.

The judge determined that the artists were independent contractors and that this was not a work for hire, which would be excepted under the act. He also found that the artists possessed honor and reputation worthy of protection, which would be damaged if the work were destroyed, modified, or mutilated. He accepted the testimony of expert witnesses that the work was of recognized stature.

The artists were entitled to a permanent injunction (having earlier received an interim or preliminary injunction) prohibiting Helmsley-Spear Inc. from distorting, mutilating, or modifying the work. The artists demonstrated that removing the work would result in "distortion, mutilation, or modification" because elements of the work could not be removed without being destroyed. The court also enjoined Helmsley-Spear Inc. from destroying the work.

The artists also raised a copyright-infringement claim. However, the court noted that registration, although not a prerequisite to copyright protection under the Copyright Act, was a prerequisite to bringing an action for infringement. The artists never obtained nor sought to register copyright in their work; therefore, the court did not have jurisdiction to decide the infringement claim.

The statute did not give the artists the right to complete or engage in further work on the installation, and Helmsley-Spear Inc. refused to permit the artists to finish the work. That refusal, the court held, did not constitute distortion, mutilation, or other modification. As a result, Helmsley-Spear Inc. was prevented by this preliminary injunction from taking any action to "alter, deface, modify, or mutilate the sculptures and installations at issue," but the artists did not have the right to enter and complete the work. This resulted in an undesirable impasse.

On appeal to the Court of Appeals for the Second Circuit, the court reversed and vacated the grant of the injunction to the plaintiffs and affirmed the dismissal by the district court of the plaintiffs' other claims as well as the dismissal of the defendant's counterclaim for waste. The court decided that there was more than sufficient evidence to demonstrate that the artists were employees, and the sculpture was therefore a work 'made for hire' as a matter of law, and therefore was not protected under the Visual Artists Rights Act since works made for hire are excluded from the operation of the act.

Moreover, because the sculpture was not protected by the Visual Artists Rights Act from removal resulting in its destruction or alteration, the court did not address the plaintiffs' contention that the act entitled them to complete the unfinished portion of the artwork and that they were entitled to reasonable costs and attorney's fees. The court also did not deal with the claim of the artists that the appellants tortuously interfered with the artists' contract with Sig and the limited partnership.

In the case of *Martin v. City of Indianapolis,*[40] the federal district court held that the city of Indianapolis violated the rights of artist Jan Randolph Martin by destroying his large outdoor stainless steel sculpture. The case confirmed that the act and the right of integrity provided him the right of the author to prevent any destruction of the work of recognized stature, and any intentional or grossly negligent destruction of that work is a violation of that right and it is actionable unless covered by specific exception under the act. Since the city destroyed the work, the only remedy available to the artist was a claim in damages for an amount to be determined by the parties or settled by further litigation.

State Legislation

Various American states have proclaimed moral-rights legislation. They include New York, with the New York Authorship Rights Act,[41] and California, with the California Art Preservation Act.[42] In all, at least thirteen states have some form of moral-rights legislation. These acts coexist with the federal act; in case of conflict, they are preempted by the federal act. (The provisions of the California statute served as models for the federal act.)

New York Authorship Rights Act

The New York act covers works of fine art, including paintings, sculptures, drawings, and works of graphic art and print. The act prohibits a person other than the artist or one acting with the permission of the artist from the knowing display in a public place of a work of fine art or a limited-edition multiple of not more than three hundred copies or a reproduction thereof, in an altered, defaced, mutilated, or modified form, if that work is displayed as the work of the artist and if damage to the artist's reputation is likely to result (Section 1403). There is a three-year limitation period on any action to be brought by an artist.

In a relevant case, the artist Phillip Pavia had been commissioned to create a sculpture for the lobby of the Hilton Hotel in New York City.[43] The sculpture comprised three large, standing forms and one smaller form lying on its side. In 1988, the work was removed from the lobby, and two of its four sections were redisplayed at a parking garage on the Avenue of the Americas in New York City. All this was done without the knowledge or consent of Pavia.

Once he became aware of what had happened, he brought an action against the owners of the Hilton Hotel and of the parking garage, alleging that they violated the New York Arts and Cultural Affairs Law as well as the federal Visual Artists Rights Act. The defendants brought a motion to dismiss the action. The trial judge dismissed that part of the action brought under the Visual Artists Rights Act but permitted it to proceed under the New York Arts and Cultural Affairs Law for damages resulting from a display of the two sections independent of the others.[44]

The federal law does not prohibit displays but prohibits acts of distortion or of modification. In respect to the display of the work, the defendants asserted that the New York statute of limitations had run, as there is a three-year limitation period. As the sculpture was removed from the hotel in 1988 and Pavia did not bring his action until 1995, the defendants argued that the case was barred by the three-year limitation period. However, the judge reasoned that the law prohibits the display of an altered or modified work, and that each day was a new display of the work; therefore, the limitation period did not apply, and the artist could proceed with the action.

The New York State Sculpture Law

New York adopted a sculpture bill effective January 1, 1991, to provide certain essential information to buyers of sculpture produced and sold in multiples, according to the state's attorney general.[45]

The purpose of the act was to require full disclosure in the sale of sculpture, which was defined as a three-dimensional fine art object produced, fabricated, or carved in multiple from a mold, model, cast, form, or other prototype, other than in glass, that is sold, offered for sale, or consigned in, into, or from the state for an amount in excess of $1,500.

The act provides that an art merchant shall not cause a catalog, prospectus, flyer, or other written material or advertisement to be distributed in, into, or from the state, soliciting a direct sale by inviting transmittal of payment for a specific multiple, unless it clearly sets forth, in close proximity to the place in such material where the multiple is described, the descriptive information required by the act, for the appropriate time period. In lieu of this required information, such written material may be set forth in a statement sent prior to or with the delivery of the multiple to the purchaser. The act also covers multiples of prints, photographs, and objects produced in more than one copy offered for sale in excess of more than $100.

The law requires disclosure of the identity of the artist, the artist's signature, the medium, whether the multiple is a reproduction, when the multiple was produced, the use of the master that produced the multiple, and the number of multiples in the edition. Various rights are given to prospective purchasers in respect to obtaining this information from the vendor-dealer even after payment.

In respect to a sculpture, the information to be given includes the title of the sculpture, the foundry, the medium, the dimensions, the time it was produced, the number of the cast, whether it was a posthumous or lifetime cast, the use of the master, whether and how the sculpture and the edition are numbered, the size of the edition or proposed edition, and the size of any prior editions of the sculpture.

It must also detail whether any sculpture casts have been produced in excess of the stated size of the edition or proposed edition; the total number of such excess casts produced; and whether and how they are or will be numbered, according to the stated intentions of the artist, or that the artist has not disclosed either a limitation on the number or numbering of sculpture casts to be produced in excess of the stated size of the edition or proposed edition, or the total number of such excess casts produced or proposed to be produced and how they will be numbered.

Other details are required for copies of sculptures not made from the master and produced after January 1, 1991. The act permits the attorney general to bring action against violators. Anyone who engages in repeated violations of the act shall be deemed to have demonstrated the persistent fraud or illegality necessary to invoke additional penalties (Section 15.17).

Every unique sculpture produced, fabricated, or carved on or after January 1, 1991, must contain, in a clear and legible fashion and in an easily accessible location, a distinctive mark that identifies the foundry or other production facility where the sculpture was made and the year in which the sculpture was made (Section 14.05).

It is unlawful for a foundry or other production facility to fail or to refuse to affix such marks or to affix a false identifying mark or incorrect year to any sculpture produced by it. It is unlawful for any person to deface, mark over, or tamper with the identifying mark or date. It is also unlawful to produce, offer for sale, sell, or consign an unauthorized sculpture cast unless it is imprinted in a legible fashion with the words "This is a reproduction."

There are special recordkeeping rules in regard to the production and sale of sculptures after January 1, 1991, for both foundries and dealers. There are civil penalties of up to $5,000 per work that can be imposed on foundries that mislabel or fail to identify their works with both the mark of the foundry and the year the sculpture was made. There are also penalties for defacing or tampering with the foundry marks, giving rise to possible criminal prosecution and a civil fine of up to $5,000.

The act does not cover sculptures made in glass.

California Art Preservation Act[46]

California was the first American state to enact legislation dealing with moral rights. The California Civil Code deals with the preservation of works of art (Section 987). Under the act, the physical alteration or destruction of fine art that is an expression of the artist's personality is considered detrimental to the artist's reputation. Also, artists have an interest in protecting their works against any alteration or destruction, and there is a public interest in preserving the integrity of cultural and artistic creations. Fine art is defined as being "an original painting, sculpture, or drawing or an original work of art in glass of recognized quality."[47] It does not include work prepared under contract for commercial use by its purchaser.

Therefore, the act provides that no person except an artist who owns and possesses a work of art created by him or her shall intentionally commit or authorize the intentional commission of any physical defacement, mutilation, alteration, or destruction of the work. Also, no person who frames, conserves, or restores a work of fine art shall commit or authorize the commission of any defacement, mutilation, alteration, or destruction of the work by any act constituting gross negligence.

The act gives the artist the right to claim authorship and, for just and valid reason, to disclaim authorship of the work. It also gives the artist the right to protect that right by injunction, damages, and punitive damages as well as to receive reasonable attorney's fees, expert fees, and any other relief that the court may deem proper. The right exists for the lifetime of the artist plus fifty years—that is, a right of survivorship. (The New York statute is silent on the right of survivorship.) In the European Union, the term of the moral right as well as the copyright has been extended to the life of the artist plus seventy years. The right of the artist must be enforced within one year of discovery or within three years of the act complained of, whichever is later. The right may be waived but not assigned, and it must be in writing and signed by the author.

The act also deals with the removal of fine art from a building without substantial physical defacement, mutilation, or destruction of a work, in terms similar to those of the federal act.

Pursuant to this statute, the artist David Botello brought an action against the Shell Oil Company in respect to the destruction of a wall to which a mural was affixed.[48] Shell had hired Botello and others to paint the mural on the wall of a service station in East Los Angeles. The mural, called *Filling up on Ancient Energies*, covered about 1,200 square feet.

In 1988, Shell, without notifying the artist, authorized the destruction of the wall to which the mural was affixed; most of the wall was destroyed.

Botello and the other artists brought an action against Shell Oil under the California Art Preservation Act. The issue then arose as to whether a mural was a painting within the meaning of the statute. The appellate court, reversing the trial judge's ruling, determined that "a mural was a type or subset of painting, much as a rose is to flowers or a ring is to jewelry or a sonnet to poetry."[49] However, the judge noted that there still appeared to be a question as to whether the work could have been removed without damage, which would require notice to be given to the artist; if the work could not be removed without damage, the artist was deemed to have waived his rights under the statute, unless there was an expressed reservation of rights in a written, recorded instrument.

Moral Rights Statutes

Are moral rights statutes necessary? Consider the two Australian entrepreneurs who, in 1986, purchased a Picasso drawing entitled *Trois Femmes*. They cut the drawing into five hundred one-inch squares and sold each square for $135 as an original Picasso.

Or consider Kenneth Snelson, who spent two years creating a sculpture for the New York World Fair in 1964. When the fair was over, he received a telephone call from a scrap-metal dealer who had purchased the sculpture at the close of the fair. He was anxious to know what alloy had been used by Snelson in the chunks of scrap, which were all that remained of the award-winning work.

Or the case of *Crimi v. Rutgers Presbyterian Church*,[50] in which artist Alfred Crimi won a commission to paint a mural, twenty-six feet wide by thirty-five feet high, for the church. It appears that a number of the parishioners objected to the mural, feeling that Crimi's portrayal of Christ with so much of his chest bare placed more emphasis on his physical attributes than on his spiritual qualities. When the church was redecorated, the mural was painted over without notice to the artist. Upon learning what had been done, the artist brought action against the church

1. to compel the church to remove the paint from the mural; or
2. to allow Crimi to take the mural from the church at the cost and expense of the church; or
3. in the event that the mural cannot be removed, for judgment against the church for $50,000.

The artist lost on all counts. Even though the moral rights of the artist were raised, there were no U.S. statutes to protect these rights in 1949, when the case was brought, nor was the United States a signatory to the Berne Copyright Convention at that time. The court indicated that in order to have such rights, the artist would have had to reserve them at the time of the drawing of the contract with the church. As no rights in the mural were so reserved by the artist, the work became the property of the church, and all rights had been lost by the artist.

CANADIAN LAW

Moral Rights

In Canada, the moral rights of authors are covered by the Copyright Act.[51]

1. Moral rights exist independent of copyright and even after the sale of copyright. The author has the right to claim authorship of a work as well as the right to restrain any distortion, mutilation, or other modification of the work that would be prejudicial to the author's honor or reputation.
2. The author has the right of integrity to the work. This right is infringed if the work is, to the prejudice of the honor or reputation of the author, distorted, mutilated, or otherwise modified or used in connection with a product, service, cause, or institution prejudicial to the honor or reputation of the author.
3. Prejudice is deemed to have occurred as a result of any distortion, mutilation, or other modification of a painting, sculpture, or engraving. However, a change in the location of a work, the physical means by which a work is exposed, the physical structure containing the work, or steps taken in good faith to restore or

preserve the work shall not alone constitute a distortion, mutilation, or other modification of the work.

4. The author has the right, where reasonable in the circumstances, to be associated with the work as its author, by name or under a pseudonym, and also to remain anonymous.

5. Moral rights (in Canada and the United States) may not be assigned but may be waived in whole or in part. An assignment, including a licensing of copyright in a work, does not alone constitute a waiver of moral rights. Any waiver must be in writing and signed by the author.

6. The rights and remedies available for breach of copyright are also fully available for infringement of moral rights. The term of moral rights is the same as copyright, namely, the life of the author plus fifty years, and moral rights are descendable to the artist's beneficiaries and estate. (This is different from the U.S. law, under which the moral right expires on the death of the creator.)

7. Both civil penalties and criminal sanctions are available (in Canada and in the United States) for breach of moral rights, as they are for breach of copyright.

In 1979, Michael Snow, a well-known Canadian artist, was commissioned to create a hanging sculpture, called *Flight Stop,* for Toronto's Eaton Centre shopping mall. It depicted sixty Canada geese in flight, and it was hung from the ceiling under the supervision of the artist.

Later, as part of a Christmas promotion for the mall, the geese were "be-ribboned without the knowledge or consent of the plaintiff"[52]: the birds had red ribbons tied around their necks as bow ties. The sculpture was also reproduced in this fashion in posters and advertising materials as part of a Christmas sales campaign.

The artist brought an application to remove the ribbons under the Canadian Copyright Act and "in particular that part which gives the author the right to restrain any distortion, mutilation, or other modification of his work that would be prejudicial to his honor or reputation."[53]

It was conceded that the sculpture is a "work" within the meaning of the Copyright Act. The judge stated that

> the words 'prejudicial to his honor or reputation' involve a certain subjective element or judgment on the part of the author so long as it is reasonably arrived at. The plaintiff is adamant in his belief that his naturalistic composition has been made to look ridiculous by the addition of ribbons, and suggests it is like dangling earrings from the *Venus de Milo.* While the matter is not undisputed, the plaintiff's opinion is shared by a number of other well-respected artists and people knowledgeable in this field.[54]

The judge was satisfied that the ribbons did distort or modify the artist's work and that Snow's concern that this would be prejudicial to his honor or reputation was reasonable under the circumstances. The court granted the application and the injunction and forced the owners to remove the ribbons.[55]

Special Considerations: Copyright and the Valuer

A relatively recent development in Canada is the right of exhibition in favor of the artist. The Copyright Act[56] provides to the artist the sole right to "present at a public exhibition for a purpose other than sale or hire, an artistic work created after June 7, 1988, other than a map, chart, or plan." The artist generally receives a fee for each such showing.

In the event of a loss or destruction of a work, not only may the owner of the work claim a loss but the creating artist may also have a possible claim for loss of earnings from future public exhibition of the work (as well as the loss of reproduction rights fees if there are no existing transparencies or photographs of the work available for such purposes). Valuers now must consider this additional right in Canada as an additional value for works lost or destroyed, especially for insurance claims.

A further consideration in copyright arises: Is the work free of copyright protection? Can it be reproduced by others? If so, does this make the work more valuable or less valuable?

Additional concerns for the valuer are: How do you value the copyright aspect of the donated work? What parameters should be used to justify value? Is the work free of moral rights claims by the creator under the copyright acts of Canada and Mexico and free of moral rights claims under the relevant U.S. legislation? If so, does this have an impact on the value of the work? Is the copyright subject to any existing copyright licenses to third parties? What is the value of the licenses? Do the licenses restrict the sale or other uses of the copyright? These are some of the questions that must be answered by the experienced appraiser. A valuer should be familiar with international laws of copyright and moral rights, as well as local legislation. These are concerns also for insurers in loss and damage claims.

MEXICAN LAW

Copyright

In Mexico, the author is the first owner of copyright and has the right to exploit the work personally and by authorized third parties. Copyright is granted for fifteen categories of original works including pictorials, drawings, dramatic, literary, dance, comics, sculptures and plastic characters, architectural, photography, and works of applied art.

The copyright remains in force for the life of the creator plus seventy-five years. However, if there are no heirs on the death of the artist, the work enters the public domain. Posthumous works have copyright protection for seventy-five years from the date of publication. Performer and producer rights are protected as well, but only for fifty years. Proprietary rights are assignable for periods up to fifteen years only with exceptions permitted for computer programs and books. In the case of joint authors, there is protection for the lifetime of the authors plus seventy-five years from the death of the last author.

Though registration of copyright is permissive and is not required for the protection of the copyright, a proper notice of copyright must appear on the property to be protected. The phrase "derechos reservados" or the abbreviation "D.R." is required, followed by the symbol ©, together with the name and address of the owner and the first year of publication. The name and address of the publisher, the number of copies printed, and the date of completion of the printing must also appear. If these requirements are not followed, it does not destroy the copyright, but the publisher/editor may be liable.

Mexico has limitations on copyright by "fair use" or "fair dealing," permitting scientific, literary, educational, and artistic criticism exceptions.

The federal executive may restrict a copyright and authorize publication of a work in circumstances in which the work has not been available for a period of time or has been available only at a price that is prohibitive to the general public. A compulsory license can be issued and a fee set where the work is necessary or of importance for the advancement of public education or national culture when the prior consent of the copyright holder cannot be obtained.

Copyright is registered with the Public Registry of Copyright for Author's Rights and is administered by the National Institute of Author's Rights, which is in charge of the registration of copyrights for works submitted by authors, including agreements or contracts that may extinguish, transfer, or modify patrimonial rights of the author as well as powers of attorney.

Moral Rights

Moral rights are dealt with under Mexico's Copyright Act, which is a federal statute.[57]

The author is entitled to

1. recognition and protection of his or her authorship, with the right to determine publication as well as withdraw the work from commerce, and

2. the right to oppose deformations, mutilations, or modifications of his or her work and any actions detrimental to same or to the author's honor and reputation, excluding scientific, literary, or artistic criticism.

These rights are personal, perpetual, and inalienable and are not subject to the statute of limitations. They are passed to the author's heirs or testamentary beneficiaries. The works protected include literary, scientific, juridical, didactic, musical, choreographic, pictorial, architectural, photographic, and cinematographic works; computer programs; works for broadcasting and television; and any other works that, by analogy, can be regarded as artistic or intellectual productions. They must, however, be expressed in a form of writing, engraving, or other objective and durable form capable of reproduction or communication to the public.

They may not be surrendered or attached.

Rights of Foreigners

Foreigners who reside permanently or temporarily in Mexico enjoy the same rights and privileges as a Mexican national. Foreign works are protected if the author is a national of a state with which Mexico has a treaty or convention. Special rules apply to creators who are residents of nontreaty countries.

Both civil actions (including injunctive relief) and criminal penalties are available as remedies for breach of copyright in appropriate circumstances.

Under the Copyright Act, various creators' associations are permitted to represent members of a particular group, to act as a collective for fees and royalties, and to enter into contracts with foreign associations on behalf of members of their association.

Mexico signed the Inter-American Convention on Copyright and Literary Property in 1946, promulgated in 1947.[58] It ratified the Universal Copyright Convention of 1957 in 1971 and, in 1974, ratified the Act of Paris of the Berne Convention of July 24, 1971.

NOTES

1. *Berne Convention for the Protection of Literary and Artistic Works*, September 9, 1896; completed at Paris on May 4, 1896; revised at Berlin on November 13, 1908; completed at Berne on March 20, 1914; revised at Rome on June 2, 1928; revised at Brussels on June 26, 1948; revised at Stockholm on July 14, 1967; and most recently revised at Paris on July 24, 1971. The Paris Text is reprinted in Melville B. Nimmer and David Nimmer, *Nimmer on Copyright* (New York: Matthew Bender & Co., 1983), App. 27.

2. *Copyright Revision Act of 1976*, codified as amended at 17 U.S.C.A. §101 (West 1996).

3. *Canada Copyright Act*, R.S.C. 1985, chap. C-42, s. 10(2).

4. *Sonny Bono Copyright Term Extension Act*, S. 102(b) (115th Cong. 2nd Session, 1998).

5. Ibid., S. 505. See also *Entertainment Law Reporter* 20, no. 6 (November 1998): 8–9.

6. *Federal Law of Author's Rights (Ley Federal del Derechos de Autor)* D.O. 12-24-96, effective March 24, 1997, Article 19 and amendments.

7. *Berne Convention Implementation Act of 1988*, Pub. L. No. 100-568 102 Stat. 2853 (1988), Section 7(a)(4).

8. Under the *1976 U.S. Copyright Amendment Act*, the omission of the notice or an erroneous notice no longer invalidated the copyright, and it could be corrected by registration of publication within five years and the owner making a reasonable effort to add the notice to all copies publicly distributed in the United States. This applies to works distributed in public prior to March 1, 1989.

9. Architectural plans or drawings were already protected by the *U.S. Copyright Act*, but the *1990 Architectural Works Copyright Protection Act,* Pub. L. No. 101-650, tit. VII, 104 Stat. Section 133 (1991), expanded that protection as enumerated above. The new act also covers architectural works of art.

10. However, a case before the U.S. courts brought by the Rock and Roll Hall of Fame attempted to prevent a photographer from selling posters he created containing a photograph of its museum building, designed by renowned architect I. M. Pei, as being a breach of its trademark in the museum name, which was also used on the poster, and being also a breach of its copyright in its building design. A preliminary injunction was granted by the trial judge against the photographer and his poster. However, the court of appeals vacated the injunction on the basis that the evidence presented did not establish a strong likelihood that the photographer made an infringing trademark use of the museum's name or building design. Also, the museum may not have established its trademark on the building, for various reasons, and the court felt it unlikely the museum would prevail in its trademark infringement claim. In addition, the court was of the view that the use of the museum's name on the poster could well constitute "fair use" and not be actionable. See *Rock and Roll Hall of Fame and Museum Inc. v. Gentile Productions,* 134 F.3d 749 U.S. App. LEXIS 722 (6th Cir. 1998) also E.L.R. 20:9. Trademarks have been registered for other buildings, especially in New York City—such as the Art Deco spire of the Chrysler building (No. 1126888) and the Neoclassical facade of the New York Stock Exchange (No. 1761655). See *The [Toronto] Globe and Mail,* September 12, 1998, C21.

11. However, a case in the Canadian courts was brought by the architect Douglas Cardinal suing to prevent an addition being added to a building designed by him. He argued that the addition would be a violation of his moral rights. The application for an interim injunction to restrain construction was refused "where the claim was based on novel legal grounds, which needed to be tested at trial." See *Cardinal v. Parish of the Immaculate Conception*, F.C.J. No. 1609 (F.C.T.D. 1995).

12. Universal Copyright Convention, in Nimmer and Nimmer, *Nimmer On Copyright*, Section 17.01[B](2).

13. This was also true under the *U.S. Copyright Act*, prior to the *1988 Berne Convention Implementation Act.*

14. *Letter Edged in Black Press Inc v. Public Building Commission,* 320 F. Supp. 1303 (N.D. Ill. 1970).

15. Ibid.

16. *The Bridgeman Art Library Ltd. v. Corel Corp.*, 25 F. Supp. 2d 421 (S.D.N.Y. 1998).

17. Ibid., 426.

18. Ibid. §2.08[E][1], 2-130.

19. *Ibid.* §2.08[E][2], 2-131.

20. *Feist Pub., Inc. v. Rural Tel. Serv. Co.*, 499 U.S. 340, 350–53 (1991).

21. *Bridgeman Art Library v. Corel*, 430.

22. Ibid., 431.

23. See *The Bridgeman Art Library, Ltd. v. Corel Corporation*, 97 Civ. 6232 (LAK), United States District Court for the Southern District of New York, 25 F. Supp. 2d 421; 1998 U.S. Dist. LEXIS 17920; 49 U.S.P.Q. 2d (BNA) 1091.

24. *Rogers v. Koons*, 960 F.2d 301 (2d Cir. 1992), aff'g, 751 F. Supp. 474 (S.D.N.Y. 1990), amended on reh'g, 777 F. Supp. 1 (S.D.N.Y. 1991), cert. denied, 113 S. Ct. 365 (1992).

25. Ibid.

26. *United Features v. Koons*, 817 F. Supp. 370 U.S. Dist. Lexis 3479 (S.D.N.Y. 1993).

27. *Campbell v. Koons*, 1993 U.S. Dist. Lexis 3957 (S.D.N.Y. 1993).

28. *Rogers v. Koons.*

29. More usual than the *Koons* cases would be one in which a sculptor or painter sues a photographer for an unauthorized photograph of an original painting or sculpture.

30. *The [Toronto] Globe and Mail*, October 4, 1995.

31. *California Resale Royalties Act*, California Civil Code S. 986 (West 1982 and Supp. 1997).

32. Ibid.

33. *North American Free Trade Agreement*, August 13, 1992 (Canada: Ministry of Supply and Services Canada, 1993).

34. *Law for the Promotion and Protection of Industrial Property* (*Ley de Fometo y Protección de la Propiedad Industrial*) D.O. (June 27, 1991).

35. *Federal Law of Author's Rights* (*Ley Federal del Derechos de Autor).*

36. *Visual Artists Rights Act of 1990*, Pub. L. No 101-650 (tit.VI) 104 Stat. 509, 5128-33 (1990), 17 U.S.C., 101 ff. (Supp 111, 1991).

37. *John Carter, John Swing and John Veronis v. Helmsley-Spear Inc.*, 474431 861 F. Supp 303 (S.D.N.Y. 1994) 71 F. 3d 77, Associates 138 A.L.R. Fed. 711, 83 (2d Cir. 1995).

38. Ibid., 304.

39. Ibid., 303.

40. *Martin v. City of Indianapolis*, 982 F. Supp. 625, 1997 U.S. Dist. LEXIS 17073 (S.D. Ind. 1997).

41. *New York Authorship Rights Act*, Section 14.03 of New York Art and Cultural Affairs Law (McKinney Supp. 1993).

42. *California Art Preservation Act 1979*, California Civil Code, §987 (West 1982 and Supp. 1997).

43. *Pavia v. 1120 Avenue of the Americas Associates*, 901 F. Supp. 620 (S.D.N.Y. 1995).

44. *New York Arts and Cultural Affairs Law*, §§11.01, 14.05–14.08 inclusive, 15.01, 15.03, 15.05, 15.07, 15.09, 15.10–15.13 inclusive, 15.15 (McKinney 1984 and Supp. 1997).

45. Ibid.

46. *California Art Preservation Act 1979.*

47. Ibid.

48. *Botello v. Shell Oil Co.*, 280 Cal. Rptr. 535 (App. Ct. 2d Dist. 1991), respondents' petition for review denied, LEXIS 3348, Cal. Sup. Ct., July 24, 1991.

49. Ibid., 545.

50. *Crimi v. Rutgers Presbyterian Church*, 194 Misc. 570, 89 N.Y.S. 2d 813 (Supp. Ct. 1949).

51. *Canada Copyright Act*, Sections 14.1, 14.2, 28.1, and 28.2.

52. *Snow v. The Eaton Centre Ltd.*, 70 C.P.R. (2d) 105 (1982).

53. Ibid.

54. Ibid, 106.

55. Ibid.

56. *Canada Copyright Act*, S. 3(g).

57. *Federal Law of Author's Rights (Ley Federal del Derechos de Autor)*.

58. *Inter-American Convention on Copyright and Literary Property*, signed in Washington on June 22, 1946, revised July 24, 1971, in Paris.

· 7 ·

Insurance

This chapter is a general discussion of insurance as it relates to personal property, fine art, and cultural objects. It will address the various concerns that impact on insurance as it affects the creator, valuer, dealer, collector, museum, borrowers, and lenders to exhibitions and institutions. It is necessary that the basic concepts of insurance, the insurance policy, and its terms be understood.

The insurance agreement or contract gives rise to a contractual relationship between the insurer and the insured. The terms of that contract or policy will govern such a relationship.

THE CONCEPT OF RISK

From the viewpoint of the insurer, the major concern is that of the *risk* to be taken by the insurer and the consequences of such risk. Risk is the chance or possibility of loss, including damage. Risk has several components: *uncertainty,* implying doubt and concern about the future, and the *frequency* of damage.[1] Risk must also be looked at from the viewpoint of the insured, and this is where *risk management* plays its part.

RISK MANAGEMENT

The risk manager's task is to minimize property loss by identifying, measuring, and then attempting to control risk. Every collector and every collecting or lending institution must be a risk manager (or charge its insurance broker with this responsibility) and consider the following:

1. the consequences of risk;
2. the financial loss that would occur if all or a part of the collection were destroyed or lost;
3. ways to reduce the chances of having a loss;
4. how to recoup losses in the event of a disaster.

Identifying Risk

In identifying risk, insurers consider several factors:

1. How might a loss to the collection occur? Events giving rise to a loss are called *perils*. They include flood, earthquake, fire, theft, vandalism, accident, explosion, and the collision or overturn of a transporting conveyance. Perceived perils are the ones to be insured against by any creator, institution, or collector.
2. What conditions might cause a peril to occur? These conditions are called *hazards*. They do not cause losses, but they can increase the likelihood of a peril occurring or making a loss more severe.

Physical hazards are those pertaining to the physical state of a property (physical risks). Examples of physical hazards are proximity of a flood plain or an earthquake zone to the place of storage of an artwork or great distance of the storage place from a hydrant or fire station; absence of fire, smoke, or central burglar alarms; failure to maintain air-conditioning and heating systems; and widespread publicity about the location of a valuable collection.

Moral hazards pertain to the characteristics of the individuals—the creator, collector, or dealer who seek the insurance (the human risk). Examples of such moral hazards are dishonesty, carelessness, and unethical behavior on the part of the policyholder. Moral risks also include theft or attempted theft, malicious damage, vandalism, and conversion.

Insurers attempt to assess the attitudes of the insured, particularly toward loss prevention and insurance, to avoid insuring poor moral risks; however, it is an inexact science. Insurers ask questions such as: Does the insured run a clean, well-organized establishment, guided by common sense and adherence to municipal building codes, fire regulations, and so forth? Does the insured underinsure to reduce premiums? Does the insured try to recover premiums by submitting many claims? Does the insured have any previous record of criminality or insurance fraud?

Insurance policies protect insurers from moral risks. For example, the term *theft* is defined broadly, and insurance policies exclude theft by persons to whom property is entrusted. (Without this exclusion, insurers would be guaranteeing the honesty of everyone to whom an insured has entrusted its property.) Other clauses that reflect concerns about assuming unknown moral hazards include exclusions for incidents not reported to the police and unexplained loss from mysterious disappearances.

Exposure is the danger of loss, particularly by fire, arising from another risk close by. For example, a home, gallery, or museum near a business with a high fire risk, such as a gasoline station or welding shop, would have increased exposure.

Measuring Risk

From an insurer's viewpoint, some risks (events) are considered more likely to occur than others. The likelihood of perils such as earthquake, fire, theft, and flood differs as to both location and frequency. For example, an earthquake is more likely in California than in New York; theft may be more likely in New York than in North Dakota; flood might be more common on the coast than inland. The likelihood of each peril—fire, theft, flood—differs as to both location and frequency. There also is generally a greater probability of fire than of flood. The greater the risk, the higher the premium or the greater the possibility an insurer will refuse the risk.

Controlling Risk

Collectors, dealers, and museums must always attempt to reduce or otherwise control risk.

Some physical hazards can be addressed by reducing exposure. For example, a collector can move from a flood plain or earthquake zone, closer to a fire hydrant, or out of an area of frequent thefts. The installation of fire, smoke, and burglar alarms, as well as regular maintenance of air-conditioning and heating systems, will reduce risk, as will dividing a collection among several locations.

After risk has been reduced or eliminated, the collector, gallery, museum, or dealer must decide whether to purchase insurance against possible future loss or to self-insure (that is, to assume the risk itself). The self-insured must have sufficient funds to withstand a loss—often of both the collection and the building that houses it—in the event of fire, earthquake, flood, and so forth. Sometimes a collector will purchase insurance but become self-insured to the extent of having a high deductible. The deductible will be the responsibility of the insured, must be manageable, and will help reduce the cost of insurance premiums: the higher the deductible, the lower the premium, as the insurance company will neither pay a claim for what is less than the deductible nor incur the expense of processing such a claim.[2]

The Insurance Industry

Insurers

Insurance is distributed by two distinct types of organizations in Canada: private and government-run insurers. Private insurers may operate in the form of stock companies, mutuals, cooperative associations, or reciprocal exchanges. Government-run operations are generally government agencies or Crown corporations. Insurance companies may be licensed provincially or federally. They may operate within a narrow area, nationally, or internationally. They may specialize in a particular class of insurance aimed at one group of consumers, or they may offer a number of classes of insurance to appeal to a broad clientele.

In the United States, most insurers are private insurance companies, mutuals, or cooperative associations. Cooperative associations are generally in business to provide protection rather than to make a profit. They may be for a specific group, business, or region.

Some insurers deal directly with the public. The consumer can purchase insurance by mail, by telephone, or from a company representative. Usually an application of insurance is made by a consumer such as an owner, collector, or institution and submitted directly, or more usually through an agent or broker, to the insurer.[3]

Underwriters

The underwriter is the professional who acts on behalf of insurers to evaluate applications for insurance made by or on behalf of an applicant such as an owner, collector, or institution. The underwriter decides how to classify the risk, to accept or reject the risk, or to make it subject to conditions. The underwriter also evaluates personal information about the applicant and details the physical hazards of exposures and specific factors pertaining to the class of risk or type of insurance. If the underwriter believes the risk is too great, the insurance will be refused or offered with a large deductible and a surcharged premium.

Reinsurers

If an insurer's reserves are insufficient to cover a particular risk or group of risks, it may protect itself by contracting with another insurer to assume part or all of the risk that is passed on to it. Although the risk is thus shared between the two companies either on a proportional (quota share) or excess basis, the original insurer retains the liability to the customer. The second insurer in an arrangement of this type is a *reinsurer*.[4]

One of the largest private-sector insurance organizations is the Lloyds Syndicates. Lloyds is an insurance exchange where the actual risk is assumed by one or more underwriting syndicates. Although Lloyds is not an insurance company and does not accept insurance risks, its individual and corporate underwriting members do. Individual syndicate members are personally liable to the full extent of their personal assets.[5]

Adjusters

Once a loss occurs and a claim is made by an insured party, an adjuster will usually be assigned to investigate the loss and/or negotiate the settlement of the claim. Usually adjusters act on behalf of insurance companies; they are generally salaried employees of the insurers. There are also self-employed adjusters for hire used by insurance companies; they are usually licensed by provincial or state authorities. Independent adjusters are often used for specialized or large claims; they may also assist insured parties in a dispute with an insurer.

Industry Regulation

Canada

In Canada, the conduct of the property- and casualty-insurance business is supervised and regulated by both federal and provincial governments. The Federal Office of the Superintendent of Financial Institutions is concerned primarily with the solvency and stability of insurance companies, which are registered under federal statutes. The key statutes are the Office of the Superintendent of Financial Institutions Act and the Insurance Companies Act. Insurance brokers are regulated by provincial legislation and broker associations.

In Canada, insurance companies are usually incorporated federally, if they wish to do business across Canada. From time to time, provincially incorporated companies are created, primarily to operate in only one province or as a cooperative.

Foreign insurance companies are generally subject to the same restrictions and provisions as those applied to Canadian companies, as long as equal treatment is given to Canadian companies in the home jurisdiction of the foreign corporation.[6]

In Quebec, the civil court applies to the conditions of formation of insurance contracts and to the interpretation and enforcement of those contracts pursuant to the Quebec Civil Code (Articles 1378ff.).

United States

In the United States, most industry regulation (such as insurance company incorporation; the appointment of agents, brokers, premium rates, commissions, and investments by insurance company; etc.) is done by the insurance commissioner of each state. However, as insurance affects interstate commerce, it is also subject to federal regulation.

Mexico

In Mexico, administration of all laws relating to insurance is federal.

Mexican insurance companies are corporations with authorization or concession granted, with discretion, by the Secretariat of the Treasury and Public Credit to operate in the financial field. Mexican insurance carriers are governed by the Law of Insurance Institutions[7] and the law concerning insurance contracts. They are supervised and under the control of the National Banking and Insurance Commission, a division of the Secretariat of the Treasury and Public Credit. Insurance companies in Mexico are permitted to use authorized insurance agents, who are government regulated.

Insurance companies can operate in such areas as civil liability and occupational risks, maritime and transportation, and fire, as well as other areas outside the purview of this book.

Foreign insurance companies are allowed to have branches in Mexico as long as they comply with the general law governing foreign and domestic companies. This includes authorization from the federal government based on normal operations of the insurer for at least five prior years and qualification to operate in accordance with the laws of the country of origin. The company must also have legal representation in Mexico in accordance with the Civil Code and must conform to certain minimum capital requirements and other specific regulations.

The National Banking and Insurance Commission controls and supervises the investment of insurers' reserves; authorizes and supervises agents; authorizes transfers of assets; establishes limits on the risks that may be insured in each group; and approves policy forms, rates, and advertising.

Insurance contracts between the insurer and the insured require the same basic information as is required in such contracts in Canada and the United States.

Insurance is available covering damages to the economic interest a person may have if some mishap occurs. In such insurance, the insurance company is liable for damages only to the limit of the amount and real value insured.[8]

AGENTS AND BROKERS

Insurance of cultural property is generally sold through agents or brokers. Often the terms *insurance agent* and *insurance broker* are used interchangeably; however, they are significantly different in law.

An *agent* solicits business for a particular insurer and transmits the application for insurance to the insurance company on behalf of the customer. If the company accepts the risk, a policy of insurance will be issued, effective on delivery to the insured.[9] An agent also participates on behalf of the insurance company in the negotiation or renewal of insurance agreements. Generally, insurance agents are permitted to represent only one insurance company for a particular kind of insurance, although this is not the case in all jurisdictions. When a client deals with an agent, in essence he or she is dealing with a representative of the insurance company. Agents are licensed by the local state or provincial government.

Brokers are self-governing professionals (except in those jurisdictions that require licensing) who deal with any number of insurance companies to obtain the best insurance at the best price for the client. They have no allegiance to any particular insurance company. In most jurisdictions (excluding Ontario and Quebec in Canada), brokers are regulated.

Just as the agent is the representative of the insurer, so the broker is the representative of the party seeking insurance—the client. As agent for the client, the broker has a professional responsibility to act with due care for and on behalf of the client. Insurance brokers have a duty "to exercise a reasonable degree of skill and care to obtain policies in the terms bargained for and to service those policies as circumstances might require."[10]

For example, consider the theft of Marc Chagall artworks left by a collector with an art gallery located in a residential home. The collector relied on the insurance broker (described as insurance agent in the court decision) for the gallery to arrange insurance on the art while in transit and while in the gallery. In arranging the insurance, the broker misinformed the insurer, Lloyds of London, of material facts and also misrepresented the level of security and protection at the gallery located in the residential home. After the theft occurred, the insurers denied liability to the owner after a claim was made on the basis that the statements made by the broker to Lloyds were "material to the risk policy" and were false. The broker was acting for and on behalf of the owner of the artworks and was not an agent for the insurance company and, therefore, Lloyds was not responsible for his misconduct. The broker, however, was held responsible for negligence and the breach of duty he owed to the owner of the artworks.[11]

Because of the confusion in the use of the term *agent* and the term *broker,* courts have usually determined that the question of whether an insurance broker is the agent of the insured or of the insurer is one based on fact in each particular case.[12]

TYPES OF INSURANCE FOR PERSONAL PROPERTIES

The Insurance Policy

The insurance policy is a legal contract defining the duties and responsibilities of both insurer and insured.

Legal Elements

The policy must contain all legal elements of a private agreement.

1. The parties to the contract must be competent to contract.
2. The party insuring the property must have an insurable interest in the property—some type of ownership or other stake in the well-being of the property. (In other words, the party would be financially prejudiced by the loss of or damage to the property and financially benefited by its continued existence.) Owners, bailees, custodians, lien holders, and mortgagees all have an insurable interest in the property.
3. There must be an agreement between the parties on the important terms, including the amount and duration of the contract.
4. There must be a subject of the contract (that is, a property involved) and at least one risk covered as well as the amount of the coverage provided by the policy.
5. The consideration (money) payable by way of premium must be set out for the coverage.
6. There must be a mutuality of obligation between the parties. In this case, the insurer underwrites the risk in exchange for payment of the premium.

The insurance policy is one of indemnity; it protects the insured against loss and returns the insured to his or her financial position before the loss. The insured cannot recover more than the amount of the loss.

Fraud and Good-Faith Covenants

In insurance contracts, there are implied covenants of good faith and fair dealing: neither party may impair the ability of the other to receive the benefit of a fair bargain. There must be disclosure of all relevant information by the insured, from the first negotiations leading to the application for insurance until the risk has been accepted by the insurer. The insured is also obliged to inform the insurer of any relevant changes to those facts and to avoid misrepresenting any relevant fact. (The insured or the insured's agent might present incorrect information; any information presented by such an agent of the insured is binding on the insured and would allow the insurance company to avoid payment.[13]) Misrepresentations can occur through oversight, innocence, carelessness, or fraud.

When it is discovered that a contract has been obtained by misrepresentation or nondisclosure, the insurer has three options:

1. rescinding or voiding the insurance contract, which means returning the premium and treating the contract as void from the beginning;
2. disregarding the misrepresentation or nondisclosure and continuing with the contract;
3. reforming or changing the contract.

The third option generally occurs when the contract does not express the actual agreement of the parties. For example, a collector may innocently insure work later discovered to be a forgery. When the loss occurs, the collector will receive the lower value for the work, unless it is a scheduled item. In such a case, a problem arises as to whether payment has to be made in full, as the insurance company had the opportunity to review and assess the insured work before the policy was issued.[14]

Interpretation

Because a standard-form policy is usually non-negotiable, U.S. and Canadian courts interpret them in favor of the insured, if there is ambiguity in the wording or exceptions and limitations.[15]

What to Look for in an Insurance Policy

For a policy to be effective, the insured (be it an owner, collector, or institution) must consider what is required for protection and how much is available for premiums.

In order to protect a work, the insured must provide the following:

1. an adequate description of the work;
2. the location of the work, construction details, burglar, fire, smoke alarm certificates;
3. the insurable value of the work (that is, have it appraised), with appraisal report attached, and the type of value insured, for example, replacement, cost, reproduction, substitution, etc.;[16]
4. any other financial interests involved in the work (such as mortgagees who must be protected);
5. whether the work travels (if it does, should it be covered for transportation independent of the coverage of the transportation company, which will have only minimal coverage except at extremely high premiums);
6. past five-year loss experience;
7. previous insurance carrier;
8. reasons why the insured is changing insurers (such as cancellation, etc.);
9. whether the object does not have to be scheduled or listed as it is not sufficiently expensive;
10. if the standard territorial limits in the policy are sufficient (A policy may cover art objects only in the location or home of the owner unless otherwise specified; most policies can be expanded to cover a greater area without a substantial increase in insurance. How broad a geographic area should be covered? This should be taken into account if a work is lent for exhibitions or is moved between a summer and winter residence.); and

11. if a work is fragile or deteriorating and may therefore be subject to a policy exception.

In respect to the policy itself, there are a number of matters to consider.

1. Is the policy an all-risks policy?
2. Is the full replacement cost covered?
3. Will it cover the geographic area required?
4. Is it wall-to-wall and nail-to-nail insurance? (Does it cover from the time the artwork is taken off the insured's wall, to the time it is on loan or in exhibition, to the time it is rehung on the insured's wall?)
5. Do I have to be concerned with depreciation?
6. What are the exclusions, and are they relevant? For example, a collector of porcelain or glass might have more concerns in respect to an exclusion relating to breakage than would a collector of metal sculpture.
7. Do I have the appropriate appraisals? If not, do I need them now?
8. Does the insurance company have salvage rights?
9. Can I get the salvage should I so wish?
10. In the event of a later recovery of a stolen work, can I buy it back for what was paid to me by the insurer?[17]
11. Are copyright and moral rights covered?

All-Risk Policy

The consumer (be it the owner, collector, or dealer) must purchase a policy of insurance from the insurer. The most common type is the "all-risk scheduled or blanket (subject to a list on file with the insurer) fine art policy." In an all-risk fine art policy (a form of "inland marine insurance"), every work of art or object is scheduled or itemized. Information includes title, artist, date, and type of appraised insurable value (for example, replacement cost, substitution, reproduction, etc.). The premium covers the full amount of the appraised value for each object; thus it is considered a *valued* policy—one that, in the event of a total loss, pays a predetermined amount agreed on by the insurer and the insured at the time the contract was made. In other words, the amount to be recovered for injury is predetermined by the agreement of the parties.

Professional valuations are usually required at the time the policy is issued, and the amount of insurance coverage for each object is based on such professional valuation. Such contracts are usually made for jewelry, fine art, antiques, stamps, and coin collections. The policies are usually location-specific, and coverage is provided only at that site. However, coverage is available for unknown locations (subject to a limit).

An interesting case concerning an all-risk policy is the *Art Gallery of Toronto and Eaton re Aetna Insurance Company*.[18] The Aetna Insurance Company had issued to the Art Gallery of Toronto and Mrs. R. Y. Eaton a policy of insurance covering certain artworks against all risks of loss or damage except as excluded by the policy. The property covered was divided into three classifications, set out in Schedules A, B, and C. Schedule A covered items of fine art, each valued at $3,000 or more. This schedule included paintings, described by the name of the artist and title, and ascribed an insured value. Schedule B covered sculpture in a similar fashion. Schedule C covered miscellaneous articles neither listed in detail nor scheduled; it provided for total coverage of $175,000, with a limit of $3,000 in respect of any object insured under the schedule.

Six paintings listed in Schedule A were thereafter stolen from the Art Gallery of Toronto (now the Art Gallery of Ontario); they had an insured value of $640,000. The paintings were recovered three weeks later. Each painting had been cut from its stretcher and rolled up to facilitate transport. Rolling resulted in substantial cracking and chipping on each painting.

The insured filed a proof of loss form claiming the market value of the six paintings at the time they were stolen to be $1,045,000. The value of the paintings when recovered was $631,900, leaving a loss of $413,100. The amount claimed by the insured under the policy was $394,100. (The difference between the whole loss and the amount claimed was the result of one of the paintings, with an insured value of $120,000, having been damaged to the extent of $139,000.)

The insured contended that they were entitled to recover the actual loss on each item up to its insured value as listed in the policy. The insurer, however, submitted that the policy was a valued policy, and therefore its liability should be determined by calculating the percentage of depreciation. (This is done by assessing the insured value of the paintings at the time of the loss and the market value at the time of recovery and applying this proportion to the insured value.)

Paragraph 9 of the policy read, "This company shall not be liable for more than the amount set opposite the respective articles covered hereunder, which amounts are agreed to be the values of the said articles for the purpose of this insurance."

The insured parties contended, among other things, that the policy was not valued but one of indemnity against all loss or damage to the property by theft up to the scheduled amount. They were therefore entitled to be fully indemnified so far as the policy permitted.

The court found that the wording of paragraph 9 was clear and unequivocal and that there was nothing in the policy to indicate it should be given anything but its plain and ordinary meaning.

As Justice Donnelly stated:

The insurer and insured have agreed that, though the items listed in Sections A and B, be of greater or lesser value, in all cases of indemnity their value is to be taken to be the amounts set opposite the respective articles... an owner may insure an article below its actual value and provide that as between him and the insurer it shall be taken to be only of the value upon which they have agreed. This [is what] the insured have done in this case. There is no provision in the policy that the agreed value shall apply only in the event of a total loss.[19]

In this case, the court accepted the position of the insurer with respect to the meaning of the policy terms and held that the sum to be paid to the gallery and Eaton for the partial loss sustained was to be determined by applying the proportion of depreciation resulting from the theft to the agreed values set out in the policy. The court did not accept the position of the insured that the policy could be treated as an unvalued policy.

Transit of Objects

Consideration must be given by owners and bailees of art objects to coverage of works while in transit. If works are damaged or lost in transit and there is no applicable insurance on the objects by the owner, the transit company will be responsible for only a small sum, often based on the weight of the goods being transported and often to a maximum of only a few hundred dollars. Therefore, transit coverage should be added to an all-risk policy. Also, by declaring the full insured or replacement value (new or comparable) to the transit company, it will provide coverage to the full value of the object at an additional cost.

Exclusions

Personal property insurance covers partial loss as well as total loss, subject to various exclusions. As mentioned, most policies are all-risks policies, which protect fine art against such major threats as fire, theft, water, vandalism, etc. One of the major exclusions is *breakage*. This exclusion can be deleted on ceramics, porcelains, etc., by paying an additional premium on the specific items affected by the exclusion. However, standard exclusions are losses due to war, nuclear damage, insects, vermin, wear and tear, gradual deterioration (which may be particularly important in some contemporary works), damage to fragile items, and damage that occurs during restoration or repair of the work. It is important to remember this last exception when works are given to a restorer for repair.

Valued Policy

In the valued, scheduled fine art policy, reimbursement is on an "agreed value basis," that is, on the values established by the most recent scheduled value. If the schedule indicates that an item is worth $100,000, that is the amount paid even if the appraised scheduled value is many years old and no longer reflects the market. It is, therefore, important to revisit appraisals and appraised values regularly if you hold this type of policy.

Open or Unvalued Policy

As indicated above, the valued policy indemnifies the insured for the full current worth of the lost property up to a specified limit.[20]

In an *open* or *unvalued* insurance policy, a current value has to be determined at the time of the loss. In effect the appraisal occurs after the loss rather than before the loss, and the compensation is based on what the object is worth at the time of the loss.

Individual-Risk Policy

Individual-risk policies—for example, a policy insuring against fire only—are available. However, these are not generally taken out by collectors, museums, and dealers, as they would usually wish to have all-risk coverage to protect from exposure of various risks.

Homeowner's Policy

Collectors can insure artworks under a homeowner's policy, which insures the residence and its contents against a number of risks. Generally, a homeowner's policy has strict limits as to the amount to be paid for any loss within a given category, unless particular objects are specifically listed and a separate premium paid. For instance, the limits might be a $1,000 limit on money and postage stamps; $5,000 limit for theft of firearms, jewelry, watches, furs, collectible coins and stamps, and precious and semi-precious stones; and $10,000 limit for loss of silver-plated ware, silverware, goldware, gold-plated ware, and pewterware, including tea sets, trays, and trophies. Thus, in the case of theft of silverware worth many thousands of dollars, the insured would recover only $10,000 in total. The insured should examine the policy wording for dollar limitations that may apply to certain classes of property and the relevance of any peril exclusions relevant to the objects to be carried in the policy.

Personal-Property Replacement—Cost Endorsement

Cost endorsement modifies a homeowner's policy to provide replacement-cost coverage. Generally, however, it does not apply to antiques and fine arts. These must be dealt with by way of scheduled personal-property endorsements for any amount above the limits permitted by the policy for each category. The insured must replace the item rather than receive a cash settlement to obtain settlement on a replacement-cost basis policy.

Schedules

Scheduled personal-property endorsements, in which the value of each item is predetermined and scheduled in the policy, include coverage for nine classes of property: jewelry, furs, cameras, musical instruments, silverware, golfers' equipment, fine arts, postage stamps, and rare and current coins.

Fine Arts Schedule

The fine arts schedule includes paintings, etchings, pictures, tapestries, art-glass windows, and other bona fide works of art, such as valuable rugs, statuary, marbles, bronzes, and antique furniture; rare books and manuscripts; antique silver, porcelain, and rare glass; and bric-a-brac of rarity, historical value, or artistic merit.[21]

Fine arts are usually subject to more restrictive exclusions than other classes of personal property covered by the scheduled personal-property endorsements. (These exclusions result from the nature of the property insured.)

1. The insurer does not have to pay for losses that result from the insured's own carelessness or the carelessness of others who perform, repair, restore, or retouch the work.
2. Publicly displayed items that are especially vulnerable to loss are not covered.
3. The endorsement does not cover breakage of property such as glassware, porcelain, marble statues, and art-glass windows that are highly vulnerable, unless the breakage results from fire or lightning; explosion; air crash or collision; windstorm, earthquake, or flood; malicious damage or theft; or derailment or overturn of conveyance. However, coverage for such breakage can usually be added for an additional premium.

Three special conditions apply to the fine arts schedule coverage:

1. Coverage applies only in the United States and Canada. Special coverage would be required and an extra premium payable for transport and exhibition of the artwork elsewhere. Insurance coverage for traveling exhibitions of expensive museum art is virtually prohibitive, so governments either finance the insurance or self-insure such exhibitions.
2. When damage occurs to one of a pair or set of objects, the full scheduled amount will be paid only if the insured surrenders the remaining piece or pieces of the set.
3. The insured must agree that the insured property will be packed and unpacked by competent packers.[22]

Object Identification

The Getty Information Institute in partnership with the United Nations Educational, Scientific and Cultural Organization (UNESCO), the Council of Europe, the International Council of Museums (ICOM), the United States Information Agency (USIA), and the Getty Conservation Institute have been working on a project to "collectively address issues relating to documentation practices and the implementation of international standards."[23] The participating organizations are working to establish an international, multi-sector agreement on the essential information required to identify an object.

The project, when properly implemented, will be of major benefit to both owners and insurers of art objects and cultural property. It will make it easier to describe objects when stolen or lost and to relay the information to the necessary parties almost immediately after the original notification of the event.

The project has two premises:

> First, a stolen object cannot be returned to its rightful owner unless it has been adequately documented; second, in case of theft, the information about the object needs to travel faster than the object itself. Both premises require agreement on what information constitutes an adequate record for identifying an object. And such an agreement must reflect broad collaboration that extends across national, agency, institutional, and organizational boundaries and that finds equal acceptance in the public and private sectors.[24]

Project participants have agreed on a core standard called Object ID. Ten categories of information plus an image are used to identify a cultural object. It is hoped that this core documentation standard will be implemented in the various communities that are involved in combating the illicit trade in cultural objects.

From the outset, the project worked collaboratively with organizations in six key communities:

1. cultural heritage organizations (including museums, national inventories, and archaeological organizations),
2. law enforcement agencies,
3. customs agencies,
4. the art trade,
5. valuers, and
6. the insurance industry

This project's contribution has been to identify a minimum standard for describing cultural objects, to encourage the creation of descriptions of objects in both private and public ownership, and to bring together organizations that can encourage the implementation of the standard, as well as those that will play a part in developing networks along which this information can circulate.

Object ID is best defined in terms of the ways in which it can be implemented.

1. It provides a checklist of the information that is required to identify stolen or missing objects.
2. It is a documentation standard that establishes the minimum level of information needed to identify an object.
3. It is a key building block in the development of information networks that will allow diverse organizations to exchange descriptions of objects rapidly.[25]
4. It provides a key component in any training program that teaches the documentation of objects.

The intent of Object ID is to complete a checklist that will help to provide the information necessary to identify an object. The information consists of photographs and the following checklist:

1. type of object (this short descriptive phrase describes the object, including object type and object name);
2. measurements;
3. materials and techniques;
4. inscriptions and markings;
5. date or period;
6. maker;
7. subject of the picture or object (for example, a landscape);
8. title of the picture or object;
9. distinguishing features (including damage, repairs, or defects); and
10. a short textual description.

Additional categories are recommended for those organizations and institutions that are developing automated documentation systems. They are as follows:

1. Object ID number,
2. related written material,
3. place of origin or discovery,
4. cross-reference to related objects, and
5. date documented (the date on which the description of the object was made).

Photographs are of vital importance in identifying and recovering stolen objects. In addition to overall views, it is recommended that close-ups be taken of inscriptions, markings, and any damage or repairs. If possible, a scale or object of known size should be included in the identification image.

Ideally, the information that can identify a stolen or an illegally exported object should be able to travel at least as fast as the object itself. This will mean that the information may have to cross national borders and be circulated among a number

of organizations. The development of electronic networks makes this effort techni-
cally possible. The project is now establishing the standards that will make it possible to exchange information in a form that is intelligible to both the systems and the
people who use them.[26]

Partial Loss or Loss of Value

Partial loss is the loss of value resulting from damage and subsequent restoration
to an art object. Where a work is so damaged, the insurer will pay the restoration
expert to bring it back to its best condition; but even if the work looks very good
after restoration, it will probably have lost a percentage of its value. It will be up to
an independent valuer to provide an estimate of the value of the restored work as
contrasted to the value of the work prior to damage.[27]

If an insured wished to have coverage that would replace an object with another similar one in case of loss, the valuation basis and sum of insurance should reflect
that intention. The insured value should also reflect additional costs such as auction
fees, taxes, delivery and transit insurance, installation, and so forth.

Temporary Insurance

Sometimes an insurer may agree to insure the risk but does not yet have sufficient information or the confirmations required to issue the policy. Temporary
coverage may then be granted under what is known as a *binder*. This is a legally
binding coverage, whether oral or in writing. It is usually a memorandum of agreement to insure for a particular risk, often for a short period of time pending issuance of the policy. The policy will usually be issued as soon as all necessary information is available to the insurer, and it is effective as of the date of the binder.

Oral binders are fraught with difficulties in respect to:

1. the agent's authority to bind the insurance company;
2. the actual subject matter of the binder;
3. the terms agreed on for the binder.

For example, if objects are being sent on tour, has the complete itinerary been given
to the agent? Have all the objects been described so that they can be identified in the
event of difficulty? For what period of time will they be away? What are their insurable or
replacement values, and how much coverage is required? Are there to be deductibles?

A commercial gallery will often put a binder on new works as they come into the
gallery. The insured value is usually between fifty percent and seventy percent of the
retail price. This reduces the premium payable and covers the loss or indemnification to the artist. The gallery's commission, usually between thirty-five percent and
fifty percent of the retail price, is often not insured.

The Blanket or Broad Coverage Policy

This is an insurance policy under which objects are insured on a blanket basis; it is generally purchased by museums and owners of large collections, as the policy covers a collection as a whole. It is especially useful if a collection is spread over more than one location, and it obviates the necessity of scheduling each of the many objects. However, the collection must be described precisely enough to ensure that the policy covers the intended works. Identifiable groups of works within the collection (for example, all sculptures, all paintings, or all ceramics) can be insured for separate amounts.

Some museums are self-insured; they do not buy insurance, except for specific insurance on works borrowed for an exhibition. (Such insurance is often a condition of the loan agreement with the lender.) Usually museums have blanket insurance policies with face amounts of many millions of dollars, often with fairly large deductibles, to avoid minor claims and reduce premium payments.

The usual exclusions to a broad coverage policy are

1. loss or damage caused by wear and tear;
2. gradual deterioration;
3. insects, vermin, inherent vice, or war damage;
4. confiscation by order of government or public authority;
5. loss due to contraband or illegal transportation or trade;
6. nuclear accident.

There may also be other exclusions. For instance, flood damage may be excluded and require coverage under a separate policy at higher rates. Also, the three exclusions applicable to fine art objects discussed earlier in this chapter—travel restrictions, components of a set, and packing—are usual exclusions. A further exclusion in most art and art objects policies deals with loss or damage caused during repair or restoration of the property. Policies may also be location specific.

SALVAGE

When insured property, be it fine art or cultural property, is badly damaged, it is up to the insurance company to determine whether there has been a total or partial loss. The insurer may decide to treat the damage as total destruction and pay the insured party as if it were a total loss. (This happens when the insurers determine that it may cost more to repair than to replace the work.) The work is then written off, just as an automobile is written off or "totaled" in a severe automobile accident.

However, the damaged goods may still have some value. Someone may be prepared to purchase and restore the work; or the work may be so important or valuable that even in its damaged state it has value in the marketplace.

Once the insured has been paid in full for the work, the insurer wants to take ownership of the insured property. However, for this salvage right to be exercised it must be in the policy and the insurer must have paid the insured for the full value of the loss. Therefore, if there is a deductible, the insurer must pay the deductible as well as the coverage to the insured. The insured may bid on the salvage.

There is usually a policy requirement that after damage has been incurred, the insured must take reasonable steps to protect the property from further damage, known as *mitigating the loss.* (This permits the insurance company to receive salvage goods in the best possible condition.)

SUBROGATION

Subrogation is the right of an insurer, after paying or agreeing to pay a loss, to assume the rights of the insured to recover the loss from a third party responsible for the loss.

If the insured has a source of compensation for the loss other than or in addition to that with the particular insurance company, the insurer has a right of subrogation to prevent over-recovery by the insured. For example, if the damage was caused by a third party who is insured, the owner of the object cannot collect from both his or her insurance company and the company insuring the third party. However, the right of subrogation does not arise until the insured has been fully indemnified for the loss.[28]

COINSURANCE

Some insurance policies have a coinsurance clause, under which the insured by way of good faith must maintain insurance representing a certain percentage of the value of the property (usually 80 percent). When a loss occurs, the insured can recover the amount of the loss up to the face value of the policy, only in the event of a total loss. The partial losses are subject to the coinsurance clause.

Although the coinsurance clause is expressed in words, it is really a mathematical formula, as follows:

amount of insurance applicable × coinsurance percentage × loss = claim value at time of loss

However, for a partial loss the insurer would be liable only for an amount in direct proportion to the ratio of the coverage to the full value; thus the insured shares any partial loss with the insurer. A personal-property floater ordinarily does not contain coinsurance provisions; however, a commercial floater does and is subject to negotiation.

Considering the importance of the insurance contract and the technical aspects of insurance coverage for art objects and cultural properties, it is imperative that proper professional advice be obtained by any owner or collector of art or art objects to make certain that the policy contains the expected terms, coverage, and amounts. Adequate records and appraisal reports must be kept by the insured to properly protect his or her interests. To do otherwise would be foolhardy.

COPYRIGHT AND MORAL RIGHTS

A loss, be it total or partial, affects the artist and his rights under the copyright acts of various countries.

1. Canada provides an exhibition right as part of the copyright owned by a creator. In the event of a total loss, the exhibition right of the artist is lost. A claim, therefore, may be brought by an artist for the loss of future earnings from a work, especially if it already has an exhibition history. The relevant parties will have to be determined; for example, the owner of the work, the party causing the damage or destruction, the insured, or all three.[29]
2. A work may be so damaged as to be a virtual write-off. In that event, the insurance company will pay for a total loss and may want salvage in the work. The artist may take the position that the repaired work brought into the marketplace would be prejudicial to his or her reputation and violate his or her moral rights. The artist may demand that the work be destroyed, regardless of the contract between the insured and the insurance company.

An example of this occurred in Toronto involving a painting by the respected American "color field" painter Kenneth Noland. A house painter, while painting an apartment wall on which the painting was hanging, accidentally sprayed paint on the canvas. In an attempt to remove the paint, the painter rubbed the canvas in a circular fashion in two places, resulting in permanent circular marks on the brushed canvas surface. The painting was deemed irreparable by independent experts, and the insurance company paid for a total loss and demanded salvage. Noland took exception to the work coming back onto the market, even at a reduced price, because the image had been so distorted or mutilated as to be prejudicial to his honor and reputation. The work was then destroyed in the presence of representatives of the owner, the insurance company, and Noland.

APPRAISAL CLAUSE

A dispute as to value that cannot be settled amicably is often settled by way of a clause in most policies dealing with "settlement by appraisal." Either party may demand an appraisal of the loss. Each party will then chose a valuer, and the two valuers will then choose an umpire. The valuers do independent appraisals and submit their written reports to the insurance company. If the valuers fail to agree upon the value, the two opinions are submitted to the umpire, who then determines the amount of the loss. This process is generally more efficient and less expensive than a court action between the parties. However, if an umpire cannot be agreed on, the matter is then determined by a judge of the appropriate court in the province or state where the insured premises is located or the loss occurred.

Reasonable fees for valuers, lawyers, and other professionals to assist in settling claims may be covered by a rider to the policy, which is usually worthwhile.

SETTLEMENT OF CLAIMS

A loss must first be reported by the insured to his or her respective insurance company or the company's agent in a timely fashion. A proof of loss form is filled out by the insured and filed within the time frame required by the policy. The majority of such claims are settled and paid or referred to one of four types of *adjusters* for settlement.

1. **Telephone Adjusters** are salaried employees of the insurer. They process large volumes of claims, usually for small amounts of money, that do not require face-to-face interviews.[30]
2. **Staff Adjusters** are salaried employees of the insurer. They investigate, negotiate, and settle claims for their employers and have the authority to commit the insurer to a settlement.
3. **Independent Adjusters** operate as independent businesses and accept assignments of claims from numerous insurance companies.
4. **Public Adjusters** are independent adjusters engaged by insureds to represent their interests during a claim. They are often used if there is a conflict between the insured and the insurers. They are paid by the insured, usually a percentage of the claim recovered.

If the loss is significant or if there are outstanding questions, an adjuster is appointed by the insurer. The adjuster will make certain that there is no fraud involved in the claim being made and will verify the damage, the loss, and the circumstances of the case.

Questions may arise as to whether the loss or damage is covered by the policy. It is often at this point that difficulties and/or possible actions arise between insurers and insureds, agents, and brokers over allegations that the agent or broker had misrepresented terms or conditions of the policy of insurance to the insured.

In the event of a question regarding coverage, the insurer will often ask the insured to sign a nonwaiver agreement. This states that, although the insurer is investigating the loss, it is not voluntarily waiving its rights to deny liability under the insurance policy.

In ordinary circumstances, the loss is investigated, the amount of the loss established, and payment made based on the amount stated in the policy, the insured's interest in the policy, or the cash value of the policy.

A release is then requested from the insured. When the insurer receives the release from the insured, the funds are paid to the insured.

CONTACTING A LAWYER

An insurance lawyer should be contacted if questions arise as to policy coverage in the event of a loss. An experienced insurance lawyer can be invaluable in the review of a proof of loss form, in negotiating a settlement amount with the adjuster and/or insurer, and in reviewing any release of interest requested from the insured. Where a claim is being denied in full or in part by an insurer, an insurance lawyer should be contacted to determine a course of action, be it negotiation, mediation, arbitration, litigation, or acceptance of the denial of the claim.[31]

NOTES

1. The Insurance Institute of Canada, *Principles and Practice of Insurance* (Toronto: The Insurance Institute of Canada, 1996), 1-2 to 1-4.

2. Professional insurance brokers may be of some assistance to guide an insured in the event of a potential claim. Often they will advise about the process of submitting a claim; the feasibility of recovering, from the insurer, a settlement once a claim is submitted; and the chances of the insurer enjoining the insured in a subrogation that will recover the deductible and reduce the "claims against" record of the insured.

3. Representatives, most often known as "agents," are paid by the insurance company, often on a commission basis. Other insurers market through independent brokers, sometimes called "agencies" or "agency companies." They have their own clients and deal with a number of insurers in each of the areas of insurance coverage in which they operate.

4. Craig Brown and Julio Menezes, *Insurance Law in Canada,* 3d ed. (Toronto: Carswell, 1997), 51.

5. Insurance Institute of Canada, *Principles and Practice of Insurance,* 4-18 to 4-23.

6. In Canada, reciprocity agreements may apply and may be obtained through the Ontario Insurance Commission or the Insurance Bureau of Canada.

7. *General Law of Insurance Institutions (Ley General de Instituciones de Seguros),* (August 30, 1935; Diario Oficial, September 13, 1935).

8. For a discussion on the laws of Mexico relating to insurance, see Joseph Wheless, *Compendium of the Laws of Mexico,* 2d ed. (St. Louis: Thomas Publishing Company, 1938). See also Organization of American States, Secretariat for Legal Affairs, *A Statement of the Laws of Mexico in Matters Affecting Business,* 4th ed. (Washington, D.C.: Pan American Union, 1970); William E. Mooz Jr., *An Introduction to Doing Business in Mexico* (Irvington, N.Y.: Transnational Juris Publications Inc., 1995); and *Mexico Business, The Portable Encyclopedia for Doing Business with Mexico* (San Rafael, Calif.: World Trade Press, 1994).

9. For a discussion on insurance, see Scott Hodes, *What Every Artist and Collector Should Know About the Law* (New York: E. P. Dutton & Co. Inc., 1974), 162–63.z

10. See *Fine's Flowers Limited et al. v. General Accident Assurance Co. of Canada et al.* (1977), 81 D.L.R. (3d) 139 (Ont. C.A.), at 149. The "broker" was called "agent" in this case, continuing the confusion of the two terms.

11. See *Bell v. Buschlen/Mowatt Fine Art Investments Ltd.* [1988] B.C.J. No. 2014 (B.C.C.A.)(QL).

12. *Davidson v. Comet Casualty Company,* 89 Illinois App. 3rd 720, 412 NE 2nd 19 (1980).

13. See *Bell v. Buschlen/Mowatt.*

14. The insured may also be able to recover the excess insurance premiums paid in the mistaken belief that the work had a higher value.

15. *Consolidated Bathurst Export Ltd. v. Mutual Boiler and Machinery Insurance Co.* [1980] 1 S.C.R. 888, at 899.

16. See Henry Babcock, *Appraisal Principles and Procedures* (Herndon, Va.: American Society of Appraisers, 1980), 90–91, for a discussion of "Insurable Value" where he states, "There is a widely accepted principle that states that a subject whole property cannot be worth, at a specified date and place, more than it would cost to replace it at that date and place. It is therefore argued that the cost of replacement sets an upper limit on the value… and is a useful check on the value-figure. This is true in those cases in which the replacement can be immediately accomplished—for example, by purchase and immediate delivery and installation of a replacement unit—but it is not true, in general, if the replacement property must be produced (by assembly, construction, fabrication, manufacture, etc.) or if the delivery and installation of a purchasable replacement involves any appreciable loss of time. Of course, the criterion is useless in the case of an irreplaceable property or one with irreplaceable parts."

17. Franklin Feldman and Stephen E. Weil, *Art Works Policy Practice* (New York: Practicing Law Institute, 1974), 699.

18. *Art Gallery of Toronto and Eaton re Aetna Insurance Company* (1961) O.R. 329 (Ont. H.C.).

19. Ibid., 334.

20. *Saint Paul Fire and Marine Insurance Company v. Pure Oil Company,* 63 F.2d 771 (2d Cir. Ct. of Ap. 1933).

21. William H. Rodda, James Trieschmann, Eric Wiening, and Bob A. Hedges, *Commercial Property Risk Management and Insurance: Volume II*, 2d ed. (Malvern, Penn.: American Institute for Property & Liability Underwritings, 1983), 34.

22. See Karen Hamilton and Donald S. Malecki, *Personal Insurance Property and Liability*, 1st ed. (Malvern, Penn.: American Institute for Chartered Property Casualty Underwriters, 1994), 141.

23. Robin Thornes, *Protecting Cultural Objects in the Global Information Society* (Los Angeles: The Getty Information Institute, 1997), vii.

24. Ibid., 2.

25. Ibid.

26. Ibid., 1.

27. Rodda et al. *Commercial Property Risk Management*, 99–100.

28. See *National Fire Insurance Company v. McLaren* (1886), 12 O.R. 682 (Ch. D). For a discussion of subrogation, see Craig Brown, *Canadian Insurance Contract Law in a Nutshell* (Toronto: Carswell, 1995), 95.

29. To date, however, there has been no reported case on this point.

30. Insurance Institute of Canada, *Principles and Practice of Insurance.*

31. Many local governing bodies for lawyers provide a lawyer referral service that can be of assistance in obtaining an insurance lawyer that practices in the area of property loss.

· 8 ·

Taxation

Tax can take many forms. There may be a tax on income, on the gain from the sale of a capital property, on gifts of valuable property made during one's lifetime, and on bequests made from one's estate. In addition, there are direct and indirect taxes, by different levels of government, on various goods and services.

This chapter restricts itself to the tax consequences in Canada, the United States, and Mexico of the gifting of art and art objects, primarily for charitable purposes, during the lifetime of the donor or by his or her estate. It deals with the general concepts employed by the federal governments of the three countries to encourage donations through tax benefits and to restrict those benefits by specific rules and regulations.[1]

There are numerous excellent tax texts available to readers who wish more tax information,[2] and professional tax advisors may be consulted for specific advice. As taxation rules and regulations change frequently, this discussion will not deal with specific tax rates or with the intricacies of making donations and the instruments used for such donations. Sadly, much tax legislation is political in nature and changes with the political party in power and its political agenda; often exceptions are built into the taxing statutes, both in Canada and in the United States, because of political pressure. The only constants are that governments require money, and taxation is the way money is raised.[3]

Historically, most museums and public institutions have received their finest works through donations of collections from both the rich and famous and the not so rich and not so famous. Often the donations are made, at least in part, for the tax benefits available to the donor. Rarely, however, will a donation of an important object at fair mar ket value net the donor as much as if the work had been sold at fair market value, even after a capital gains tax has been applied, as most tax rates are fifty percent or less and the after-tax benefit of a donation would be less than the funds received from a sale at the same fair market value. Therefore, altruism is as vital to the concept of a donation as are any tax benefits. Whether a donor's impetus is social standing or a genuine desire to share the works with the designated institution, its members, and the general public for the greater good, any tax regime that does not recognize the benefit to the community of such donations is short-sighted and ultimately harmful to the nation it serves.

Unfortunately, taxing authorities rarely have an understanding of aesthetics and culture, which gives rise to frustration, both in the arts community and in the taxing authorities. Moreover, from time to time there are those who wish to abuse the system by using tax loopholes, which are subsequently attacked by the taxing authority, often resulting in ill will toward the cultural communities. Overall, however, donors of art objects make a major contribution and enhance both the culture and the cultural history of nations for the benefit of all.

DONATIONS IN CANADIAN LAW

Tax Credit

The Income Tax Act of Canada[4] provides significant benefits to individuals and corporations making certain charitable donations to qualifying donees. A qualifying gift will generally exist when

1. property is transferred to a permitted donee;
2. the transfer is voluntary; or
3. the transfer is made without expectation of return or receipt of benefit other than a benefit of nominal value.[5]

The sum of gifts donated in a year is referred to as *total gifts.*

Qualifying gifts have been classified into four categories:

1. charitable gifts—made to registered charities, Canadian municipalities, the United Nations or an agency thereof, certain prescribed foreign universities, and certain foreign charitable organizations that have received gifts from the Crown up to two years prior to the gift;
2. Crown gifts—made to the federal or a provincial government;
3. ecological gifts—land designated ecologically sensitive, made to a Canadian municipality or a registered charity, and approved by the minister of national revenue as having conservation and environmental protection as one of its main purposes;
4. cultural gifts—cultural property given to a designated institution, both determined pursuant to the Cultural Property Export and Import Act.

Property is certified as *cultural property* by the Canadian Cultural Property Export Review Board. In order to qualify for tax benefits, the donee or the purchaser must be a *designated institution*. The board designates two categories of institution:

1. institutions that normally handle property of the type (galleries and museums will usually be given permanent classification as designated institutions for the type of property they deal with) and
2. institutions that, in the particular circumstances of a specific gift, the board holds to be in a position to care for the gift (this designation is specific to the particular gift).

The board makes determinations with respect to the "outstanding significance and national importance of objects or collections."[6] The criteria listed in the Cultural Property Export and Import Act[7] for a contribution to be found of "outstanding significance and national importance" (Section 11) are

1. close association with Canadian history or national life;
2. aesthetic qualities; and
3. value in the study of the arts or sciences.

These factors are considered in relation to both the mandate and the geographical location of the institution to which the property is being donated.[8]

In the case of an individual, relief consists of a tax credit of seventeen percent of the value of total gifts up to $200 and twenty-nine percent of the value in excess of this amount (Section 118.1[3]). However, the true value of the tax credit is much higher, as it precludes applicable surtaxes and provincial taxes that, with the federal tax, total a maximum of fifty percent to fifty-four percent of taxable income, depending on the province of residence of the donor. Thus, the tax credit is virtually equivalent to a deduction from income of the fair market value, apart from the first $200. (See chapter 9 for a discussion of cultural property legislation).

A claim of up to one hundred percent of annual income can be made by an individual for

1. gifts made in the year of death. If the value of the gift is in excess of one hundred percent of income, the excess can be carried back for one year (Section 118.1[3],[4],[5]).
2. gifts of certified cultural property donated to a designated institution pursuant to the Cultural Property Export and Import Act. Any excess can be carried forward up to five years after the year of the gift (Section 118.1[1]).
3. ecological property gifts having the same benefits as cultural property gifts (Section 118.1).

In all other cases, including gifts to Her Majesty in Right of Canada or a province or to Crown corporations, the limit on donations eligible for the tax credit that may be claimed in any given year (and may be carried forward for five years) is as follows:

1. seventy-five percent of the donor's income; plus
2. twenty-five percent of the taxable capital gain in respect of a gift of property to a qualified donee; plus
3. twenty-five percent of any recapture of depreciation in respect of property donated to a qualified donee. (Section 118.1[1]).

The formula is based on the notion that the taxable capital gain in respect to gifted property is added to income in the usual fashion, but the maximum annual claim is adjusted upward to ensure that the additions to income are more than eliminated by the increased donation limit.

The same general rules apply to corporate donors; however, rather than tax credits, a corporation is entitled to deductions from income under the federal rules. In certain situations, provincial rules may differ for corporations.

Capital Gains—Canada

As a general rule, when artwork and other similar property is gifted to a charity, the artwork is deemed to have been disposed of at its fair market value (Section 69[1]). Where the property has appreciated in value, the donor will normally realize a capital gain on the transfer. Only seventy-five percent of a capital gain is taxable.

However, no capital gain is recognized with respect to a donation of certified cultural property to an institution designated pursuant to the Cultural Property Export and Import Act (Income Tax Act, Section 39[1][i.1]), either by testamentary disposition (under a will) or by gift. If depreciation has been taken on the art (capital cost allowance), this must be brought back into income and is not forgiven under the act.[9]

A commercial gallery or art dealer is not able to have inventory certified as cultural property and thereby avoid a capital gain or income. Additionally, where the disposition is of property that is "listed personal property" (for example, a painting, sculpture, antique, etc.), no capital gain is recognized in respect of the first $1,000 of value on the particular property (Sections 40[2][g][iii], 41, 54).

Receipt of Benefit

It is the general rule that receiving any economic benefit in return for a donation will cause the donation to lose its status as a gift for which a tax credit is available. One exception has been accepted administratively. Where a ticket is purchased to a charity dinner, ball, concert, show, or like event and food, entertainment, etc., is provided, two payments are considered to have been made [Revenue Canada Interpretation Bulletin IT-110R3, par 5.]. That part of the total ticket price that is the fair market value of the admission is considered to be nondeductible; the balance is considered a gift to the charity [Revenue Canada Interpretation Bulletin IT-110R3, par. 6]. Revenue Canada has made no concessions for other partial gifts.

Valuation

The Canadian Cultural Property Export Review Board has been authorized under the Income Tax Act of Canada to set values for cultural gifts, for which it issues certificates (Section 118.1[10]). Auction sales are an important benchmark in the board's determination of value. For gifts that have been purchased recently, the price paid for the object will be the predominant factor. The board has reduced values of donated works purchased within three years of the date of the gift.[10]

For other types of property, a valuation by a reputable valuer should be obtained in writing. However, the opinion of a valuer will not be accepted as estimating value in all cases. In the case of property held for less than one year, Revenue Canada may argue that any increase in value is not reflective of the fair market value.[11] In the case of property purchased with the intention of making a donation shortly thereafter, Revenue Canada may also argue that any gain on the transaction should be treated as income, not a capital gain.[12] The benefits of making a gift may also be reduced if the property is income property.

Valuations inflated by reason of fraud or negligence, which therefore result in an under-reporting of income, may be subject to a penalty equal to $100 or fifty percent of the difference in tax liability, whichever is greater (Section 163[2]).

The Canadian Cultural Property Export Review Board has taken the position that its aim should be to reflect, not establish, the current market for the cultural property it certifies. Appraisals therefore have to address value in terms of recent sales, if any, of comparable objects in an open and unrestricted marketplace. Previous board determinations are not acceptable to the board as a basis on which a valuer estimates fair market value of works by the same artist or other copies of prior-valued and certified works by the artist (for example, another copy of an earlier appraised and value-accepted lithograph of the artist donated previously to another institution and approved by the board).

The board has accepted the definition of fair market value established in *Henderson Estate, Bank of New York v. Ministry of National Revenue.*[13]

The board has also determined that the role of auctions in the art market is increasingly important. Once considered wholesalers, auction houses are now active participants in the retail market. Therefore, the board considers prices achieved at auction (including the hammer price plus buyer's premiums, but not taxes). Auction results are important benchmarks for the board because they are evidence of sales at a given place and time; in some cases, they are the only verifiable indication of market value.[14]

The board also confirms the time and price paid by the donor or vendor to be relevant to market value, especially if the purchase is recent. However, in *Friedberg v. Canada*,[15] the trial judge approved the views of the court in *Conn v. M.N.R.* as follows:

> Fair market value does not seem to pay any attention to cost of acquisition, only what might be obtained in the market at the time of disposition. Costs of acquisition can vary greatly, as has been illustrated, even for the same item, and such a cost or an adjusted cost base might affect income tax but in my opinion does not affect fair market value.

U.S. courts have also looked at recent purchases as being relevant.

The concept of *blockage* has also been utilized by the board to reduce values. Blockage is discussed later in this chapter.

Civil Penalties for Misrepresentation by Third Parties

The 1999 Budget of Canada has proposed new civil penalties against those who knowingly or in circumstances amounting to gross negligence make false statements or omissions in respect to another person's tax matters. The new penalties will apply after Royal Assent. Revenue Canada has the burden of proof of establishing the facts necessary to apply these penalties.

The new penalty applies to tax shelter and other tax planning arrangements. It provides that any person who knowingly plans, promotes, or sells an arrangement that includes a false statement or omission is subject to the penalty, which is equal to the greater of $1,000 or one hundred percent of the gross revenue derived, or to be derived, by the person from the activity. The example given in the budget paper is as follows:

> Promoter X organizes an art scheme whereby taxpayers acquire art at its fair market value (FMV) of $100 and donate it to Charity Y at an inflated appraised value of $1,000 as appraised by Valuator Z. Charity Y issues a charitable donation receipt for the $1,000 providing taxpayers with a tax savings of $500 (assuming a fifty percent top marginal tax rate) which exceeds their cost of $100 for the art. Charity Y auctions off the art at its FMV of $100. The penalty would be levied against Promoter X for the false statement on the value, Valuator Z for furnishing false valuations, and Charity Y for issuing false receipts if it knew that the valuations were incorrect. Charity Y's registration as a charity could also be revoked. The taxpayer's donation receipt would presumably be reduced from $1,000 to $100. In addition, the taxpayer could be subject to the existing negligence penalty if he or she knew that the $1,000 appraised value was inflated.[16]

Contents of the Appraisal

The board has determined certain rules for appraisals, as follows:

1. No in-house appraisals are acceptable for gifts of any value to an institution.
2. All appraisals must be "at arm's length," i.e., completed by an independent appraiser not associated with any of the parties or the objects being donated and having no financial interest in the transaction.[17]
3. There must not be any prior association or affiliation between the valuer and the donor and/or the management of the recipient institution. If valuers have had business associations with clients or artists, the board expects such relationships to be openly acknowledged in the appraisal report. However, disclosure of such a relationship does not exclude the valuer.
4. Where more than one appraisal for the same object is sought (objects having a fair market value above $10,000 (CAN) require two appraisals), each appraisal must be prepared independently. Should a particular circumstance warrant a deviation from this procedure, the board secretariat must be consulted beforehand.
5. Appraisals are acceptable only if made by persons qualified and knowledgeable about market values, such as professional valuers or dealers in or valuators of the type of cultural property being appraised.
6. Only one appraisal is required if it is provided by a committee of a professional association, such as antiquarian, art, or antique-dealer associations.
7. All appraisals must state that they establish the estimated "fair market value" of the object. Valuations for "insurance purposes" or for "probate purposes" or simply for "value" are not acceptable. In addition, the valuer should define fair market value in its short form: "the highest price, expressed in terms of money, that the property would bring in an open and unrestricted market between a willing buyer and a willing seller who are both knowledgeable, informed, and prudent and who are acting independently of each other."[18]
8. Appraisals must be prepared by individuals or corporations who are actively buying and selling and who are professionally qualified valuers of the type of property concerned. They should be experienced and known for their expertise in the appropriate area. If the board is unsure of the expertise of a valuer in a given area, it may require information about the qualifications of the valuer, or an additional evaluation may be requested. However, the board does not publish a list of acceptable valuers and does not guarantee the acceptance of any appraisal.
9. Whether the cost of the appraisal should be borne by the donor or the recipient is not a direct concern of the board. (Often the institution is made responsible for payment, and the donor makes a donation to the institution for the amount of the appraisal, thereby making it tax-deductible.)

For a full discussion of valuers and appraisals for cultural property purposes, see chapter 9, "Cultural Property Legislation."

Election of Donated Value—Non-Artists

If the fair market value of donated property exceeds its cost for tax purposes, the taxpayer making the donation may pick a value anywhere between the cost and the fair market value of the property (Section 118.1[6] for individuals; Section 110.1[3] for corporations). Both the donation tax credit and the proceeds of the sale are deemed to be equal to this elected amount. The election is available for both gifts and bequests. Making an election can be helpful when the full charitable deduction cannot be utilized: the capital gain can be reduced with no effect on the amount of the charitable deduction claimed. As noted above, there is no capital gain on gifts of cultural property. There is, therefore, no election in respect to such gifts.

Election of Donated Value—Artists

The general provision described above pertains to capital property, not to inventory or other property that gives rise to ordinary income. In the case of an artist who creates a piece of artwork, it is part of the artist's inventory; therefore, any gain on disposition is income, not capital gain. Like all other ordinary income, it is taxed fully. A separate election enables an artist to reduce his or her taxable income arising on certain donations.

When making a qualifying donation of one's work as a charitable gift or a Crown gift, the artist may elect a value between the cost and the fair market value. This value will be considered to be the proceeds of the disposition of the item and the amount of the gift for tax-credit purposes (Section 118.1[7]).

When the gift is a cultural gift (that is, one made by the artist pursuant to the Cultural Property Export and Import Act), there is no need to make the election: the "proceeds" of the donation are deemed to be equal to the cost, resulting in no income (Section 118.1[7.1]). The amount of the gift for the donation tax credit is equal to the fair market value. The ultimate result is that an artist making a gift of cultural property will be in the same position as any other person making such a gift. No income will be deemed recognized on the transfer, and a donation tax credit equal to the full fair market value of the object will be available. With regard to a gift that is not cultural property, the artist can

1. elect to donate the work at its fair market value, which will result in a realization of the full inherent gain on the work (and therefore the maximum capital

gain) but receive a corresponding tax credit based on a donation value equal to the fair market value;

2. elect to donate the work at its cost amount, which will result in no realization of the inherent gain (and therefore no taxable capital gain) but receive a tax credit that is based on a donation value equal only to the cost amount; and

3. elect to donate the work at a value greater than its cost amount but less than the fair market value, which will result in a partial realization of the inherent gain on the work and receive a tax credit that is based on this elected amount, higher than cost but lower than fair market value.

A donation of copyright in any of the artist's works is outside the jurisdiction of the Cultural Property Export and Import Act and is dealt with under general tax laws (as would a donation of copyright by any other party). The act deals only with a donation of "things" and not with a donation of intellectual property. The incentives clearly favor donations that take the form of cultural gifts.

A proposed amendment provides that if property is the subject of a gift that is made within two years of the Canadian Cultural Property Export Review Board's valuation and is claimed as a charitable donation that is not a gift of cultural property, the board's valuation will nevertheless be deemed to be the fair market value of the property for purposes of the charitable donation deduction (proposed section 118.1 [10.1]). The board's valuation is also deemed to be the proceeds of disposition, subject to an election being made at a different amount.

Carry-Over of Excess Credits

The value of Crown gifts, cultural gifts, and ecological gifts may be claimed in the current year or in one of the preceding five years. In other words, any credit in excess of the income limitation may be used in any of the five following years, subject to the income limitation in that year. In the case of charitable gifts, any excess credit may be carried forward forever (Section 118.1[1]).

In some circumstances, six years may not be enough to exhaust the entire value of a gift. In such a case, a phased gift (a gift of partial interest) may be acceptable to Revenue Canada. While this is acceptable, for example, in the case of land, Revenue Canada does not yet recognize partial interests in, for example, a painting.[19]

Charitable Remainder Trust

It is possible to receive an immediate donation tax credit for property that does not become available to the recipient until the donor dies. This is done through gifting an equitable interest in a trust to a permitted donee. Revenue Canada has described an equitable interest in a trust as being that interest "created upon the transfer of any property (including real property) to a trust with the requirement that the property be distributed to a beneficiary at some future date (for example, when an income interest of another person ends)."[20] A gift will be considered to have been completed when the transfer of property to the trust has been completed and the interest in the trust has vested in the donee.[21] Such a gift will generally qualify for a donation tax credit equal to the fair market value of the equitable interest at the time of the transfer.

The valuation of such equitable interest may be problematic, however. The value of the equitable interest is the present value of the interest distributed to the donee, who is the ultimate beneficiary under the trust. This requires both an estimation of the duration of the intervening income interest of the beneficiary and an appropriate discount factor for that period. It will then be necessary to estimate the value of the item at the time of death. For works of art, determining the current value of an item is complex; estimating the value at a future date may be nearly impossible. Where the value cannot reasonably be determined, Revenue Canada has stated that no tax credit will be allowed.[22]

Estate Tax

There is no estate tax per se in Canada. However, property such as artwork is deemed to have been disposed of immediately before the death of the owner for proceeds equal to fair market value (Section 70[5]). This will cause any accrued gains to be realized and to be brought into the income of the deceased. The exception is property transferred on death to the surviving spouse or to a trust solely for the benefit of the spouse (Section 70[6]). Such a transfer is deemed to occur at the cost amount of the property transferred. Therefore, no capital gain will arise until the transferred property is disposed of by the surviving spouse.

It is possible to make donations out of a decedent's estate, thereby reducing the amount of tax payable on the deemed disposition. Gifts made by individuals in the year of death are deemed to be made by the individual in the preceding tax year to the extent that the gift has not been deducted in the year of death (Section 118.1[4]). Thus, executors may make gifts on which the donation tax credit described above can be claimed. The annual tax credit limitation for total gifts is one hundred percent of the individual's income for the year in which he or she dies or the following year.

Gift Tax

There is no gift tax in Canada. However, several provisions result in many gifts being subject to tax. Where a gift is made to any person during the donor's life, the gift is deemed to have been made for proceeds equal to the fair market value. To the extent that the property has increased in value, there will be a capital gain on this disposition. If the gift is a charitable or Crown gift and is to a qualified recipient, then the election described above is available and can be used to reduce any capital gain. The recipient of the gift is deemed to have acquired the property at its fair market value. However, as is the case for testamentary (estate) transfers to spouses, an *inter vivos* (lifetime) transfer between spouses will generally not trigger any tax. Such a transfer is deemed to occur at the cost amount, which is both the proceeds for the transferor/donor and the acquisition cost for the acquirer/recipient (Section 73[1]).

Gifts between certain related persons may also trigger the *income attribution* rules. When these rules come into play, income from the property transferred will "attribute" back to the transferor, who will be required to include it in his or her income. Any income or loss from property transferred to or for the benefit of a spouse will be deemed to be income of the transferor spouse (Sections 74.1[1]and 74.2[1]). As well, any capital gains realized on property transferred to a spouse will be attributed to the spouse who made the transfer (Section 74.2[1]). Income from property transferred to related minors (persons younger than 18 years for the whole of the year) will be attributed back to the transferor (Section 74.1[2]).

Attribution can be avoided by selling the property for its fair market value. In addition, to avoid attribution on spousal transfers, the deferral of recognition of capital gain, which applies automatically on these transfers, must be waived (Sections 73[1] and 74.5[1]). Of course, in avoiding attribution, the gift aspect of the transfer is eliminated.

DONATIONS IN UNITED STATES LAW

In the United States, donors who contribute works of art and other art objects to a charitable organization are generally entitled to a charitable deduction from income. Both corporations and individuals may deduct from income an amount equal to the fair market value of qualifying charitable contributions as required under the Internal Revenue Code of 1986. To qualify for the charitable contribution deduction, a transfer must constitute a contribution or gift within the meaning of the code. No definition of *contribution or gift* is found in the code. One test developed by the courts is that of "donative intent." The U.S. Supreme Court applied the test, holding that the transfer must be motivated by detached and disinterested generosity or by charitable motives rather than by expected economic benefit.[23] It is also relevant whether the donor received or expected to receive a quid pro quo for the transfer to the recipient (that is, some substantial benefit in return).[24] A receipt or expectation of quid pro quo benefit will disqualify the deduction.

A charitable contribution of artwork and other art objects for which a full deduction will be available generally consists of a transfer of long-term capital gain property to a permitted donee (for example, a museum) that is both voluntary and without receipt of or expectation of any economic benefit, where the property is put to a related use, and where the property is valued in accordance with certain standards.

Transfer of Property

Whether a gift has been made is a matter of state law, but it generally depends on the passing of "dominion and control" over the contribution to the donee.[25] If the donor retains an ownership interest, he or she will not be treated as having parted with the property and will not be able to claim a charitable deduction. For example, the long-term loan to a museum of an art object would not qualify, as the lender still owns the object and has no intention of parting with ownership.

Thus, conditional gifts may not qualify for deduction as charitable contributions. With respect to a gift subject to a condition subsequent (that is, one that may occur after the gift has been made and will void the gift), a deduction is allowable if the occurrence of the conditional event "appears on the date of the gift to be so remote as to be negligible" [Reg. Sec. 1.170A-1(e)]. In the case of gifts subject to a condition precedent (a condition that must first occur), no charitable contribution is considered to exist until the condition has been met. A deduction will be allowed only if the possibility that the charitable transfer will not become effective is so remote as to be negligible [Reg. Sec 1.170A-1(e)].

A gift consisting of the right to use property or an interest that is less than the entire interest held by the taxpayer generally will not qualify for deduction (Code Sec. 170[f][3][A]). However, among the exceptions to this prohibition are gifts of an undivided portion of the donor's entire interest (Code Sec. 170[f][3][B][ii]). This allows gifts of, for example, one-fourth of a painting to be made. In this way, a gift may be spread out over a number of years. Where an interest is gifted in this manner, the donee will thereafter become entitled to possession. For example, if one-fourth of a painting is donated to a museum, the museum will become entitled to possession of the whole painting for one-fourth of the year.

If this exemption from the partial-interest prohibition is used to claim a deduction while maintaining possession, it may violate the prohibition against future interests. A right to possession by the donee will determine whether the interest is a present one, which qualifies for deduction, or a future one, which does not.[26] However, it has been suggested that no more than a year should pass between the gift and the period of initial possession by the donee.[27]

In the case of a work of art, a donor who also owns the copyright to the work must donate both the work and the copyright to the charity in order to qualify for the charitable income tax deduction (Reg. Sec. 1.170A-7[b][1]). Generally, only complete interests will entitle the donor to a deduction. A work of art and the copyright therein are not treated as two distinct properties but as two interests in the same property (Reg. Sec. 1.170A-7[b][1]). These are separate properties under copyright law and under the provisions dealing with estate tax, which may lead to some confusion. However, if a donor owns only the work of art, his or her donation need not include the copyright to be eligible for deduction, as the contribution is the donor's entire interest in the property and therefore does not offend the prohibition against partial interests (Code Sec. 170[f][3][A]; Reg. Sec. 1.170A-7[a][2][i]).

Long-Term Capital Gain Property

Tangible personal property may be contributed and a deduction taken for the sum of the cost of the item plus any appreciation in value considered to be a long-term capital gain (that is, capital gains realized on capital assets held for more than twelve months). Capital property includes tangible personal property, which comprises items such as works of art, collectibles, antiques, and jewelry (Code Sec. 1221).

All charitable contributions of ordinary income property are required to be reduced by the amount of ordinary income that would have resulted had the contributed property been sold at its fair market value at the time of contribution (Code Sec. 170[e][1]). Ordinary income property is "property any portion of the gain on which would not have been long-term capital gain if the property had been sold by the donor at its fair market value at the time of its contribution to the charitable organization" (Reg. Sec. 1.170A-4[b][1]). Ordinary income property would generally consist of property held for less than one year (Code Sec. 1221[3]; Code Sec. 170[e][1][A]). However, property held for more than one year may not qualify for a deduction if, on the facts, the gain on the sale of the property would not be a long-term capital gain. This would be the case if the property were not held as capital property. Examples of ordinary income property include

1. property held by the donor primarily for sale to customers in the ordinary course of the donor's trade or business (a dealer);
2. a work of art created by the donor; and
3. a capital asset held by the donor for less than one year (a speculation) (Code Sec. 1221[3][a]; Code Sec. 170[e][1][A]).

Property that is received as a gift from the artist is not a capital asset, and any donation of the property so received will not therefore qualify as a charitable deduction equal to the fair market value (Code Sec. 1221[3][C]). It will be ordinary income property, subject to the relevant restrictions. If the property is not received by way of gift but is purchased, the fact that it was purchased from the artist will not restrict the charitable deduction. In the case of a gift, the cost for both parties is the same. In the case of a purchase, the cost for the purchaser (the price paid) will usually be more than the cost to the artist. It is the equivalency of "tax cost" in the first case that offends the code and prevents a deduction from being taken.

Donees

Permitted Donees

For the purposes of determining the deductibility of a contribution by an individual, the term *charitable contribution* is defined (Code Sec. 170[c]) as a contribution or gift by an individual to or for the use of any organization included in the following categories:

1. a state, a possession of the United States, or any of their political subdivisions, the United States or the District of Columbia, if made for exclusively public purposes;
2. a corporation, trust, community chest, fund, or foundation
   a. created or organized in the United States or in any possession thereof or under the law of the United States, any state, the District of Columbia, or any possession of the United States;
   b. organized and operated exclusively for religious, charitable, scientific, literary, or educational purposes, for the prevention of cruelty to children or animals, or to foster national or international amateur sports competition (if no part of its activities involves the provision of athletic facilities or equipment);
   c. in which no part of the net earnings inures to the benefit of any private shareholder or individual;
   d. that is not disqualified from tax exemption by reason of attempting to influence legislation and does not participate in, or intervene in (includ-

ing the publishing or distributing of statements), any political campaign on behalf of (or in opposition to) any candidate for public office;

3. a post or organization of war veterans or an auxiliary unit or society of, or trust or foundation for, any such post or organization
   a. organized in the United States or any of its possessions or
   b. no part of the net earnings of which inures to the benefit of any private shareholder or individual;
4. a domestic fraternal society, order, or association operating under the lodge system, if such contribution or gift is to be used exclusively for religious, charitable, scientific, literary, or educational purposes, or for the prevention of cruelty to children or animals; or
5. a cemetery company owned and operated exclusively for the benefit of its members, or any corporation chartered solely for burial purposes as a cemetery corporation and not permitted by its charter to engage in any business not necessarily incidental to that purpose, if such corporation is not operated for profit and no part of the net earnings of such company or corporation inures to the benefit of any private shareholder or individual.

Restricted Donees

Gifts to charitable organizations that are permitted donees may nonetheless not be deductible. If the gift is subject to restrictions concerning its application, its deduction may be denied. Examples of such restrictions include:

1. contributions to a class of beneficiaries specifically designated by the donor or by the donee's charter. As the class becomes smaller, the charitable purpose of the donee begins to look private rather than public. Contributions are not deductible when the donee organization is even partially operated for the taxpayer's private or personal purposes.[28]
2. certain individuals who often benefit from gifts made to a charitable organization. The determination of whether such gifts are deductible is usually based on whether the donee organization has full control of the donation and discretion as to its use, so as to ensure that it will be used to carry out the organization's functions and purposes. Provided that the donee has such control and discretion and that the gift is used to further the organization's exempt purposes, the charitable gift ordinarily will be deductible, notwithstanding the donor's wish that the gift be applied for the benefit of a particular individual (for example, Rev. Rul. 61-66, 1961-1 C.B. 19).

Ineligible Donees

No deduction will be allowed for contributions to certain organizations, including:

1. contributions made directly to foreign organizations by U.S. individuals or corporations (Sec. 170[c][2][A]). Deductions to Canadian charities may be deductible under the Canada-U.S. Income Tax Treaty.[29] To obtain this deduction, the donor will generally need to have Canadian-source income. Deductions may also be available for contributions to certain Mexican charitable organizations under an income tax treaty with Mexico. Contributions to U.S. organizations that transfer property to foreign charities may be deducted if the U.S. organization controls the use of the funds.
2. organizations with racially discriminatory policies (Rev. Rul. 71-447; Rev. Rul. 75-231).
3. communist controlled organizations (Code Sec. 170[k]; Reg. Sec. 1.170A-1[h][3]).
4. certain other organizations that have engaged in prohibited transactions (Reg. Sec. 1.170A-1[h][2]; Code Secs. 508, 4948).
5. organizations that attempt to influence legislation or that participate in political campaigns (Reg. Sec. 1.170A-1[h], [f]).

Economic Benefit

If the donor receives or is deemed to have received partial consideration in exchange for the appreciated property, a deduction of the full fair market value is not available. This is sometimes referred to as a *bargain sale*. In such a case, the excess of fair market value over the actual selling price—the bargain—may be treated as a charitable contribution (Code Sec. 1011 [b]). The fair market value of the property is reduced by the fair market value of property received in consideration of the transfer in determining the amount of the deduction (Reg. Sec. 170A-4[c][2])

Donated tangible personal property must be related to the purpose or function of the donee in order to qualify for full fair market value deduction. If it is not, the amount of the gain that would have been the long-term capital gain if the property had been sold at the time of the contribution is reduced by one hundred percent (Code Sec. 170[e][1][B][i], also Reg. Sec. 1.170A-4[b][3]). A donor may treat his or her gift as being put to a related use only if

1. the donor establishes that the property is not put to an unrelated use by the donee (that it is used for the actual purposes of the donee organization), and

2. at the time of the contribution or at the time the contribution is treated as made, it is reasonable to assume that the property will not be put to an unrelated use by the donee. For example, a gift of a valuable painting to a cemetery company may not qualify, whereas a gift of a valuable historic funeral urn may qualify (Reg. Sec. 1.170A-4[b][3][I],[ii]).

The donor will file Form 8283 to report certain required information about noncash charitable contributions above $500 to obtain a permitted deduction for the donation.

If an object such as a work of art is donated to the donee and the donee sells the work within two years thereafter, then the donee must file a Form 8282. If it is determined that the donation has been made for a use unrelated to the purposes of the institution, it could be disallowed (S. 170 [e][1][A][i]).

Valuation of the Deduction

Generally, the amount of a charitable donation for a contribution of property is the property's fair market value (Reg. Sec. 1.170A-1[c][1]). Fair market value is "the price at which the property would change hands between a willing buyer and willing seller, neither being under any compulsion to buy or sell and both having reasonable knowledge of relevant facts" (Reg. Sec. 1.170A-1[c][2]).[30]

It has been ruled that the fair market value of property purchased at a discount and contributed to charity should be the purchase price rather than the nondiscounted value for purposes of determining the amount of the deduction (Rev. Rul. 80-69; Rev. Rul. 80-69).

Most revenue rulings on valuation have focused on the economic reality of the transaction (a willing buyer and willing seller analysis). The case law has reflected the IRS focus on economic reality as well. The courts have used the retail market to determine the correct valuation but have recognized that there may be more than one retail market. The market that most closely resembles the activities of the taxpayer is the market that will be examined.[31] In determining value a number of factors are examined, including the item's condition, how unique or rare it is, its authenticity, and the market for comparable items.[32]

Often an item is purchased, then donated a short time later. If it is clear that the purchase was at a discount to the actual value of the item, a large difference between purchase price and deduction will more likely be accepted.[33] In the absence of unusual facts in such a situation, the purchase price will be the best indicator of the value of an item if the purchase was within the last twelve months.[34]

Section 7517 of the code provides that the IRS must furnish, on written request by a donor or executor, a written statement explaining the basis on which the IRS has determined or proposes to determine a valuation of property that is different from the valuation submitted by the donor or executor. This section applies to all valuation issues. The section goes on to deal with the timing for such a statement to be furnished as well as the contents of the statement.

Substantiation of the Donation

Charitable contributions are required to be substantiated by the donor in order to qualify for deduction (Code Sec. 170[a][1]). The specifics depend on the nature of the asset and the value of the deduction claimed.

Contributions of Property: less than $250

A receipt must be obtained showing the name of the charitable organization, the date and location of the contribution, and a reasonable description of the property. The donor must keep written records in addition to the receipt. These records should show

1. the name and address of the organization contributed to;
2. the date and location of the contribution;
3. a reasonable description of the property;
4. the fair market value of the property and the method by which this figure was obtained;
5. the cost basis (the cost for tax purposes) of the property should the amount of the deduction be reduced;
6. the amount claimed as a deduction if less than the entire interest is contributed;
7. the terms of any conditions attached to the gift; and
8. the amount claimed as a deduction for the year.

Contributions of Property: $250–$499

All gifts of property for which the deduction is greater than $250 require that the donee provide a written acknowledgment of the gift. The acknowledgment must include the same information as the receipt above and further must

1. be written;
2. provide a description of the property, whether the organization provided any goods or services in return, and a description and estimate of the value of the goods or services so provided; and
3. be obtained on or before the earlier of (a) the date the return is filed for the year in which the contribution is made or (b) the due date for filing the return.

Contributions of Property: $500–$5,000

In addition to the written acknowledgment and the written records described above, the taxpayer must submit Form 8283, completing Part A, with his or her tax return (Reg. Sec. 1.170A-13[b][3]). There is no appraisal requirement (Reg. Sec. 1.170A-13[b][2][ii]). In addition to the written records above, written records are required containing details as to how the property was acquired; the approximate date of the acquisition or substantial completion; and the cost basis of the property. An explanation should be attached if there is reasonable cause for not providing information on acquisition date or cost basis.

Contributions of Property: $5,000–$20,000

Certain additional requirements apply if the deduction claimed for an item and all similar items of property contributed by the donor in one year exceeds $5,000. This would apply, for example, if a group of paintings contributed in a year had an aggregate fair market value of $10,000, even though none of the paintings had a value in excess of $1,000. These requirements are that a qualified appraisal be obtained; a complete appraisal summary be attached to the return on which the deduction is claimed; and the written records described above be maintained.

A qualified appraisal, as defined in Reg. Sec. 1.170A-13(c)(3),

1. relates to an appraisal made no more than sixty days prior to the time of the contribution of property;
2. is prepared, signed, and dated by a qualified appraiser (*qualified appraiser* is defined in Reg. Sec. 1.170A-13[c][5]);
3. does not involve a prohibited appraisal fee (a *prohibited appraisal fee* is one in which the whole or part is based on the appraised value of the property before or after an IRS audit) (Reg. Sec. 1.170A-13[c][6][i]); and
4. contains the following information:
   a. a sufficiently detailed description of the property;
   b. physical condition of tangible personal property;
   c. date or expected date of the contribution;
   d. terms of any agreement entered into that relates to use, sale, or disposition of the property;
   e. name, address, and taxpayer identification number of the qualified appraiser and, if applicable, that of a partnership or person employing the appraiser;
   f. qualifications of the appraiser;
   g. a statement that the appraisal was prepared for income-tax purposes;
   h. valuation date of the property;
   i. appraised fair market value; and

j.   the method used in the valuation, plus the specific facts used, and the reason for their use, in the application of such method.

An appraisal summary is made on Form 8283 and is essentially a summary of the qualified appraisal. It must be signed by the appraiser (Reg. Sec. 1.170A-13[c][4]).

Contributions of Art Valued at More than $20,000

A copy of the complete appraisal report prepared by a qualified appraiser is required. A photograph must be provided on request, of a size and quality to show the object fully, preferably an eight-by-ten-inch color print or color transparency no smaller than four by five inches.

The qualifications of the appraiser who signs the appraisal must be included. These would include, for example, the background, experience, education, and professional memberships in appraisal or related organizations. The appraiser cannot be the donor or donee; a party to the transaction in which the donor obtained the object (that is, the dealer or an employee of the dealer); or anyone having a real or perceived conflict of interest.[35]

IRS Appraisal Review

Because of the uncertainties inherent in valuing certain types of contributed property, the IRS has created and published Revenue Procedure 96-15. If at least one of the items has a value of $50,000 or more, a taxpayer can, before reporting a deduction on an income tax return, request that the IRS provide a statement of value to establish the value of contributed property. A fee of $2,500 for the first three items and $250 for each thereafter is payable for this service. The taxpayer must first obtain a qualified appraisal by a qualified appraiser for each item of property. A request may be made only after the property has been transferred by contribution, gift, or death but before the taxpayer has filed the return.

The Art Advisory Panel, a panel of experts, has been constituted by the IRS to assist in determinations of the reasonableness of valuations of art.[36] The panel will classify valuations as being justified, questionable, or clearly unjustified. The panel will usually be requested by the local IRS audit office to review valuations that exceed $20,000.[37]

The panel is voluntary, comprising various art experts with particular knowledge of the cultural areas of objects being evaluated. They include art dealers, museum curators and directors, historians, and critics; and they are appointed by the commissioner for the Internal Revenue Service. Currently, the panel has twenty-five members and meets twice a year in Washington, D.C. Its meetings are closed to the public. It assesses the documentation submitted by taxpayers in support of values being proposed. The recommendations of the panel are then submitted to the IRS with an explanation of the valuations it has determined.

Taxpayers may requisition a reconsideration of any value that has been readjusted by the committee only if the taxpayer provides new information deemed to be relevant. In such cases, the matter is then resubmitted to the panel.

As indicated earlier, the United States Internal Revenue Code (Section 6662) provides penalties for "substantial valuation misstatements" and "substantial estate or gift-tax valuation understatements." As well, interest and penalties (defined and categorized within Section 6664) are imposed on the taxpayer. Therefore, it is extremely important that a valuer be accurate and responsible in providing appraisals, especially when the appraisals are being used for tax purposes. Both the appraiser and his or her client are liable to penalties for irresponsible appraisal values.

Penalties

If property is valued in excess of its actual fair market value, an accuracy-related penalty or a fraud penalty may apply. A penalty is imposed on the portion of any underpayment of tax attributable to one or more of the following (Code Sec. 6662[b]):

1. negligence or disregard of the rules or regulations;
2. substantial understatement of income tax;
3. substantial valuation misstatement for income tax purposes.

An underpayment is generally equal to the amount of tax imposed less the amount of tax shown on the taxpayer's return (Code Sec. 6664[a]). The penalty is twenty percent of the underpayment of tax in respect of the overstatement of value (Code Sec. 6662[a]). A substantial misstatement occurs when the value of any property claimed is two hundred percent or more of the amount determined to be the correct fair market value (Code Sec. 6662[e][1]). The penalty will not apply unless the portion of the underpayment attributable to substantial valuation misstatement exceeds $5,000 (Code Sec. 6662[e][2]).

Where there is a gross valuation misstatement (where the value of any property claimed is four hundred percent or more) of the amount determined to be the fair market value and the underpayment of tax is more than $5,000, the penalty is equal to forty percent (Code Sec. 6662[h]).

In addition, a fraud penalty equal to seventy-five percent of any underpayment of tax that is due to fraud may be applicable.

Contribution Limits

For the purposes of limiting the amount of charitable contributions that may be deducted in a year, permissible donees have been divided into two types of charities: fifty percent limit organizations and thirty percent limit organizations.

Fifty Percent Limit Organizations

The fifty percent limit organizations include public charities (such as museums) (Code Sec. 170[b][1][A][i]-[vi]; 170[b][1][A][viii]); most churches; certain educational institutions; certain hospitals and medical research organizations; university endowment funds, governmental units and publicly supported organizations; private operating foundations; and two types of nonoperating foundations.

A *private operating foundation* is a private foundation that makes qualifying distributions to be used directly in the conduct of its exempt activities. Such qualifying distributions must equal at least eighty-five percent of its adjusted net income or its "minimum investment return" (Code Secs. 509[a]; 4942[j][3]; 4942[g]; 4942[f]; 4942[e]).

One type of nonoperating foundation is a distributing foundation, which must distribute one hundred percent of its received donations (Code Sec. 170[b][1][E][ii]; Reg. Sec. 1.170A-9[g][1][ii] and [iii]). The other type is an organization that maintains a common fund of received donations but that does not qualify to be exempt from tax because certain donors may direct where such donations are to be distributed. Such a foundation will qualify as a fifty percent limit organization if it distributes all received donations (Code Sec. 170[b][1][A][vii]; 170[b][1][E][iii]).

Contributions to fifty percent limit organizations are subject to two limits. The first limit is an overall limit on deductions of charitable contributions equal to fifty percent of the taxpayer's contribution base for the year. (In Code Sec. 170[b][1][F], *contribution base* is defined as an individual's "adjusted gross income" [AGI] before deducting any "nonoperating loss" carryback for that year.)

The next limit is with respect to deductions of contributions of cash and ordinary income property to fifty percent limit organizations. An individual's limit is fifty percent of the individual's contribution base. The limit for contributions of capital gain property is thirty percent (Code Sec. 170[b][1][A] and 170[b][1][C]).

Thirty Percent Limit Organizations

The thirty percent limit organizations include permissible donees that do not qualify as fifty percent limit organizations.

Contributions to thirty percent limit organizations are subject to a thirty percent limit, except for appreciated capital-gain property, which is subject to a limit
of twenty percent. These limits also apply where the contribution is for the use of
either type of charity (Code Sec. 170[b][1][B] and 170[b][1][D]; Reg. Sec. 1.170A-
8[c]). The phrase "for the use of" was held by the U.S. Supreme Court to require
that the gift be made in trust for the benefit of the organization.[38]

A donor may elect to treat donated capital-gain property that meets the relat-
ed-use rule, subject to a deduction limit of thirty percent, as being subject to a
deduction limit of fifty percent. If the donor makes the election, the deduction
will be limited to the cost of the property (Code Sec. 170[b][1][C][iii]). This
election may be used if a deduction for donation at fair market value could not be
utilized and the cost amount is substantial.

Carry-Over

There are four separate carry-over provisions. The first applies to contributions to fifty percent limit organizations in excess of fifty percent of a taxpayer's
contribution base, which excess is treated as a contribution to public charities in
each of the five succeeding years or until no excess exists (Code Sec. 170[d][1]).

The second carry-over provision applies to contributions of thirty percent capital gain property to fifty percent charities. These may be carried over to the extent
such contributions exceed thirty percent of the taxpayer's contribution base (Code
Sec. 170[b][1][C][ii]).

A five-year carry-over also exists for contributions in excess of 30 percent of the
contribution base to, or for the use of, thirty percent charities (Code Sec.
170[b][1][B]). In addition, a five-year carry-over exists for excess twenty percent
capital-gain property contributions to the use of fifty percent charities and to, or
for the use of, thirty percent and fifty percent charities.

Capital Gains—U.S.

Generally, on the transfer of tangible personal property to a permissible donee, any inherent capital gain will not be recognized. Capital gains will be recognized in two specific situations:

1. if partial consideration is received or deemed to have been received in ex-
    change for the property. In such a situation, the cost for tax purposes of the
    property is allocated between the sale proceeds and the charitable contribution
    according to their proportion of the fair market value of the property (Code Sec.
    1011[b]; Reg. Sec. 1.1011-2; Reg. Sec. 1.170A-4[c][2][i]). For example, if an

artwork with a tax cost of $10,000 and a fair market value of $25,000 is bargain sold for $20,000, the deduction would be $5,000 ($25,000 less the proceeds received or $20,000). The tax cost would be allocated four-fifths ($20,000/ $25,000) to the sale proceeds and one-fifth ($5,000/$25,000) to the deduction of $5,000. Therefore, only $8,000 of tax cost allocated to the sale proceeds, yielding a capital gain of $2,000.

2. if the charity sells the property shortly after the transfer. If this sale is found to be part of an "overall plan," the charity may be treated as the donor's agent in selling the property, with the result that the donor is treated as if he or she sold the property for cash (Rev. Rul. 60-370). Any capital gain inherent in the property would therefore be realized by the donor. A deduction is still available for the cash contribution, but the income of the donor is increased by the amount of the capital gain.

Alternate Minimum Tax (AMT)

At one time, deductions in respect of charitable contributions were considered to be tax preference items. Therefore, the benefits of making such a contribution were often offset by a corresponding increase in liability under the Alternate Minimum Tax (AMT), often with the net effect of completely eliminating the value of the deduction.[39] However, the paragraph deeming the deduction to be a tax preference item was deleted in 1993.[40] As a result, claiming the deduction will no longer affect one's AMT calculation.

Gift Tax

Gift tax is imposed on gratuitous *inter vivos* (lifetime) transfers of property by an individual to a donee in exchange for less than full consideration, in money or money's worth. The tax is imposed on the donor, not the donee (Reg. Sec. 25.2510-1[b], 25.2511-2[a]). A gift for gift-tax purposes is not necessarily the same as a gift for income-tax purposes. A gift for gift-tax purposes is "any transaction in which an interest in property is gratuitously passed or conferred upon another" (Code Sec. 2511[a]), while a gift for income-tax purposes requires all the ingredients mentioned earlier. The transfer may be in trust, and it may be direct or indirect (Code Sec. 2511[a]). Whether a transfer is a gift for gift-tax purposes depends on:

1. whether ownership has sufficiently shifted from the donor to the donee (if the donor retains no legal right or economic benefit in the transferred property);[41]
2. whether the donor received less than adequate and full consideration in money or money's worth (Reg. Sec. 25.2511-1[g][1]), for example, a sale of a valuable object to an owner's friend for minimal consideration.

If property is transferred for less than adequate and full consideration in money or money's worth, the value of the transferred property in excess of the consideration received is a gift for gift-tax purposes.

Section 25.2512-1 of the Gift Tax Regulations provides that the value of property is the price at which the property would change hands between a willing buyer and a willing seller, neither being under any compulsion to buy or to sell and both having reasonable knowledge of the relevant facts.

Revenue Procedure 96-15 provides a procedure for taxpayers to request advance review of art valuations for income, estate, and gift tax returns.

In determining taxable gifts, the following should be noted:

1. A donor may exclude the first $10,000 of present (not future) interests in property gifted to each donee in each year (Code Sec. 2503[b]).
2. A marital deduction is allowed for all qualifying gifts to a spouse who is a U.S. citizen (Code Sec. 2523). Non–U.S. citizen spouses are not entitled to the marital deduction. Gifts to non–U.S. citizen spouses are subject to a $100,000 annual exclusion (Code Sec. 2523[i]).
3. An unlimited deduction is allowed for certain gifts to governmental entities and charitable organizations (Code Sec. 2522).
4. A unified credit is allowed equivalent to an exemption from tax of $625,000 in 1998; $650,000 in 1999; $675,000 in 2000; $700,000 in 2002; $850,000 in 2004; $950,000 in 2005; and $1 million in 2006 (Code Secs. 2010, 2001[c], 2505).
5. Married donors may split gifts. If both spouses are U.S. citizens or residents and both consent, the gift may be considered to be made one-half by each spouse (Code Sec. 2513[a]; Reg. Sec. 25.2513-1).

Estate Tax

Federal estate tax is levied on the taxable estate on the death of an individual. The taxable estate is equal to the gross estate (the value of all property transferred or deemed to have been transferred at death), less certain deductions.

The Charitable Deduction

A charitable deduction from the taxable estate is allowed for the value of property transferred to or for the use of certain charitable, religious, scientific, literary, educational, and public organizations (Code Sec. 642[c]). Although the deduction is not subject to any percentage limitations (unlike an income-tax charitable deduction), property for which the deduction is taken must be included in the decedent's gross estate. For U.S. citizens or residents, the deduction is not limited to transfers to domestic corporations or associations.

The categories of beneficiaries that are qualified to receive deductible bequests include (Code Sec. 2055[a][1]):

1. the United States, a state, a political subdivision of a state, or the District of Columbia, as long as the transfer is for exclusively charitable purposes;
2. any corporation or association organized and operated exclusively for religious, charitable, scientific, literary, or educational purposes (the deduction is not allowed if any portion of the organization's earnings benefits any private individual);
3. trusts and fraternal societies, orders, or associations operating under the lodge system, as long as the property is to be used exclusively for religious, charitable, scientific, literary, or educational purposes; and
4. veterans' organizations incorporated by an act of Congress or any of its departments, local chapters, or posts, as long as none of its net earnings benefits any private individual.

Unlike the charitable contribution deduction discussed above, it is possible to transfer the ownership of a piece of art without the related copyright for estate-tax and personal-property law purposes.

Valuation

Although valuation for estate-tax purposes is generally the same as that for other tax purposes, there are differences of note. According to Revenue Procedure 65-19, 1965-2 C.B. 1002, valuations for estate tax can be based on actual sales of tangible personal property of the estate through classified advertising in newspapers or at a public auction—if the sale is made within a reasonable period following the valuation date and if there is no substantial change in market conditions. These are considered to be retail sales at retail prices.

The value of the gross estate of a decedent is determined by including the value at the time of death of all property wherever situated (Code Sec. 2031). Section 20.2031-1(b) of the regulations provides that the value of property included in a decedent's gross estate is its fair market value at the time of the death of the decedent.

Section 20.2031-6(a) provides that the fair market value of a decedent's household and personal effects is the price that a willing buyer would pay to a willing seller, neither being under any compulsion to buy or sell and both having reasonable knowledge of the relevant facts. A forced sale is not a fair market sale, nor is a sale outside of the market most commonly used for the sale of the object.

Section 20.2031-6(b) of the regulations provides that if articles having market, artistic or intrinsic value of a total in excess of $3,000 are included among the household and personal effects, an appraisal completed by an expert or experts under oath must be filed with the estate tax return.

Section 20.2031-6(d) provides that if expert appraisers are employed, they must be reputable and of recognized competency to appraise the particular class of property involved.

There is a penalty for valuation understatements. A valuation understatement occurs if the value of any property claimed on the estate tax return is $66^2/_3$ percent or less of the amount determined to be the correct valuation. If there is such an under-payment of estate tax because of the understatement, an addition to tax of up to thirty percent of the underpayment may be assessed. This, however, does not apply to underpayments of less than $1,000. Also, there is a waiver limitation in that the IRS may waive all or any part of the additional tax if it can be shown that there was a reasonable basis for the valuation claimed and it was made in good faith.

In valuing large blocks of property of the same type for estate tax, a *blockage discount* is often applied. (This concept has been specifically recognized for sales of artwork.)[42] This discount recognizes that the size of the block of property may be such that it would depress the market for those goods if the block were to be sold as a whole. The amount of the discount depends on the size of the block, the relative prices of the pieces of art, the size of the market, any discounts that need to be offered, and the estimate of time it would take to sell the whole of the block.[43]

The application of a blockage discount was key to a recent multimillion-dollar suit brought by attorney Edward Hayes against the Andy Warhol estate and the Andy Warhol Foundation for Visual Arts. Hayes was the estate's former attorney. After he was fired, he sought up to $14 million in legal fees from the estate and foundation. The estate, the foundation, and the Charities Bureau of New York State Attorney General's Office countered that Hayes had received $4.85 million, which was payment in full. The difference lay in the two dramatically different valuations of Warhol's work owned by the estate and transferred to the founda-tion. Hayes' contract gave him a fee of two percent of the estate's value, which Hayes claimed was about $600 million. (Experts for Hayes included private New York art dealers and a former Christie's photography specialist.) The estate and foun-dation, however, stated the value of the estate at $220 million, based primarily on Christie's 1991 Date of Transfer appraisal of the artworks willed by Warhol to the foundation. Christie's valued the art portion at $95 million, as against the $226 million determined by Hayes' expert witness. Christie's had applied a blockage dis-count to reduce the value of the art assets for estate-tax purposes.

In determining the amount of the legal fees payable to Hayes as executor in the administration of the estate, the retainer agreement between the parties had to be reviewed. It was found to be unenforceable on technical grounds. The next question was: What was reasonable compensation for the services provided throughout the administration of this very complex and diverse estate?

The court indicated that what constitutes reasonable compensation "requires consideration of the nature of the services rendered, the size of the estate, the responsibility undertaken, the difficulty of the legal issues, the ability of the attorney, and the amount of time spent."[44] Based on these criteria, the court awarded $7.2 million to lawyers Edward Hayes and Francis Harvey Jr. for the fees as executor in the administration in the estate.[45] The fees were reduced on appeal to $3.5 million on the theory that the executor was not an expert or specialist in the art field but an attorney, and the original award would have compensated him at an exorbitant hourly rate.[46]

In order for blockage to be relevant, a number of factors must be considered.

1. What is the block of works?
2. Will the size of the block have any significant affect on the market? A factor of size is the medium of the works: Are all the works in the same medium?
3. What is the size or sizes of the work?

If the works are of different sizes and in different media, and thus might be available for different markets, what may have been considered to be a block may not really be one.

In the Canadian case of *Zelinski v. Her Majesty the Queen,* the court refused to accept a blockage discount of fifty percent put forward by one of the expert witness valuers, stating that:

> The hypothetical open market in which fair market value is determined contemplates purchasers and vendors acting without pressure to buy or sell. There is no evidence that these appellants, the donors of the artworks to museums, were under any pressure to dispose of the Morrisseau art. In fact, their evidence was to the contrary, and I believe them. The fact that they decided to give away all of the Morrisseau art within a twenty-four month period does not mean that they would attempt to sell it within the same period if they had decided to follow the sale route.[47]

The judge, however, went on to say: "I shall without hesitation use the cost of the Morrisseau art to the appellants as a relevant fact in my quest for fair market value."[48]

In respect to valuations, he stated:

> I am troubled by the fact that the Professional Art Dealers Association of Canada appraisal was performed in the midst of the valuation years without any apparent inquiry as to where Morrisseau was at that time, whether he was producing new works of art, whether the new works were being sold, and if so, where and to whom.

These questions must be relevant when determining the fair market value of paintings by a contemporary artist who appears to have been highly productive in the midst of the valuation years.[49]

In the field of art objects, blockage discounts originated for determining the value of art objects in a collection or the value of the art inventory of a deceased artist for estate-taxation purposes. It has now been applied from time to time to charitable contributions as well, both in the United States and Canada.

Copyright and Moral Rights

Other considerations in determining fair market value reach into the area of copyright and moral rights. Does the work donated also contain the copyright of the artist and a waiver of the moral rights of the artist? If it is so included, does this give an increased value to the work donated? And, how does one determine a copyright value?[50]

California Resale Royalties Act

Another possible issue in determining value is the California Resale Royalties Act,[51] which applies to the sale of works of fine art that take place in California after January 1, 1997. The act grants to artists who are American citizens or residents of California for two years a residual right to five percent of the sale price on the sale by a seller residing in California and/or if the sale takes place in California. This right exists for the life of the artist and for twenty years thereafter. No waiver of this right is permitted by the act. The act covers sales of fine art sold at auction or by a gallery, dealer or broker, museum, or other person acting as the agent for the seller. These are relatively new areas for the consideration in determination of value by valuers and tax authorities.

Charitable deductions are not eligible if:

1. at the time of the decedent's death, a transfer to a charitable organization is dependent on an act or an event before it is effective, unless the possibility that the charity might not receive the property can be considered negligible (Reg. Sec. 20.2055-2[b]). For example, if a work of art was bequeathed to a museum only if the decedent's daughter fails to have children, the gift will become effective only when the chance of the daughter having a child becomes negligible.
2. a legatee or trustee is given power to divert the property to a use that would not qualify for a charitable deduction if the property were bequeathed directly by the decedent for that use (Reg. Sec. 20.2055-2[b]).

3. there are unseverable charitable and noncharitable interests in the same property. An estate-tax charitable deduction is allowed for the value of a charitable
interest only if such interest is currently ascertainable and, thus, severable
from the noncharitable interest (Code Sec. 2055[e][2]; Reg. 20.2055-2). A
deductible interest would qualify if there were a transfer of an undivided portion of an entire interest for the entire term of the interest, where it is not
transferred in trust. For example, the transfer of an undivided one-half share of
the full ownership of a piece of artwork would qualify. Transfers subject to a
power to divert such property to noncharitable purposes are not deductible.

Marital Deduction

If property in the gross estate passes to a surviving spouse, a marital deduction
for such property may be available. The deduction will be available where the
property

1. is part of the decedent's gross estate;
2. in fact passes to a surviving spouse; and
3. is not a "terminable interest" (one limited by years or in which the remainder
interest in the property has not passed).

A copyright interest, for example, is a terminable interest. While an outright
transfer of a property will qualify for deduction, a terminable interest will qualify
only if it meets certain technical requirements (Code Sec. 2056[b]; Reg. Sec.
20.2056[b]).

Computation of Tax

A unified rate schedule applies for determining both estate and gift taxes,
from eighteen percent for the first $10,000 in taxable transfers to fifty-five percent
for those in excess of $3 million. The benefits of the graduated-rate structure are
phased out for transfers in excess of $10 million but not exceeding $21.4 million
by adding a five percent surtax.

Tax is computed by first applying the unified rate schedule to the total of (1)
the taxable estate and (2) the total amount of taxable gifts made by the decedent
after 1976 not included otherwise in the gross estate (Code Sec. 2001[b][1]).

Tax previously paid on taxable gifts is then deducted from this amount. The
difference less the unified credit and other deductions with respect to previous
estate tax paid and foreign-state death taxes is the net estate tax (Code Secs. 2010
to 2014). The unified credit is equivalent to a deduction from the gross estate
and/or gifts of $625,000 in 1998; $650,000 in 1999; $675,000 in 2000;

$700,000 in 2002; $850,000 in 2004; $950,000 in 2005; and $1 million in 2006 (Code Secs. 2010, 2001[c], 2505).

Generation-Skipping Transfer (GST) Tax

At one time it was possible to avoid estate or gift taxes by transferring property directly or in trust to grandchildren or great-grandchildren. As a result, generation-skipping transfer (GST) tax was imposed on certain events that result in the transfer of property to a person two or more generations below the transferor (Code Sec. 2611[a]). These events are:

1. the termination of an interest in a trust with the effect of vesting all interest in the trust in a person two or more generations below that of the transferor;
2. a distribution from a trust to or for the benefit of a person two or more generations below that of the transferor; or
3. a direct transfer of property to a person two or more generations below that of the transferor (a "direct skip").

Every individual is entitled to a $1 million exemption, which may be allocated to any property for which the individual is the transferor. Any allocation is irrevocable (Code Sec. 2631). There is also an annual exclusion of $10,000 available for certain direct-skip transfers made in trust (Code Sec. 2503[b]; Reg. Sec. 26.2642-1[c][3], [d]).

DONATIONS IN MEXICAN LAW

In Mexico, inheritances and bequests received by individuals are exempt from income tax.[52] Also exempt are gifts of cash or property from nonresidents of Mexico, except if the gift is of Mexican real estate or a share or other interest in a company. These are subject to a flat-rate tax of twenty percent on officially appraised value. (Gifts from residents are discussed below.) For the most part, income subject to tax consists of wages and salary. Income may also arise on transfers of property for both the transferor and the transferee.

Income Tax on Transfers of Property

Where capital property, including artwork, is sold, income is considered to arise equal to the consideration received for the transfer (Mexican Income Tax Law, Article 95). A deduction for the cost of acquisition, after certain adjustments (Article 96), is allowed in computing the profit from the sale (Article 97). If no consideration is given for a transfer, income is determined according to the value determined by a person authorized by the Secretariat of Finance and Public Credit to make such valuation (Article 95). However, where the property was transferred by way of donation, whether or not consideration was received, no income is recognized (Article 95).

The profit or "capital gain" realized on a disposition is treated as income; that is, the full amount is included, and usual rates of tax apply. There is an income withholding tax requirement on sales proceeds received on sales by agents/vendors such as auction houses. The present special low tax rate is eight percent of the sales price received and without deduction. The sales price for this special tax treatment is segregated from other taxable income, and the eight percent tax is a "final" tax on this sum. The withheld tax funds must then be remitted to the government by the agent (auction house) on behalf of the original owner/seller.

Gains derived by legal entities (for example, corporations) are usually included in gross income and are subject to tax at usual rates (up to thirty-four percent of their annual accumulated income less permitted deductions). Gains realized by individuals from the transfer of personal property, other than shares and other investments, are exempt from tax to the extent that the gains derived do not exceed three times the general minimum salary for the taxpayer's geographic area (the country is split into regions and a minimum salary is applicable in each) for the year (Article 77, Section XVII).

When a person acquires property, that person may be considered to receive income. Income from the acquisition of property is considered to arise where property is acquired

1. in a transfer by way of donation,
2. in a transfer of an object of worth,[53] or
3. in a transfer for consideration that is more than ten percent below the value determined in an appraisal by a certified public broker or credit institution authorized by the secretariat (Article 104).

The income for donations and items of worth is equal to the appraised value of the property. With respect to the third item, income is equal to the difference between the appraised value and the consideration given to the seller (Article 104).

Certain entities in Mexico are tax exempt and will, therefore, not be subject to tax on income, including income arising on a transfer of property to it. These entities include (Article 70)

1. labor unions and their federations;
2. employer associations;
3. chambers of commerce and industry; and agricultural, stock-breeding, fishing, or forestry associations and their federations;

4. professional associations and their federations;
5. civil associations and limited-liability companies of public interest with decentralized administration of irrigation districts or units;
6. authorized public welfare and aid institutions and civil associations or companies authorized to receive donations under income tax rules that do not individually designate beneficiaries and that are active in
    a. providing attention to the poor and/or physically disabled persons;
    b. the operation of specialized centers for homeless and abandoned children, the elderly, the poor, and/or physically disabled persons;
    c. rendering medical or legal assistance, social orientation, or funeral services to the poor, especially minors, the elderly, and/or physically disabled persons;
    d. the social readaption of criminals; or
    e. the rehabilitation of poor, drug-dependent persons;
7. consumer cooperatives;
8. organizations that legally associate cooperative companies;
9. mutual companies that do not operate with third parties and do not incur expenses such as premiums and commissions;
10. civil companies and associations dedicated to teaching that are authorized or recognized under the Federal Education Law;
11. registered civil associations or companies organized for cultural purposes (the promotion of the arts), those dedicated to scientific or technological research, and public museums and libraries;
12. civil institutions or companies created solely to administer savings funds or savings plans;
13. parents' associations registered under the Federal Education Law;
14. public-interest authors' companies created under the Federal Copyright Law;
15. civil associations or companies organized for political, athletic, or religious purposes;
16. civil associations or companies that grant scholarships authorized under the Income Tax Law;
17. tenants' civil associations and civil associations exclusively dedicated to the administration of jointly owned buildings; and
18. civil companies and associations dedicated to preserving the natural environment in certain designated areas.

Donations

Donations within Mexico to the entities listed below will provide a donor with a deduction from tax (Article 140, Section IV). The delivery of property to an authorized donee, resulting from the death of the holder or owner (by bequest), is also deemed to be a donation.[54] In order for a donation to be deductible by an individual, it must be strictly indispensable for the purposes of the taxpayer's activity except in the case of donations that are not onerous or compensatory and that are donated to the following entities (Article 140, Section IV):

1. the federation, federated entities, or municipalities;
2. foundations, patronages, and other entities whose purpose is to economically support the activities of entities authorized to receive deductible donations, provided that
   a. they direct all their income to the purposes for which they were created and
   b. at liquidation they direct their entire worth to the entities authorized to receive deductible donations;
3. the entities referred to in item 18 above; and
4. the entities referred to in items 6, 10, and 11 above, provided that
   a. a substantial part of their income is derived from donations or other public sources, with no excessive income from sources unrelated to their purpose, and
   b. they do not attempt to influence legislation or become involved in political campaigns.

A list of authorized donees is published in the *Official Gazette*. Parties must file a statement with the tax authorities to be included on the list of authorized donees.

Recipients of Donations or Gifts

An individual is not exempt from tax, and an individual is not entitled to receive deductible donations. However, a donation will not be included in income if (Article 77, Section XXIV)

1. it is between spouses or direct descendants or ascendants or
2. all other donations (gifts) received in the year do not exceed three times the annual general minimum salary for the taxpayer's geographical area; however, any excess is subject to tax and must be included in the resident's taxable base.

Value Added Tax

There is a value added tax (VAT) payable by the owner/vendor on sales through corporations (commercial galleries) as well as on the commission portion of a sale at auction. At present, the tax is fifteen percent. The tax is not chargeable on chattels sold at auction as they are considered to be used goods and do not fall within the tax.

The consignment of personal property to a factor, agent, auctioneer, or broker who receives a fee or payment on the sale is considered a rendering of personal services, and the VAT is payable and becomes due when the consideration for the sale is paid. VAT collected by the agent is remitted monthly to the government. The assessed basis for calculating the tax due is on the total amount of the consideration stipulated, including any advances made on the works sold. (For example, on a price received on a sale at auction of $1,200 with a commission of ten percent or $120.00, the VAT is fifteen percent of the commission or $18. Also, a withholding tax of eight percent on $1,062.00 equals $84.96. The total deductions equal $222.96. Therefore, the sales net to vendor is $977.04.)

In the case of art objects imported for sale in Mexico under consignment agreements, if the artworks are not sold, VAT paid on that importation can be credited afterward so that the importer does not bear the cost of the tax.

Tax by Professional Artists

On October 31, 1994, a decree was published in the official record of the federation that gave a special right to creators (people dedicated to the creation of plastic arts) to pay their tax with works of art of their own production—paintings, etchings, prints, and sculpture. This is known as payment in kind. This decree, in addition to assisting the creators, sustains the cultural patrimony of the nation and allows the state to conserve and exhibit examples representative of the art of the time. Some of the works are given to the Federal Ministry of Treasure and Public Credit, and others are given to cultural and nonprofit organizations under Article 70, Section XI, of the income tax law, including museums in accordance with Article 70-B and 70-C of the tax law establishing organizations that may receive donations. A formula is established as to how many works must be given by an artist in satisfaction of tax payable; it is based on the number of works sold by the artist into the marketplace in that calendar year (e.g., for up to five works sold, a transfer of one work; for sales of six to eight works, a transfer of two works; for sales of nine to eleven works, a transfer of three works, etc.). The works must be selected from those created in that calendar year or from any of the two years prior and must also be of similar size and workmanship to those sold during the previous three years.

Some of the works may be auctioned off by the ministry, in which case the funds obtained are used for current government art collections. At these auctions, other artists may be invited to participate with a condition that ten percent of the proceeds of the sale of the works of the participating artist will be directed to the maintenance and upkeep of federal art collections and ninety percent will be given to the artist.

For paintings to be donated, the painting must be signed, dated, framed, and wired. If it is an original print it must be signed, dated, framed and wired; the number of the series must be shown; and the print must be of an edition that does not exceed one hundred prints, the matrix or master of which has been destroyed or cancelled before the work is presented. In the case of a sculpture, it must be signed, dated, and numbered; the number in the series also must be indicated.

Residents of Canada and the United States are not obliged to pay income tax, even when the work of art has been produced totally or partially in Mexico.

Importation and Export of Art—Taxation

There is no tax on the export of cultural objects. There is also no tax on the temporary import of cultural objects that come into the country for exhibition or that are under cultural exchanges, provided that they are being brought in for nonprofit public exhibition and provided that the import does not harm the integrity of the arts in the country. The works are permitted to remain in the country for a specific period of time and with a specific goal, but they must be returned to the exterior in the exact same condition in which they came into Mexico.

On August 23, 1994, the tariff on the general import tax was amended. Thereafter, paintings, etchings, prints, original lithographs, sketches, original statues, or sculpture in any material were free to enter Mexico without payment of any import tax.

These tax rules and regulations in all three countries are subject to changing government fiscal policies and needs as well as pressure on government from various special interest groups. As a result, there is ongoing review and revision of tax legislation and constant change.

NOTES

1. In addition, many individual states and provinces have their own tax statutes and tax payable.
2. Commerce Clearing House (C.C.H.) distributes numerous tax loose-leaf services, including *The Federal Tax Guide of the United States, Canadian Income Tax,* and *Income Tax Worldwide,* which includes Mexican tax laws. In addition, various other legal publishers such as Butterworths and West Publishing also provide tax services. *The Tax Management International Journal* is a monthly journal on tax management produced by Tax Management Inc.,

Washington, D.C. Another service is *Tax News Service,* a bimonthly loose-leaf report on taxation worldwide, created and distributed by the International Bureau of Fiscal Documentation—Amsterdam. Also, The Practicing Law Institute provides seminars and text updating various tax issues that arise through amendment to tax legislation and court interpretations. See also Peter W. Hogg and Joanne E. Magee, *Principles of Canadian Tax Law* (Toronto: Carswell, 1995) and J. M. Dodge, J. C. Fleming Jr., and D. A. Geier, *Federal Income Tax: Doctrine, Structure and Policy* (Charlottesville, Va.: The Michie Company, 1995).

3. In all three countries, different tax treatment is given to corporations and individuals. For example, a donation of personal property is given favorable tax treatment, whereas a donation of business inventory or business property is given substantially less beneficial treatment. See Revenue Canada, Interpretation Bulletin IT-110R3: *Gifts and Official Donation Receipts* (June 20, 1997).

4. R.S.C. 1985 (5th. Supp.) c.1, as amended.

5. Revenue Canada, Interpretation Bulletin IT-110R3: *Gifts and Official Donation Receipts* (June 20, 1997).

6. Ministry of Public Works and Government Services Canada, *Cultural Property Export and Import Act Applications for Certification of Cultural Property for Income Tax Purposes Information and Procedures* (Ottawa: Ministry of Public Works and Government Services Canada, 1997), 2.

7. *Cultural Property Export and Import Act,* R.S.C. 1985 c. C-51 and amendments thereto.

8. A more extensive discussion of the factors that contribute to "outstanding significance and national importance" can be found in Government of Canada, *Applications for Certification of Cultural Property for Tax Purposes* (October 1996).

9. Section 1102(1) of the Income Tax Regulations permits artwork (a print, etching, drawing, painting, sculpture, or other similar work of art) acquired by a taxpayer (a corporation, individual, or partnership) to qualify as a class 8 asset eligible for capital cost allowance at a rate of twenty percent provided certain conditions are met. These conditions include:

   a. the artwork was acquired for the purpose of gaining or producing income;

   b. the artwork is not described in the taxpayer's inventory;

   c. the cost of the artwork to the taxpayer was $200 or more;

   d. the individual who created the artwork was a Canadian; and

   e. the property was acquired after November 12, 1981, in an arm's length transaction.

   For the purposes of this subsection, *Canadian* is defined to mean an individual who was at all relevant times:

   a. a Canadian citizen as defined in the Citizenship Act and

   b. a permanent resident within the meaning of the Immigration Act, 1976 and amendments.

   Artwork acquired for personal enjoyment is considered "personal use property" and would not qualify for capital cost allowance.

10. This approach was rejected in *Whent et al. v. The Queen,* (1996) E.T.C. 444 (TCC). But the Canadian Cultural Property Review Board has raised the threshold to a three-year hold.

11. Arthur Drache, *Canadian Taxation of Charities and Donations* (Scarborough: Carswell, 1998), 12–14.

12. Ibid., 12–15.

13. *Henderson Estate, Bank of New York v. Minister of National Revenue,* (1973) C.T.C. 636 at 644 (Fed. T.D.); affirmed (1975) C.T.C. 495, 497 (Fed. C.A.); and affirmed.

14. However, see chapter 5, "Auction and Other Marketplaces," for a discussion of the concerns in accepting auction results as being "fair market value" without further inquiries and without investigating other markets.

15. *Friedberg v. Canada* (1989) 89 D.T.C. 5115 (Fed. Ct. T.D.), 29; also [1989] 1 C.T.C. 274; reversed 92 D.T.C. 6031 (Fed. C.A.); affirmed 93 D.T.C. 5507 (S.C.C.).

16. The Federal Budget, February 16, 1999, Canadian Tax Reports, Special Report No. 1405 Extra Edition.

17. *Friedberg v. Canada* (1989) 89 D.T.C. 5115 (Fed. Ct. T.D.), 29; also [1989] 1 C.T.C. 280; reversed 92 D.T.C. 6031 (Fed. C.A.); affirmed 93 D.T.C. 5507 (S.C.C.).

18. *Applications for Certification of Cultural Property for Income Tax Purposes, Information Procedures Revised October 1997* (Ottawa: Ministry of Public Works and Government Services, 1997), 22.

19. Drache, *Canadian Taxation*, 12–27.

20. Revenue Canada Interpretation Bulletin IT-226R.

21. Revenue Canada Interpretation Bulletin IT-226R, par 4.

22. Revenue Canada Interpretation Bulletin IT-226R, par 6.

23. *Comr. v. Duberstein*, 363 U.S. 278 (1960).

24. *U.S. v. Transamerica Corp.*, 392 F.2d 522 (9th Circ. 1968).

25. *Pauley v. U.S.*, 459 F.2d 624 (9th Circ. 1972).

26. *Winokour v. Commissioner*, 90 T.C. 733 (1988).

27. Ralph E. Lerner and Judith Bresler, *Art Law,* 2nd ed. (New York: Practicing Law Institute, 1998), 1203.

28. *DuBois v. Comr.*, 31 B.T.A. 239 (1934); *Charleston Chair Co. v. U.S.*, 203 F. Supp. 126 (E.D. S.C. 1962).

29. *The Convention between Canada and the United States of America with Respect to Taxes on Income and on Capital*, signed at Washington, D.C. on September 26, 1980, as amended by the protocol signed at Ottawa on June 14, 1983, and the protocol signed at Washington on March 28, 1984.

30. See chapter 1, "Title," for a full discussion of "fair market value."

31. *Anselmo v. Commissioner,* 80 T.C. 872 (1983); aff'd, 757 F.2d 1208 (11th Circ. 1985).

32. *Heriberto A. Ferrari v. Commissioner*, 58 T.C.M. (CCH) 221 (1989).

33. *Bernard Lightman et al. v. Commissioner*, 50 T.C.M. (CCH) 226 (1985).

34. In re Stanley P. De Lisser 71A A.F.T.R., 2d 93-3706, 90-2 USTC P50, 352.

35. See chapter 4, "Role and Responsibility of Valuers," for a full discussion of qualified valuers and the contents of proper appraisals.

36. IRS News Release, IR-68, February 1, 1968. A panel also exists for purposes of valuing art prints.

37. Lerner and Bresler, *Art Law,* 1151.

38. *Davis v. U.S.*, 110 S. Ct. 2014 (1990), aff'g 861 F.2d 558 (9th Circ. 1988), aff'g 664 F. Supp. 468 (D. Idaho 1987).

39. Ralph E. Lerner, "Income Tax Benefits From Private Funding for the Arts," *Entertainment and Sports Lawyer* 4, no. 3 (Fall 1995), 3.

40. *Revenue Reconciliation Act of 1993*, s. 13171(a), 1993 RRA P.L. 103-66.

41. *Sanford Est. v. Comr.*, 308 U.S. 39 (1939); *Burnet v. Guggenheim*, 228 U.S. 280 (1933); Reg. Sec. 25.2511-2(b).

42. *Estate of David Smith v. Commissioner*, 57 T.C. 650 (1972); aff'd, 510 F.2d 479 (2d Cir.); cert. denied 523 U.S. 827 (1975).

43. Lerner and Bresler, *Art Law*, 1354; *I.R.S. Valuation Guide for Income, Estate and Gift Taxes*, Std. Fed. Tax Rep. (CCH) no. 4 (January 28, 1994).

44. Estate of Warhol, 224 A.D. 2d 235, 637, N.Y.S. 2d 708.

45. Matter of Estate of Warhol, 165 Misc 2d 726, 629 N.Y.S. 2d 621.

46. Ibid, 224 A.D. 2d 235, 637 N.Y.S. 2nd 708.

47. *Robert E. Zelinsky v. Her Majesty the Queen* [1996], 50 D.T.C. 1594 (T.C.C.).

48. Ibid., 1611.

49. Ibid., 1614.

50. Copyright and moral rights are discussed in chapter 6, "Copyright."

51. *California Resale Royalties Act*, California Civil Code, S.986 (West 1982 Sup. 1997). For a more complete discussion of this act, see chapter 6, "Copyright."

52. *Mexico Income Tax Law*, Article 77, Section XXIII.

53. Abraham Eckstein and Enrique Zepada Trujillo, *Mexican Civil Code* (St. Paul, Minn.: West Publishing Co., 1996). Article 875 defines objects of worth as the hidden deposits of cash, jewels, or other art objects whose legitimate origin is unknown.

54. Rule 3.14.3—General donee requirements, Miscellaneous Resolution, 1997.

· 9 ·

Cultural Property Legislation

Throughout history, art, antiquities, and cultural property have been taken as war booty, moved about the world, or sold internationally. Over the centuries, invading armies have taken their plunder back to the successful nation as a reward for the victors and a punishment for the defeated nation.

Until World War II, Napoleon's armies were the world's greatest plunderers of national patrimony. Major cultural and historical objects were uprooted during his campaigns, from Egypt to Russia. The museums of France were filled with the "treasure" brought home by its successful forces. But even Napoleon's treasure hunts didn't hold a candle to the cultural plundering by the Nazis. Numerous books have now documented the art thefts by the invading armies and generals of Germany.[1]

During and immediately after World War II, invading and occupying forces of various countries were involved in seizing and carrying off the treasures of other countries. During the past half century, the current location of some of this art has come to light, giving rise to difficult political and legal questions. Where did these works come from? Who has title? Who has right of possession? What if they once belonged to public institutions? What if they belonged to private collectors? What if the collectors were killed and there is no trace of their families? What if title to the works was obtained by force? What are the rights of heirs of deceased owners? What is the responsibility of dealers, collectors, and countries to establish true ownership and to give up possession of works to the true owners?

Compounding this problem is the export of cultural treasures from Third World, art-rich nations to wealthy collectors in rich nations. Many poorer countries also are losing their cultural patrimony because of theft or insurrection. Every time there is a "local war," cultural property is affected; whether it is looting of archaeological sites in Nicaragua, the National Museum of Kuwait, or the cultural objects of Africa, treasures are sold to dealers and collectors abroad.

INTERNATIONAL AGREEMENTS REGARDING WAR BOOTY

Pre–World War II

The Hague Convention of 1907[2]

The only comprehensive international agreement before World War II that dealt with cultural property stolen during wartime was the Convention Respecting the Laws and Customs of War on Land, commonly known as the Hague Convention of 1907. Ratified by some forty countries including France, the United States, Germany, Great Britain, and Russia, the convention sets out, in the words of the preamble, "a general rule of conduct for the belligerents in their mutual relations and in their relations with the inhabitants." The convention therefore deals with the wartime treatment of cultural property as part of its general subject matter.

In particular, the convention states that all seizure or destruction of private property (including the property of municipalities and institutions dedicated to religion, charity, education, the arts, and the sciences, even where it is state property) is forbidden (Article 56). An army of occupation can take only cash and funds that are strictly the property of the state (Article 53). The convention also provides remedial measures: all seizure or damage prohibited under the convention must be made the subject of legal proceedings (Article 56); in addition, a belligerent that violates the rules set out in the convention is liable to pay compensation (Article 3).

The Treaty of Versailles[3]

The Hague Convention failed to prevent the destruction of cultural property during World War I. Nonetheless, after the war, the principles embodied in the Hague Convention did help the victorious nations to bring about the return of cultural property plundered during the war. Instrumental to the efforts of these nations was the Treaty of Peace with Germany, also known as the Treaty of Versailles, signed in 1919 by twenty-eight nations, including France, Germany, and the United States. The treaty not only provides for the ordinary remedy of restitution (the return of the looted property), it also provides for the replacement of lost objects that have been destroyed with objects of comparable nature and value. In addition, the treaty recognizes no limitation periods. Therefore, under this treaty, France was able to force Germany to return cultural property it took out of France during World War I.

The Roerich Pact

In 1936, twenty-one nations, including the United States of America and the Latin American countries—but none of the European countries—signed the Treaty on the Protection of Artistic and Scientific Institutions and Historic Monuments,[4] known as the Roerich Pact. The treaty provides that historic monuments; museums; and scientific, artistic, educational, and cultural institutions be considered neutral, accorded respect, and protected in time of war as well as peace. The treaty provides also for a distinctive flag to be used to identify institutions to be protected.

The Declaration of London

In January 1943, the Inter-Allied Declaration against Acts of Dispossession Committed in Territories under Enemy Occupation and Control,[5] known as the Declaration of London, was made by the French National Committee, the United States, Canada, Great Britain, and the Soviet Union, among other nations. The declaration issued a formal warning to all, including neutral countries, against transactions involving looted objects. It stated that such objects were to be returned regardless of whether the transactions were sanctioned by local laws.

The Declaration of London was widely adopted in postwar Western Europe and became quasi-common law; but such effect did not last long, and the law was not systematically applied to acts committed during World War II.[6]

Post–World War II

The Hague Convention and Protocol of 1954

The United Nations Educational, Scientific and Cultural Organization (UNESCO) was founded in 1945 to specialize in the protection of cultural property. One of its early accomplishments was the adoption of the UNESCO Convention and Protocol for the Protection of Cultural Property in the Event of Armed Conflict, known as the Hague Convention and Protocol of 1954.

The 1954 Hague Convention, which defines *cultural property* as "movable or immovable property of great importance to the cultural heritage of every people,"[7] included, among other things, works of art, manuscripts, books, and other objects of artistic, historical, or archaeological interest. It stipulates that the parties to the convention undertake to prohibit any form of theft, pillage, or misappropriation of cultural property in armed conflict and refrain from acquiring such property. The convention further provides that certain designated cultural property enjoy immunity from seizure or capture and that the parties to the convention undertake to prosecute and impose penal or disciplinary sanctions on those who commit a breach of the convention.

The Protocol to the 1954 Hague Convention is similar to the Declaration of London in the principles it articulates, and it has been adopted by eighty-seven countries including Mexico; it has not been adopted by the United States or Canada.[8] It deals with the removal of cultural property from occupied territory and its return. It provides, among other things, that cultural property taken from an occupied territory must not be detained as war reparations.

In March 1999, the UNESCO conference in the Hague adopted a new protocol proposing that attacks on cultural property in wartime be qualified as criminal acts and criminal prosecutions of organizations and individuals be permitted.[9]

INTERNATIONAL AGREEMENTS FOR THE PROTECTION OF CULTURAL PROPERTY

Today it is recognized that "countries of origin" of plundered and exported works have unique claims; that some works have a historical integrity and relationship to these countries that transcend conventional concepts of ownership. This recognition has led to international conventions on prohibiting and preventing the illicit import, export, and transfer of ownership of the cultural property of nations.

The UNESCO Convention[10]

The UNESCO Convention on the Means of Prohibiting and Preventing the Illicit Import, Export and Transfer of Ownership of Cultural Property, which was opened for signature in 1970, does not aim primarily to address the protection of cultural property during wartime. However, the convention states that "the export and transfer of ownership of cultural property under compulsion arising directly or indirectly from the occupation of a country by a foreign power shall be regarded as illicit" (Article 11). The member countries agreed that no article of cultural property documented as stolen from a member country and as belonging to a museum, a religious or secular public monument, or similar institution may be imported into another member's country. It also states that a member country whose archaeological or ethnological property forming part of that country's national patrimony is in jeopardy from pillage may request that other member countries impose import restrictions. The UNESCO Convention operates from the time of ratification of the relevant member country.

The UNESCO Resolution[11]

UNESCO also adopted by 1978 a resolution called the Statutes of the Intergovernmental Committee for Promoting the Return of Cultural Property to Its Countries of Origin or Its Restitution in Case of Illicit Appropriation. Known as the UNESCO Resolution, it established an intergovernmental committee responsible for, among many other things, promoting multilateral and bilateral cooperation regarding the restitution and return of cultural property to its countries of origin. It provides that a member state of UNESCO may request the restitution or return of cultural property of fundamental significance to the spiritual values and cultural heritage of the people of the member state, which has been lost as a result of illicit appropriation.

Convention of San Salvador

Though not specifically about wartime conduct, the Convention on the Protection of the Archaeological, Historical, and Artistic Heritage of the American Nations,[12] known as the Convention of San Salvador, adopted in 1976, addresses the looting and plundering of the native cultural heritage of Latin American countries. The convention identifies its purpose as identifying, registering, protecting, and safeguarding the cultural heritage of the American nations in order to prevent illegal exportation or importation of such property, and promoting cooperation among the American states for mutual awareness and appreciation of their cultural property. The convention provides that each state party will undertake whatever measures are effective to prevent and curb unlawful exportation, importation, and removal of cultural property, as well as those necessary for the return of removed property to the state to which it belongs.

The UNIDROIT Convention

The UNIDROIT Convention of 1995[13] deals with stolen or illegally exported cultural objects. Though not specifically concerned with wartime conduct, it does attempt to establish minimum common legal rules for the restitution and return of cultural objects between contractive states, with the objective of improving the preservation and protection of the cultural heritage in the interest of all.

Other Agreements

Germany and the former Soviet Union have entered into agreements germane to cultural property stolen during wartime. The treaty between the Federal Republic of Germany and the Union of Soviet Socialist Republics on Good-Neighborliness, Partnership and Cooperation provides that the parties will advocate the preservation of cultural treasures of the other in their territory. The parties agreed that lost or unlawfully transferred art treasures located in their territories will be returned to their owners or their successors (Article 15).[14]

Similarly, in the 1992 Agreement between the Government of the Federal Republic of Germany and the Government of the Russian Federation on Cultural Cooperation, the parties agreed that lost or unlawfully transferred cultural property located in their sovereign territory will be returned to its owners or their successors. Nevertheless, it is unclear whether works of art and historical documents taken out of Germany by the Soviet Union during World War II will be returned to Germany, as the overwhelming public opinion in Russia is that the works and documents constitute war reparations.[15]

U.S. LAWS REGARDING WAR BOOTY

The United States military law regarding war booty[16] provides

1. that it is the policy and tradition of the United States that the desire for battlefield souvenirs in a combat theater not blemish the conduct of the combat operations or result in the mistreatment of enemy personnel, the dishonoring of the dead, or other unbecoming activities;
2. that when forces of the United States are operating in a theater of operations, enemy material captured or found abandoned must be turned over to appropriate United States or allied military personnel; and
3. that a member of the armed forces may not (except in accordance with regulations prescribed by the secretary of defense) take from a theater of operations as a souvenir an object formerly in the possession of the enemy.

In addition, each state has penal laws governing offenses related to theft and possession of stolen property. For example, the Penal Code of the State of New York contains provisions (Sections 165.40–165.54) for five classes of criminal possession of stolen property. Criminal possession of stolen property in the first degree is committed where the value of the property exceeds $1 million.

The California Code of Civil Procedure contains a unique stipulation that the cause of civil action in the case of theft of any article of historical, scientific, or artistic significance is not deemed to have accrued until the discovery of the whereabouts of the article by the aggrieved party (Sections 338[c]). The provision does not require the aggrieved party to make an effort to discover the location of the lost article.

The UNESCO Convention

The Convention on the Means of Prohibiting and Preventing the Illicit Import, Export and Transfer of Ownership of Cultural Property[17] was to provide nations with a common framework within which to counter abuses in the international trade of cultural property. It was the first comprehensive multinational agreement to protect cultural property.

As of July 1996, there were eighty-six signatory nations, including Canada and the United States. But, with the exception of the United States, which required separate bilateral or multinational agreements, the major art-importing nations were conspicuously absent from the list. Of the major European "importing countries," only France has ratified the UNESCO Convention, and Switzerland is in the process of doing so, much to the consternation of its art dealers, auction houses, and collectors.

The direct impetus for the convention was the appeals by Mexico and Peru for action to protect cultural property after these countries experienced massive losses of heritage objects.

The convention includes a detailed description of the cultural property that qualifies for protection, including

1. flora and fauna;
2. minerals;
3. paleontology specimens;
4. property relating to the history of science, to technology, and to military and social history;
5. objects acquired from archaeological excavation, monuments, or archaeological sites;
6. antiquities more than one hundred years old;
7. ethnological objects;
8. pictures, paintings, drawings, sculptures, prints, and decorative arts more than one hundred years old;
9. rare manuscripts and books;
10. postage and revenue stamps; and
11. archives, including sound-recording, photographic, and cinematographic archives.

The protection proposed by the act is to prevent the removal and illicit trafficking in these objects. Each state must decide what is licit and what is illicit to export. It then establishes regulations regarding the movement and transfer of ownership of cultural property within its territory.

The signatory countries agree to

1. prevent museums within their territories from acquiring cultural property that has been illegally exported;
2. prohibit the import of cultural property stolen from a museum; and,
3. at the request of the state of origin, recover and return any cultural property stolen or illegally imported.

The convention recognizes the rights of a bona fide purchaser, and if a bona fide purchaser agrees to return the object, he or she may be entitled to financial compensation.[18]

The UNIDROIT Convention

The UNIDROIT Convention on Stolen or Illegally Exported Cultural Objects[19] was adopted by representatives of seventy-five countries in June 1995. The convention is intended to complement the 1970 UNESCO Convention.

UNIDROIT (the International Institute for the Unification of Private Law) was founded in 1926 for the purpose of creating an internationally accepted common ground in private law. It has conducted about seventy studies, mostly concerning trade law. In 1995, UNIDROIT consolidated the efforts of UNESCO, the European Union, the Council of Europe, and the International Council of Museums to address illicit trafficking in cultural property. As of January 1997, twenty-two states had signed the resulting convention. The convention will not enter into force, however, until six months after five of those states have ratified it in their respective countries.

Content of the Convention

The preamble states that the UNIDROIT Convention is

determined to contribute effectively to the fight against illicit trade in cultural objects by taking the important step of establishing common, minimal legal rules for the restitution and return of cultural objects between contracting states, with the objective of improving the preservation and protection of the cultural heritage in the interest of all.

The Scope of Application

The UNIDROIT Convention stipulates (chapter 1) that the convention applies to two types of claims of an international character:

1. claims for the restitution of stolen cultural objects, which may be made by individuals; and

2. claims for the return of "illegally exported cultural objects" (objects removed from the territory of a contracting state contrary to its law regulating the export of such objects). *Cultural objects* are defined as objects that are of importance for archaeology, prehistory, history, literature, art, or science and that belong to one of the categories specified in the convention. There are eleven categories: rare collections; specimens of fauna, flora, and minerals; objects of ethnological interest; postage; sound, photographic, and cinematographic archives; articles of furniture more than one hundred years old; and property of artistic interest. The definition of cultural property is the same as that in the 1970 UNESCO Convention.

Rules Regarding Restitution of Stolen Cultural Objects

The convention stipulates that the possessor of a cultural object that has been stolen must return the object.[20] It also states that claims for restitution are to be brought within fifty years of the theft and within three years of the time when the claimant knew the location of the cultural object and the identity of its possessor. However, the fifty-year limit does not apply to claims for restitution of an object that is an integral part of a monument or archaeological site or that belongs to the public. For such claims, there is no time limit. It is of note, however, that despite these general rules, any contracting state may declare that a claim is subject to a time limitation of seventy-five years "or such longer period as is provided in its law." These rules may affect existing limitation laws.[21]

A contracting state may request that the court or other competent authority of another contracting state order the return of a cultural object illegally exported from the territory of the requesting state. The court is to order the return of the object if the requesting state establishes that the removal of the object from its territory significantly impaired one or more of the following interests: the physical preservation of the object or of its context; the integrity of a complex object; the preservation of information of a scientific or historical character; and/or the traditional or ritual use of the object by a tribal or indigenous community.

A possessor of a cultural object who acquired the object after it was illegally exported is entitled to payment of fair and reasonable compensation from the requesting state, provided that the possessor neither knew nor ought reasonably to have known at the time of acquisition that the object had been illegally exported. The cost of returning the cultural object is to be borne by the requesting state.

The convention does not apply retroactively (Article XVIII).[22] Thus the provisions apply only to objects stolen after the convention comes into force in the state where the claim is brought and only to objects illegally exported after the convention enters into force for the requesting state. No reservations are permitted except those expressly authorized in the convention.

The convention has been met with strong objections from many countries, especially Britain, the United States, and Switzerland. They fear that the implementation of the convention will have serious implications for the art world in general and, in particular, for the museums and art markets in their countries. They are concerned that the effect of implementing the convention would be to freeze international trade in cultural objects: the requirements of the convention, they argue, would render trading in cultural objects too risky and unattractive even for those involved in legitimate trade.

This assessment is based on several observations. First, the convention would affect an immense segment of international trade—dealers, collectors, and museums—all the more so because the convention's broad definition of cultural objects sweeps in a huge range of cultural property. Second, the proposal would result in collectors, museums, and dealers being conspicuously engaged in costly legal battles against states with superior financial resources. Third, the adoption of the convention would radically change the long-standing practice of preserving the confidentiality of buyers and sellers. Fourth, the due diligence requirement of buyers, under the compensation provisions, is so stringent as to impose an immense amount of research on legitimate trade.

Those who favor the implementation of the convention point to the defects of the existing system, under which efforts to recover stolen cultural property can be seriously hampered by the differences among national legal systems, many of which contain loopholes for illicit trade. They argue that, by harmonizing the private legal systems of the world (the systems dealing with private rights), the convention would go far toward achieving the goal of preventing the illegal trade of stolen cultural property. In addition, they point out that the convention provides for the compensation of good-faith purchasers and that a state cannot recover an object unless it proves its case before the court.

It is worth noting that viewpoints on the convention diverge not only regarding the predicted practical effects of implementing the convention but also on ideological grounds. The convention is seen by some to be promoting ethnocentrism; others emphasize the urgent need to reduce the theft of "cultural patrimony," thereby preserving the cultural heritage of each state. Whether these radical differences of opinion can be reconciled remains to be seen.

To date, the convention has been signed by France, Finland, Holland, Italy, among others; Switzerland is in the process of signing.[23]

COMMONWEALTH PROTECTION SCHEME

In 1993, the commonwealth justice ministers of the British Commonwealth as constituted at that time—consisting of fifty-four nation-states, including Australia, Bahamas, Barbados, Cameroon, Canada, Cyprus, Malaysia, New Zealand, Nigeria, Pakistan, the United Kingdom, and Uganda—adopted a plan to protect commonwealth cultural heritage. The intent was to redress some of the losses of cultural property suffered by various colonies of Great Britain, both during the colonial period and when the colonial government withdrew following independence.

The agreement scheme governs the return of items of cultural heritage among commonwealth countries. It applies to both export and import and is intended to complement both the 1970 UNESCO Convention and the UNIDROIT Convention. It covers all items of cultural heritage classified by the protection scheme and subject to export control by the country of origin. Each country is required to prohibit the export of items covered by the scheme and may make it an offense to import items of cultural heritage unlawfully exported from another party to this agreement.

If the country of origin requests the assistance of a country of location in the return of an object, the country of location must take the appropriate steps in accordance with its own laws to secure and safeguard the item, even if it has not imposed import restrictions. The country of location must then notify the holder of the item that unless his or her title is established by the courts, the item will be returned to the country of origin; alternatively, either the country of location or the country of origin may institute legal proceedings to obtain return of the item.

A court may order the return of the item, but only after determining whether the holder is a bona fide purchaser. If he or she is, the court may order fair and reasonable compensation; the object does not have to be returned until the compensation is paid.

The commonwealth protection scheme is not yet in force in Canada. A review is under way to determine if amendments are necessary to the Cultural Property Export and Import Act and other legislation before the scheme can be implemented.[24]

CANADIAN LAW

The Cultural Property Export and Import Act[25] came into force in 1977, implementing the UNESCO Convention. It establishes rules for the export of culturally important objects from Canada and establishes both the benefits of compliance and the penalties for noncompliance with the act.

The purposes of the act are as follows:

1. to give the state in appropriate cases the right to prevent the export of objects of high importance;
2. when export is prevented, to ensure the owner an offer to purchase at a fair price;
3. to strictly confine export control to limited categories of objects of high importance;
4. to have a time period during which the natural free flow of commerce in recently imported objects is allowed;
5. to have offers to purchase come from the marketplace rather than from government wherever possible; and
6. to establish a special fund to be drawn on to assist in financing the purchase of cultural property determined to be of national importance, for retention in appropriate Canadian institutions.

The Canadian Cultural Property Export Control List

An export permit is generally required for any object or work in the groups of the control list unless the object is less than fifty years old or its creator is still living. The act is not restricted to Canadian-made objects. The groups are as follows:

Group I: Objects recovered from the soils or waters of Canada, including mineral specimens, paleontological specimens, and archaeological objects of various values.

Group II: Objects of ethnographic art or ethnography:
1. Objects made, reworked, or adopted for use by an aboriginal person of Canada that have a full market value in Canada of more than $3,000.
2. Objects made, reworked, or adopted for use by an aboriginal person of what is now the United States, Greenland, or that part of the former Union of Socialist Republics east of 135 degrees east longitude that have a fair market value in Canada of more than $10,000.
3. Objects made, reworked, or adopted for use by an aboriginal person of a territory other than those listed above that have a fair market value in Canada of more than $20,000.

Group III: Military objects that have a value of more than $3,000.

Group IV: Objects of applied and decorative art:

1. Objects other than the ethnographic art of Group II in which principles of design, ornamentation, enrichment, or decoration are incorporated in functional and utilitarian objects or architectural features such as pottery, glassware, earthenware, porcelain work, etc. These works must be more than one hundred years old, made in Canada, and have a fair market value in Canada of more than $1,000. This category also includes antique furniture, sculptured works in wood or precious metals, and other objects of decorative art that have a fair market value in Canada of more than $4,000.
2. Religious or sacred carvings made in Canada, more than fifty years old, that have a value in Canada of more than $3,000.
3. Decorative art made outside of Canada, by a person who at any time ordinarily resided in Canada, that is more than fifty years old and has a value in Canada of more than $6,000.
4. Canadian coins, preproduction proofs of Canadian stamps, and medals more than fifty years old that have a value in Canada of more than $3,000.
5. Decorative art made outside of Canada that has a direct association with Canada either through the artist's theme or the work's history. It must be more than fifty years old and have a fair market value in Canada of more than $8,000.
6. Applied and decorative art other than those described above that was made outside Canada, is more than fifty years old, and has a fair market value in Canada of $15,000 or more.

Group V: Objects of fine art:

1. Objects of fine art made within or outside the territory that is now Canada by a person who at any time was ordinarily resident in Canada. Such drawings or prints must have a value of more than $5,000 in Canada. Such paintings or sculpture must have a value of $15,000 or more in Canada. Multimedia objects or objects that are not paintings, sculpture, drawings, or prints must have a value of $5,000 or more.
2. Objects of fine art made outside of the territory that is now Canada that were commissioned by a person who at any time normally resided in Canada, incorporate a Canadian theme or subject, or are identified with a prominent person, institution, or memorable event related to the art history or national life of Canada. Such drawings or prints must have a fair market value in Canada of more than $7,500. Such paintings or sculpture must have a fair market value in Canada of more than $20,000. Multimedia objects or objects that are not paintings, sculpture, drawings, or prints must have a value in Canada of $7,500 or more.

3. Objects other than those described above made outside Canada. Such drawings or prints must have a fair market value in Canada of more than $15,000. Such paintings or sculpture must have a fair market value in Canada of more than $30,000. Multimedia objects or objects that are not paintings, sculpture, drawings, or prints must have a value in Canada of $20,000 or more.

Group VI: Scientific or technical objects, including scientific instruments, machines, and vehicles, above a fair market value in Canada of $3,000.

Group VII: Books, records, documents, photographic positives and negatives, and sound recordings. This group includes photographs and photographic art, cinematographic works, and motion pictures of all kinds. The different types of works in Group VII have different requirements as to fair market value and where and by whom they were made. It is important to ascertain into which group a particular work falls, as different criteria apply to each category to determine whether an export permit is necessary.

Group VIII: Musical instruments valued above various fair market values.

How the Act Operates

A person wishing to export an object in the classes of objects covered by the control list must apply for an export permit. The information required in such an application is set out in the Cultural Property Export Regulation.[26] This regulation also sets out the time period for which the permit is valid and the process for renewing the permit.

An export permit must be obtained whether the object is being exported for gift or sale purposes. Only a person ordinarily resident in Canada or a corporation having its head office or establishment in Canada may apply for an export permit. However, a Canadian resident can apply as the exporter on behalf of a nonresident.

The application form may be obtained from any Canadian Customs office or from the Office of the Department of Canadian Heritage. The completed form must be submitted to the permit officer at the designated customs office. If he or she determines that the work is not on the control list, a permit will be issued immediately[27] if it is established that:

1. the work was imported into Canada within the preceding thirty-five years and was not exported under a permit issued under the act prior to that importation date;
2. it was lent to an institution or public authority in Canada by a nonresident; or

3. it is to be removed from Canada for purposes prescribed by the Cultural Property Export Regulation for a period of time not exceeding the period prescribed (not more than ten years). For example, a work may be removed for display or exhibit outside the country, for restoration, or for display in another home of the owner, on a signed undertaking that it will not be sold abroad. A temporary export permit will be issued.

If the permit officer does not know whether to issue the permit, he or she will call a designated examiner,[28] an appointed expert from a local museum or gallery. If the object is on the control list, the expert examiner will consider the following criteria to determine if the permit should be issued.[29]

1. Is the cultural property of outstanding significance under the act because of its close association with Canada, its historical or national life, its aesthetic qualities, or its value in the study of arts or sciences?
2. Is the object of such a degree of national importance that its loss to Canada would significantly diminish the national heritage?

If the expert examiner determines the object is not of outstanding significance or national importance, he or she will advise the permit officer to issue the export permit.[30]

If the expert examiner determines that the object is of outstanding significance or national importance, he or she will advise the permit officer not to issue the permit.[31] The permit officer then so advises the applicant, listing the reasons why the work of art cannot be exported.

If the applicant is dissatisfied with the expert's finding, he or she may appeal the decision within thirty days to the Cultural Property Export Review Board.[32]

General and general open permits are available to the "trade" but are rarely issued. They are "open-ended permits" generally available to museums and galleries that take into account the ongoing needs of such institutions for the borrowing and lending of artworks across borders for exhibition purposes.

The Canadian Cultural Property Export Review Board

The Cultural Property Export and Import Act requires that the Canadian Cultural Property Export Review Board be an arm's length agency composed of government-appointed members including a chairperson and one member from the public at large; four individuals who are or have been officers of art galleries, museums, archives, or libraries in Canada; and four individuals who are or have been dealers in or collectors of art, antiques, or other objects that form part of the national heritage.[33]

Review of Applications for Export Permit

A board must determine, using the same criteria as the expert examiner,[34] whether the object in question is:

1. included in the control list;
2. of outstanding significance by reason of its close association with Canadian history or national life, its aesthetic qualities, or its value in the study of the arts or sciences; or
3. of such a degree of national importance that its loss would significantly diminish the national heritage.

If the review board determines that the object fails to meet any of the above criteria, it directs the permit officer to issue the export permit.[35]

In 1991–92 (the most recent year for which this information is available), the review board heard eight appeals. In all cases, it agreed with the recommendation of the expert examiner; permits were not issued.

If the board determines that the object meets the criteria and that a fair offer to purchase the object might be made by an institution or public authority in Canada within six months of its determination, it establishes a delay period (of two to six months) during which the export permit will not be issued.[36] A government grant and loan program is available to assist institutions in making such purchases.[37]

If the review board establishes a delay period, it gives written notice to the applicant and to the heritage minister.[38] The minister then advises appropriate institutions and public authorities of the object and of the delay period.

If no request is made by a designated institution or public authority for the object within the delay period, an export permit is issued.[39]

If an offer is made by an institution and is acceptable to the collector, the transaction is made. However, if the offer is not acceptable to the collector, the institution may request that the review board determine a fair cash offer.[40] The review board notifies the collector of the fair market value it establishes. If the collector refuses a cash offer equal to that set by the review board, no export permit will be granted for two years. After this time, the collector may reapply for a permit.

In all other cases, the review board directs the permit officer to issue the export permit.[41]

Certifying Cultural Property for Income Tax Purposes

The Cultural Property Export and Import Act and the Income Tax Act, by providing tax exemptions, encourage private owners of cultural objects to donate or sell their cultural property to designated public institutions.

If a work of certified cultural property is sold to a designated institution, the vendor will receive the proceeds of the sale free of any tax on a capital gain. Tax would ordinarily be payable on three-quarters of the gain above $1,000 cost or tax-free zone if the cost was below $1,000.

If a work of certified cultural property is donated to a designated institution, a one hundred percent tax credit (or deduction for a corporate donor) is given for the fair market value of the donation under the Income Tax Act, and no deemed taxable gain accrues to the donor. The full benefits of the donation may be used for the year of donation; any excess may be spread over an additional five years or utilized at any time within the six-year period at the option of the donor.

The review board deals with proposed donations, donations, and sales to designated institutions under the act. In order to be eligible for tax benefits of the act, the donated work must be certified by the review board. The work need not be on the control list, or more than fifty years old, or the work of a deceased artist to qualify for a certificate. The work must, however, be of outstanding significance to Canada and of such national importance that its loss to Canada would significantly diminish the national heritage. Often works that are significant to a specific region, municipality, or location are considered to be of sufficient significance to qualify under the act.

All applicants for certification of works must be accompanied by an explanation from the recipient institution as to the "outstanding significance and national importance" of the work submitted for certification to the review board.[42] Works by both Canadian and non-Canadian living artists have been certified; works that might not themselves meet the criteria for certification may be certified because they are part of a collection of importance.

The benefits available for gifting are available to artists by way of specific amendment to the act; the artist is treated in the same fashion as a collector.[43]

Estimation of Fair Market Value

On December 17, 1991, Bill C18, an act amending the Income Tax Act and twelve other acts of Parliament, including the Cultural Property Export and Import Act, received Royal Assent and was proclaimed. The board uses as its basis for the definition of fair market value the decision in *Henderson Estate, Bank of New York, v. M.N.R.,*[44] which reads as follows:

> The highest price an asset might reasonably be expected to bring if sold by the owner in the normal method applicable to the asset in question in the ordinary course of business in a market not exposed to any undue stresses and composed of willing buyers and sellers dealing at arm's length and under no compulsion to buy or sell. I would add that the foregoing understanding as I have expressed it in a general way

includes what I conceive to be the essential element which is an open and unrestricted market in which the price is hammered out between willing and informed buyers and sellers on the anvil of supply and demand.

The amendment authorized the review board to determine the fair market value of gifts of certified cultural property for Revenue Canada purposes.[45]

To assist the board in determining the fair market value of the object proposed to be donated or already donated, all applications for certification must be accompanied by appraisals from professionally qualified valuers of the property concerned.

When the board receives such application for certification for income-tax purposes, if it is still concerned about the valuation of the object being donated, it will normally request that the applicant institution or donor provide additional information to support the valuation.[46] The board may also obtain independent arm's length appraisals. Specific appraisal rules are set out by the board.[47]

If the board is convinced that the original valuation is appropriate, it will issue an income-tax certificate. If it remains unconvinced, it must then determine the value of the work.

In 1998–1999, the board accepted the applicant's submitted appraisal of fair market value in ninety-one percent of the 1,033 applications for certification, which totaled approximately $100 million.[48]

The Cultural Property Export and Import Act, the Income Tax Act, and the Tax Court Act of Canada were amended effective July 12, 1996, to provide for an appeal to the Tax Court of Canada by any person who irrevocably disposed of an object to a designated institution or public authority when the fair market value was predetermined by the review board within ninety days of the certificate from the review board being issued. However, it is a precondition to such appeal that the donor has resubmitted the application for a redetermination by the review board and still is dissatisfied with the result and with having made the "irrevocable gift." The court may confirm or vary fair market value for the purposes of the Income Tax Act. Should an applicant fail to bring the appeal within the limitation period, he or she may apply to the tax court for an order extending the limitation period. There have been seven appeals to date; four were settled at the pretrial stage, and the others are continuing.[49]

The act was further amended in 1998 to establish that where at any time after February 23, 1998, the Canadian Cultural Export Review Board makes a determination of the fair market value of a property, the amount of the determination is deemed to be the fair market value of that property for the purposes of all provisions of the act (the Income Tax Act) relating to charitable donations and gifts of property for a period of two years from the date of the determination.

A further revision provided that from and after February 23, 1998, the period during which an institution or public authority will incur liability to pay a tax penalty under Part XI.2 of the act, if it disposes of a property that it received as a gift of certified cultural property, is increased from five years to ten years from the date of acquisition of the property (unless to another similar designated institution).

Movable Cultural Property Program

The Movable Cultural Property Program provides administrative services to the Canadian Cultural Property Export Review Board, and it carries out the ministerial responsibilities under the act.

Designations

Under the act, tax certificates and grants are given only to designated institutions and public authorities.

Institution is defined as one that is publicly owned and operated for the benefit of the public and not for the benefit of a private person.[50] It is established for educational or cultural purposes, and it conserves objects and exhibits them or otherwise makes them available to the public.

Public authority is defined as Her Majesty in right of Canada or a province, and agent of Her Majesty in either such right; a municipality in Canada; a municipal or public body performing a function of government in Canada; or a corporation performing a function or duty on behalf of Her Majesty in right of Canada or a province.[51] An institution or public authority may be designated either indefinitely or for a limited time and either generally or for a specific purpose.[52]

The movable Cultural Property Program designates an institution as either Category A or Category B. In Category A, Canadian institutions or public authorities are designated indefinitely and for general purposes relative to their mandate to collect and preserve or to cause to be collected and preserved movable cultural property.[53] In Category B, Canadian institutions or public authorities are designated indefinitely in relation to a specific cultural property that a person proposes to donate or sell to it. Designation may be revoked at any time.[54]

Cultural Property Grants

The minister may make grants and loans to designated institutions and public authorities to purchase objects for which export permits have been refused or cultural property outside of Canada that is related to the national heritage.[55]

The Canadian Cultural Property Export Review Board advises the minister on the awarding of these grants.

Export Control

All cultural property export permits are processed through the permit officer and expert examiner networks. Export permits are issued by officials of Canada Customs in twelve Canadian cities; the expert-examiner function is performed by more than 350 academics, curators, archivists, and librarians in local institutions. The program also maintains records concerning illegal exports and imports and advises the Royal Canadian Mounted Police (RCMP) and Canada Customs on enforcement.

Permits

The program may issue to any resident of Canada a general permit to export objects on the control list subject to any terms and conditions the program requires.[56] The program may amend, suspend, cancel, or reinstate any permit at any time.

The program may, with the concurrence of the minister of industry, issue to all persons a general permit to export objects within any class of objects on the control list that is specified in the permit, subject to such terms and conditions as the program requires.[57] With the concurrence of the minister of industry, these permits may at any time be amended, suspended, cancelled, or reinstated.

Implementation of the UNESCO Convention

The Cultural Property Export and Import Act provides that Canada may enter into international agreements relating to illicit international traffic in cultural property.[58] This enabled Canada to become a signatory to the UNESCO Convention on the Means of Prohibiting and Preventing the Illicit Import, Export and Transfer and Ownership of Cultural Property. Canada ratified the convention in 1970.

For cultural property to be considered illegally imported, the state seeking the recovery of its cultural property must be a *reciprocating state,* defined as a foreign state that is party to a Cultural Property Agreement.[59]

Under the act, the government of a reciprocating state may submit a written request to the minister for the recovery and return of any foreign cultural property imported into Canada illegally and in the possession or under the control of any person, institution, or public authority in Canada. The attorney general of Canada may then institute an action for the recovery of the property by the reciprocating state.

If, after affording all persons who have an interest in the action a reasonable opportunity to be heard, the court is satisfied that the property has been illegally imported into Canada and that compensation, if appropriate, has been paid, the court can make an order for the recovery of the property or any other order sufficient to ensure the return of the property to the reciprocating state.

The act protects the interest of a bona fide Canadian purchaser, and the courts can decide what compensation, if any, is to be paid to such a purchaser by the reciprocating state for the object to be returned to that state. The court may fix any amount it considers just in the circumstances.

The act provides that any object on the control list is designated by Canada as being of importance for archaeology, prehistory, history, literature, art, or science for the purposes of Article 1 of the UNESCO Convention.[60] This means that any of the objects included in the control list are illegal imports into countries with which Canada has a cultural agreement, as well as under the UNESCO treaty, unless the work was exported from Canada with a proper cultural property export permit.

Offenses and Punishments

It is an offense under the act to export or attempt to export from Canada any object on the control list, except with a permit issued under this act.[61] It is also an offense for a person authorized to export an object out of Canada to transfer to, or allow the relevant permit to be used by, a person who is not so authorized.[62] It is an offense for a person to willfully furnish any false or misleading information, or knowingly to make a misrepresentation in applying for, procuring the issue of, or use of a permit.[63]

No person may import or attempt to import into Canada any property that it is illegal to import into Canada under the act and the UNESCO Convention.[64] It is an offense to export or attempt to export from Canada any property that is the subject of an action[65] or the recovery of which has been ordered by the court.[66]

Penalties for export or attempted export offenses under the act[67] are:

1. for a summary conviction, a fine of up to $5,000 and/or imprisonment up to twelve months, and
2. for conviction on an indictment, a fine of up to $25,000 and/or imprisonment up to five years.

If a corporation commits an offense under the act, any officer, director, or agent of the corporation who directed, authorized, consented to, acquiesced in, or participated in the commission of the offense is a party to and guilty of the offense and is subject to the penalties under the act,[68] whether or not the corporation has been prosecuted or convicted.

The limitation period for prosecution of a summary offense is three years from the time when the subject matter of the complaint arose.

Return of Illegal Imports

Since the implementation of the convention, there have been few requests from foreign governments for the return of illegal imports.

The first was received in March 1981 from the government of Mexico, asking Canada to return two pre-Columbian statuettes illegally exported from the country and being held by Canada Customs in Montreal. The statuettes had been forfeited pursuant to the Customs Act. The Ministry of Revenue ordered that they be turned over to the minister of communications. They were then handed over to the Mexican Embassy in Ottawa.

The second request came in December 1981. A Nok terracotta sculpture had been brought into Canada from the United States. At the request of the government of Nigeria, it was retrieved by the RCMP. Three people, two of them U.S. art dealers, were charged under the Cultural Property Export and Import Act with illegally importing a cultural object.

The judge discharged all three accused, as evidence indicated that the sculpture had left Nigeria prior to 1970. The UNESCO Convention specifically states that exportation becomes illegal when the signatories entered into the agreement: Canada entered into the agreement in 1978; Nigeria in 1972. The judge was of the opinion that the Canadian statute was ambiguous on the issue of when the exportation from the reciprocating state becomes legal.

On appeal to the Supreme Court of Alberta, the preliminary hearing was ruled invalid and was quashed, because the judge had heard evidence in the absence of the accused. On further appeal by the government, the appeal was dismissed and all criminal charges were dropped. A civil action for recovery and return of the sculpture to Nigeria, begun in the Federal Court of Canada at the request of the Nigerian government, was also discontinued.

A third request was received in June 1983, from the government of Peru, for the return of five pre-Columbian ceramic and stone sculptures seized by Canada Customs at the Port of Toronto. The request was dealt with through the forfeiture provisions of the Customs Act, and the objects were returned to the Peruvian Consulate on October 12, 1983.

In 1983, the Hellenic Ministry of Culture advised that a Greek icon seized by the RCMP in Victoria, B.C., after being smuggled into Canada, had not been properly exported. However, in 1996, the Greek government advised Canada that the matter was resolved and that it had now approved the export.

The first import case under the act to go through a complete trial in Canada was that of Canadian Roger Yorke. He was convicted under the Cultural Property Export and Import Act and fined $10,000 for illegally importing Bolivian artifacts—including weavings, wood carvings, clothing, and other textiles—in June 1996.

The federal government launched a civil case to make Yorke forfeit the artifacts, discovered in a raid on Yorke's home in 1988, so they might be returned to Bolivia. The RCMP were alerted to Yorke's possible offenses when his name was connected with that of U.S. businessman, Richard Burger, who was being investigated by a U.S. grand jury on similar charges.[69] The Canadian case included a three-year Charter of Rights and Freedoms struggle regarding the search and seizure issue. The issue went all the way to the Supreme Court of Canada before Yorke lost on appeal.[70]

Compensation for the Innocent Purchaser

In the case of *Union of India v. Bumper Development Corp.,*[71] an Indian temple had obtained a judgment in England holding that its title to a twelfth-century bronze sculpture was superior to that of the defendant. The defendant, an Alberta company, had purchased the sculpture in good faith from an English dealer. The object had not been imported into Canada; it was returned from England to India.

The plaintiff brought an action in Alberta to enforce the English judgment; the defendant then claimed a right to compensation under the Cultural Property Export and Import Act. The court rejected the claim, as the sculpture had been repatriated not under the UNESCO treaty but under private civil law, as Britain was not a signatory to the treaty.

In November 1997, Canada returned a total of 124 objects to the governments of Peru, Mexico, and Colombia. These objects included historical Peruvian vessels, textiles, and feathered objects; Mexican ceramic vessels and figurines that date from 200 B.C. to A.D. 250; and Colombian material consisting primarily of pre-Columbian gold jewelry dating from roughly A.D. 1000 to 1500.

The 124 objects are believed to have been looted from tombs and graves in the three countries in question. According to the Canadian Heritage News Release dated February 20, 1998:

> The objects were intercepted and seized by Revenue Canada customs officers because their importation into Canada was in violation of the Customs Act and the Cultural Property Export and Import Act. The three governments had taken the position that the artifacts were exported illegally from their countries and had formally requested the return of the material.[72]

The Province of Ontario also has passed the Foreign Cultural Objects Immunity from Seizure Act (R.S.O. 1990, Chapter F.23), which gives immunity from seizure to certain foreign cultural objects while in Ontario if brought into the province pursuant to an agreement between the foreign owner or custodian and the government of Ontario or any cultural or educational institution in Ontario providing for the temporary exhibition or display of the works in Ontario. The institution must be operated or sponsored without profit.

No proceedings are permitted to be taken in any Ontario court, and no judgment, decree, or order can be enforced in Ontario to have the effect of depriving the government of Ontario—or any institution or carrier engaged in transporting such work or object into Ontario—of custody or control of a work or object if, before the work or object is brought into Ontario, the lieutenant-governor in council determines and publishes an Order in Council that the work or object is of cultural significance and the temporary exhibition or display of that object in Ontario is in the interest of the people of Ontario.[73]

UNESCO Intergovernmental Committee for Promoting the Return of Cultural Property to Its Countries of Origin or Its Restitution in Cases of Illicit Appropriation

This committee was established by UNESCO in 1978 to assist in these areas of concern. The committee is composed of twenty-two members elected for four- year terms, which are renewable. Canada was first elected in 1983, reelected in 1988, and reelected again in 1995.

The mandate of the committee is as follows:

1. to seek ways and means of facilitating bilateral negotiations for the restitution or return of cultural property;
2. to promote multilateral and bilateral cooperation for the restitution or return of cultural property;
3. to foster a public information campaign on the nature and scope of the problem;
4. to guide and plan UNESCO's activities with regard to the return of cultural property;
5. to encourage the establishment of museums and other institutions for the conservation of cultural property; and
6. to promote exchanges of cultural property.[74]

In 1996, it was noted by a curator of the Royal Ontario Museum in Toronto that there was a rare Mazer bowl in a Sotheby's silver auction. Research indicated that the bowl had been consigned to Sotheby's by Canadians who had failed to apply for the necessary export permit under the Cultural Property Export and Import Act.

The museum notified Sotheby's of the oversight, and the bowl was withdrawn from the sale and returned to Toronto. An export permit was then applied for, but because of the importance of the bowl, the permit was denied. The museum was able to negotiate the purchase of the work through Sotheby's thereafter. Mazer bowls are usually of turned maple wood with an intricate grain. They were used as communal drinking vessels during the Middle Ages by the upper middle classes and nobility or religious orders, guilds, or colleges. To effect the purchase by the museum, the minister of Canadian heritage provided half the purchase price under the Canadian Heritage Preservation Endowment account.

The Canadian Heritage Preservation Endowment Account

The Cultural Property Export and Import Act established the Canadian Heritage Preservation Endowment Account,[75] which is available for the repatriation of Canadian heritage objects and to prevent the export of heritage objects from Canada by purchasing them.

All monies received by Her Majesty, by gift, bequest, or otherwise, for grants to institutions and public authorities under the act are credited to the account. If the gift or bequest is received in the form of securities, all monies received by Her Majesty as income on or as proceeds from the sale of these securities are credited to the account, as is interest received on the principal of the account. Grants to institutions and public authorities to purchase objects related to the national heritage for which export permits have been refused under the act or which are situated outside of Canada may be taken from this account.

Cultural property situated outside of Canada is considered to be related to the national heritage of Canada if it was made or found in Canada; was made outside Canada for use in Canada or commissioned by a person who resided in Canada; or incorporates a Canadian theme or subject or is identifiable with a prominent person, institution, or memorable event in the history or national life of Canada. Such cultural property must be of "outstanding significance"[76] or of "national importance"[77] as determined by the review board.

The extent to which the applicant is willing to provide funds of its own toward the purchase price and, if necessary, has explored other sources of funding will also be considered.

Numerous applications for funds have been approved by the minister, both for the repatriation of heritage objects and for the purchase of works approved for export but delayed to allow an institution to apply for funds and purchase the work.

Treaty between the Governments of Canada—British Columbia and the Nisga'a Nation

On August 4, 1998, a historic "Final Agreement" was initialed by the government of Canada, the province of British Columbia, and the Nisga'a people of the Nass Valley in the province of British Columbia. The Final Agreement deals with various Nisga'a land claims, self-government, rights, and financial matters. It also requires Canadian museums to return more than 250 artifacts to the Nisga'a people.[78] These are sacred and nonsacred artifacts located in Canadian museums having been purchased, gifted by collectors, or otherwise obtained over many years. The initial museums involved are the Canadian Museum of Civilization[79] and the Royal British Columbia Museum.[80] Under the terms of the Final Agreement, the museums will return the artifacts to the Nisga'a Nation as soon as practicable following a Nisga'a request, and if there has not been such a request and if no other date has been agreed to, then the return is to be ten years after the effective date that the Final Agreement takes effect or the date that the artifact is included in the appendices attached to the Final Agreement, whichever date is later. An artifact originally obtained from a Nisga'a person, a Nisga'a community, or a Nisga'a heritage site is presumed, in the absence of proof to the contrary, to be a Nisga'a artifact (paragraph 6).

Future acquisitions of Nisga'a artifacts by the museums are also affected by the Final Agreement (paragraphs 12 and 27). Arrangements are also provided to deal with future discoveries of Nisga'a artifacts, whether on Nisga'a lands or elsewhere in British Columbia or under British Columbia control (paragraphs 40 to 42 inclusive).

Curatorial and disposal arrangements with the institutions may also be negotiated for artifacts left in the institutions as outlined in appendices to the Final Agreement. Additional arrangements may be negotiated pertaining to the replication of certain Nisga'a artifacts and to technical and professional training for Nisga'a citizens in "museum skills and conservation expertise."[81] Also, Canada and British Columbia agreed to use reasonable efforts to facilitate Nisga'a Central Government access to Nisga'a artifacts held in other public and private collections.[82]

A further portion of the Final Agreement deals with the protection of archaeological and other heritage sites, including identification of such sites, assessment of significance of the sites, and taking appropriate protective or management measures for the sites in the future and the costs thereof.[83]

In addition, the Final Agreement deals with the removal of Nisga'a human remains from heritage sites.[84]

The Nisga'a Treaty was ratified by the province of British Columbia and, at the time of writing, awaits federal government ratification. The treaty may well set the standard for other outstanding treaty negotiations in Canada and elsewhere.

Heritage Surplus Assets Agreement

In January 1980, the National Museums of Canada and the Crown Assets Disposal Corporation signed the Heritage Surplus Assets Agreement, under which Canadian institutions may acquire objects of heritage significance declared surplus by federal government departments.[85]

A list identifying objects suitable for Canadian museums collections is circulated. If the value of the asset is $7,000 or more, it is referred to the review board for a ruling on its significance. If the board agrees that it meets the criteria of the act for certification, the object is transferred without charge to the appropriate museum. A committee, set up under the agreement, deals with assets valued at less than $7,000.

Quebec

The province of Quebec has its own Cultural Property Act.[86] The minister of cultural affairs can classify cultural property located in Quebec, and a register is kept of all "recognized" and classified cultural property. Neither can be transported out of the province without the authority of the minister.

U.S. LAW

The United States had serious reservations about the UNESCO Convention, and it took more than eleven years to pass the implementation legislation. Being a "cultural property importing nation," the United States was obviously concerned with the impact of the convention on objects already purchased by institutions and on the substantial trade by American dealers and collectors in the art and cultural objects of other nations.

Implementing the UNESCO Convention

The Convention on Cultural Property Implementation Act[87] implemented Articles 7 and 9 of the UNESCO Convention. The United States commissioner of customs issued regulations under the Cultural Property Act that went into effect on March 31, 1986.

Article 7 prohibits the importation of stolen cultural property into the United States, if that property is part of the documented inventory of a museum, religious or secular public monument, or similar institution. It applies only to cultural property stolen after April 12, 1983, the effective date of the act.

Article 9 permits restrictions to be applied to the importation of archaeological and ethnological components of a country's national patrimony in jeopardy of pillage. However, this is available only to member countries and only after a specific request for that protection has been submitted to the president of the United States. Restrictions may also be imposed expeditiously in emergency situations.

Once import restrictions are in place, artifacts are denied entry into the United States unless accompanied by an export certificate issued by the country of origin. A request for import restriction under the act is submitted by the member country to the director of the United States Information Agency (USIA), which determines whether the request merits the imposition of restrictions.

The Cultural Property Advisory Committee is responsible for investigating requests made by nations for bilateral agreements and emergency import restrictions. (The committee is appointed by the president.) The committee comprises eleven private citizens and experts in archaeology, anthropology, and the international sale of cultural property; they represent the interests of museums and the general public. The USIA provides technical and administrative support; its director considers the recommendation of the Cultural Property Advisory Committee in arriving at a decision.

United States import restrictions were first imposed on September 11, 1987, as a response to an emergency request submitted by the government of El Salvador. To date, the United States has imposed emergency import restrictions on the following categories of cultural property:

1. pre-Hispanic archaeological material from the Cara Sucia archaeological region of El Salvador;
2. antique Aymar textiles from Coroma, Bolivia;
3. Moche artifacts from the archaeological region of Sipan in northern Peru;
4. Mayan archaeological material originating in the Peten region of Guatemala; and
5. archaeological material from the Ike Bandiagara Escarpment region of Mali.

In 1996, the UNESCO Convention was first applied. In response to a request from the Italian authorities, the United States attorney in New York seized a first-century sculpture of Artemis. The piece had originally been in the convent of Santa Maria Immaculata in Naples. It was exported in 1988 to Britain, where it was acquired at Sotheby's by a London antiquities dealer. He later sold the piece to a New York art dealer, Richard Feigen, who brought it into the United States. It was consigned to Sotheby's in New York for a sale of antiquities in June 1995. A photograph of the piece in the Sotheby's sale catalog put the Italian authorities on notice that the work was in the United States.

The U.S. attorney executed proceedings in New York, applying various U.S. customs law provisions that had been amended in 1983 to implement the UNESCO Convention. These import and customs laws prohibit anyone from importing into the United States any article of cultural property that has been stolen from a museum, a religious or secular public monument, or a similar institution in any country that is a signatory to the convention. Cultural property is defined in accordance with the convention itself. The lawsuit was successful, and the sculpture was returned to Italy.

Prior to the passage of this legislation and even afterward, various countries have brought actions against U.S. owners or possessors of cultural property removed from that country without permission. Some examples are set out below.

Guatemala v. Hollinshead[88]

The government of Guatemala brought an action for the recovery of a Mayan stela. Guatemala had enacted a statute vesting ownership of all cultural properties in the government to prevent their destruction. This allowed Guatemala to have standing in the U.S. court.

Künstsammlungen zu Weimar v. Elicofon[89]

The defendant had purchased two paintings from a U.S. serviceman in 1946 for $450. The portraits were by Dürer and were valued at more than $3 million dollars each.

The paintings were displayed in the Künstsammlungen zu Weimar until 1943, when they were removed to a nearby castle for safekeeping. It is believed the paintings were stolen from the castle by U.S. soldiers during the war.

The Grand Duchess of Saxony; Weimar; the Federal Republic of Germany; the government of West Germany and the Künstsammlungen zu Weimar, representing the interests of the German Democratic Republic; and the government of East Germany all sued Elicofon to recover the Dürers.

The district court held that the Künstsammlungen was the rightful owner of the paintings. On appeal the decision was upheld.

The court found that the plaintiffs were not barred by statute of limitation. Notwithstanding the defendant's status as a good-faith purchaser for value, the defendant could not acquire title to stolen property.

Government of Peru v. Johnson[90]

The Peruvian government based its claim on Peruvian statutes that provide that pre-Columbian objects located in Peru are the property of the state and removal of such objects from Peru without government permission is theft. The district court found for Johnson, reasoning that

1. Peru did not prove that the objects came from Peruvian territory.
2. Peru did not prove that the objects were removed while the Peruvian statutes under which title was claimed were in force.
3. As Peru never sought to exercise its ownership rights, the laws of Peru had no more effect than export restrictions.

There was no claim under the convention, as there was no proof that the property was stolen from a museum, religious or secular public monument or similar institution. This case indicates that the United States will allow the recovery of a stolen work of art but will not enforce the export laws of a foreign country.[91]

Other Claims

More and more claims are being brought forward in respect to artworks and art objects that disappeared or were forcibly taken during the Second World War. Recently the Budapest Museum of Fine Arts laid claim to a sixteenth-century painting by Vasari, *The Marriage Feast of Cana,* painted in 1566, now in the collection of the Montreal Museum of Fine Arts. The Montreal Museum believes it properly owns the painting. It was acquired in 1963 from a Canadian-resident daughter of a Hungarian collector who had purchased it in 1961 from the Hungarian government.

However, Hungarian records indicate that the painting was on loan to the Ministry of Finance building in Budapest, later destroyed by bombing in 1945. The museum believed the painting had been destroyed and was shocked to find that the work was in the collection of the Montreal Museum. The Budapest Museum takes the position that the work is stolen goods and truly belongs to it. The matter remains outstanding at the time of writing.[92]

In the United States, a claim was brought by Holocaust survivors' heirs to two Egon Schiele paintings on loan by an Austrian lender, the Leopold Foundation, to the Museum of Modern Art for an exhibition of works by the artist. The heirs claimed the works were owned by their families in Austria prior to the Second World War and then stolen from the families. Manhattan District Attorney Robert N. Morgenthau issued a subpoena requiring the museum to hold the paintings, which were on the way back to Austria. The New York State Supreme Court was asked to decide whether the subpoena issued by the attorney general violated the New York law prohibiting the seizure of artworks on exhibit in a museum as above noted.[93]

Judge Laura Drager, who heard the matter, determined that the New York Arts and Cultural Affairs Law (Section 12.03) exempting from seizure works of art on loan to nonprofit institutions in New York State was valid and applied even in criminal cases. The judge also ruled that there was no conflict between the New York statute and the federal Immunity from Seizure Act. The Manhattan attorney general appealed the decision.[94] The attorney general took the position that this is a criminal matter and outside the purview of the New York seizure legislation. He also claimed that the federal act has preempted the New York State statute, and he appealed as well on other technical grounds.

The appeal from the decision of Judge Drager was heard by Judge Richard T. Andrias, who accepted the argument of the attorney general that Section 12.03 does not apply to a subpoena issued as part of a criminal investigation and it was unnecessary to examine the issue of whether such statute is preempted by federal law, specifically the Federal Immunity from Seizure Act (22 USC §2459). Accordingly, the decision of Judge Drager was reversed by Judge Andrias on March 16, 1999.

The Museum of Modern Art then brought a motion for leave to appeal the decision to the court of appeals; this motion was granted on May 10, 1999. The grounds raised by the Museum of Modern Art for the appeal included that the appeal required the construction of Section 12.03 of the New York Arts and Cultural Affairs Law and involved issues of substantial public importance that the appellant division decided in a manner contrary to the plain language of the statute.

On September 21, 1999, the Court of Appeals of New York, in a six-to-one decision, reversed the decision of the Appellate Division, FIRST Department, ruling that the New York Arts and Cultural Affairs Laws, Section 12.03, did apply to both civil and criminal actions and quashed the subpoena. The museum was thus prepared to return the paintings to Austria's Leopold Foundation.[95]

However, immediately after the decision, U.S. Attorney Mary Jo White issued a seizure warrant for one of the two Egon Schiele paintings, "Portrait of Wally," preventing the return of that work to the Leopold Foundation. At the time of writing, the return of the art is yet to be determined.[96]

These are but two of the many claims emerging as more information becomes available as to the whereabouts of art objects thought lost, stolen, or forcibly taken during the Second World War.

Bilateral Cultural Agreements

U.S.–Canada Agreement concerning the Imposition of Import Restrictions on Certain Categories of Archaeological and Ethnological Material

In April 1997, the United States and Canada signed an agreement restricting import into the United States from Canada of aboriginal, archaeological, and ethnographical artifacts, including Inuit, Sub-Arctic, Plateau, Plains, Woodlands, and Northwest Coast aboriginal material. The agreement also restricted the import of nonaboriginal material from historical shipwrecks at least 250 years old, unless such items are accompanied by an export permit issued in accordance with Canada's Cultural Property Export and Import Act. The U.S. government will also attempt to recover any such material in the United States and return any material on the designated list forfeited to the U.S. government.

In exchange, the Canadian government has agreed to cooperate with the United States in recovering archaeological cultural objects that have entered Canada illicitly from the United States. *Archaeological* is defined by the Archaeological Resources Protection Act;[97] *cultural items* are defined in the Native American Graves Protection and Repatriation Act,[98] and *archaeological items recovered from shipwrecks* are defined by the Abandoned Shipwreck Act.[99]

U.S.–El Salvador Agreement

The U.S.–El Salvador Bilateral Cultural Property Agreement protects several categories of El Salvador's rich pre-Hispanic archaeological heritage.

This is the first bilateral cultural property agreement within the framework of the 1970 convention as created by the U.S. Cultural Property Act. It was signed on March 8, 1995, and a descriptive list of the type of artifacts subject to import restrictions was published on March 10, 1995, in the *Federal Register* by the U.S. commissioner of customs.

The agreement restricts importation into the United States of the types of artifacts on the list unless accompanied by an export permit issued by the government of El Salvador.[100]

U.S.–Mexico Treaty

On July 17, 1970, the United States and Mexico signed a treaty of cooperation providing for the recovery and return of stolen archaeological, historical, and cultural properties.[101] Ratified by both countries and entered into force, the treaty defines the properties subject to protection as pre-Columbian cultural art objects and artifacts of outstanding importance to the national patrimony of the two countries.

The parties undertook

1. to encourage the discovery, preservation, and study of archaeological sites;
2. to deter illicit excavations of such sites;
3. to facilitate the circulation in both countries of details of the protected properties;
4. to enhance mutual understanding; and
5. to permit legitimate international commerce in art objects.[102]

The parties agreed to employ, at the request of the other party, the legal means at their disposal to recover and return from its territory cultural properties, removed from the territory of the requesting party after July 17, 1970, the date of entry into force of the treaty.

The costs for the return of the property requested under the treaty are to be borne by the requesting party, and no person is to have any right to compensation for damage or loss resulting from the return.[103] The treaty thus makes no provision for compensation to innocent purchasers.

U.S.–Peru Treaty

The terms of the agreement for the Recovery and Return of Stolen Archaeological, Historical, and Cultural Properties[104] are similar to those of the U.S.–Mexico Treaty above noted. It covers archaeological remains from 12,000 B.C. to A.D. 1532.

A 1997 "memorandum of understanding" deals with ethnological material from A.D. 1532 to 1821.

In 1997, FBI agents recovered a two-thousand-year-old solid gold item of armor. It was believed to have been stolen from the tombs of the Moche civilization of Peru. The FBI obtained the armor through a sting operation that resulted in the arrest of two Miami businessmen. When the prosecutions are completed, the armor will be returned to Peru, pursuant to the agreement.[105]

Special U.S. Legislation

The American Indian Religious Freedom Act

The relevant portion of the act reads:

It shall be the policy of the United States to protect and preserve for American Indians their inherent right of freedom to believe, express, and exercise the traditional religions of the American Indian, Eskimo, Aleut, and Native Hawaiians, including but not limited to access to sites, use and possession of sacred objects, and the freedom of worship through ceremonials and traditional rites.[106]

The key words are "use and possession of sacred objects."

The purpose of the act is to prevent actions that would violate Native Americans' First Amendment rights. In order to be such a constitutional violation, the offending activity must be a government action and, as several federal court cases have held, must inhibit a central or indispensable part of the religion. However, the issue of centrality to religion can present serious problems of proof.

The act has not changed the legal mechanisms available to Native Americans who seek the return of culturally significant artifacts; however, it has focused attention on such claims.

Native American Graves Protection and Repatriation Act[107]

This act requires federal agencies and all museums that have possession or control over holdings or collections of Native American human remains and associated funerary objects to compile an inventory of such items and, to the extent possible, based on information possessed by such entities, identify the geographical and cultural affiliation of such items.[108]

Inventories must be completed in consultation with tribal governments, native Hawaiian organization officials, and traditional religious leaders within ten years of the act's enactment. Museums must also supply existing records of the geographic origin, cultural affiliation, and other basic facts relevant to the acquisition and accession of Native American human remains and associated funerary objects. Any museum failing to comply with the act will be subject to civil penalties.

If a cultural affiliation of any Native American human remains and associated funerary objects is established with a particular tribe, the federal agency or museum must expeditiously return such remains and associated funerary objects on the request of a known lineal descendant of the Native American or the tribe.[109]

National Stolen Property Act

Enacted in 1934, the act was created as part of title 18 (Crimes and Criminal Procedure), chapter 113 (Stolen Property), of the U.S. Code provisions regarding, among other things, transportation and sale or receipt of stolen property.[110]

Under the act,

1. whoever transports in interstate or foreign commerce any goods of the value of $5,000 or more, knowing the goods to have been stolen, converted, or taken by fraud, will be fined and/or imprisoned for up to ten years (Section 2314);
2. whoever receives, possesses, conceals, stores, or sells any goods of the value of $5,000 or more, or pledges or accepts as security for a loan any goods of the value of $500 or more that have crossed a state or U.S. boundary after being

stolen, knowing the goods to have been stolen, will be fined and/or imprisoned for up to ten years (Section 2315); and

3. it is a federal offense to "transport in interstate or foreign commerce goods of a value of $5,000 or more known to be stolen or to receive, conceal, or sell such goods" (Section 2314) (it must, however, be shown that the accused had knowledge that the property was stolen).

United States v. Hollinshead[111]

As described earlier, Clive Hollinshead, an art dealer, was prosecuted for the interstate transport of a Mayan stela from Guatemala. The defendant knew that the stela had been stolen. It was not necessary to show whether the defendant knew that the title was vested in the State of Guatemala under its law.

USA v. McClain[112]

Once an object has been exported from a country in contravention of its laws, that country generally has limited recourse, because the object and its possessor are then beyond the country's jurisdiction. In the absence of any international commitment to enforce relevant foreign laws, the importing country frequently is reluctant to secure the return of the object.

A U.S. court usually will not entertain a criminal charge against the alleged thief or enforce fines and other penalties based on foreign law.

In the case of *USA v. McClain,* a group of U.S. citizens engaged in transporting movable pre-Columbian artifacts from Mexico into the United States. They were arrested and indicted for violating and conspiring to violate the National Stolen Property Act. The prosecution argued that the artifacts were considered stolen under Mexican law and that the courts should give full faith and credit to the foreign law.

The group was convicted. The court found it necessary to determine whether the laws of Mexico merely imposed export requirements or whether they vested title to the artifacts in the Mexican government. If the laws vested title, then removal of the artifacts from the control of the government would constitute theft.

The appeals court did not agree with the opinion that the Mexican law vested title to the artifacts in the government and remanded the case to the lower court for a new trial.

The group was convicted again. At the second appeal, the court agreed to give full faith and credit to the 1972 Mexican statute, which in its opinion clearly claims state ownership of all pre-Columbian antiquities, but not to prior laws, which the court felt were ambiguous as to title.

U.S. v. An Antique Platter of Gold Known as a Gold Phiale Mesomphalos[113]

In November 1997, a decision was handed down by the District Court of the Southern District of New York dealing with the importation and forfeiture of an antique gold platter known as a phiale mesomphalos (phiale). The phiale was a fourth century B.C. antique gold platter of Sicilian origin. It began its circuitous path to the United States sometime around 1980, when a private dealer in Sicily approached a professor of Greek history for an expert opinion regarding the authenticity of the work, which was in the dealer's collection at the time. The professor concluded the phiale was authentic and Sicilian in origin.

Later, the dealer traded the phiale to a Sicilian coin dealer/art collector, who later stated to an employee of the Monuments of Fine Arts Bureau in Palermo, Sicily, and an Italian photographer that the work had been found in Sicily during the completion of some electrical work by an Italian utility company. The coin dealer/art collector also gave a photograph of the work to an art dealer and personal friend who owned an art dealership in Zurich, Switzerland. The Swiss dealer was a specialist in antiquities and later acquired the work from the coin dealer/art collector. The Swiss dealer then brought the phiale to the attention of an American art dealer, Robert Haber, who was a dealer in ancient art in New York City. Haber traveled to Sicily to see the phiale and believed that his New York client, Michael Steinhardt, might be interested in acquiring it. Haber had previously sold Steinhardt twenty to thirty objects totaling $4 million to $6 million, and he advised Steinhardt that this particular phiale was the twin of one belonging to the Metropolitan Museum of Art in New York and that its seller was a Sicilian coin dealer.

Thereafter, Steinhardt, with Haber as an intermediary, agreed to purchase the phiale: Steinhardt would pay more than $1 million in two weeks, and he would wire transfer a further installment plus an additional fifteen percent commission fee, for a total of $1.2 million purchase price. The first installment was paid.

The document outlining the terms of sale provided that if the object was confiscated or impounded by customs agents or a claim was made by any country or governmental agency whatsoever, full compensation would be made immediately to the purchaser. A letter was also to be written by the professor of Greek history stating that he had seen the object fifteen years earlier in Switzerland. Later, the professor claimed that he had never agreed to certify that the phiale was authentic, nor that it was of Swiss origin, nor that he had seen it in Switzerland.

After the first installment was sent for the purchase of the work, Haber flew to Switzerland and obtained the work in a town near the Swiss-Italian border. He then came back to New York with the phiale and with customs forms that had been prepared showing the phiale's country of origin to be Switzerland and its value to be $250,000, despite the fact that it had been sold for more than $1 million. The form made no mention of the phiale's Sicilian origin or of its Italian history. Shortly thereafter, the phiale was taken to the Metropolitan Museum of Art in New York, which declared the work authentic and returned it to either the dealer or the ultimate purchaser. Thereafter, the second installment was wired in payment of the work. Also, the art dealer's fifteen percent commission was paid.

From 1992 to 1995, Steinhardt possessed the phiale and displayed it in his home. In February 1995, the Italian government requested the legal assistance of the government of the United States, pursuant to the Treaty on Mutual Legal Assistance on Criminal Matters, to investigate the circumstances surrounding the exportation from Italy of the phiale and its importation into the United States. The Italian government also asked that the phiale be confiscated and returned to Italy.

In November 1995, United States customs agents obtained a warrant and seized the work from Steinhardt's home in New York. On December 13, 1995, the United States filed the current civil action, seeking forfeiture of the phiale pursuant to 18 U.S.C. §545 and 981(a)(1)(c) and to 19 U.S.C. S. 1595(a)(c). The government's complaint, as amended, alleged that (1) the phiale had been illegally imported into the United States due to the materially false statements provided by the dealer in the customs form relating to the phiale's country of origin and (2) the phiale had been exported illegally from Italy pursuant to Article 44 of Italy's laws of June 1, 1939, No. 1089, regarding the Protection of Objects of Artistic and Historic Interest. Pursuant to the Italian law, archaeological finds and objects of antiquity belong to the Italian state unless a party can establish private ownership of the object pursuant to a legitimate title that predates 1902, the year in which the first Italian law protecting antiquities went into effect.

In December 1995, Steinhardt filed a motion for summary judgment against the United States in the forfeiture action, claiming the phiale was not subject to forfeiture under the aforesaid legislation on the grounds that any misstatements by the art dealer at the time of the importation of the work were not "material" as required by the statute. He also alleged that he was an innocent purchaser as a matter of law under each of the statutes and that the forfeiture of the phiale violated the Excess Fines Clause of the Eighth Amendment.

The court dismissed all of his claims and affirmed the forfeiture of the work on the following basis.

Section 545 of Title 18 of the United States Code prohibits the importation of merchandise in a manner contrary to law. The dealer violated this section by making materially false statements on the customs form in violation of 18 U.S.C. S. 542, specifically, the false identity of the country of origin as Switzerland rather than Italy. It went on to state that Section 542 of Title 18 of the United States

Code prohibits the making of false statements on various documents, including customs forms (n. 27, 18 U.S.C. S. 542).

The government also cited the cases of the *United States v. Holmquist* (36F. 3d. 154, 157 [1st Cir. 1994] cert. denied, 514 US 1084, 131 L. Ed. 2d 724, 115 S.CT. 1797 [1995]) and the *United States v. Bagnall* (907 F. 2d. 432, 435 [3d. Cir. 1990]) as establishing what is material being "not only if it is calculated to effect the impermissible introduction of ineligible or restricted goods, but also if it affects or facilitates the importation process in any way." They also argued that a false statement is material "if it has the potential, significantly to affect the integrity or operation of the importation process as a whole."

Applying the "materiality standard," the court found that the statements in the customs forms misidentifying Switzerland as the country of origin were materially false and in violation of Section 542. Customs procedures provide the country of origin as a significant factor in determining whether customs officials should admit an object; hold it for further information; or seize it as a smuggled, improperly declared, or undervalued item. Certain countries have stringent laws to protect their cultural and artistic heritage; identification of such a country raises a red flag for customs officials reviewing customs forms. Italy is known to be such a country; Switzerland is not. Truthful identification of a country of origin on the customs forms would place the customs service on notice that an object of antiquity dated circa 450 B.C. was being exported from a country with strict antiquity-protection laws; such information would tend to influence the customs service's decision-making process. It was the court's determination that the government had met its burden of establishing that there was probable cause to believe the phiale was subject to forfeiture as merchandise imported contrary to law in violation of 18 U.S.C. S. 542.

In respect to the innocent-owner defense under 18 U.S.C. S. 545, the court disagreed with this concept, finding that S. 545 does not afford an innocent-owner defense. Property may be subject to forfeiture regardless of the guilt or innocence of its owner.[114]

On an alternative basis, the government argued that the phiale was subject to forfeiture pursuant to 19 U.S.C. Section 1595A(c) n.33 as stolen property imported contrary to law in violation of 18 U.S.C. Section 2314, the National Stolen Property Act.

N. 33, Section 1595(a)(c) provides that "merchandise which is introduced or attempted to be introduced into the United States, contrary to law, shall be seized and forfeited if it is stolen, smuggled, or clandestinely imported or introduced."

The United States Code prohibits the importation of merchandise known to be stolen at the time of import (N. 34, 18 U.S.C. Section 2314). Under this section, an object may be considered stolen if the foreign nation has assumed ownership of the object through its artistic and cultural patrimony laws.[115] It also provides that "Whoever transports, transmits, or transfers in interstate or foreign commerce any goods, merchandise or money of the value of $5,000 or more, knowing the same to have been stolen, converted, or taken by fraud, shall be guilty of a crime."

Having reviewed the relevant Italian law in submissions of the parties, including expert opinion, the court concluded that the phiale belonged to Italy pursuant to Article 44 of Italy's law of June 1, 1939, No. 1089. Accordingly, the court found that the phiale was stolen within the meaning of Section 2314.

Also, based on the undisputed facts of the case, the court found probable cause to believe that the dealer knew the phiale was stolen when he imported it. Accordingly, the government met its burden of showing that the phiale was subject to forfeiture pursuant to 19 U.S.C. Section 1595(a)(c) as stolen merchandise imported in violation of 18 U.S.C. Section 2314.

The government also found that Steinhardt's claim about his rights under the Eighth Amendment in respect to the allegation that the forfeiture was excessive was without merit, and it too was dismissed.

The case was then appealed by Steinhardt with the support of the Association of Art Museum Directors and the American Association of Museums. However, it was opposed by various archaeological groups, including the Archaeological Institute of America.

On February 13, 1998, the *Boston Globe* stated that

Ashton Hawkins, the legal counsel for the Metropolitan Museum of Art in New York, said the Association of Art Museum Directors, in its decision to support the appeal by New York financier and art collector, Michael H. Steinhardt, is not in any way endorsing the smuggling and falsification of customs documents by Steinhardt's dealer. Instead, Hawkins said the Association of Art Museum Directors feels that the judge's decision to enforce Italian law barring archaeological exports was wrong and sets a 'very dangerous' precedent."[116]

The appeal was heard by the Federal Court of Appeals for the Second Circuit.[117] Chief Judge Winter, speaking for the court, summarized the appeal as follows:[118]

Steinhardt contends that: (i) the false statements on the customs forms were not material under 18 U.S.C. §542, (ii) stolen property under the National Stolen Property Act ("NSPA") does not encompass property presumed to belong to the state under Italian patrimony laws, (iii) both statutes afford him an innocent owner defense, and (iv) the forfeiture violates the Eighth Amendment. We hold that the false statements on the customs forms were material and, therefore, need not reach issue (ii). We further hold that there is no innocent owner defense and that forfeiture of the Phiale does not violate the Eighth Amendment.

In a comment on the case for the International Foundation for Art Research, the author, Sharon Flescher states:

> The current appeals court decision addressed only that part of the lower court ruling dealing with whether the U.S. had the right to seize the phiale because of the false information on the customs forms relating to country of origin. Because the appeals court found the false information "material" to the import process (Steinhardt argued it was not), it let the lower court's ruling stand. Much of the appeals court discussion focused on the standard for determining materiality. The Court of Appeals did not address the more controversial issue of whether the U.S. government had the right to seize the platter as "stolen property," that is, whether U.S. law, which constitutionally forbids governmental taking of private property without just compensation, should recognize Italy's claimed title to the phiale predicated on Italy's declared ownership under its Patrimony Law.

Specifically, the appeals court stated:

> "We hold that importation of the phiale violated 18 U.S.C. §545 because of the false statements on the customs forms. We need not, therefore, address whether the NSPA [National Stolen Properties Act] incorporates concepts of property such as those contained in the Italian patrimony laws." Cf. United States v. McClain, 545 F. 2d 988, 994-97 (5th Cir. 1977) (adopting broad definition of property under NSPA).

It was concern for the ramifications of the latter issue, which gives the Customs Service authority to seize an object and makes "the burden of proof and cost of appeal ... the responsibility of the museum," that led the AAM to file their *amicus curiae* on behalf of Steinhardt. In its members newsletter written after the appeals court decision, the AAM promised to "monitor" the situation and "voice its concern" if the U.S. government takes similar actions again." [119]

Importation of Pre-Columbian Monumental or Architectural Sculpture or Murals Act [120]

The Importation of Pre-Columbian Monumental or Architectural Sculpture or Murals Act authorizes seizure and forfeiture by the U.S. Customs Service if any architectural sculpture or mural or fragment thereof from a pre-Columbian Indian culture enters the United States without a proper export license. The work does not have to be stolen to be considered illegally exported. The act gives effect to the export laws of thirteen Latin American countries.

Temporary Import

From time to time various works are borrowed by American institutions for temporary exhibition in the United States. There may be a concern by the lender that ownership claims may be made against the work by American residents or through the American courts. In order to facilitate such temporary public exhibitions, the United States has passed legislation dealing with immunity from seizure of such cultural objects. The Immunity from Seizure Act[121] provides immunity from seizure under judicial process of cultural objects imported into the United States for temporary exhibition or display.[122]

The Immunity from Seizure Act also provides that:

> Whenever any work of art or other objects of cultural significance is imported into the United States from any foreign country, pursuant to an agreement entered into between the foreign owner or custodian thereof and the United States or one or more cultural or educational institutions within the United States, providing for the temporary exhibition or display thereof within the United States at any cultural exhibition, assembly, activity, or festival administered, operated or sponsored without profit by any such cultural or educational institution, no court of the United States, any state, the District of Columbia, or any territory or possession of the United States may issue or enforce any judicial process, or enter any judicial decree or order for the purpose or having the effect of depriving such institution, or any carrier engaged in transporting such work or object within the United States, of custody or control of such object if before the importation of such object, the president or his designee has determined that such object is of cultural significance and that the temporary exhibition or display thereof within the United States is in the national interest, and a notice to that effect has been published in the *Federal Register*.[123]

Pursuant to executive order, the director of the United States Information Agency serves as the president's designee under the act.

The legislation goes on to deal with any pending judicial proceeding and the right of the United States attorney to intervene on request made by the institution adversely affected or on the direction of the attorney general if the United States is adversely affected for the denial, quashing, or vacating of any judgment or decree.

Theft of Cultural Objects

Under American Law 18 U.S.C. S. 668, passed in 1994, the theft of objects of cultural heritage has been criminalized. Under the law, a person who is found guilty of stealing from a museum an object that is more than one hundred years old and worth more than $5,000 or one that is worth at least $100,000, irrespective of its age, faces up to ten years in prison.

In the recent case of the *United States of America v. Helard J. Gonzales O'Higgins*, the court upheld the constitutionality of the law.[124] In that case, the defendant was charged with stealing a leaf from a piano minuet by Wolfgang Amadeus Mozart from the New York Public Library for the Performing Arts that had an estimated market value of $50,000. He was also charged with stealing an essay and three lectures by composer Richard Wagner from that library. The defendant contended that the law was unconstitutional because Congress had exceeded its power to legislate under the Commerce Clause.

The judge stated, "recent cases before this court have involved the possession and attempted sale in the United States of many valuable works of art stolen from museums."[125] The Isabella Stewart Gardner Museum in Boston and the Peabody Museum in Salem, Massachusetts, are among two of the better-known institutions victimized by art thieves in the 1990s. The court found that there can be no doubt that the theft of a world-famous Rembrandt would substantially affect interstate commerce through its impact on the value of other works of art and the cost of insurance.

The defendant's motion to dismiss was denied.

MEXICAN LAW

International Agreements

The significant cultural international agreements signed by Mexico include:

1. the 1970 UNESCO convention;
2. a bilateral agreement with the United States, discussed earlier in this chapter;[126] and
3. a signatory to the Hague Convention of 1954, dealing with the protection of movable cultural property (in force as of August 7, 1956).

Domestic Statutes

The federal law of Archaeological, Artistic and Historic Monuments and Zones was passed in 1972; the regulations were published in the *Official Gazette* on December 8, 1975.[127] The act deals primarily with the protection of archaeological, artistic, and historic monuments and of monument areas. It states the following:

1. Privately owned historic or artistic monuments may be exported temporarily or permanently by way of a permit issued by a competent institute in accordance with the regulations.[128]
2. The exportation of archaeological monuments is prohibited, except in the form of exchanges or gifts to foreign governments or scientific institutes; these require the agreement of the president of Mexico.[129]
3. Two public registers of archaeological and historic monuments and areas are established: those under the auspices of the National Institute of Anthropolo-

gy and History and those under the auspices of the National Institute of Fine Arts and Letters.[130]

4. Archaeological monuments, both movable and immovable, are deemed to be inalienable and the property of the nation.[131]

5. All movable or immovable property that is the product of the cultures existing prior to the establishment of the Hispanic culture in the National Territory, as well as human, animal, and plant remains relating to those cultures, are defined as *archaeological monuments*.[132] Anyone who finds archaeological objects must inform the nearest civil authority thereof.[133]

6. Works of outstanding aesthetic value are considered *artistic monuments*.[134] Except for Mexican mural paintings, the works of living artists should not be declared monuments. Outstanding murals are to be conserved and restored by the state.

7. A national commission on artistic areas and monuments is to be established. Its task will be to propose that the works of a deceased Mexican artist be declared to be artistic areas or monuments. The commission will also keep a register of movable artistic works, as of their first exhibition in the country, with regard to the provisions of the Federal Copyright Law.[135]

8. All properties linked with the nation's history from the time of the establishment of Hispanic culture in the country are considered historic monuments, according to the terms of the relevant declaration or by the determination of the law.[136]

9. The act outlines current law determining that historic monuments comprise, among other items, buildings constructed between the sixteenth and nineteenth centuries and intended as churches, archbishops' or bishops' palaces, seminaries, convents, and various other public and religious buildings, as well as objects found within such buildings including documents, manuscripts, crafts, tools, and artifacts.[137]

10. The act outlines the procedures to establish areas comprising immovable archaeological, artistic, and historic works as monument areas and to have such areas entered into the appropriate register.[138]

11. Anyone who executes any archaeological work by excavation, removal, or any other means on immovable archaeological monuments or in archaeological monument areas without authorization is liable for imprisonment for one to ten years and a fine of 100 to 10,000 pesos.[139]

12. Anyone who has received a contract or commission to carry out archaeological work from the National Institute of Anthropology and History, which is to enforce this portion of the act, and who appropriates any movable archaeological monument for himself or herself or for another is liable for imprisonment for one to ten years and a fine of 3,000 to 15,000 pesos.[140]

If these offenses are committed by a government official responsible for the application of the act, the sanctions will be imposed independently of those to which the official is liable under the law concerning the responsibilities of civil servants and government employees.

13. Anyone who executes any act of transfer of ownership or sale of a movable archaeological monument, and anyone who transports, exhibits, or reproduces it without permission and appropriate registration, is liable for one to ten years' imprisonment and a fine of 1,000 to 15,000 pesos.[141]

14. Anyone who illegally possesses an archaeological monument or movable historic monument found on or originating in an immovable monument site to which Section 1, Article 36, refers, is liable for one to six years' imprisonment and a fine of 100 to 50,000 pesos.[142]

15. Anyone who takes possession of a movable archaeological, historic, or artistic monument without the consent of the person entitled to it by law is liable for one to ten years' imprisonment and a fine of 3,000 to 15,000 pesos.[143]

16. Anyone who by means of a fire, flood, or explosion damages or destroys an archaeological, artistic, or historic monument is liable for two to ten years' imprisonment and a fine equal to the value of the damage caused. Anyone who by any other means damages or destroys any archaeological, artistic, or historic monument is liable for one to ten years' imprisonment and a fine equal to the value of the damage caused.[144]

17. Anyone who by any means removes or attempts to remove from the country an archaeological, artistic, or historic monument without permission from the appropriate institute is liable for two to twelve years' imprisonment and a fine of 100 to 50,000 pesos.[145]

18. Repeat offenders committing any of the illegal acts described in the law will incur prison sentences of an additional two-thirds to twice the sanctioned term of imprisonment. Also, persistent offenders will be fined two or three times the amount imposed for the original offense.

19. For the purposes of the law, traffickers in archaeological monuments will be considered persistent offenders.

Extensive regulations are attached to the act, establishing the procedures and responsibilities for carrying out the act and for its enforcement.

Cultural property has in recent years become an important element in the national patrimony of many countries as there evolves a greater understanding and awareness of the need for cultural identity. As a result, we can expect greater involvement and communication among countries, both the countries of export and of import, to control the international trade of national heritage objects.

NOTES

1. Charles De Jaeger, *The Linz File: Hitler's Plunder of Europe's Art* (New York: John Wiley and Sons Ltd., 1981); L. H. Nicholas, *The Rape of Europa: The Fate of Europe's Treasures in the Third Reich and the Second World War* (New York: Knopf, 1994); Hector Feliciano, *The Lost Museum: The Nazi Conspiracy to Steal the World's Greatest Works of Art* (New York: Basic Books, 1995); William H. Honan, *Treasure Hunt: A New York Times Reporter Tracks the Quedlinburg Hoard* (New York: Fromm International Publishing Corp., 1997).

2. International Peace Conference (2d, Hague, Netherlands: 1907), *Convention Respecting the Laws and Customs of War on Land* ("The Hague Convention of 1907") (Washington, D.C.: The Endowment, 1915).

3. *The Treaty of Peace with Germany,* commonly known as *The Treaty of Versailles,* 225 Can. T.S. 188.

4. *The Protection of Artistic and Scientific Institutions and Historic Monuments*, April 15, 1935, 168 L.N.T.S. 289.

5. United Nations 1942–1945, *Inter-Allied Declaration against Acts of Dispossession Committed in Territories under Enemy Occupation and Control 1943* (London: H.M.S.O., 1943).

6. Lyndel V. Prott, "Principles for the Resolution of Disputes Concerning Cultural Heritage Displaced during the Second World War," *The Spoils of War: WWII and Its Aftermath: The Loss, Reappearance, and Recovery of Cultural Property,* ed. Elizabeth Simpson (New York: Harry N. Abrams, Inc., 1997).

7. The UNESCO Convention and Protocol for the Protection of Cultural Property in the Event of Armed Conflict, May 14, 1954, 249 U.N.T.S. 215. Also reproduced in *The Spoils of War,* ed. Elizabeth Simpson, 287ff.

8. Harvey E. Oyler III, "The 1954 Hague Convention for the Protection of Cultural Property in the Event of Armed Conflict—Is It Working?" and "A Case Study: The Persian Gulf War Experience," *Columbia - VLA Journal of Law and The Arts* 23, no. 1 (1999), 55.

9. "Attacks on Cultural Property Criminalised Author: Jean-Marie Schmitt," *The Art Newspaper* #93 (June 1999): 6.

10. *The UNESCO Convention on the Means of Prohibiting and Preventing the Illicit Import, Export and Transfer of Ownership of Cultural Property*, November 14, 1970, reported 823 U.N.T.S. 231 (1972); 9 I.L.M. 289. Reproduced in *The Spoils of War,* ed. Elizabeth Simpson, Appendix 11, 297.

11. UNESCO, *Intergovernmental Committee for Promoting the Return of Cultural Property to Its Countries of Origin or Its Restitution in Case of Illicit Appropriation*, guidelines for the use of the standard form concerning requests for return or restitution, April 30, 1986.

12. *The San Salvador Convention on the Protection of the Archaeological, Historical, and Artistic Heritage of the American Nations*, Organization of American States, Proceedings of the General Assembly, Sixth Regular Session, Santiago, Chile, June 4–18, 1976, vol. I.

13. *Final Act of the Diplomatic Conference for the Adoption of the Draft UNIDROIT Convention on the International Return of Stolen or Illegally Exported Cultural Objects,* Rome (June 24, 1995).

14. *Treaty between the Federal Republic of Germany and the Union of the Soviet Socialist Republics on Good-Neighborliness, Partnership and Cooperation*, 1990, F.R.G.-U.S.S.R., 30 I.L.M., 505. Also reproduced in *The Spoils of War,* ed. Elizabeth Simpson, Appendix 14, 304.

15. *1992 Agreement between the Government of the Federal Republic of Germany and the Government of the Russian Federation on Cultural Cooperation,* December 16, 1992, signed in Moscow, entered into force May 18, 1993. Approved English translation reproduced in *The Spoils of War,* ed. Elizabeth Simpson, Appendix 15, 307.

16. *United States Military Law,* 10 U.S.C. Section 2579 (War Booty: Procedure for Handling and Retaining Battlefield Objects).

17. *The UNESCO Convention on the Means of Prohibiting and Preventing the Illicit Import, Export and Transfer of Ownership of Cultural Property.*

18. David Walden, "International Agreements for the Protection of Cultural Property," *Personal Property Journal with Gems and Jewelery* 9, nos. 1–2 (Winter/Spring 1997), 45.

19. *Final Act of the Diplomatic Conference for the Adoption of the Draft UNIDROIT Convention.*

20. Ibid., chapter 2.

21. See chapter 3, "Limits on Ownership," for a review of limitation laws and cases.

22. *Final Act of the Diplomatic Conference for the Adoption of the Draft UNIDROIT Convention.*

23. For a summary of the UNIDROIT Convention, see Walden, "International Agreements."

24. Ibid.

25. *Cultural Property Export and Import Act,* R.S.C. 1985, c. C-51, as amended.

26. *Cultural Property Export Regulation,* C.R.C., c. 449.

27. *Cultural Property Export and Import Act,* s. 7.

28. Ibid., s. 8(3).

29. Ibid., s. 11(1).

30. Ibid., s. 11(2).

31. Ibid., s. 11(3).

32. Ibid., s. 29(1).

33. Ibid., s. 18.

34. Ibid., s. 29(3).

35. Ibid., s. 29(4).

36. Ibid., s. 29(5)(a).

37. Ibid., s. 35.

38. Ibid., s. 29(6).

39. Ibid., s. 30(4).

40. Ibid., s. 30(1).

41. Ibid., s. 29(5) and (6).

42. The criteria are outlined in Minister of Public Works and Government Services Canada 1996, "Applications for Certification of Cultural Property for Income Tax Purposes," *Information and Procedures* (revised October 1996), Canadian Cultural Property Export Review Board, Ottawa.

43. Ibid., 8.

44. *Henderson Estate, Bank of New York v. M.N.R.,* C.T.C. 636, 644 (Fed. T.D. 1973); affirmed C.T.C. 485, 497 (Fed. C.A. 1975).

45. The concept of "fair market value" is dealt with in detail in chapter 4, "Role and Responsibility of Valuers," and is here dealt with in a fashion specific to the Canadian Cultural Property Export and Import Act.

46. This may include data on sales of comparable objects or collections to substantiate the original valuation.

47. Minister of Public Works and Government Services, "Applications for Certification of Cultural Property," 20–27.

48. Ian Christie Clark, chair of the Cultural Property Export Review Board, "Donations—How To Get It Right," seminar sponsored by the Professional Art Dealers Association of Canada on May 31, 1999, Toronto, Ontario.

49. Ibid.

50. *Cultural Property Export and Import Act*, s. 2.

51. Ibid., s. 2(1).

52. Ibid., s. 32(2).

53. Ibid., s. 32(2).

54. Ibid., s. 32(3).

55. Ibid., s. 35.

56. Ibid., s. 17(1).

57. Ibid., s. 17(2).

58. Ibid., s. 37.

59. Ibid., s. 37(1).

60. *The UNESCO Convention on the Means of Prohibiting and Preventing the Illicit Import, Export and Transfer of Ownership of Cultural Property.*

61. *Cultural Property Export and Import Act,* s. 40.

62. Ibid., s. 41.

63. Ibid., s. 42.

64. Ibid., s. 43.

65. Ibid., ss. 44(1) and 37(3).

66. Ibid., s. 44(2).

67. Ibid., s. 45.

68. Ibid., s. 46.

69. The case against Burger later failed.

70. *R. v. Yorke,* 3 S.C.R. 647. See also 134 N.S.R. (2d) 100 (1993).

71. *Union of India v. Bumper Development Corp, (*1995) 29 Alta. L.R. (3d) 194; affirmed (December 4, 1995) (Alta. C.A.), leave to appeal denied (1996) 9 W.W.R. xlvii (note).

72. "Canada Returns Seized Heritage Artifacts to Peru, Mexico and Columbia. *Canadian Heritage News Release,* 20 February 1998, Government of Canada, Department of Heritage and Citizenship, Ottawa.

73. Foreign Cultural Objects Immunity from Seizure Act, R.S.O. 1990, Chapter F. 23.

74. Ibid.

75. *Cultural Property Export and Import Act,* s. 36.

76. As set out in para. 11, sub 1(a) of the act.

77. As set out in para. 11, sub 1(b) of the act.

78. *Nisga'a Treaty Final Agreement,* pages 108–112, Federal Treaty Negotiation Office, Vancouver, British Columbia.

79. Ibid., paragraphs 4–13.

80. Ibid., paragraphs 14–21.

81. Ibid., paragraph 34.

82. Ibid., paragraph 35.

83. Ibid., paragraphs 36–38.

84. Ibid., paragraph 43.

85. Heritage Surplus Assets Agreement, Cultural Property Export and Import Act, *Annual Report, 1984–85,* Canadian Cultural Property Export Review Board, Ottawa, p. 38.

86. *Cultural Property Export and Import Act,* R.S.Q. 1997, c. B-4.

87. *The Convention on Cultural Property Implementation Act,* 19 U.S.C. §2601–2613 (1982).

88. *Guatemala v. Hollinshead,* no. 6771 (Cal. Super. Ct. 1972).

89. *Künstsammlunger zu Weimar v. Elicofon,* 536 F. Supp. 829 (E.D.N.Y. 1981); affirmed, 678 F.2d 1150 (2d Cir. 1982).

90. *Government of Peru v. Johnson,* 720 F. Supp. 810 (C.D. Cal 1989), affirmed in an unpublished decision (unofficially published in 1991 U.S. App. LEXIS 10385) (9th Cir. 1991).

91. For a full discussion of this and other preconvention cases, see Ralph E. Lerner and Judith Bresler, *Art Law,* 2d ed. (New York: Practicing Law Institute, 1998).

92. See Mathew Hays, "Montreal Museum Accused of Bad Faith in Painting Dispute," *The [Toronto] Globe and Mail* (March 7, 1998), C13.

93. In the *Matter of the Application to Quash Grand Jury Subpoena,* Duce Tecum served on the Museum of Modern Art, 677 N.Y.S. 2d 872, 1998 N.Y. Misc. LEXIS 387 (Sup. 1998).

94. *Matter of the Application to Quash Grand Jury Subpoena,* 1999 N.Y., App. Div. Lexis 2969.

95. "People v. Museum of Modern Art," *New York Law Journal* 39 (September 22, 1999), 1.

96. Ibid.

97. *Archaeological Resources Protection Act 1979,* as amended 16 U.S.C.A., §470ee (West 1985 and Supp. 1996).

98. *Native American Graves Protection and Repatriation Act,* Pub. L. No. 101-601, Section 2, 104, Stat. 3048 (1990), codified at 25 U.S.C.A. §§3001–13 (West Supp. 1996).

99. *Abandoned Shipwreck Act 1987,* 43 U.S.C. 2101 et seq.

100. For a full discussion of the U.S. position, see Lerner and Bresler, *Art Law,* note 83, and United States Information Agency, "Protecting Cultural Property" brochure (undated).

101. *Treaty of Cooperation between the United States of America and United Mexican States Providing for the Recovery and Return of Stolen Archaeological, Historical and Cultural Property,* July 17, 1970, 22 U.S. T. 494, T.I.A.S. no. 7088 [hereinafter *U.S.–Mexico Treaty*].

102. Ibid., Article II.

103. Ibid., Article IV.

104. *Treaty of Cooperation for the Recovery and Return of Stolen Archaeological, Historical and Cultural Property,* September 15, 1981, United States–Peru, T.I.A.S. No. 10136.

105. See National News in Brief, *Artnews (*December 1997), 54.

106. *The American Indian Religious Freedom Act,* Pub. L. no. 95-341, 92 Stat. 469 (1978), codified at 42 U.S.C.A. §1996 (West 1994 & Supp. 1996).

107. *Native American Graves Protection and Repatriation Act,* note 88.

108. 25 U.S.C.A. §§3001–13 (West Supp. 1996), §3003(A).

109. See Section 3003(b), 3007 and 3005 (AN) 1. See also Marilyn Phelan, "A Synopsis of the Laws of Protecting Our Cultural Heritage," *New England Law Review* 28 (Fall 1993), 63.

110. See *National Stolen Property Act,* 18 U.S.C. s.2314 (1982).

111. *United States v. Hollinshead,* 495 F.2d 1154 (9th Cir. 1974).

112. *USA v. McClain,* 545 F.2d 988 (5th Circ. 1977); *USA v. McClain* , 593 F.2d 658 (5th Cir. 1979) [hereinafter *McClain*].

113. *U.S. v. An Antique Platter of Gold known as a Gold Phiale mesomphalos 400 B.C. defendant in rem, Michael Steinhardt, Claimant and the Republic of Italy, Claimant,* 1997 U.S. Dist. LEXIS 18851, 95 Civ. 10537.

114. See *Bennis v. Michigan*, no. 94-8729, 116 S. Ct. 994, 998–1000.

115. See *USA v. McClain,* 664–65.

116. Quoted in the Museum Security Network, Museum Security Mailing List Reports, February 15, 1998.

117. 184 F. 3d 131 (2d. Cir. 1999); 1999 U.S. app. LEXIS 15679

118. 184 F. 3d 133

119. Sharon Flescher "Long-Awaited Ruling In The "Steinhardt Case", *IFAR* (International Foundation For Art Research) *Journal,* Volume 2, Number 3, Summer 1999, p. 3.

120. *Importation of Pre-Columbian Monumental or Architectural Sculpture or Murals Act*, 19 U.S.C. §§2091–95 (1988).

121. *The Immunity from Seizure Act*, 22 U.S.C.A. §§2459 (West 1990).

122. Ibid., s. 2459(a).

123. Ibid.

124. *Unites States of America v. Helard J. Gonzales O'Higgins*, 1998 US Dist. Lexis 15668, 98 Cr. 358 (RPP).

125. Ibid., 367. See *U.S. v. Koga*, No. 97 Cr. 930 (S.D.N.Y. filed Sept. 17, 1997) (RPP).

126. *Treaty of Cooperation between the United States of America and United Mexican States.*

127. See *Federal Law of Archaeological, Artistic and Historic Monuments and Zones, Official Gazette*, December 8, 1975.

128. Ibid., Article 16.

129. Ibid.

130. Ibid., Article 21.

131. Ibid., Article 27.

132. Ibid., Article 28

133. Ibid., Article 29.

134. Ibid., Articles 27–33 in particular.

135. Ibid., Article 34.

136. Ibid., Article 35.

137. Ibid., Article 36.

138. Ibid., Chapter 4.

139. Ibid., Chapter 6.

140. Ibid., Chapter 6, Article 48.

141. Ibid., Chapter 6, Article 49.

142. Ibid., Chapter 6, Article 50.

143. Ibid., Chapter 6, Article 51.

144. Ibid., Chapter 6, Article 52.

145. Ibid., Chapter 6, Article 53.

· 10 ·

Import and Export

NORTH AMERICAN FREE TRADE AGREEMENT

On January 1, 1994, the North American Free Trade Agreement (NAFTA) came into force, establishing a single trade zone in North America.[1] It liberalized the movement of goods across borders and also dealt with intellectual property and services throughout North America.

NAFTA is an international treaty negotiated among Canada, the United States, and Mexico. The text consists of more than a thousand pages plus supplementary agreements on environment, labor, and emergency actions. It was signed in 1992; a supplementary agreement was added in September 1993. Domestic legislation implementing the NAFTA obligations, which was necessary under the laws of Canada, Mexico, and the United States, was then passed by each of the three signatories.

NAFTA had its origins in the General Agreement of Tariffs and Trade (GATT) of 1948, which deals with the reduction of trade barriers and tariffs, subsidies, and dumping of goods, as well as with intellectual-property concerns.[2] It was also influenced by previous free-trade agreements, first that between the United States and Israel and then the U.S.-Canada Free Trade Agreement, which provided much of the content for the NAFTA agreement.

The objectives of the agreement included the elimination of barriers to trade in goods and services; the promotion of "conditions of fair competition" within the free-trade area, increasing investment opportunities within the free-trade area; the protection and enforcement of intellectual-property rights; and the creation of a framework for further cooperation to enhance the benefits of the agreement.

INTELLECTUAL PROPERTY

NAFTA provides protection for intellectual property, as well as an enforcement mechanism for the protection of these rights (chapter 17). It is based on preexisting intellectual-property agreements such as the Berne Convention on copyright and the Uruguay Round of negotiations for Trade Related Aspects of Intellectual Property Rights (TRIPS).[3]

In order to fulfil its obligations under NAFTA, Mexico implemented the terms of the Berne Convention and established procedures for both copyright protection for creators and equality of domestic creators and creators of signatory states to the copyright convention. It also removed any formalities or conditions of acquiring rights in respect to copyright and related rights. Since Mexico has implemented the Berne Convention, the transfer and movement of intellectual property in North America will likely become easier and result in greater trade in this area between the various countries.

IMPORT AND EXPORT OF FINE ART OBJECTS

Art objects are imported duty-free under NAFTA; there may, however, be domestic taxes applicable to such objects. For instance, the Canadian Goods and Services Tax (GST), currently at seven percent of the purchase estimate of the goods, is payable at the border on the importation of various goods, including artworks. Delays in the payment of the tax may be allowed for art dealers when a substantial number of works or substantial value of works is entering the country, such as if the work is part of a shipment of imported art on consignment and the total value of the shipment is determined in accordance with section 215 of the act to be at least $250,000 (Section 3F). The delay is permitted to enable the works to be sold and the funds generated for payment of the tax.

GST is not payable on goods imported by a charity in Canada and donated to the charity (Schedule VII, sections 213–217). This would include works imported for donation to the major museums and public art galleries in Canada.

DUTY-FREE TREATMENT OF ART

NAFTA incorporates the "Harmonized Tariff Schedule" (HTS) approved by GATT. The vast majority of original works of art are routinely classified as such, thereby qualifying for duty-free status. Chapter 97 of the tariff of both the United

States and Canada specifically enumerates most forms of art. Issues still arise occasionally regarding objects that are not clearly classifiable as art or objects that are classified elsewhere in the tariff schedule and therefore subject to the duties or tariffs required by that schedule. However, on January 1, 1998, most duties were eliminated on goods among the three countries. Certain tariffs will be eliminated in 2003, and the few remaining tariffs will be removed in 2008, fifteen years after the initiation of the agreement. This should result in greater and easier import and export of art among the three countries.

As of January 1, 1998, internal taxes and charges may not be applied in a way that gives protection to domestic production at the expense of the other countries in the agreement. Charges are permitted on imported goods only if they are similarly charged on the domestic product. This obligation extends also to state and provincial governments, unless the country was permitted to negotiate a reservation to that particular NAFTA obligation. For the most part, provincial and state governments must treat the goods of another NAFTA country just as they treat the goods of any producer in any state or province of their own country.

Although NAFTA has reduced many of the difficulties in trade among the three countries, it does not create a common market (that is, authorize the free movement of goods among the three countries). Customs administrations still exist, and customs officers still enforce the laws of import and export. Importers and exporters have to comply with complex laws and regulations in all three countries. Most often, this necessitates the use of customs brokers and related professionals to expedite the movement of goods.

Mexico has a particularly complex import and export procedure, even though NAFTA customs administration requires a common certificate of origin (for all goods in excess of $1,000 U.S.) and sets up procedures for the certificate.

Exporters of Mexican goods must have a valid certificate (Article 510 [4]), and importers must have a certificate for all goods on which they want to claim NAFTA treatment (Article 502[2][a]). The certificates cover one importation or multiple importations of the same goods for one year and remain valid for four years from the date of issue.

PROFESSIONAL SERVICES

No internationally acceptable professional standards are in place, nor is there free trade within the NAFTA countries in this regard.

Under NAFTA (appendix 1210.5) the signatories encourage professional bodies in signatory countries to develop mutual and acceptable standards for licensing professionals and reciprocal recognition. However, recognition of standards is entirely up to the professional bodies. NAFTA does not impose any standards or commitments apart from requiring professional associations to be fair in their review of and answer to applications by nationals of other NAFTA countries for professional licensing.

Professional services is defined (article 12.13) as "services, the provision of which requires specialized post-secondary education, or equivalent training or experience and for which the right to practice is granted or restricted by a party, but does not include services provided by trades-persons or vessel and aircraft crew members."[4]

CULTURAL INDUSTRIES

The cultural industries of Canada related to five types of activity were excluded from the Canada-U.S. Free Trade Agreement. This exception was carried into the NAFTA agreement. The cultural industries excluded are

1. printed publications,
2. film and video (which may relate to film and/or video used in artworks),
3. music recording,
4. music publishing, and
5. broadcasting.

There was no exception for original fine and decorative art.

ENDANGERED SPECIES

Although art and art objects are affected only peripherally by endangered-species protection acts, various materials used in art and art objects may be affected (for example, whalebone, ivory, quills, and skins of animals). Therefore, such legislation must be examined carefully to avoid possible civil and criminal penalties. Related acts and conventions include the International Convention for the Regulation of Whaling[5] and the U.S. Marine Mammal Protection Act,[6] which allowed native subsistence harvesting to make items for personal use only.

NAFTA takes priority over all other international agreements (Article 103[2]) unless otherwise stated in NAFTA. One such exception is the 1973 Convention on International Trade in Endangered Species of Wild Fauna and Flora (CITES), amended June 22, 1979.[7]

CITES

CITES was signed by the United States in March 1973 and became effective in the U.S. on July 1, 1975. Canada joined CITES in July 1975, and Mexico joined in October 1991.

This international agreement was created to protect certain animal and plant species against overexploitation by international trade. More than 110 countries have joined CITES and are controlling trade in more than 48,000 species and subspecies of animals and plants, their parts, and products manufactured from them. The treaty acknowledges the different degrees of vulnerability of various species. Control is exercised through a permit system that reflects how severely endangered the species might be. Each species is listed under one of three appendices, depending on its vulnerability; the restrictions on trade differ for each appendix.

1. Appendix 1: species "threatened with extinction, which are or may be affected by trade." International trade in specimens of these species is subject to strict regulation.
2. Appendix 2: wildlife whose survival may be endangered unless trade in them is subject to strict regulation.
3. Appendix 3: species identified by any member country as regulated within its jurisdiction for the purpose of preventing exploitation.

Trade conditions respecting appendix 2 and 3 species are less stringent than those that apply to appendix 1 species.

Some consider that there is a defect in the language of CITES in that it allows reservation clauses. These permit any member nation to enter a reservation at the time the species is listed on an appendix, making that country a nonparty to the agreement insofar as that species is concerned. It appears that these clauses contribute to the continued commercial exploitation that threatens certain endangered species.

Canadian Law

In Canada, CITES is applied through the Export and Import Permits Act (EIPA),[8] which reflects the CITES appendices listings. It also is covered under the Wild Animal and Plant Protection and Regulation of International and Interprovincial Trade Act (WAPPA),[9] assented to on December 17, 1992.

U.S. Law

The Endangered Species Preservation Act[10] of 1966, later expanded by the Endangered Species Conservation Act[11] of 1969, was passed to protect, conserve, restore, and propagate selected species of native fish and wildlife threatened with extinction. The Endangered Species Act of 1973[12] and its expansion into the Endangered Species Act[13] of 1988 (ESA) was more comprehensive than these earlier statutes in recognizing that threatened and endangered species of wildlife and plants are "of aesthetic, ecological, educational, historical, recreational, and scientific value to the nation and its people." This statute was the first to include flora and to provide a program of conservation for threatened and endangered plant species.[14]

The Endangered Species Act prohibits the importation, taking, exportation, and sale of, or interstate or foreign commerce in, any listed species. It requires the United States to participate and cooperate in any international attempts to protect endangered species. This ultimately led to the CITES legislation.

The ESA empowered the secretary of state to work with foreign countries for the conservation of fish, wildlife, and plants, including endangered species and threatened species listed pursuant to the act (Section 1533); to enter into bilateral or multilateral agreements with foreign countries to provide for such conservation; and to work with foreign persons involved in these areas to develop and carry out, with such assistance as the secretary may provide, conservation practices designed to enhance such fish, wildlife, or plants and their habitats.

It is prohibited to import any such endangered species of fish or wildlife into the United States; to take any such species within the United States or the territorial sea of the United States; to possess, sell, deliver, carry, transport, or ship any such species by any means; and to deal or offer for sale such species in interstate or foreign commerce (Section 1538).

This act has been used to block both the attempted importation into the United States of artworks and art objects carved in ivory and whalebone and the use of various animal skins in works of art and art objects.

Certain exceptions are permitted by the act, with the onus on the party claiming the exemption (Section 1539[h]). These include certain antique articles (articles more than one hundred years of age), articles that have not been repaired or modified with any part of any species on or after December 28, 1973, and certain other specific exemptions.

Civil and criminal penalties provided by the act include fines up to $12,000 for each violation. Each violation is a separate offense. Criminal violations may include fines of up to $50,000 and/or imprisonment for a maximum of one year.

A defense includes the right of the defendant in good faith to protect himself or herself or a member of his or her family from bodily harm from any endangered or threatened species.

Prosecutions

There have been few prosecutions under these statutes, and the penalties imposed on conviction have been fairly minor. For instance, in the case of *Rittenberry v. U.S. Fish and Wildlife Service*,[15] a tourist imported a polar bear skin rug and a gray wolfskin rug, both appendix 2 species, from Canada into the United States without the requisite export permits. The administrative-law judge from the Interior Department Office of Hearings and Appeals imposed only a $200 penalty. Even this was appealed by the respondent.

The relevant section of the ESA

> applied a strict liability standard to the violation since Congress did not intend to make knowledge of the law a prerequisite to imposition of a civil penalty. Nonetheless, the appeals board focused exclusively on the intent of the importer in reaching its order, which imposed only a $2 penalty, a dollar for each violation of the ESA.[16]

Similarly, in *U.S. Fish Wildlife v. Kinger*,[17] a professional fur dealer imported from Canada into the U.S. thirty-nine river otter skins, which were appendix 2 species. He did not obtain the appropriate reexport certificate. He was assessed only a $1 penalty as the "importer's reliance on other people to obtain proper documentation suggested that the trader did not intentionally evade the CITES regulations, and since the purpose of a civil penalty is deterrence, there was no need to impose a fine."[18]

IMPORT AND EXPORT OF CULTURAL PROPERTY

The UNESCO Convention on Cultural Property[19] is discussed in detail in chapter 5, "Auction and Other Marketplaces," as are specific U.S. statutes in respect to the importation of cultural property and the various agreements between the United States and Canada, the United States and Mexico, and various other South American countries.

NOTES

1. *North American Free Trade Agreement*, August 13, 1992 (Canada: Ministry of Supply and Services Canada, 1993).
2. *General Agreement of Tariffs and Trade*, 55 U.N.T.S. 308 (1947).
3. This area is discussed in detail in Chapter 6, "Copyright."

4. For an excellent overview and examination of NAFTA, see Barry Appleton, *Navigating NAFTA, A Concise User's Guide to A North American Free Trade Agreement* (Toronto: Carswell, 1994).

5. *International Convention for the Regulation of Whaling*, signed on December 2, 1946, in Washington and adopted at the twenty-fourth meeting of the International Whaling Commission, London (June 26–30, 1972).

6. *U.S. Mammal Marine Protection Act, 1972* as codified in 16 U.S.C. §1362.

7. *Convention on International Trade in Endangered Species of Wild Fauna and Flora*, signed March 3, 1973, in Washington. D.C., and amended June 22, 1979, as cited in U.N.T.S., no. 14537, vol. 993 (1976).

8. *Export and Import Permits Act*, R.S.C. 1985, c. E-19.

9. *Wild Animal and Plant Protection and Regulation of International and Interprovincial Trade Act*, S.C. 1992, c. 52.

10. *The Endangered Species Preservation Act of October 15, 1966* (P.L. 89-669, 80 Stat. 926), as amended by the *Endangered Species Conservation Act of December 5, 1969* (P.L. 91-135, 83 Stat. 275).

11. *The Endangered Species Conservation Act of 1969*, 16 U.S.C. §688 (1969), repealed by *The Endangered Species Act*, 16 U.S.C. §§1531–43 (1982).

12. *The Endangered Species Act of 1973*.

13. *The Endangered Species Act, 16* U.S.C. §§1531–44 (l988).

14. See Carlo Balistrieri, "CITES: The ESA and International Trade," *Natural Resources and Environment* 8, no. 1 (Summer 1993), 33.

15. *Rittenberry v. U.S. Fish and Wildlife Service*, 2 O.R.W. 2089 (1980).

16. Ibid.

17. *U.S. Fish and Wildlife v. Kinger,* 40 R.W. 239 (1985).

18. Meena Alagappan, "The United States' Enforcement of the Convention of International Trade in Endangered Species of Wild Fauna and Flora, A Comment," *Northwestern Journal of International Law and Business* (Winter 1990), 541–68.

19. *The UNESCO Convention on the Means of Prohibiting and Preventing the Illicit Import, Export and Transfer of Ownership of Cultural Property*, November 14, 1970, 823 U.N.T.S. 231 (1972).

Index

A

American Society of Appraisers, 98
AMT. *See* Alternate minimum tax
Andy Warhol Foundation for Visual Arts, 244-245
Anns and Others v. London Borough of Merton, 59
Anselmo v. Commissioner, 103
Antiquities Act of 1906, 82
Appraisal contracts, components of, 97-98
The Appraisal Foundation
  function of, 95-96
  Uniform Standards of Professional Appraisal Practice, 18
Appraisal Institute of Canada, 96
Appraisal reports
  defined, 95
  elements of, 103-104
  restrictions on use of, 109
Appraisal Standards Board, 95
Appraisals. *See also* Valuers
  content of tax appraisals, 224-225
  defined, 95, 101
  insurance appraisal clauses, 214
  IRS appraisal review, 237-238
Appraiser Qualifications Board, 95
Appraisers. *See* Valuers
AQB. *See* Appraiser Qualifications Board
Archaeological, defined, 288
Archaeological items recovered from shipwrecks, defined, 288
Archaeological resources, defined, 83
Archaeological Resources Protection Act, 82-83
Architectural Works Copyright Protection Act, 17, 163
Art Advisory Panel, 237-238
Art faking, 2
Art Gallery of Toronto and Eaton re Aetna Insurance Company, 204-205
Art Loss Register, 51
The Art of Using Expert Evidence, 112
Art theft. *See also* Abandonment
  California legislation, 70-71
  copyright theft, 50
  counterfeiting, 50
  demand and refusal rule, 60-61
  disclaimers, 54

C

California
  Art Preservation Act, 17, 152, 184-185
  art theft legislation, 70-71
  Code of Civil Procedure, 262-263
  Resale Royalties Act, 41-42, 125-126, 174-175, 246-247
Campbell, Barbara, 172
Canada
  abandoned property legislation, 85-88
  auction legislation, 127-128, 140
  contract law, 3-5
  copyright legislation, 188
  cultural property agreement with U.S., 288
  cultural property legislation, 267-283
  defamation law, 11-12
  endangered species protection, 310
  export control, 276
  export control list, 268-270
  fraud or deceit, 13-14
  Goods and Service Tax, 307
  injurious falsehood, 15
  insurance industry regulation, 198
  moral rights of artists, 16, 186-188
  negligent misrepresentation, 14
  Sale of Goods Act, 4
  tax legislation, 219-228
Canada Shipping Act, 86
Canadian Copyright Act, 16
Canadian Criminal Code, 54
Canadian Cultural Property Export and Import Act, 31
Canadian Cultural Property Export Review Board, 220, 222-223, 226
Canadian Heritage Preservation Endowment Account, 281
Candle auctions, 122
Capital gains
  Canadian legislation, 221
  U.S. legislation, 230-231, 240-241
Catalogs for auction sales, 122-124
Caveat emptor, 9, 51, 130
Central Trust Co. v. Rafuse et al., 59

Crimi v. Rutgers Presbyterian Church, 186
Criminal Code of Canada, 140
Crown gifts, 219-221
Cultural gifts, 219-221
Cultural industries, NAFTA exclusion of, 309
Cultural items, defined, 288
Cultural objects
  defined, 265
  theft of, 297-298
Cultural property
  bilateral agreements, 288-289
  Canadian Cultural Property Export and Import Act, 31
  Canadian legislation, 267-283
  certification of, 220
  commonwealth protection scheme, 267
  defined, 259-260
  estimating fair market value, 273-275
  expropriation of, 90
  grants, 275-276
  international protection of, 258-262
  Mexican legislation, 298-300
  Movable Cultural Property Program, 275
  Object ID, 208-210
  protection of, 260-262
  U.S. legislation, 283-298
  war booty, 257-260, 262-266
Cultural Property Act, 283-284
Cultural Property Advisory Committee, 284
Cultural Property Export and Import Act, 220, 267-281
Cultural Property Export Regulation, 270
Cultural Property Export Review Board, 271-276
Customs Administration, 177

D

Damp bidding, 138
Davis, David J., 56-57
Dawson v. Malina, 10
Dealers

E

F

Financial Institutions Reform, Recovery and Enforcement Act, 96
Fine art
  categories of, 1
  defined, 175
  import and export of, 307
  insurance schedules, 207
FIRREA. *See* Financial Institutions Reform, Recovery and Enforcement Act
Floating charges, 44
Floating liens, 44
Foreign Cultural Objects Immunity from Seizure Act, 279-280
Forgeries, 2
Found property, 83
Foxley, William C., 134-136
Foxley v. Sotheby's Inc., 97
Fragmented title, 37
Fraud, 13-14
Fraudulent misrepresentation, 13-14
Friedberg v. Canada, 223

G

General Agreement of Tariff and Trade (GATT), 306
Generation-skipping transfer tax, 248
Gerber, Ellen, 64
Germany, cultural property agreements with the Soviet Union, 262
Gertrude Stein Gallery, 56-57
Getty Conservation Institute, 208
Getty Information Institute, 208
Gifts
  Canadian tax legislation, 219-228
  carry-over of excess credits, 226
  carry-over of provisions, 240
  categories of, 219
  charitable remainder trust, 226-227
  content of tax appraisals, 224-225
  contribution limits, 239-240
  estate taxes, 227, 242-247
  gift taxes, 228, 241-242
  Mexican tax legislation, 248-253

H

I

J

K

L

M

Marital property, 36
Market value, 149-150
Martin v. City of Indianapolis, 181
Masters, defined, 39
Mel Steinberg Inc., 139
Menzel, Erna, 55-56
Menzel v. List, 55-56, 60
Merchantability, defined, 54
Merchants, defined, 19
Mexico
  abandoned property legislation, 88-90
  art theft legislation, 78-80
  auction legislation, 142-144
  burden of proof, 21
  capital gains tax, 114
  commercial transactions, 18-19
  conflict of laws, 24
  contracts, 20
  copyright legislation, 188-189
  cultural property agreement with U.S., 288-289
  cultural property legislation, 298-300
  defamation law, 22
  disclosure statutes, 45
  general law of torts, 22-24
  insurance industry regulation, 199
  intellectual-property rights, 175-177
  limitation period, 21
  moral rights of artists, 22, 189-190
  negligence, 22-24
  ownership, 42-43
  pawnshops, 115-116
  protection of valuers, 24
  public brokers, 113-114
  recovery of possession, 44
  rights of foreigners, 190
  security interests, 44-45
  slander, 22
  statute of frauds, 21-22
  tax legislation, 248-253
  title, 42-43

statutory proposal concerning art theft, 71-72
Newcomb-Macklin Art Gallery, 34-36
Nisga'a Treaty, 282-283
Noland, Kenneth, 213
North American Free Trade Agreement, 175-177, 306-309

O

Object ID, 208-210
Occupancy, obtaining title by, 81
Office of the Superintendent of Financial Institutions Act, 198
O'Keeffe, Georgia, 68-69
O'Keeffe v. Snyder, 68
Ontario Business Practices Act, 140
Ontario Personal Property Security Act, 5-6
Open insurance policies, 206
Opinions of authenticity. *See* Authenticity
OPPSA. *See* Ontario Personal Property Security Act
Ownership
  abandoned goods, 80-90
  Mexican law, 42-45
  obtaining title, 28-37
  rights, 27
  stolen objects, 47-80
  U.S. legislation for buying or selling fine art, 38-42

P

Patry, William, 168
Pavia, Phillip, 182
Pawnshops, Mexican, 115-115
Payment in kind, 252-253
Peixeiro v. Haberman, 59
Penal Code of the State of New York, 262
Perfected security interest, 5-6
Perils, defined, 195
Perls, Klaus, 55-56
Personal property rights, 159

of stolen art, 51
Purdue v. Commissioner, 103

Q

Quebec
  Civil Code, 87-88
  Cultural Property Act, 283
Quid pro quo benefits, 229
Quo Vadis, 34-36

R

Real property rights, 159
Receipt of benefit, 221-222
Reciprocating states, defined, 276
Recovery of possession, 44
Registration of copyright, 173
Reinsurers, 197-198
Replacement-cost insurance coverage, 206-207
Replevin actions, 67-68
Reproductions
  copyright issues, 148-149, 160-161
  limited-edition works, 38
Repudiating contracts, 4-5
Resale rights, 41-42, 125-126, 173-175
Reserve bids in auctions, 123-124, 138
Reserve prices, 94
Restoration of works, 147, 210
Retail vendors, purchases from, 28-29
Right of attribution, 179
Right of integrity, 179-181
Right of return, 134-136
Right of survivorship, 37
Ring control of auctions, 138-139
Risk management, 194-199
Rittenberry v. U.S. Fish and Wildlife Service, 312
Rizik, Jacqueline, 62-68

Rizik, Phillip, 62-68
Roerich Pact, 259
Rogers, Art, 171-172
Rogers v. Koons, 171-172
Rudman, Isaac, 139

S

Sale, defined, 4, 8
Sale by description, 8
Sale of Goods Acts, 4-5, 52-53, 127-128, 137
Sale on approval, 29
Salvage rights, 211-212
Sculpture
  casts, 183
  copyright issues, 164-166, 171-172
  foundry marks, 184
  Importation of Pre-Columbian Monumental or Architectural Sculpture or
    Murals Act, 296
  moral rights issues, 180-181
  multiples, 182-183
  New York Arts and Cultural Affairs Statute, 40-41
  New York Sculpture Law, 182-184
  public commissions, 150-152
Security interests
  Mexican law, 44-45
  perfected, 5-6
Sellers, protection of, 17-18
Serra v. The United States General Services Administration, 152
Sherman Antitrust Act, 139
Shipwrecks
  defined, 81
  ownership of property, 82-83, 288
Sig Management Company, 180-181
Slander
  defined, 11
  Mexican law, 22
  of title, 14-15
Snelson, Kenneth, 185

T

transactions in Mexico, 18-24
void and voidable, 53-58
warranty of, 129-130
by way of exchange, 32-33
Trade libel, 15
Trade Related Aspects of Intellectual Property, 307
Transit of art objects, 205
Trap bidding, 137
Treasure of Salvors Inc. v. Unidentified Wrecked and Abandoned Vessel, 82
Treasure trove, 82, 86-87, 89-90
Treasure Trove Act, 86
Treaty of Versailles, 258-259
Treaty on Mutual Legal Assistance on Criminal Matters, 293
TRIPS. *See* Trade Related Aspects of Intellectual Property
Trusts
auction proceeds, 131
beneficial trusts, 31-32
Mexican law, 44

U

UCC. *See* Uniform Commercial Code
Underwriters, 197
UNESCO. *See* United Nations Educational, Scientific and Cultural
Organization
UNESCO Convention, 260-261, 263-264, 276-278, 280-281, 283-285
UNESCO Resolution, 261
The UNIDROIT Convention, 261, 264-266
Uniform Commercial Code
art theft, 51
auction law of sale, 128-129
purchases from artists or retail vendors, 29
sale by description, 8
seller warranties, 6-7
statutes of frauds, 8-9
statutes of limitations, 7
Uniform Standards of Professional Appraisal Practice, 18, 95-96, 99-100,
103-104
Union of India v. Bumper Development Corp., 279

V

W

X

Z